P9-CSA-140

Multimedia: Interactive Video Production

Throughout this endeavor, my family—Fah, Vishi, and Anna— were constantly with me behind the scenes, helping, encouraging, and believing in my effort. I cannot adequately thank them for their understanding.

Multimedia:

Interactive Video Production

Reza Azarmsa

California State University, Bakersfield

An imprint of Wadsworth Publishing Company

I(T)P® An International Thomson Publishing Company

Belmont • Albany • Bonn • Boston • Cincinnati • Detroit • London • Madrid •
Melbourne Mexico City • New York • Paris • San Francisco • Singapore • Tokyo •
Toronto • Washington

Mutimedida Editor: Kathy Shields
Assistant Editor: Tamara Huggins
Production Editor: Pat Waldo
Designer: Reza Azarmsa
Print Buyer: Karen Hunt
Permissions Editor: Bob Kauser
Copy Editor: Carol Carreon Lombardi
Cover Design: Stephen Rapley
Composition: Reza Azarmsa

We would like to thank the following reviewers:

Steven G. Jackson, Boise State University
Brenda C. Litchfield, University of South Alabama
Susan Michael, University of Kentucky
Ken Quamme, University of North Dakota - Williston
Judith E. Wakefield, University of Central Oklahoma

Copyright © 1996 by Wadsworth Publishing Company
A Division of International Thomson Publishing Inc.
The ITP logo is a registered trademark and Integrated Media Group is a trademark under license.
Printed in the United States of America
1 2 3 4 5 6 7 8 9 10

All rights reserved. No part of this work covered by the copyright hereon may be reproduced or used in any form or by any means—graphic, electronic, or mechanical, including photocopying, recording, taping, or information storage and retrieval systems—without the written permission of the publisher.

Library of Congress Cataloging-in-Publication Data
Azarmsa, Reza.
    Multimedia--interactive video production / Reza Azarmsa.
       p. cm.
    Includes bibliographical references and index.
    ISBN 0-534-25416-0
    1. Multimedia systems.   2. Interactive video.   I. title.
QA76. 575.A93   1996
778.59--dc20   95-25008
                                                        CIP

ISBN 0-534-25416-0
For more information, contact Integrated Media Group:

Integrated Media Group
Wadsworth Publishing
10 Davis Drive, Belmont, California 94002, USA

International Thomson Editorés
Campos Eliseos 385, Piso 7
Col. Polanco, 11560 México D.F. México

International Thomson Publishing Europe
Berkshire House 168-173, High Holborn
London, WC1V 7AA, England

International Thomson Publishing GmbH
Königswinterer Strasse 418, 53227 Bonn, Germany

Thomas Nelson Australia
102 Dodds Street
South Melbourne 3205, Victoria, Australia

International Thomson Publishing Asia
221 Henderson Road, #05-10 Henderson Building
Singapore 0315

Nelson Canada
1120 Birchmont Road
Scarborough, Ontario, Canada M1K 5G4

International Thomson Publishing Japan
Hirakawacho Kyowa Building, 3F
2-2-1 Hirakawacho, Chiyoda-ku
Tokyo 102, Japan

Table of Contents

CHAPTER 3

CHAPTER 4

CHAPTER 5

Preface

The term "multimedia" has roots preceding the computer. The word has been used for decades to describe productions incorporating multiple slide projectors, video monitors, audio tape decks, synthesizers, and other standalone media devices. Upon the arrival of the microprocessor, the hardware tools used in various media disciplines became programmable. This meant that various combinations of settings could be stored and recalled on demand. The same technology made it possible for devices to control each other with greater intimacy and to synchronize their respective parts of the multimedia production more accurately. The combination of these factors led to far more ambitious productions and a maturing market for multimedia.

As the personal computer began taking its place in the world, it was quickly put to use controlling various media devices. Standards and protocols for device control evolved quickly, and suddenly the computer was controlling entire video editing suites, recording studios, and more.

Simultaneously, the more powerful computers and workstations were being used for computer graphics, animation, and digital audio. As the price-performance ratio of computing technology improved, personal computers assumed those abilities at moderate levels of quality.

Interactive videodiscs combine the power of a computer, the sensory impact of television, and the quality and flexibility of laser recording and playback. No other single method or medium can offer the advantages of an interactive videodisc.

Interactive videodiscs are powerful and effective because of viewer involvement. Users actually control and respond to the prerecorded program. This two-way communication offers many benefits:

- Hands-on participation and self-paced instruction contribute to high comprehension and retention.

- Ease of use, random access, immediate feedback, and automatic or manual review make the program effective regardless of subject complexity, user experience, or knowledge levels.

- The nature of the presentation demands undivided attention, turning passive observers into active participants, drawing them totally into the learning process.

- Interactive instruction is fun, exciting, and stimulating. High interest levels ensure a positive learning experience, helping users learn quicker.

- Freeze-frame and slow-motion features help simplify complicated concepts.

- The quality of video images on videodiscs is stable and does not deteriorate during the copying process.

The potential applications for interactive videodiscs are practically unlimited. They can effectively teach students in even the most complex subjects, train inexperienced personnel in almost any field, or help accomplished professionals hone their skills. They can sell products and services and safely store thousands of images and other pieces of information for quick and easy access.

In education and training, interactive videodiscs are being used to create powerful, self-paced instruction programs. They provide training when the user needs it and without straining the instructional staff. They make it fast and easy for users to review an explanation they did not understand or to skip past material they already know.

At retail, videodiscs are being used for point of purchase displays. Visual menus and branching programs allow potential customers to access information on particular products or processes that interest them.

In medicine, videodiscs are being used for patient case simulations, basic medical science, and surgical procedures. Special programs have been developed on mental health issues, such as teenage suicide prevention.

In museums and publishing, videodiscs are being used to create image banks of thousands of geographic maps, works of art, photographs, motion pictures, and manuscripts.

Videodiscs are being used for recording movies and even for creating jukeboxes of music videos.

OVERVIEW

This book consists of eight chapters.

Chapter 1 presents an overview of multimedia. It defines multimedia, reviews CD-ROM and videodisc, explains levels of interactivity, elaborates on hypertext and hypemedia, and details some applications for multimedia in education.

Chapter 2 deals with planning a multimedia production. In this chapter topics such as understanding learning theories, developing objectives, defining audiences, writing treatments, and evaluating resources are discussed.

Chapter 3 explains video technology and how digital technology affects the production of multimedia. This chapter also includes technical information about resolution, video format, types of cameras, and nonlinear editing systems.

Chapter 4 provides information about video production for interactive video. This chapter offers tips on lighting techniques, special effects, camera shots, and on-location production.

Chapter 5 covers audio technology—the other half of multimedia production. In this chapter, digital audio, types of microphones, audio recording techniques, music selection, and sound mixing are explained.

Chapter 6 describes the process of videodisc mastering and replication. To ensure the quality of videodisc, certain steps should be taken prior to the mastering and replication stage. This chapter clarifies these steps.

Chapter 7 offers a brief overview of HyperCard, an authoring system for interactive video. HyperCard is considered to be one of the simplest yet most capable authoring systems for creating interactivity. This chapter shows readers the layout of the HyperCard program.

Chapter 8 presents the HyperCard commands used to connect the computer to the videodisc player. These commands are explained and examples are given.

The appendixes consist of multimedia resources, a glossary of terms, and an index.

The following conventions are used in Chapters 7 and 8:

- Menu and dialog box names as well as sections from menus and dialog boxes appear in *italic* type.

- Window names, tools, button, and keyboard keys have initial capitals and are in plain (roman) type.

- Commands and syntexes typed into the computer program are in Courier type.

Acknowledgments

Special acknowledgment goes to the individual companies that made this book possible. They sent me computer software, product pictures, clip art, and product literature. They granted permission to use their material and offered endless support. I would like to thank them all for the time and courtesy they offered me in this project:

Asymetrix
Canon U.S.A., Inc.
Data Translation
Hitachi Denshi America, Ltd.
Intel Corporation
JBL Professional
JVC Professional Products Company
Lowel-Light Manufacturing, Inc.
NewTek, Inc.
Panasonic Broadcast & Television System Company
Pioneer
Shure Brothers, Inc.
3M
T/Maker Company
Voyager Company

I wish to express my special thanks to Kathy Shields, Integrated Media Group Publisher, for her insight and continuous support; Tamara Huggins, assistant to the editor, for putting matters in order; Pat Waldo, production manager, for pulling things together; Carol Carreon Lombardi for her skillful copy editing and her suggestions; and the reviewers for their constructive and helpful ideas.

Chapter 1

An Overview of Multimedia

Multimedia is a powerful tool that can change both the way we look at knowledge and our educational system. Multimedia can affect education by providing instructors, students, and others with a dramatic new environment for presentations. Multimedia holds great promise for improving the quality of education by providing the ability to illustrate ideas with visual, audio, text, or any combination of media so that users can create new ways of communicating ideas. Teachers will be freed from the constraints of textbooks and chalkboards. Multimedia allows the user to be an active learner, controlling access to and manipulating vast quantities of information with a computer.

Multimedia will provide teachers and students with a dramatic new environment for presentations. They will no longer be bound by the limits of illustrating processes on a chalkboard or in slide collections. Vast libraries of audio, video, and text material will be easily accessed by the computer.

WHAT IS MULTIMEDIA?

Multimedia refers to the integration of text, audio, graphics, still images, and motion pictures into a computer-controlled multimedia product. In other words, multimedia uses the computer to integrate and control diverse electronic media such as computer screens, videodisc players, CD-ROM discs, and speech and audio synthesizers.

If teachers make logical connections among those elements and make the entire package interactive, then they are working with *hypermedia.* Computers vary in their abilities to handle the various elements of multimedia, but just about any modern computer can handle text processing, display images, and produce sound.

> Multimedia is the convergence of computers with motion, sound, graphics, and text. It is described as a "technological loom" that weaves media together.

Many educators believe that multimedia technology can be an important element in improving the quality of education. The single most significant benefit multimedia materials have to offer education is the one most often cited—interactivity. Learners do not just sit in front of the computer screen watching a presentation someone else has prepared; they interact with the materials.

CD-ROM

Today a multimedia application typically requires a computer-controlled compact disc read-only memory (CD-ROM) player. CD-ROM is considered by many educators to be a major solution for the storage and rapid access and retrieval of instructional materials.

CD-ROM is a digital data-distribution medium that uses laser optic technology to record and read any kind of digital information including text, images, and digital audio. Because of its large capacity and low cost, CD-ROM currently provides the most cost-effective distribution method for digital data. Since a compact disc never wears out, it is ideal for educational applications in which the system may be in operation 24 hours a day, 7 days a week. Further, since there is no contact between the pickup head and disc, access to different information on the disc can be achieved easily at high speed.

The audio/video signal, which is eventually read from the CD-ROM by a laser beam, is originally recorded on the disc by a laser beam as well. The information is recorded on the disc in the form of tiny pits arranged in a spiral from the inside to the outside of the disc.

A major difference and improvement of CD-ROM over videodisc is that it stores data in a digital format, whereas videodisc images are stored in an analog format.

> CD-ROM technology is rapidly changing the way we store and access information.

The extremely high recording density means that the disc is capable of storing the equivalent of about 1,200 floppy disks, 250 large reference books, 2,400 full screen photos, or 500 megabytes (MB) of storage.

Just think about the archive of educational material that can be stored on a disc and retrieved by browsing a computer index or searching information by a database of key words. For example, a textbook publisher could provide the math department in a school district a single CD-ROM that contains their textbook series (K–12) with all of the accompanying resource materials, such as workbooks and supplemental worksheets.

To read and display the information on a CD-ROM disc, you must connect the CD-ROM player to a computer. Most players are designed to be connected to either a Macintosh or an IBM-compatible computer.

To facilitate access to the information on the disc, most CD-ROM applications provide software programs to search and retrieve the desired information.

Some CD-ROM players require that the CD-ROM disc be placed into a caddy before it is inserted into the player (Figure 1.1). These caddies are usually interchangeable among various CD-ROM players.

When purchasing a CD-ROM application for an IBM computer, be sure that the program is compatible with your computer monitor. If the CD-ROM program offers color graphics and photographs, a VGA (video graphics array) monitor is often required. If the program is text only, a monochrome or CGA (color graphics adapter) monitor will probably be sufficient.

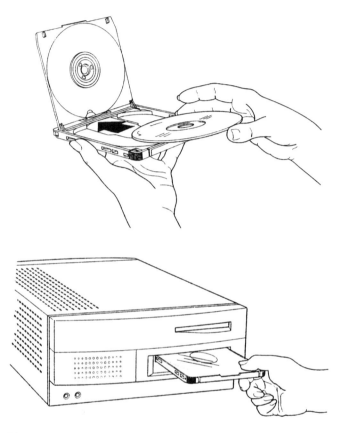

Figure 1.1. Caddy for CD-ROM.

CD-ROM discs and drives have a number of features that make them well suited for educational settings.

When a CD-ROM player is connected to an IBM-compatible computer, an additional card (board) must usually be installed in the computer. After the card has been installed, an interface cable connects the CD-ROM player to the card. CD-ROM players for IBM-compatible computers come in many shapes and sizes. For example, some players are external and are designed to fit between the monitor and the computer; others may be built into the computer as an internal drive (Figure 1.2). The internal drives require less space on the desktop, but

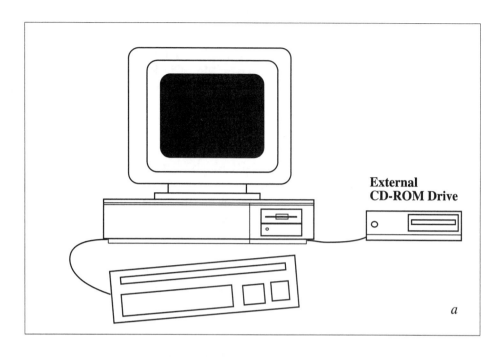

**External
CD-ROM Drive**

a

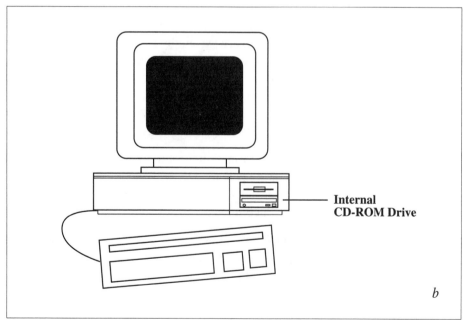

**Internal
CD-ROM Drive**

b

Figure 1.2. IBM or compatible with (a) external and (b) internal CD-ROM drive.

they are permanently installed in the computer and limit the portability of the player. Most CD-ROM players have the ability to play CD-quality audio, and many of the applications incorporate audio into the programs.

TYPES OF CD-ROM

The success of CD-ROM has fostered the creation of many other technologies that incorporate compact discs. Although most of the technologies use the same size disc, in many cases they are incompatible across platforms.

> CD-ROM technology has established a strong base in the educational system because of its large storage capacity and low cost.

- Compact Disc Interactive (CD-I) is a specification by Philips for an interactive audio, video, and computer system based on compact discs as the storage medium. CD-I players contain a built-in computer, and the output will display on a standard television set. CD-I has a wide range of capabilities and is focused at the consumer market, where low cost is important.

- Commodore Dynamic Total Vision (CDTV) is a multi-media delivery system by Commodore that combines digital audio, graphics, and video on a compact disc. CDTV is very similar to CD-I in that it will display on a standard television set and does not require an external computer. CDTV provides entertainment and educational titles for the consumer market.

- Video Information System (VIS) is a Tandy-Microsoft standard for home interactive compact disc players. Similar to CD-I and CDTV, a VIS player contains a built-in computer.

- Digital Video Interactive (DVI) is a technology for compressing and decompressing video and audio to create multimedia applications. DVI can store 72 minutes of full-motion video on a compact disc.

- CD-ROMXA (Compact Disc-Read Only Memory eXtended Architecture) is a special CD-ROM disc that interleaves (mixes) the audio and the graphics/text. A standard CD-ROM must store the text and audio in different formats on segregated parts of the compact disc. To play music and display a graphic, this technology first displays the graphic, and then the laser beam searches for and plays the audio. With CD-ROMXA, the audio and graphics can be stored in adjacent areas, providing a much smoother display.

- CD+G (Compact Disc plus Graphics) is a system to produce discs with limited graphics to complement music. These discs will play in a regular audio compact disc player, without displaying the graphics. To view the graphics, you must use a special CD+G player or another player that can read both the audio and the graphics. Both CD-I and CDTV players can play CD+G discs.

- Photo CD (Photographic Compact Disc) is Kodak's compact disc technology to store photographic images. Customers can have their pictures developed and placed on a compact disc. The compact disc can then be played through a special Photo CD player (or compatible player, such as CD-I or CD-ROMXA) and displayed on a home television set. Consumers can also alter the sequence of the photos to create a "slide show" effect with the photos.

- CD + MIDI music discs play in standard CD audio players and can also accompany themselves with additional MIDI (Musical Instrument Digital Interface) if the player is MIDI-compatible. The unique feature of CD + MIDI is that the MIDI information can be altered before it is played through the MIDI instrument. In other words, a listener can change instruments, key signature, and other MIDI information as the music is being played.

- Sony Data Discman is a portable compact disc player that uses a miniature CD-ROM disc. The Data Discman is designed to play interactive books or to serve as a portable reference guide. The player weighs less than 2 pounds and has a 3.4-inch pop-up screen.

> CD-ROMs provide almost instant access to over 650 megabytes of text, graphics, video, or sound.

- WORM (Write Once-Read Many), in contrast to "read-only," is a special technology that can record (but not erase) a compact disc. It works well if you have a lot of information you need to store and you only need a few copies of it. For example, a school system might decide to use WORM technology to preserve all its past student records.

- Rewritable compact discs are available that allow you to write, erase, and rewrite on a compact disc. These drives use a combination of the technique used to save information on a hard drive (magnetic) and the technique used to store information on a CD-ROM (optical). Therefore, they are often referred to as *magneto-optical drives.* At present, magneto-optical drives are quite expensive and considerably slower than hard drives. The most common uses of rewritable drives are for backup of hard drives, storage of very large files (such as graphics), or portability of files.

ADVANTAGES OF CD-ROM

CD-ROM technology offers many benefits to schools and libraries. Following are some of the features of CD-ROM technology for education:

> The educational applications for CD-ROM cover a wide range of programs, from electronic encyclopedias to multimedia databases.

- Each CD-ROM disc can hold about 680 megabytes of data, graphics, or sound. That capacity is equivalent to hundreds of floppy disks and more than an entire printed encyclopedia.

- CD-ROM discs are small and lightweight, making them an ideal medium for transporting data.

- CD-ROM discs are encoded in plastic and are very durable. Although they should be handled with care, fingerprints and slight scratches will not usually impair their performance. In addition, the discs are read with a laser beam, so there is no direct contact or wear on the disc as it is played.

- CD-ROMs cost only pennies to reproduce after the master is created. CD-ROM technology has the potential to save money and trees.

- The cost of CD-ROM drives has decreased dramatically in the past few years.

- The number of CD-ROM titles has increased recently. The several thousand commercial titles now available include a wide range of reference materials, multimedia applications, and government documents.

- Although the access time of CD-ROM drives is slower than that of hard drives, the speed of the search time compared to other methods is very impressive.

INTERACTIVE VIDEODISC

Educational applications of videodisc technology have increased tremendously in the past few years. Videodisc players are now affordable for schools and a wide variety of commercial programs are available. The tremendous potential of this technology makes learning about videodiscs a necessity for all educators.

Most videodiscs are the same size as a 33-rpm record (12 inches in diameter). They are a strong, durable medium for storing and displaying video information. Videodiscs are read by a laser beam; this provides the ability to randomly search any segment and play it at slow or fast speeds. Videodiscs provide almost instantaneous access to full-motion video and quality sound.

> Videodisc technology offers great potential to add new dimensions to classrooms.

Although videodisc technology has been used in military and industrial settings since the 1970s, it is just beginning to emerge as a major educational medium. One of the reasons for its growing popularity is the myriad of reasonably priced educational discs that are appearing on the market. Thousands of educational videodiscs are now available, and the number continues to grow as corporate giants, such as ABC News and Turner Broadcasting, enter the videodisc arena.

Another reason videodisc technology is sweeping into the schools is that teachers are discovering that videodiscs are an ideal medium for teaching dynamic events. Whether conducting a complex chemistry experiment or analyzing the formation of a hurricane, videodiscs allow teachers complete control of the sequence, rate, and duration of the presentation. Figure 1.3 shows a videodisc player.

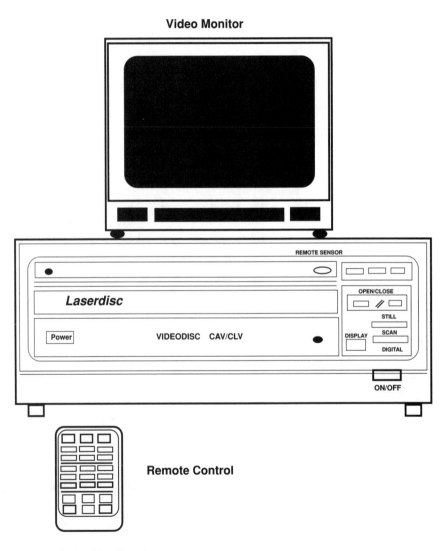

Figure 1.3. A videodisc player.

Videodisc Format

The video material on the disc is produced in exactly the same manner as a videotape (with video camera and editing equipment). The difference is that after a master videotape is edited (to 30 or 60 minutes per side), it is sent to a mastering studio to produce the videodisc. Once the videodisc is mastered, it cannot be changed in any way.

Both videotapes and videodiscs consist of a series of many frames or pictures. When the tape or disc is in the "play" mode, it moves at a standard rate of 30 frames per second to create the illusion of motion. The difference between the storage of frames on a videotape and a videodisc is that on a videotape, video frames are stored in a linear pattern. You must fast forward or rewind to locate the section you want. However, on a videodisc, frames are stored in concentric circles that are read with a laser beam. Each circle represents an individual frame, and the beam can easily jump from one frame to another to provide almost instant access.

> Interactive systems allow learners to take control of—and hence, responsibility for—their learning process.

Another advantage of the disc storage format is that a still frame (picture) can be displayed. That means you can stop the videodisc on any single frame and display it for as long as you want, without causing any damage to the videodisc. This ability to "still frame" provides individual access to every single frame on the disc. There are 30 minutes of motion on each side of the disc at 30 frames per second; therefore, one can access up to 54,000 individual frames if the disc is full (30 frames per second x 60 seconds per minute x 30 minutes per side = 54,000 frames per side).

To make access easy, each frame on the videodisc has a unique number in the range from 1 to 54,000. These numbers are automatically placed on the disc when it is made. If you know the number of a desired frame, you can use the remote control unit or the computer to access it. Another feature of a videodisc is that you can "step" (move forward or back by just one frame) by using the remote control unit or the videodisc player panel. You can also "scan" (fast forward through the disc) and "play" at various speeds, forward or reverse.

The sound (audio) on a videodisc is stored in two separate audio tracks that can be played separately or together (for stereo). This feature provides the potential of having two different languages for the same video content or for having one track for the students and one for the instructor. The audio will play only if the videodisc is moving forward at the standard rate (30 frames per second). If you are playing the disc faster, slower, or in reverse, there will be no sound.

TYPES OF VIDEODISC

There are two different videodisc formats. The format discussed up to this point (with 54,000 frames) is called *CAV* for constant angular velocity. This type of disc is most frequently used in education and training because of its versatility. The CAV format allows maximum interactivity through features such as still frames, step frames, and multiple speeds.

> Videodisc branching capabilities could allow the learner to progress from concrete to more abstract content.

The other format used for videodiscs is *CLV,* which stands for constant linear velocity. A CLV disc is the same size as a CAV disc, but the video frames are stored in a different configuration; instead of having one frame on each concentric circle, the frames are stored in a spiral pattern and several frames or parts of frames may be on the same circle. This is both good and bad. It is good because more video can fit on a CLV disc. But it is also bad because many of the best features of videodiscs, such as the ability to still frame and step frame, are lost.

Instead of frame numbers, most CLV discs have time codes embedded on them. For example, you might search to 0:08.12, which would be 8 minutes and 12 seconds from the beginning of the disc. Because CLV discs cannot display still frames, when you search for a particular time code, the video will start playing from that point.

Both CAV and CLV videodiscs can also have chapter stops embedded on them. Chapter stops are much like chapters in a book.

ADVANTAGES OF VIDEODISC

Videodiscs offer many advantages for schools over their counterparts videotape and film.

> Videodisc provides easy access to information stored on on the disc.

- Frames and segments on a videodisc can be accessed by using a remote control unit, barcode reader, or computer. There is no need to fast forward or rewind. The access is fast and precise.

- Videodisc technology does not require the complex loading process that a film does—just open the disc drawer, lay the videodisc on the platform, close the drawer, and press "PLAY." Also, there is no need to remember to reset the counter to 0 (as for a videotape); the frame numbers on a videodisc are permanently encoded and do not change.

- Although cost varies, many videodiscs are less expensive than the same programs on tape or film.

- Because videodiscs are read with a laser beam and there is no direct contact, the images on the disc do not degenerate with use. Even after many years of use, the video will look as clean and sharp as it did the first time. Discs are made of rugged plastic and even fingerprints and small scratches do not affect them. The estimated shelf life of videodiscs is much greater than that of videotapes or film.

- Videodiscs are generally recorded with 350 lines of resolution. VHS and Beta videotapes are recorded with only 200 to 250 lines of resolution. Therefore, video discs have a sharper appearance and better quality picture.

- Videodiscs are easy to store. They take up very little shelf space when stored upright and will not warp as easily as records.

- Unlike videotape or film, a videodisc with a computer is relatively easy to control. Level III videodisc programs provide the interactivity and instant feedback of computer-assisted instruction with the visual and audio realism of a videodisc.

- It is difficult to pause a videotape, and the tape may be damaged by doing so. Videodiscs can be halted on a still frame for hours with no damage. This provides individual access to every frame on the disc.

- Two audio tracks are available on all videodiscs. This means that you can have stereo sound or two separate tracks. In many of the programs, one track is recorded in English and the other in Spanish or another language. Other programs utilize two tracks to provide different levels of narration, for instance, one for elementary students and one for high school students.

- Although there are two different video formats (CLV and CAV), all videodisc players can play all laser standard videodiscs! The VHS versus Beta versus Umatic videotape format inconsistencies do not affect videodiscs.

- Students enjoy the individualization possible with videodisc programs. They can use them for learning, research, or video reports.

LEVELS OF INTERACTIVITY

Interactive systems can provide a level of responsive feedback and individual involvement that has proven to be highly motivating in both individual and classroom learning environments.

Normally, audiovisual systems are linear in operation, that is, the program material runs from beginning to end. The high speed random access capability of videodisc makes it possible to present information on a disc in any desired order. Computer control additionally makes it possible for the videodisc player to present information according to reviewer response in any programmed sequence during a program. There are three interactivity levels: *Level I, Level II,* and *Level III.*

LEVEL I

This is the stand-alone mode of operation. In this mode the videodisc system might consist of only a videodisc player and a TV monitor. No programming capability is implied, but simple interactive applications are possible. The Level I interactivity system is illustrated in Figure 1.4. A Level I system can, for example, perform chapter search and picture stop operations. This means that the player can be instructed to go to the beginning of any chapter on the disc at any time during playback. The chapter locations on the disc are defined by special chapter codes actually recorded on the disc during manufacture.

Interactive systems can provide greater and more equal access to quality eduation.

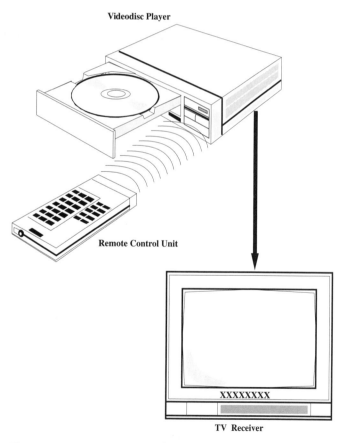

Figure 1.4. Level I of interactivity. This system consists of a videodisc player and a TV monitor.

Using only the most basic Level I system, it is possible to add impact to live presentations. Using a remote control unit, the teacher can call out specific information from the videodisc player using the chapter search function. Since the teacher is not limited to linear operation, information can be skipped or called a second time for review without unnecessary delays, thereby supporting rather than disrupting the presentation.

LEVEL II

This level includes videodisc players that have programming capability. That is, they have their own internal microprocessor, which can be programmed to perform a certain playback sequence and respond to viewer choices during the program. Several methods of programming are possible. For example, the player can be programmed manually via its remote control unit, or it can be programmed automatically. Of course, this program can then be modified or changed completely using manual programming procedures. Level II operation is ideal for many interactive applications. Figure 1.5 illustrates Level II of interactivity.

A student searching for information about a specific topic is presented with a menu listing the various related topics. The student selects the appropriate topic via a simple numeric keypad and the videodisc description. This capability of branching to different programs in response to menu selection can be utilized in a broad range of applications.

LEVEL III

In this mode the videodisc player is controlled via an external computer. The computer used could be any type. The computer itself contains the program, which responds to user input and causes the videodisc player to perform accordingly. Figure 1.6 illustrates Level III of interactivity. This type of system lends itself to the most sophisticated interactive applications.

Students studying a language sit down at a monitor and keyboard and are presented with a short dialogue in the language they are studying. The students have the opportunity to watch the actors in the actual situation in which the dialogue is occurring. Then they are asked questions about the dialogue. If the students answer incorrectly via keyboard, the player may replay the appropriate portion of the dialogue. The question is asked a second time. If the answer is still incorrect, the dialogue may be repeated.

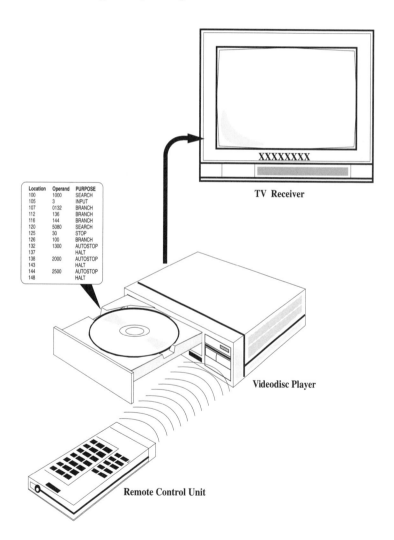

Figure 1.5. Level II of interactivity. In this level, the videodisc player has programming capability.

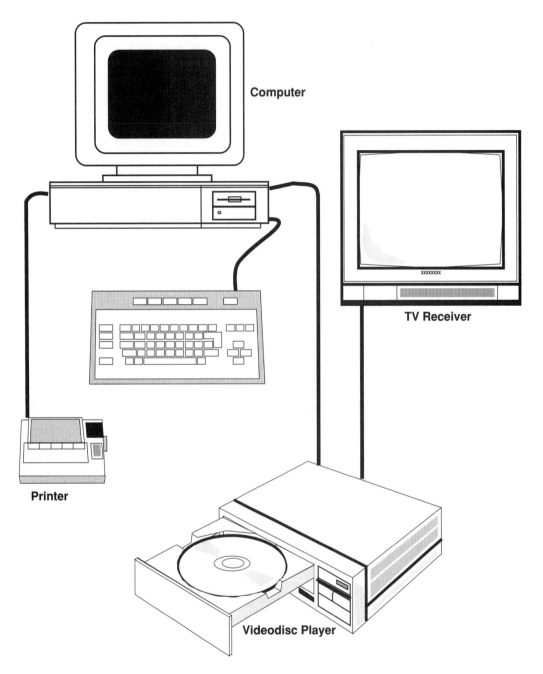

Computer

TV Receiver

XXXXXXXX

Printer

Videodisc Player

Figure 1.6. Level III of interactivity. In this level, the videodisc player is controlled by an external computer.

BARCODES

A growing number of educators, presenters, and trainers are discovering that interactive multimedia does not have to be complicated. In fact, it does not even have to involve a computer. It can be as easy as a videodisc player controlled by a barcode reader. While giving a presentation, the presenter simply holds the scanner over a barcode, which has been pasted or printed onto a script, and presses a button to send the command to the player. The player will then carry out the command, for example, "play still frames from frame 756 to frame 806," or "play frames 2,325 to 2,350 in slow motion."

The system not only allows presenters to give nicely structured presentations, it also offers a high degree of interactivity, with the ability to quickly search to any part of the disc to respond to questions or reassert important points. In some cases, the barcode system is as good as or better than the Level III (computer-controlled) videodisc systems because it's more flexible and less expensive.

Barcode

The idea is not new. National Education Corporation marketed a system called ActionCode, employing barcodes with videodisc players for training as early as 1982. In 1989, Pioneer began marketing its own system.

Pioneer targeted the K–12 education market and found overwhelming interest. In 1991, the state of Texas decreed that videodisc courses could be considered equivalent to textbooks. Since that time, California and Florida have adopted similar policies, and it's estimated that more than 100,000 videodisc players are being used in schools throughout the United States, with more than half of those equipped with barcode readers. This approach allows direct access without having to deal with all of the hierarchical menus of computer systems. There are approximately 2,200 videodisc titles, more than half with barcodes. For more information about barcodes, please see Chapter 8.

HYPERTEXT

> Hypertext is nonsequential! There is no single order that determines the sequence in which the text is to be read.

Hypertext is an approach for handling text and graphic information by allowing the users, whenever they wish, to jump from a given topic to related ideas. Reading or viewing of information thus becomes open-ended, controlled by the user. Hypertext allows users to access information in a nonlinear fashion by following a train of thought. It lets the reader control the level of detail and the type of information displayed.

All traditional text, whether in printed form or in computer files, is sequential, meaning that there is a single linear sequence defining the order in which the text is to be read. First you read page one, then you read page two, and so on. Hypertext is nonsequential; there is no single order that determines the sequence in which text is to be read.

Current hypertext programs do not use typical database record and file structures; their databases usually consist of screen-size workspaces called *nodes,* and the relations that connect nodes are called *links.* Links are the essence of hypertext because they facilitate jumping from node to node in nonlinear fashion. These nodes or computer index cards are filled with text, graphics, images, audio, and video data. Most hypertext implementations link nodes in either hierarchical or nonhierarchical fashion; some support both structures.

Currently there are two types of hypertext: static and dynamic. Static hypertext does not permit changes to the database, but it is interactively browsable. In dynamic hypertext, the user may add or subtract data and links. An important aspect of many dynamic hypertext systems is their ability to maintain multiple versions of a document as it changes over time. This allows the writer to track the history of a document and weigh alternative versions simultaneously.

Hypertext has numerous applications in education. For example, if students are learning about the civil rights movement, they are learning about what happened during the 1950s and 1960s in the United States. The students learn about the Supreme Court's 1954 *Brown vs. Board of Education* decision, about the bus

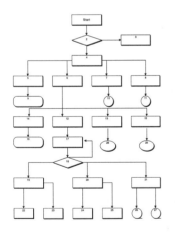

Hypertext/hypermedia flowchart

boycott, Martin Luther King and his "I have a dream" speech, school desegregation, the voting rights act, King's assassination, and so on. Without hypertext, to gather information about these subjects, the students have to go through the card catalog, find the related materials, go to the shelves, look at the indexes (if the materials are not checked out), and read the text. With hypertext, students can select the exact topic, read about it, listen to the speeches and songs, and look at pictures all by simply clicking the mouse or performing a few keystrokes.

The term hypertext is actually a misnomer, as many of the current systems allow and even encourage the inclusion of nontext data such as graphics, animations, and digitized sounds. In the future, the more precise *interactive hypermedia* will probably replace the term *hypertext* because in a digital world, sound, text, and images are all represented by the same binary signals, and microcomputers are evolving to take advantage of these new capabilities.

HYPERMEDIA

Hypermedia describes linked-information presentations that could contain several types of media, such as text, graphics, audio, and video. Hypermedia may contain several layers of information, with each layer related to many others. Hypermedia is very simply an authoring tool. Bill Atkinson, the creator of HyperCard™, the popular hypermedia system, calls it an "electronic erector set," meaning it is a tool that can help build new approaches to teaching and learning.

> Hypermedia applications can be utilized in education for database management, electronic slide shows, student projects, or interactive instruction.

Hypermedia can be like a stack of index cards, with each card having a button on it that, when touched, will automatically connect you to another card in the stack, to another stack of cards, or to a graphic that may be in some other file. For example, a computer lab coordinator is responsible to ensure the proper care of the lab equipment, which means teaching computer care rules to all students who use the lab. A hypermedia approach can teach students about the rules and etiquette of the computer lab and at the same time introduce them to a powerful new learning tool. By clicking on any one of the computer pieces on the first computer care card, students can explore the rules associated with it. Clicking on the disk, for instance, can bring up a card about how to handle disks. To explore more deeply, students can click on the disk label and learn about proper methods for labeling disks. Figure 1.7 shows an example of a HyperCard explaining computer input devices.

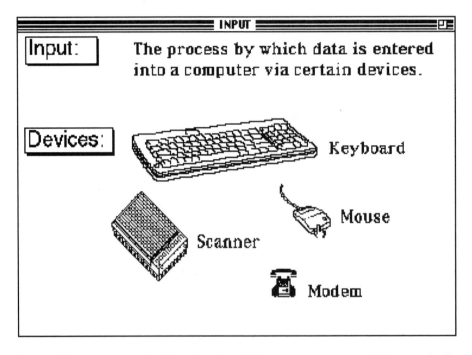

Figure 1.7. An example of a HyperCard card. Users can choose any of the icons and get detailed information about the device pictured.

Perhaps the most significant kinds of connections in hypermedia are the links that can be created between stacks. For example, students examining the computer lab rules stack can click on the school building button to connect them to other stacks that address other school rules, such as library etiquette or fire drill procedures. The connections, then, are not just between one fact and another, but between different school departments. All of school life can potentially be an integrated learning experience with the power of hypermedia.

Hypermedia has an authoring tool that allows users to organize and present information by linking or branching it to other information, graphics, or media such as CD-ROM files. One of the popular hypermedia authoring programs is LinkWay, distributed by IBM.

APPLICATIONS OF MULTIMEDIA IN EDUCATION

Multimedia has found its greatest applications in training and education as well as in presentations that lure an audience and provide information. The most widely known educational example of CD-ROM is *Grolier Multimedia Encyclopedia*. The encyclopedia on CD-ROM takes up only about 20 percent of the disc capacity, so a great quantity is still available for further supplements, such as graphics, video, or even a built-in word processor.

When students are engaged in using CD-ROM in the library, for example, using *Grolier Multimedia Encyclopedia* as a research and study tool, they browse the computerized index by subject. Encylopaedia Britanica and Jostens Learning Corporation developed *Compton Multimedia Encyclopedia*, offering students with varied learning styles a world of sound, colorful graphics, and information across the curriculum. The CD-ROM disc contains not only 26 volumes of *Compton's Encyclopedia* but also thousands of color images, audio, and moving animation. Compton is a source of information and an interactive tool for students. For example, it includes the complete *Webster Intermediate Dictionary*. When students select a key word in a passage, the full definition appears on screen and a human voice reads it. The word processor (a built-in program) enables students researching a topic in the encyclopedia to open a window, take notes, and even copy blocks of text from the article for future use in a report or composition.

> Use of multimedia technology results in significant changes in the teacher's role due to the increase in learner-controlled instruction.

Students may also use the electronic encyclopedia to solve complex and multifaceted research problems. Phillipo (1989) noted that, using the keyword search feature of the electronic encyclopedia, students can query the information database for complex and integrated information.

Marchionini (1988) stated that there are three main characteristics of hypermedia systems that have great potential for learning and teaching. First, hypermedia systems allow huge collections of information in a variety of media to be stored in an extremely compact form and accessed easily and rapidly. Thus, comprehensive and diverse materials can be assembled and delivered to learners. More importantly, these materials can be linked both explicitly and implicitly. Explicit links can be used by authors to suggest paths (and thus relationships) through the information, and learners can choose to follow them or not, in effect, creating their own interpretation of the content. Authors can include implicit links to support materials (for example, dictionaries, encyclopedias) and navigational aids (graphics of the user path, guided tours), allowing learners to apply them as needed. Comprehensive information, varied formats, and dynamic linking offer learners individualized access to rich intellectual environments.

> Multimedia can be used to enrich. Using materials such as video, still images, or audio segments from famous speeches can make the subject immediate and alive in a way that the printed page never can.

Second, hypermedia is an enabling rather than a directive environment, offering unusually high levels of learner control. Learners may choose to follow well-marked trails of explicit links or blaze new trails according to their individual abilities and objectives. Hypermedia offers not only a new way to learn course content but also new ways of learning how to learn.

Third, hypermedia offers the potential to alter the roles of teachers and learners and the crucial interactions between them. Good teachers always learn from their students, and hypermedia provides an opportunity to facilitate and formalize the human/human interaction that is central to effective teaching and learning. The flexibility of hypermedia will enable students to create unique tours and interpretations of the information in a hyperdocument. Sharing these tours and interpretations with other students and their teachers will provide richer and more challenging experiences for learners and teachers alike. The system can facilitate this exchange by saving and replaying tours and allowing these tours (the traces of the process of using the materials) to be studied and exchanged. The interactive nature of the electronic media can foster repetitive interaction between learners and instructors, thus affecting the nature of teacher/learner relationships.

A science student could query the encyclopedia for information on the "effects of ultraviolet light on green plants in a tropical environment" and "tropic." The student's research in will not only be attributable to his/her ability to write a reseach report, but also the ability to analyze a problem, think critically, and select the most appropriate words.

> The most significant benefit of multimedia is students working together. Multimedia encourages interactive education.

Multimedia emphasizes links across the curriculum by taking a topic and connecting it to the larger picture of what is happening in the world today. Events in our world, present and past, are not isolated unto themselves. They involve a combination of history, economics, and sociology. Multimedia has the capability to combine all these aspects, offering a much broader view of historical events. For example, if a teacher is doing a lesson on the Civil War, multimedia helps to connect the textbook lesson with images from that era. That gives students a more realistic view of what America was like at that time.

Multimedia contributes significantly to science. Collins (1989) noted that it could be useful for pre-lab and post-lab activities, especially when the teacher is preparing the students for comparative work on a subject such as the skeleton. Before labs, the teacher can show a full cat skeleton and then a frog skeleton. The teacher can show a close-up of any part. This helps students know what to look for and how to distinguish differences. The post-lab activity may include review and practice.

Interactive multimedia helps illustrate concepts that are difficult to show in a classroom setting. For example, the students can see a nuclear explosion or look inside nuclear reactors. Another example Collins mentioned is radiation: after seeing alpha, beta, and gamma rays, followed by radiation passing through lead plates, students can deduce which type of radiation it is, based on what they have already learned.

Keathley (1989) explained a project with interactive technology wherein the ninth grade physical science students sit in small groups and animatedly discuss a nuclear reaction they are observing from only a few feet away. They are perfectly safe. The reaction is simulated and unfolds on a computer screen. The students can also interact with the program by touching the computer screen.

Jones (1989) mentioned an example of a multimedia project about the solar system. In this project, students can activate a videodisc sequence showing the earth revolving around the sun. They may start and stop the CD-ROM player to examine the earth's position at various times of the year or the moon's location in different stages of its orbit.

Jones and Smith (1989) conducted a series of studies in the area of chemistry and engineering. In a preparatory course for students with low placement scores, the interactive videodisc lessons were tested as a replacement for audio tutorial laboratory instruction. One group of students, selected at random, used the videodisc system; the control group was taught identical content via audio tapes, a workbook, and laboratory experiments. The students were compared by means of a written quiz. In all cases, the results showed statistically significant gains for the students using the videodisc lessons.

Pina and Savenye (1992) argued that multimedia technologies offer unique opportunities to learners to access information by selecting highlighted words or icons. Choices of a word or of an icon enables the learner to select the order in which lessons are presented, skip unneeded lessons, access help screens, repeat a particular lesson, receive additional examples, or take a test. They also noted that use of multimedia technology provides the opportunity for learning experiences that would otherwise be difficult for teachers to incorporate, such as computer simulations of dangerous chemical reactions and computer software that allows medical students to practice life-and-death procedures without harm to real patients.

Borras (1993), Meskill (1993), Nummikoski and Smith (1993), and Wohler (1992) examined the effect of interactive multimedia in second language acquisition. Interactive multimedia allows students to move from text and data into the realm of graphics, sound, images, and full-motion video, thus allowing both students and teachers to use the power of the computer in new ways to accomodate the process of second language learning.

Fontana et al. (1993) described a multimedia prototype developed at George Mason University's Center for Interactive Educational Technology to foster higher-order thinking skills in social studies. As an initial step, the Civil War Interactive Project used the Ken Burns documentary, "The Civil War." The project concluded that using multimedia can produce the following results: (1) explicit instruction; (2) modeling; (3) tutoring/coaching; (4) student control of the data and the production; (5) cooperative learning; and (6) equity of access to information.

Sprayberry (1993) conducted a study to investigate the effectiveness of multimedia instruction in improving listening comprehension of high school students studying second-year Spanish. A multimedia instructional approach was adopted with 50 randomly selected students. The results showed that students were receptive to and enthusiastic about the process, and post-tests indicated significant language achievement gains over the period of treatment.

Chapter 2

Planning

The planning process is the most important step in multimedia development. During this process, planners set goals that will determine how the application will work and what content they must gather. They will begin to gather all the information they will need to continue into the project planning phase, where developers will have to tackle hard questions about resources and budget.

Desirable multimedia outcomes are usually attained through careful plans. Start with an idea, a problem situation, or a need identified within an area or a course for multimedia materials. An idea may indicate an area of interest, but the most useful ideas are those conceived in terms of a need relating to a specific group, a need for certain information or for a skill, or a need to establish a desired attitude.

Multimedia planning starts with a recognition of the broad goals of the learning program. After establishing the goals, list the major topics to be treated within the content area. A topic is a heading for a unit or a component of a multimedia program that treats subject content knowledge to be learned. Those topics, or unit headings, become the scope of the multimedia program. It becomes necessary to decide how many topics should be treated and to what depth. Consider such factors as when the program must be ready and what restrictions have been set by learner characteristics and by the limitations of budget, facilities, or resources.

LEARNING THEORIES

Two major learning theories, behaviorism theory and cognitive theory, provide directions to designing and planning instructional materials. Specifically, they provide directions to the developers of multimedia programs.

BEHAVIORISM THEORY

Of the theories supporting the use of technology in the learning process, behaviorism has historically had the greatest impact. Behaviorism was used as the basis for designing early audiovisual materials and was also the impetus behind many related teaching/learning strategies, such as the use of teaching machines and programmed texts. Thorndike's connectionism, Pavlov's classical conditioning, and Skinner's operant conditioning gave direction to early researchers who examined the impact of instructional technology on behavior and to early developers who produced teaching materials for use in the schools.

> Behaviorism states that all instruction should be based on objectives that state clearly what is expected of the learner.

The use of behaviorism in learning is based on the principle that instruction should be designed to produce observable and quantifiable actions by the learner. Behaviorists consider the mental state of a learner to be merely a predisposition. Because mental states cannot be observed, behaviorists do not believe teaching should be directed toward strengthening the mind, a common goal of educators of the early 20th century, but should be aimed at producing desirable outcomes in students. In other words, behaviorists expect any effective instructional activity, such as a computer-based tutorial, to change the learner in some obvious and measurable way. After completing a lesson, students should be able to do something that they could not do, or could not do as well, before the lesson.

Another kind of learning is called *operant conditioning*. This approach for producing behavior change uses no identifiable stimulus before a response, but rather, uses reinforcers that follow a response or that are produced by a response. These reinforcers are responsible for a behavior change. Operant conditioning includes the use of reinforcement to promote desirable changes in behavior. Reinforcement occurs after desired actions.

Behaviorists' contributions to the practice of instructional technology are numerous. They include the following techniques:

> Behaviorism is criticized as dehumanizing the teaching and learning process.

- Stating objectives in terms of desired terminal behaviors.

- Assessing a student's previously acquired behaviors before any instruction.

- Placing learners in a sequence of instruction where they can achieve at the 90% level.

- Using teaching machines to reinforce and to strengthen desired terminal behaviors.

- Recording a learner's progress through a lesson-to-gain feedback for revising the lesson.

Skinner was a vocal advocate of behaviorist principles and of the use of machines to teach. As late as 1986 he reiterated his belief that behaviorism was a critical theory for educators to understand and apply. He also advocated the use of computers in instruction because he believed that when computers were correctly programmed, they became ideal teaching machines.

COGNITIVE THEORY

Educational psychologists and learning theorists have begun to move away from the behaviorist approach and have advocated a closer look at the internal processes that take place in learners during instruction. Behaviorists tend to ignore the cognitive changes that occur internally during learning. They maintain that it is impossible to design instruction based on what happens in a learner's brain because these changes are not observable or measurable and are impossible to predict. On the other hand, cognitive psychologists, the common name for advocates of cognitive theory, focus attention on the learning process itself and attribute a greater degree of autonomy and initiative to the learner than do behaviorists.

Cognitive theory concentrates on the conceptualization of learners' learning processes. It focuses on the exploration of the way information is received, organized, retained, and used by the brain. When instruction is designed, proponents of cognitive theory believe that the cognitive structure of the learner and groups of learners should be taken into account. Several persons have been influential in advocating the cognitive approach, including Jerome Bruner, Jean Piaget, and Seymour Papert.

Cognitive psychologists have proposed that much of behavior depends on how we structure knowledge about ourselves and the world around us. Cognitive theorists believe that instruction must be based on a learner's existing state of mental organization, or schema. How knowledge is internally structured or organized by a learner has considerable impact on whether new learning will occur. New learning is based on using prior knowledge to understand new situations and changing prior knowledge structures to deal with new situations. According to cognitive theory, information must be organized in a way that helps learners connect the new information with current knowledge in a meaningful way.

> Cognitive theory advocates the importance of determining as much as possible about the learner and about the process used by the learner to internalize information so that instruction can be optimally designed.

Cognitive theorists concentrate on several concepts. First, they are interested in how knowledge is organized and structured. Second, they are interested in readiness for learning. Third, cognitive theorists value intuition. By intuition, Bruner means the intellectual techniques used for arriving at plausible but tentative conclusions without going through a sense of analytical steps. In other words, the value of the "educated guess" is recognized. Last, the importance of motivation, or desire to learn, is identified. Specifically, cognitive scientists accept the importance of students having positive attitudes toward learning.

Cognitive psychologists view the learner as an active participant in the learning process, believing that learning occurs because the learner actively participates in understanding and interpreting the learning environment. Thus, to the cognitive psychologist, education consists of enabling active mental exploration of complex environments.

Cognitive theory gives several guidelines to educators interested in designing or evaluating mediated instruction (multimedia) and to scientists interested in planning research. They are the following:

> There should be mechanisms to provide for multiple contingencies that might affect the successful completion of the lesson. Specifically, the ultimate technology-based system should be an intelligent one that "learns" as it is used.

- Predisposition to learning is important. Instruction needs something to get it started, something to keep it going, and something to keep it from being random. Jerome Bruner would call this activation, maintenance, and direction.

- The learner must be actively engaged in the learning process; students create knowledge by making connections with previously learned material. Learning environments must allow and encourage learners to make these connections.

- The structure and form of knowledge must be considered. Specifically, the body of materials to be learned should be organized in some optimal way. Cognitive theory is partially based on the concept that children are first able to understand concrete operations, then graphic representations of reality, and finally abstract verbal and numerical symbols.

> Instruction should be motivating to the learner, both cognitively and affectively. It should be both informative and interesting.

- Sequencing of instructional material is important. Sequencing must take into account the limited capabilities of learners to process information. Because a child's cognitive style may partially determine success in learning activities, many educators in recent years have begun to attempt to identify components of the cognitive styles of learners, such as their brain hemisphere dominance, their level of field dependence, and their visual processing ability.

- New information should be connected in a meaningful way to information previously learned. Use of information organizers prior to instruction provides one approach to helping students connect new learning with previously learned material.

- Discovery learning is one important technique that applies much of cognitive theory. As an educational method, discovery learning consists of inserting learners into educational situations without telling them what is already known about that situation.

Active involvement by the learner is important. Both intellectual and psychomotor involvement should be required of the learner.

In summary, cognitive theory provides educators with a missing piece of the puzzle. Where behaviorists look at outcomes, cognitive theorists look at learners and processes. Although current work in educational research is increasingly based on the paradigms of cognitive theory, both theories provide important grounding for empirical work.

Certainly, these briefs are only general explanations of behaviorism and cognitive theory. Some educators would even consider it improper to try to identify similarities between these theories. One simple yet fairly accurate way to relate them to one another is to apply each to something familiar, such as getting a good picture on a color television set. A behaviorist would be content with adjusting the knobs and controls on the television. Behaviorists work with the situation at hand and manipulate it to get results. Getting the best picture possible would be the major concern of the behaviorist. The cognitive theorist, on the other hand, would use special scopes and monitoring devices to examine every tube and transistor inside the television. The cognitive theorist would try to examine the video signal to be sure it was being correctly processed by the television's electronic parts. Faulty or weak components would be identified and replaced. How the television manipulated the signal would be of paramount importance to the cognitive theorist.

In a learning situation, the behaviorist wants to take the learner and produce the desired behaviors by controlling the learning environment. Manipulating the learner and learning situation to produce the desired outcome would be the most important to the behaviorist. The cognitive theorist would want to study the brain and its functioning to see how learning occurs. This information would then be used to produce learning in learners.

INFORMING OR INSTRUCTING

Multimedia materials can be used for either of two purposes— to inform or to instruct individuals or groups. For informational purposes a presentation would be general in nature, serving as an introduction, an overview, a report, or for background knowledge. It might employ entertainment, dramatic, or motivational techniques to attract and hold attention. When viewing and listening to informational materials, individuals are passive viewers and listeners. The anticipated response would most likely be limited to degrees of mental agreement or disagreement and to pleasant, neutral, or unpleasant feelings. Materials that are designed for informational purposes can in turn lead a person to involvement with the idea or topic on an instructional level.

A topic can be designed for a teaching situation and a general instructional purpose. But the same topic might be used with another audience on an informational level.

For instructional purposes, although the presentation of information is important, participants should also engage in mental or overt activities relating to the multimedia materials being used so that learning can take place. The materials themselves should be made more systematically and psychologically sound in terms of learning principles in order to provide effective instruction. At the same time they should be enjoyable and provide pleasant experiences. Making provisions for individuals to interact with materials by answering questions, by engaging in performance as directed by the materials, by checking understandings, and by making use of information presented are key features to consider when you plan multimedia materials for instruction.

DEVELOPING THE OBJECTIVES

Philosophers and psychologists alike have proposed and discussed two models or images of humanity. The behaviorist orientation considers human beings to be passive organisms governed by stimuli from the external environment. Through proper control of environmental stimuli, people can be manipulated, their behavior governed. According to the behaviorists, the laws that govern humans are the same as the universal laws that govern all natural phenomena. Therefore, the scientific method evolved by the physical sciences is also appropriate for the study of the human organism.

According to the phenomenological view, humans are the source of their acts; thus, they are free to make choices in every situation. The focal point of this freedom is human consciousness. Advocates of this position feel that behavior is only the absorbable expression and consequence of an essentially private, internal world of being. Therefore, only a "science of humans," which begins with experience, can be adequate for a study of the human organism.

Freud, throughout his career, hoped to reduce human behavior to chemical and physical dimensions. Freud had little interest in the social implications of his theories. He called attention to the unconscious mind and its influence on human behavior. Freud believed that our raw instincts were repressed by the artificially imposed customs and morals of society. The id and the super-ego were constantly at war with one another, and the resulting behavior came from one's ego, the part of the mind that combined the forces of the id and super-ego to determine action.

Humanistic psychologists have been critical of these traditions because they believe that behaviorism and psychoanalysis—Freudianism—offer limited views of human nature, ignoring the heights to which people have the potential to rise. Neither behaviorism nor psychoanalysis has dealt with our potential for growth, our desire to be better or more than we are.

The perceptual view of human behavior holds that the behavior of an individual is a function of his ways of perceiving. That is to say, how any person behaves at a given moment is a direct expression of the way things seem to him at that moment. People do not behave according to the "facts" as they seem to an outsider. What a person does, what a person learns, is thus a product of what is going on in his unique and personal field of awareness. Behaving and learning are products of perceiving.

CATEGORIES OF OBJECTIVES

Objectives for learning can be grouped into three major categories—cognitive, psychomotor, and affective. We need to understand these areas (or domains, as they are generally called), as referred to in the literature that discusses objectives. Understanding of the levels within each domain will help focus attention on the higher levels of learning and behavior.

These domains provide a helpful standard by which multimedia developers can evaluate the quality of their objectives. Within each of the domains there are levels, probably hierarchical, that attempt to categorize different kinds of learner behavior.

THE COGNITIVE DOMAIN

The cognitive domain has six levels. They move from knowledge, the lowest level, to evaluation, the highest level.

KNOWLEDGE. Knowledge involves the recall of specifics or universals, the recall of methods and processes, or the recall of a pattern, structure, or setting. It will be noted that the essential attribute at this level is recall. For assessment purposes, a recall situation involves little more than "bringing to mind" appropriate material.

COMPREHENSION. This level represents the lowest form of understanding and refers to a kind of apprehension that indicates that a learner knows what is being communicated and can make use of the material or idea without necessarily relating it to other material or seeing it in its fullest implications.

APPLICATION. Application involves the use of abstractions in particular or concrete situations. The abstractions used may be in the form of procedures, general ideas, or generalized methods. They may also be ideas, technical principles, or theories that must be remembered and applied.

ANALYSIS. Analysis involves breaking down a communication into its constituent parts such that the relative hierarchy within that communication is made clear, the relations between the expressed ideas are made explicit, or both. Such analyses are intended to clarify the communication, to indicate how it is organized and the way in which the communication manages to convey its effects as well as its basis and arrangement.

SYNTHESIS. Synthesis represents the combining of elements and parts so that they form a whole. This operation involves working with pieces, parts, elements, and so on, and arranging them into a pattern or structure not clearly present before.

EVALUATION. Evaluation requires judgments about the value of material and methods for given purposes. Quantitative and qualitative judgments are made about the extent to which material and methods satisfy criteria. The criteria employed may be those determined by the learner or those given to the learner.

It is probably sufficient if the multimedia developer simply divides the cognitive taxonomy into (a) the lowest level, knowledge, and (b) all those levels higher than the lowest, comprehension through evaluation. Even this rough, two-category scheme will allow a multimedia developer to identify the proportion of objectives that fall into the lowest level category. And this seems to be the most important advantage of the cognitive taxonomy—encouraging the multimedia developer to identify what proportion of objectives are at the very lowest level.

THE AFFECTIVE DOMAIN

The affective domain is subdivided into five levels. Once more, these levels may have some value in that they encourage the multimedia developer to think about different forms of objectives, but it is not recommended that the multimedia developer devote too much time in attempting to classify various objectives within these levels.

RECEIVING. The first level of the affective domain is concerned with the learner's sensitivity to the existence of certain phenomena and stimuli, that is, with the learner's willingness to receive or to attend to them. This category is divided into three subdivisions that indicate three different levels of attending to phenomena: awareness of the phenomena, willingness to receive phenomena, and controlled or selected attention to phenomena.

RESPONDING. At this level one is concerned with responses that go beyond merely attending to phenomena. The learner is sufficiently motivated that he or she is not just "willing to attend," but is actively attending.

VALUING. This category reflects the learner's holding of a particular value. The learner displays behavior with sufficient consistency in appropriate situations that he or she is actually perceived as holding this value.

ORGANIZATION. As the learner successively internalizes values, he or she encounters situations in which more than one value is relevant. This requires organizing his or her values into a system such that certain values exercise greater control.

CHARACTERIZATION BY A VALUE OR VALUE COMPLEX. At this highest level of the affective taxonomy, internalization has taken place in an individual's value hierarchy to the extent that we can actually characterize the learner as holding a particular value or set of values.

THE PSYCHOMOTOR DOMAIN

The psychomotor domain is concerned with physical abilities, such as muscular or motor skills, manipulation, and neuromuscular coordination. This domain has been classified into the following major categories:

PERCEPTION. The first step in performing a motor act is the process of becoming aware of objects, qualities, or relations by way of the sense organs. It is the main portion of the situation-interpretation-action chain leading to motor activity.

SET. Set is a preparatory adjustment for a particular kind of action or experience. Three distinct aspects of set have been identified: mental, physical, and emotional.

GUIDED RESPONSE. This is an early step in the development of a motor skill. The emphasis is upon the abilities that are components of the more complex skill. Guided response is the overt behavioral act of an individual under the guidance of another individual.

MECHANISM. At this level the learner has achieved a certain confidence and degree of skill in the performance of an act. The habitual act is a part of his or her repertoire of possible responses to stimuli and the demands of situations where the response is appropriate.

COMPLEX OVERT RESPONSE. At this level, the individual can perform a motor act that is considered complex because of the movement pattern required. The act can be carried out efficiently and smoothly, that is, with minimum expenditure of energy and time.

The difficult problem is to spell out the objectives so that learning experiences can be developed to satisfy each objective and tests or performance measurements can be designed to find out whether the learning has taken place. Once you have categorized the objectives, the next step is to write the objectives.

WRITING THE OBJECTIVES

Brainstorming is a critical part of developing multimedia. Whether you brainstorm on your own or with several other people, the method is the same. Focus on the communication objectives of the multimedia production for a predetermined amount of time. Voice every verbal and visual idea that comes to mind. Write down all of the ideas in the order they come.

Useful statements of objectives are made up of two grammatical parts. First, there is a specific action verb, such as to *identify*, to *name*, to *demonstrate*, to *show*, to *make* or *build*, to *order* or *arrange*, to *distinguish between*, to *compare*, to *apply*, and so forth. Second, content reference follows the verb, such as to name *the five steps in the process*, to kick *a football at least 30 yards*, to write *a 500-word theme*, to apply *a rule*, to solve *four of five problems*, and so forth.

Notice that in addition to the action verb and the content reference, we may add a standard of competency (at least 30 yards, 500 words, four of five problems). The standard further provides for setting an attainment level that can be measured.

You might prepare multimedia materials for many instructional purposes. Here are some major general purposes with specific examples. They are stated as objectives in terms of audience changes, from the audience's viewpoint.

- To learn about a subject; for example, "to recognize the location of five Middle Eastern countries."

- To apply the steps in a process; for example, "to locate and use the major reference books in the school library."

- To exercise a skill; for example, "to create a document using a word processing program."

- To practice a certain attitude, for example, "to form the habit of defensive driving."

- To respond to a social need; for example, "to offer my services in a fund-raising event."

In planning materials, limit yourself to no more than a few concisely stated, achievable objectives. However much you feel it necessary to cover the whole topic, you will eventually realize that limitations should be set. If you do not set limits, your materials may become too complex and unmanageable. You can maintain limits by aiming at a series of related multimedia materials, each of which includes a single phase of a large topic.

> First step: Express your idea concisely.
>
> Second step: Recognize broad general purposes.

Finally, objectives do not stand alone. It is obvious that they are dependent on the subject content that will be treated and are influenced by the needs and dispositions of the learner or intended audience.

CONSIDERING THE AUDIENCE (THE LEARNER)

The characteristics of the learner or audience—those who will be learning from and using your materials—cannot be separated from your statement of objectives. One influences the other. Audience characteristics such as age and educational level, knowledge of the subject and attitude toward it, and individual differences within the group all have a bearing on your objectives and treatment of the topic. The audience is the determinant when you consider the complexity of ideas to be presented, the rate at which the topic is developed, the vocabulary level for captions and narration, the number of examples to use, the kinds of involvement and degree of participation of the learner, and similar matters.

Generally, it is advisable to plan for one major audience group, then consider other secondary ones that also might use your materials. Describe the major audience explicitly.

You have your content organized in terms of objectives and the audience. You are aware of the kinds of multimedia materials you may consider for preparation, their characteristics and particular contributions, advantages, and limitations.

There is no single best manner in which the details of the content outline can be transformed into meaningful and related pictures and words. Two approaches have been established through experience, but they are by no means the only sound ones. First, many successful materials carry an audience from the known to the unknown; they start with things familiar to the audience (perhaps by reviewing the present level of understanding) and then lead to as many new facts and new relationships as the material is meant to achieve. Second, many materials are successfully built around three divisions: the introduction, which captures the attention of the audience; the developmental stage, which contains most of the content and in effect tells the story (or involves the viewers in active participation); and the ending, which may summarize or review the ideas presented and suggest further activity.

DEFINING THE LEARNER

It is important to give attention to learner characteristics when preparing a multimedia program. Consideration should be given to the nature of the learners, their aptitudes and preparation levels, degree of motivation, or other traits that contribute to interest and success in learning.

Obviously, the measure of success of multimedia materials will be based principally on the learning level accomplished by the learners involved. Learner populations, from elementary levels through high school and college and in training areas—whether industrial, business, health, government, or military—are composed of varied types of people. Therefore, it is essential, early in planning, to give attention to the characteristics, abilities, and experiences of the learners—as a group and as individuals.

It is well recognized that all people differ in many respects, including the ways in which they learn. Some of these differences are evident in the kinds of experiences each person requires in order to learn, and if competence in a skill is to be acquired, in the amount of time and practice each person requires. To serve either an academic class or a training group, the multimedia developer must obtain information about the capabilities, needs, and interests of the learners. This information should affect certain elements in planning, such as the selection of topics (and the level at which topics are introduced), the choice and sequencing of objectives, the depth of topic treatment, and the variety of learning activities.

When designing a multimedia plan, decide early in the initial design stages which characteristics of your learners or trainees it would be most useful to identify. Then decide how to acquire the necessary information.

ACADEMIC INFORMATION

In the design of multimedia materials, information about individual learners' academic records allows access to knowledge and skills that learners may already possess that directly relate to the subject content or skills to be learned. Much of this information can be obtained from student record files in a school's administrative office. Some of it is available on employment applications or in a personnel file.

PERSONAL AND SOCIAL CHARACTERISTICS

It is desirable to be aware of personal and social characteristics of the learner for whom the program is to be planned. To design a procedure for teaching a person anything, an instructor needs knowledge about the learner such as age and maturity level; motivation and attitude toward the subject; current employment and work experience (if any); and ability to work under various environmental conditions. Such useful data may be obtained by observation, interviews, and informational questionnaires.

MULTICULTURAL LEARNERS

Learner groups may include members from many cultures. Therefore, consideration should be given to their special characteristics during planning. Such consideration can be essential whether the learners are in an academic or a vocational training program.

In some cultures an accepted strong authority figure, like the father in a family, influences the freedom and decision-making abilities of children. If background experiences are limited, naiveté and lack of sophistication may affect a learner's readiness for and participation in a program.

Information about multicultural learners can be obtained through the usual testing, interview, and questionnaire procedures. In addition, consider obtaining help from counselors, either in an institution or from the community, who have had direct experience in working with such individuals.

DISABLED LEARNERS

The category of disabled learners includes physically handicapped individuals and others with learning disabilities such as hearing and vision loss, speech impairment, and mild mental retardation. Each type of challenged learner has unique limitations and requires special consideration. Some physically handicapped persons can participate in regular classes; others cannot.

Many physically challenged learners require special training and individual attention. Therefore, a multimedia program may require extensive modification in order to serve them appropriately.

ADULT LEARNERS

Adults are returning to colleges and universities and participating in job training or retraining for new skills in business, industry, health fields, government service, and the military. Adults enter a program with a high level of motivation and readiness to learn. Often they clearly know what goal they want to reach. They appreciate a program that is structured systematically, with elements clearly specified. They bring to a course extensive background experience from both their personal and professional lives. These experiences should be used by an instructor as major resources by helping adults relate their experiences to the topics being studied.

When plans are made for classroom or group instruction, obtain general indications of the academic and social characteristics of potential and actual learners.

Adults may be less flexible than younger learners. Their habits and methods of operation have been developed into a routine. Before they will accept change, they must see an advantage in doing so. Most adults are largely self-directed and independent. Although some adults lack confidence and need reassurance of their ability to learn, the great majority prefer to engage actively in their own learning. For them, a multimedia program should serve as informal facilitator to guide, assist, and provide encouragement as necessary.

Special attention should be given to the unique characteristics of nonconventional learners, such as individuals from different ethnic groups, learners with disabilities, and adults.

For designing individualized learning programs, data about each learner can further aid in the selection of alternative activities, resources, and the most appropriate study environment.

In planning for individual learners, the matters of learning styles, including brain hemisphere dominance, preferred learning conditions, and cognitive learning can all profitably receive attention.

PLANNING FOR INVOLVEMENT

Many investigations of the effectiveness of multimedia materials have shown the value of having the learner participate in some way during, or immediately after, the study of the material. These experiments, without reservation, have proven that active participation definitely helps learning. But most producers of multimedia materials ignore this principle.

The way to create participation is to make involvement an inherent part of the material itself. This is a key element of multimedia materials—the learner is actively doing something while studying. Here are some suggestions for developing participation in multimedia materials:

- Include questions that require an immediate written or oral response.

- Direct other written activity (explain, summarize, give other examples, and so forth).

- Require selection, judgment, or other decisions to be made from among things shown or heard.

- Require performance related to the activity or skill shown or heard.

These participation techniques often require a break in the presentation—having the learner stop the program to do something or promoting immediate activity after studying a section of the material.

Also, be sure to plan for evaluation of the participation results and provide feedback to the learner indicating the correct reply or a comparison of measurement for the level of accomplishment. If your materials are designed for information rather than for instruction, you still want a response. Possibly it is acceptance as expressed by applause, or an action to follow the viewing.

WRITING THE TREATMENT

The treatment is a written document that serves as a blueprint for the script. It should contain all the information needed to help the production staff visualize the program from start to finish. The treatment differs from the script in that it is not written in a script format and usually does not include production jargon, such as camera moves.

The treatment is the foundation upon which the script is built. At this stage, every detail must be thought through to find the right visuals, sounds, and key words that will make the program effective. For this reason it may take longer to write than the shooting script.

When the production staff reads a treatment, they should be able to piece together the program mentally. They should be able to visualize the characters and imagine how they will sound and how they will talk. The production staff should be able to hear the various types of music or sound effects the writer has chosen. Most important, they should be able to follow the story, pictures and sound, from start to finish. There should be no holes in the message.

The responsibility for writing a treatment should be allocated to the writer/producer. The slash shows that this responsibility may be allocated to one or two people.

Writing a successful treatment depends upon selling your ideas; to sell your ideas you must believe in them fully. Put those beliefs on paper and you will have an effective treatment.

The following is part of a treatment written for an international Fortune 500 company:

Title: Working with Diversity
Audience: All employees
Medium: Videotape/videodisc
Estimated length: 20–25 minutes
Objective: After viewing the videotape, employees should perceive diversity in the workforce as an asset to the company. They should also understand that it is each employee's responsibility to approach the work and co-workers with an open mind.
Key message: Demographic changes in workforce are inevitable— by the year 2000, male Caucasians will be a minority. Like the society, the company needs to incorporate ethnic diversity and people-approaches. Each individual has a responsibility to learn how to work well with diversity.

Commercial television has a great impact on the "visual literacy" of most people. We have learned to accept fast

> The treatment is the first document of the video production, and it should be easy to follow.

> The treatment acts as a blueprint for the script. A detailed treatment will allow the production staff to fully visualize what the program will be like.

pacing of commercials and dramatic programs. The sophistication that results from these experiences requires that many multimedia materials be planned to move briskly both in content treatment and visual techniques. Writing the treatment is an important step because it causes you to think through your presentation, putting it in a sequential, organized form that you and others can follow easily.

> Prepare a descriptive synopsis of the content, then a storyboard; finally, write the script—a "map" for your production.

As you develop the story, try to visualize the situations you are describing. Remember, you are preparing multimedia material—with the emphasis on the word *visual*. Most people normally think in words, but they have to reorient to learn to think in pictures—not in vague general pictures but in specific visual representations of real situations. Visualization can be aided by making simple sketches or by taking photographs (instant pictures on self-processing film are ideal for this purpose) that show the treatment of each element or sequence.

Put the sketches or pictures on cards. Use 3 x 5- or 4 x 6-inch cards or 8 1/2-x-11 inch paper. These proportions approximate the format of most visual materials, the pictures being wider than they are high. Use a card with an area blocked off for the visual and make a space for narration notes or production comments.

Every sequence should be represented by one or more cards. Include separate cards for possible titles, questions, and special directions (such as indications for learner participation). It may not be necessary to make a card for all anticipated scenes. The details, like an overall picture of a subject followed by a close-up of detail within the subject, will be handled in the script that follows.

> The treatment is another important checkpoint stage in the development of your multimedia material.

Reactions and suggestions from those involved in the project or from other interested and qualified persons are valuable at this point. Often people studying the displayed treatment point out things that have been missed or sequences that need reorganization. Rearranging scenes and adding new ones are easy when the storyboard is prepared on sheets of paper or on cards.

DEVELOPING THE SCRIPT

Once the treatment and the storyboard continuity are satisfactorily organized, you are ready to write your detailed blueprint, the script. This script becomes the map that gives definite directions for your picture-taking, art work, or filming. The script is a picture-by-picture listing with accompanying narration or captions. First plan what will be seen, then what will be said or captioned. Write the script in a two-column format, placing camera positions and shot descriptions on the left half of the page and narration on the right, opposite the appropriate scene descriptions. Figure 2.1 shows an example of script sheet.

Figure. 2.1. An example of a script sheet.

The placement of the camera for each picture, with respect to the subject, should be indicated. If the subject is to be at a distance from the camera, the shot is a long shot (LS); if the camera covers the subject and nothing more, it is a medium shot (MS); a close-up (CU) brings the camera in to concentrate on a feature of the subject. Whether the scene is to be photographed from a high angle or a low angle, or subjective (from the subject's viewpoint, as over the shoulder) can also be specified. Figure 2.2 illustrates the different shots.

Figure 2.2.a. Examples of close-up shots.

Figure 2.2.b. Examples of medium shots.

Figure 2.2.c. Examples of long shots.

At this stage the narration or captions, indicated along the right-hand side of your script, need not be stated in final, detailed form. It is sufficient to write narration ideas, or brief statements, that can be refined later. Only when an explanation requires a scene to be of a specific length must the narration be written carefully and in final form at this point.

Narration is important not only for the part it plays in explaining details as the audio of multimedia but also to call attention to relationships and indicate emphasis that should be given in some pictures (center of attention or camera position) when filming. Be alert to problems that may arise with narration. If it is not related closely to the visual so as to reinforce the visual, the narration may with interfere with or inhibit learning. Figure 2.3 shows an example of a script.

Visual	Audio
Fade up from black. The video opens with LS of an elementary school children in a classroom. We see boys and girls, different races.	<u>Music up and under.</u> Voice over : "In the next decade, these children will be entering the workforce. The workforce they meet will be quite different from today."
Cut to a MS of a male Caucasian child working with blocks at a table.	Voice over: "For the first time in history, white males will not be the majority. Seventy five percent of new workers to the workforce will be females and minorities."
Cut to CU shot of a statistic that shows the distribution of workforce by white males compared to females and minorities. Super-impose (LS) a white male child playing, a female and a minority child walk up to where this child is playing. They join him in what he's doing.	Voiceover: "The diversity of the work force will pose a great challenge to us all because we have but one choice—we either learn to work with diversity or we will be lost." <u>Dramatic music up and under.</u>
Freeze frame. *The title of the videotape appears on the screen,* **Working with Diversity**. *The title screen dissolves to a LS of employees walking through a hallway. The diversity of the people is obvious.*	<u>Music out.</u> Employees conversing with each other. Voiceover: "Diversity in the workforce in our company presents a challenge to all employ-ees—because with diversity, sometimes there are some difficulties to overcome." (pause) "Problem of language barriers."
Disolve to a (MS) minority employee in interview position.	<u>Music up and under.</u> Minority employee: "At first, I wasn't sure of how to answer the telephone because I was afread of being perceived as rude." <u>Music up and out.</u>

Figure 2.3. Example of script.

CONSIDERING THE LENGTH

The content of multimedia material affects the time needed to present it. You need to have time in mind as the script takes shape. Any estimate at this early stage is inevitably loose and approximate, but an estimate is necessary. How are you to forecast the time that will be needed? The following few facts, culled from experience, may offer some guidance:

A still image can hold attention for about 30 seconds (or it may remain on the screen for only a few seconds). The average motion-picture/video scene runs for 7 seconds; it may range from 2 seconds to 30 seconds or more. How are you to know whether the material, at whatever estimated duration, is too short, too long, or just right? There is no formula. An image series must be allowed enough time to permit adequate development of the topic, as based on the purposes, but not be so long that it will lose its effectiveness. A single-concept multimedia presentation may run for 2 or 3 minutes, whereas an orientation program may require 15 or 20 minutes. A multimedia program for primary-grade children would ordinarily be shorter than one designed for high-school or college learners. Also, available time must be considered—do not come up with a 15-minute program for a 10-minute program spot. When you (and your team) appraise your script against the amount of time desirable or available, you may need to review it to see whether the needed time can be shortened, or the content divided into two or more outlines for a series of presentations.

PREPARING THE SPECIFICATIONS

After preparing the script, you must address these questions: What specific things are to be done now, next, and thereafter until the multimedia materials are ready to be used? What is to be bought, made, decided? The answers to these are the specifications. The more complex the projected multimedia material, the more numerous the specifications. Naturally they need to be organized and classified. Some classes of specifications have no bearing on some kinds of materials; on others (slide series, filmstrips, motion pictures, videotape recordings, multi-images) all may be needed. Here are some examples of specifications, with detailed and specific points that must be considered and choices that must be made.

SETTING THE PRIORITIES

Planning for a multimedia production often seems like an exercise in mental juggling. Dozens of factors must be identified, categorized, compared, and the very act of performing this analysis sometimes seems to complicate matters rather than unravel them.

A priority list helps to evaluate and give priorities to factors of seemingly equal importance. The method is almost mechanical in application, but the decision-making process it sets in motion is dynamic. This process forces the developer to plan and to make decisions based on this plan; almost always it also forces the individual to reevaluate the plan. This refining process results in a list of requirements that will serve as firm project guidelines.

The following is a suggested list of priorities:

- Set communications objective, knowing that a communications objective must be based on a change in human behavior or thinking.

- List all presentation requirements. The initial plan should specify the basic presentation requirement such as format, target audience, budget, and so forth.

- Separate requirements into "musts" and "wants." It is at this point that decisions should be made. You have to decide what is necessary for the success of the presentation and what is merely desirable.

- Set priorities for all "musts" and "wants." To bring your requirements into sharpest focus, you should set priorities for both necessary and desired lists. The following table shows an example of a Musts and Wants list with priorities shown at the left. Your priority list may be different.

Musts	Wants
(5) Text	Color-coded text
(4) Graphics	High-resolution color graphics
(1) Motion picture	Full-screen/high-resolution motion
(2) Sound	Stereo sound
(3) Interactive	Web interaction
(7) Audience: K–adult	General population
(6) Budget: $35,000 max	Less is better
(8) User friendly	Easy to use for all
(12) Use high-quality equipment	Use professional-grade equipment
(9) Use qualified staff	Use professional staff
(11) Use special effects	Use computer-generated special effects
(10) Use experienced scriptwriter	Use professional scriptwriter and copy editor
(13) Document	Worksheets and activities

At this point, having ranked requirements, you should be prepared to evaluate the lists in light of time and budgetary limitations.

EVALUATING YOUR RESOURCES

Time is an element that cannot be altered. Just as the scope of a multimedia presentation must often be curtailed to stay within a budget, the sophistication of a production must often suffer for lack of time. And more often than not, that lack of time was brought about by unrealistic scheduling or a total lack of scheduling. It is important to estimate just how much time will be required to produce the material you are planning.

At this juncture, it would be safe to break the production schedule into four major sections:

1. Research, treatment, and scripting

2. Design, art, photography, and cinematography

3. Sound track and visual assembly

4. Programming for interactivity

There are, of course, no hard and fast rules that dictate this specific sequence of events, or even that each section must be completed before another is begun. But in general, because they involve one or more distinct skills, each section is usually dependent upon the preceding ones for direction. By analyzing the time requirements for each of these production specialties, you will be able to develop a production schedule much as you would develop a cost estimate. The result of this analysis will at least provide the assurance that your efforts are not being directed toward an impossible goal.

MONEY

Production costs depend on the length of the program, the complexity of the program, the equipment needed to produce and present the program, as well as dozens of other factors. Normally, you cannot talk about costs until you can talk specifics.

To estimate the cost of a multimedia presentation, you must begin with specifications for a particular multimedia project. You will not have a problem developing the specifications from which to calculate a budget. In fact, these specifications already exist, in broad terms, in the entries on your priority chart. If prepared correctly, that chart should tell you the length of your presentation as well as the general style of the presentation. Your next step is to assemble, on paper, the staff and equipment you will need to bring these requirements into existence. Once that is done, you have to put a price tag on these resources.

Job Category	Hourly Rate
Producer	$50+
Project Manager	$30+
Director	$60+
Writer	$30
Photographer	$50
Narrator	$30+
Actor/Model	$300/day
Composer	$50+
Audio Tech.	$40+
Videographer	$25+
Editor	$20+
Programming	$30+
Computer Artist	$30+
Other Technical Staff	$15+

Staff Costs

TO BUY OR TO RENT

How often do you plan to use the equipment? If the answer is only two or three times a year, you may be better off renting. If you are not sure, apply this simple formula: Begin by estimating how often you think you will use the equipment each year. Then multiply that figure by the number of years you expect to use the equipment before replacing it. Four years is considered average. (Equipment will usually function for more than four years but it may become obsolete sooner than that.)

Then divide the purchase price plus 20 percent for maintenance and repairs by the number of times you plan to use the equipment. If the cost per usage comes out substantially higher than the rental fee, rent the equipment.

Example:
Machine costs $500 + 20% = $600
Annual use (30 times) x (4 years) = 120 uses
$600 divided by 120 uses = $5 per usage
Cost per usage = $5; Daily rental fee = $20

If the cost of renting equipment turns out to be slightly cheaper than the cost of buying, it still may be less expensive to purchase. Remember your time is worth money. If you add up the time you spend picking up and returning rental equipment, buying may be cheaper.

SKILLS

The easiest resource to begin with is skills. Under this category you may be budgeting for any or all of the following skilled production staff:

- scriptwriters

- photographers

- video camera operators

- graphic artists

- animators

- sound recording specialists

- sound engineers

- lighting specialists

- stage directors

- computer programming specialists

- decorators

- video editors

- narrators

- stage actors

- photographic lab personnel

Which of these personnel will you need? Turn to your priority chart for the answer. Almost certainly you will need a video camera operator, maybe even more than one. Again your presentation requirements should indicate, at least roughly, the amount of video taping involved in the project. Then you are going to need a video editor. If the sequences will include on–location sound, you are also going to need someone to record, edit, and mix your final sound track. You should budget for the skill needed to write an operation manual and possibly to market the multimedia material.

EQUIPMENT

In much the same way you identified the skills you will need to complete your production, you also have to go through your priority chart to identify the equipment you will require. Following is a list of the most common equipment needed to produce and present a multimedia program.

- video camera, lenses, lights, and tripod

- sound recording gear

- video editing equipment

- video monitors

- tape recorder

- amplifier

- audio mixing equipment

- 35 mm still camera with lenses, tripod, and strobe unit

- videodisc player

- computer system (including software)

You probably have some of this equipment already. If you have a photographer and a media production specialist on your staff, you probably have the equipment they normally use. Of course, the equipment you do not have you will have to obtain, and that poses a basic question: buy or rent? Answering this question depends on your organization long-term multimedia/communication commitment.

> Purchase certain services rather than rent equipment.

Some equipment used in multimedia production is so specialized that even renting it makes little sense. One such piece of equipment is an animation copy stand. This unit is used to film or photograph artwork or photographic prints or slides in a controlled, precise way, and it takes an experienced operator to use the unit correctly. If you find you need slides or film sequences copied with such a unit, your best approach is to contract for the services of both equipment and operator.

Developing cost estimates for all the equipment you will need will take some time, but that does not mean it is a difficult task. Ask two or three audiovisual dealers in your community to give you quotes for the equipment you have to buy, then, in budgeting, use the prices from the dealer you are most likely to do business with. For the equipment you will rent, the procedure is similar—ask for prices from companies that rent audiovisual equipment and use the prices from the most likely supplier.

SUPPLIES AND MATERIALS

The next items you must budget for are the consumable supplies, materials, or services needed during production. Common items in this category include the following:

- videotape

- film (for still photography)

- audiotape

The quantity of each item you'll need depends on the length and scope of the proposed presentation. Naturally, the greater the length and complexity of the show, the greater the material costs are going to be. Once familiar with the overall goals, the production specialist will be able to develop a cost estimate for this category.

FACILITIES

Space is needed for videotaping and video editing. How much space you will need depends, of course, on your production requirements. Although the production studio provides a security blanket of engineering support and allows complete control over work space, it is only one room. The location may be any number of rooms in a home or an office, a street corner, a park, anywhere. It is the unlimited choice of location that will best serve each story or idea that gives the production its realism. Consider a tearful goodbye between two friends at a train station or a party scene aboard a sailboat. To look real, these scenes must be shot on location. But although going on location offers new creative possibilities, it also raises several logistical issues. You must search for a location and obtain permission to use it. Adequate electrical power must be available, and the cast and crew must be able to work in a secure and relatively noise-free area during the taping. Once these issues are resolved, you can easily produce a final show on location that looks as good as or better than that produced in a studio.

If you need space for an in-house production, you may have to budget for costs involved. These costs might include interorganizational charges for renting the space and costs incurred if a maintenance staff has to provide additional electric power or equipment to make the room usable. Your organization's facility management staff will be able to supply an estimate of these costs.

THE BOTTOM LINE

Add up all the cost estimates you have gathered. Then add 10 percent of that total to the estimate for contingencies. That additional money should cover the one or two small items you forgot to budget for. It will also cover the unanticipated problems you will encounter along the way. This final figure—the bottom line—is what your planned presentation is going to cost.

Now, look at that figure and ask a logical question: Is there any way I can save money? There are ways of cutting estimated costs. To make these cuts—and to get the budget to the point where you feel comfortable with it—you must go back to your Must/Want Lists with one thought in mind: Is there any way to simplify these requirements without jeopardizing the communications objective?

You can reduce the length of the presentation. And you can look at your equipment list with the idea of determining the minimum capability needed to achieve the results you want. In multimedia production it is imagination more than a room full of expensive equipment that makes multimedia effective.

Chapter 3
Video Technology

One of the most important elements of interactive multimedia is video. Video offers much potential to draw the viewer into a real world. We are accustomed to watching television to such a degree that it may have become a reality of its own. Video usually includes sound, and combining the two media gives a more powerful representation of reality.

Analog video experiences signal-path degradation, generation loss, and influence by the medium itself. Digital video promises to eliminate those problems and integrate moving images and sound more seamlessly into a computerized world.

As with many other media, video equipment undergoes a gradual transition from professional use to industrial use to consumer use. The lines between these categories continue to blur.

Regardless of subject matter or equipment used, the process of creating a video can be broken down into three main phases. Plans are made during preproduction, elements are gathered during production, and everything comes together during postproduction. Whether traditional or desktop video production tools are used, getting a handle on the techniques employed for decades by television and movie production professionals can make a big difference in creating videos that are compelling, entertaining, and informative.

ANALOG VIDEO

Most things in nature are analog. Real images and sounds are based on light intensity and sound pressure values, which are continuous functions in space and time. Conversion of images or sounds to electrical signals is done by appropriate use of sensors, also called transducers. Sensors for converting images and sounds to electronic signals are typically analog devices, with analog outputs. The world of video and sound recording is based on these devices.

> Most things in nature are analog. Real images and sounds are based on light intensity and sound pressure values, which are continuous functions in space and time.

Because the waves in sight, sound, and electricity are analog and those in computers and many other modern electronic products are digital, some method of conversion between the two technologies is required. *Analog-to-digital converters* (also referred to as *A-to-D converters* or *ADCs*) accept an analog voltage and convert it into a series of discrete numbers in a process known as *digitizing* or *sampling*. *Digital-to-analog converters* (*D-to-A converters* or *DACs*) transform a group of discrete numbers into a continuous analog voltage. These circuits are used separately or together in various multimedia components such as graphic display cards, digital audio recorders, digital video recorders, CD-audio players, digital sampling keyboards, and video digitizers.

The purpose of a video camera is to convert an image in front of the camera into an electrical signal. An electrical signal has only one value at any instant in time—it is one-dimensional, but an image is two dimensional, having many values at all the different positions in the image. Conversion of the two-dimensional image into a one-dimensional electrical signal is accomplished by scanning that image in an orderly pattern called a *raster*. With scanning, we move a sensing point rapidly over the image—fast enough to capture the complete image before it moves too much. As the sensing point moves, the electrical output changes in response to the brightness or color of the image under the sensing point. The varying electrical signals from the sensor then represents the image as a series of values spread out in time—this is called a *video signal*.

Scanning of the image begins at the upper left corner and progresses horizontally across the image, making a *scanning line*. At the same time, the scanning point is being moved down at a much slower rate. When the right side of the image is reached, the scanning point snaps back to the left side of the image. Because of the slow vertical motion of the scanning point, it is now a little below the starting point of the first line. It then scans across the next line, snaps back, and continues until all of the image has been scanned vertically in a series of lines. During each line scanned, the electrical output from the scanning sensor represents the light intensity of the image at each position of the scanning point; During the snap-back time (known as the *horizontal blanking interval)* it is customary to turn off the sensor so a zero-output (or *blanking level)* signal is sent out. The signal from a complete scan of the image is a sequence of line signals, separated by horizontal blanking intervals. This set of scanning lines is called a *frame*.

VIDEO MONITOR AND COMPUTER MONITOR

The *CRT* (cathode-ray tube) is the picture tube used in televisions, oscilloscopes, radar, video monitors, and computer monitors. The CRT consists of a screen coated with phosphorescent dots called *pixels* (short for *picture elements).* The phosphors glow when bombarded with electrons from an *electron gun* at the back of the tube. The pattern and intensity of the bombardment determines the nature of the image we discern on the screen.

> Normal video signals are analog and require analog TV monitors to interpret the signal.

The basic element of that pattern is the *scanline*—one complete horizontal line of pixels. A sawtooth current applied to one of the coils directs the flow from the electron gun so that it scans horizontally across the screen from left to right, then shuts off while moving back to the other side. After this *horizontal retrace* or *horizontal blanking interval*, the next cycle of the sawtooth wave starts the process over again. The sawtooth wave that governs the timing of the horizontal scanlines and horizontal retrace is the *horizontal sync* signal. Another slower sawtooth wave is simultaneously applied to the other coil so that the overall flow is progressively directed down the screen. This allows the horizontal scans to create a raster—a successive pattern of scanlines that fills the screen. When the last line is completed, the gun shuts off—the *vertical blanking interval*—and repositions to the upper left corner again, *vertical retrace.* The sawtooth wave that governs the timing of the vertical scanning and retrace is synchronized to the *vertical sync* signal. This *rasterizing* process repeats itself continually to refresh the screen as the phosphors fade from each previous pass.

> Like television, computer displays are measured diagonally. Monitors are also measured by the number of pixels they display.

More detailed operations differ between monitors for computers or video. Most computer monitors draw every line in sequence from the top of the screen to the bottom at a rate of approximately 60 times per second. This is called a *non-interlaced signal.* Video, television, and some computer displays employ an *interlaced signal* that draws all the even lines, then all the odd lines. A typical computer screen only scans 480 horizontal lines from top to bottom, not the 525 lines of NTSC television. Also, a computer monitor scans each line prograssively, with no interlacing; the scan is full frame at a rate of typically 66.67 Hz or higher, compared to 60 Hz for a full television frame. Each *field,* or complete set of odd or even scanlines, takes 1/60th of a second; each complete two-field screen is redrawn 30 times per second.

RESOLUTION

Resolution is referred as picture sharpness, usually measured in lines. The greater the number of lines, the sharper the picture. If someone displayed 550 straight vertical lines on a TV monitor and you could see them well enough to tell one from another, you could say that monitor had a horizontal resolution of at least 550 lines. If the vertical lines merged together so they could not be clearly differentiated from each other, the monitor then has a resolution less than 550 lines.

Four hundred lines of resolution is slightly substandard for a TV monitor; 550 is common, 800 excellent. Six hundred to 700 lines is appropriate for a TV studio monitor. Seven hundred to 800 lines makes an exceptional monitor. These numbers are for straight video signals. For RF inputs, the signals become fuzzier. Radio frequency is broadcast through the air and comes from a TV antenna. RF is a combination of audio and video signals coded as a channel number. Three hundred lines of resolution, even on good TV sets, is normal for RF signals.

Video Type	Resolution
8mm	230
VHS	240
3/4-SP	330
S-VHS	400
Hi-8	400
Betacam SP	550
MII	550
Broadcast	1,000

The picture from a camera always ends up sharper at the center than at the corner of the screen. Four hundred lines of center-screen resolution is typical of an inexpensive black-and-white camera. Five hundred and fifty is average. Eight hundred lines (with 500 in the corners) is typical of a high quality black-and-white camera. Color cameras generally have less resolution than black-and-white camera. Consumer-grade color cameras have about 250 lines of resolution.

A VCR with 240 lines of resolution will record and play back a color picture with not more than 240 lines of sharpness. Excellent resolution for a VCR would be 320 to 400 lines.

Device	Consumer/ Home grade	Broadcast/ Professional Grade
TV/Monitor	250–300	500–800
Camera	250–300	400–600
VCR	230–270	500–1,000

HORIZONTAL RESOLUTION

As the scanning point moves across one line, the electrical signal output from the sensor changes continuously in response to the light level of the part of the image that the sensor sees. One measure of scan performance is the *horizontal resolution* of the pickup system, which depends on the *size* of the scanning sensitive point. A smaller sensing point will give higher resolution.

A system that is said to have a horizontal resolution of 400 lines can reproduce 200 white and 200 black lines alternating across a horizontal distance corresponding to the height of the image.

Scanning across a pattern of vertical black and white lines produces a high-frequency electrical signal. It is important that the circuits used for processing or transmitting these signals have adequate *bandwidth* for the signal.

VERTICAL RESOLUTION

The *vertical resolution* of a video system depends on the number of scanning lines used in one frame. The more lines there are, the higher is the vertical resolution. Broadcast television systems use either 525 lines (North America and Japan) or 625 lines (Europe) per frame. A small number of lines out of each frame (typically 40) are devoted to the *vertical blanking interval*. Both blanking intervals (horizontal and vertical) were originally intended to give time for the scanning beam in cameras or monitors to retrace for starting the next line or the next frame. However, in modern systems they have many other uses, since these intervals represent nonactive picture time where different information can be transmitted along with the video signal.

> Pixels are defined as picture elements—the little dots that make a display image. For example, the Macintosh display system is based on 72 dots per inch (dpi)—monitors that have 72 pixels in an inch of screen space. People working with photographic images often prefer monitors with higher resolutions of 77, 82, 85, or 88 dpi.

COLOR RESOLUTION

The following section pertains to computer monitor and computer video card resolution. The color resolution of an image refers to the total number of colors possible for individual pixels in the image and is defined mathematically by the number of digital bits the computer uses to record the color of each pixel. Most graphics professionals refer to the color resolution as *bit depth*. One-bit graphics, for example, allow the pixel to be represented in only two possible color states—black or white.

Adding another bit doubles the range of possible colors to four, and so on. When the computer uses eight bits to represent one pixel or dot in the image, the color resolution is referred to as 8-bit. Eight-bit color is in fact one bit (two options) to the eighth power, or 2^8, which yields 256 possible colors. For reference, the math works out this way: 8-bit color represents 2^8 or 256 possible colors; 16-bit color represents 2^{16} or 65,536 possible colors; and 24-bit color translates to 2^{24} or 16,777,216 (16.7 million) colors. Table 3.1 demonstrates the relationship between bit depth, the number of possible colors, and the effects on file size. It also shows the video resolution standards that apply to the various bit depths at a 640 x 480 video resolution.

Bit Depth	Possible Colors	Video Standard (at 640x480)	Approximate File Size*
1 bit	2 colors	monochrome	37K
2 bit	4 colors	CGA	75K
4 bit	16 colors	VGA	153K
8 bit	256 colors	XGA, SVGA	307K
16 bit	65,536 colors	XGA, SVGA	614K
24 bit	16.7 million colors	True color	922K

Table 3.1. Sample file sizes at various bit depths.
*File sizes are theoretical and given for comparison only.

The specific colors that are available for reproducing the image are referred to as the *color palette*. Image reproduction generally improves as the number of colors in the total palette increases. Most people, for example, will see a visible improvement in quality when looking at a photo image drawn from a 16 million-color palette versus a 65,000-color palette, because the 16 million-color palette has more colors available to fill in the subtle gradations in hue.

Some graphic boards in the PC and Macintosh environments are capable of 24-bit color resolution delivering more than 16.7 million colors. These are sometimes referred to as *true* color boards. True color can be a significant enhancement to a multimedia presentation. If your computer processor is powerful enough and your budget allows it, a 24-bit board is a good investment in high-quality production values.

> The specific colors that are available for reproducing the image are referred to as the *color palette*.

The quality level of the graphics will directly affect the size of the file. Generally, the greater the color-bit depth, the larger the file size. The 24-bit images in particular are not only storage intensive but also tax the capabilities of a computer's central processor. An 8-bit image uses one byte of storage for every pixel. A 24-bit image uses three bytes per pixel, so the image file becomes three times larger; switching a 300K graphic from 8 bits to 24 bits increases it to 900K.

The 32-bit is considered an ultra high-quality graphics file format. These files are most frequently in one of two forms. The first is a 32-bit CMYK file (CMYK stands for the Cyan, Magenta, Yellow, and blacK inks used in four-color process printing). Although this format is commonly used for print advertising, its color system has no advantages for screen-based multimedia, which works with the red, green, and blue values of each pixel.

In the second type, formats such as the TGA (Targa) file format reproduces 32-bit color by combining 24-bit color with an 8-bit alpha channel. The alpha channel holds an 8-bit color or grayscale image that can be used to modify the 24-bit color values.

GRAPHICS STANDARDS

Most graphics boards support multiple video resolutions. Generally, the more expensive the board, the higher the resolution capability. The following standards or display protocols have been developed as guidelines for compatibility and capabilities.

VGA: The Video Graphics Array, used with IBM PC and compatibles, describes a graphics capability of 640 x 480 video resolution with 4-bit (16 colors) color.

XGA: The Extended Graphics Adapter standard, developed by IBM, provides for 8-bit color up to 1024 x 768, or 16-bit color at 640 x 480 pixels.

SVGA: Super VGA, or SVGA, was developed to answer the demand for graphics reproduction with more colors and higher screen resolution. Generally, it refers to cards capable of multiple resolutions, including 640 x 480 resolution at 4-bit, 8-bit, or 16-bit color; 800 x 600 resolution at 4-bit, 8-bit, or 16-bit color; and 1024 x 768 resolution at 4-bit or 8-bit color.

FRAME RATES FOR MOTION

In the United States, video is standardized at 30 frames per second (fps); European video-tape travels at 25 fps; and standard 35mm film uses 24 fps.

For motion video, many frames must be scanned each second to produce an effect of smooth motion. In standard broadcast video systems, normal frame rates are 30 frames per second. However, these frame rates—although they are high enough deliver smooth motion—are not high enough to prevent a video display from having flicker. In order for the human eye not to perceive flicker in a bright image, the refresh rate of the image must be higher than 50 per second. However, speeding up the frame rate to that range while preserving horizontal resolution would require speeding up of all the scanning rate. To avoid this difficulty, all television systems use *interlace*.

Interlace in a television system means that more than one vertical scan is used to reproduce a complete frame. Broadcast television uses 2:1 interlace—2 vertical scans for a complete frame. With 2:1 interlace, one vertical scan displays all the odd lines of a frame, and then a second vertical scan puts in all the even lines. At 30 frames per second (in North America and Japan), the vertical rate is 60 scans per second. Because the eye does not readily see flickering objects that are small, the 30-frame-per-second repetition rate of any one line is not seen as flicker; instead, the entire picture appears to be being refreshed at 60 per second. The use of computer-generated images, particularly graphics, sometimes causes difficulties in interlaced systems.

DIGITAL VIDEO

Digital technology has significantly altered the way video is shot, processed, and edited, and promises to continue to do so at a tremendous rate. Standard analog video signals consist of smoothly varying voltage levels that closely mirror the original image. Digital technology, on the other hand, divides a signal into tiny segments of time and measures the quality of the signal within each segment. The segments themselves and their measurements are expressed in binary digits—complex series of positive (one) and null (zero) values. Binary digits are more easily processed than analog signals and can be copied without the generational loss of quality that occurs with analog signals.

> Digital video, when properly implemented, offers benefits such as cost savings, enhanced interactivity, cleaner duplication and editing, and storage flexibility.

Digital technology in video depends on converting analog signals to digital signals. Analog-to-digital converters and digital-to-analog converters accomplish these functions. Graphics thus may be created in the digital domain and integrated into an analog system. Similarly, most original video images and audio are inherently analog; conversion is always required to use original material in a digital system.

Most video systems are analog-based, which is currently cheaper and easier to manage. However, three primary digital formats are in use, with many more envisioned. Like analog video recording, digital video can be composite. The D1 recording format, developed by Sony, is not composite. The D2 and D3 formats, developed respectively by Ampex and Panasonic, feature composite recording. Because the composite signal requires less processing, D2 and D3 are less expensive than Dl. Yet Dl offers superior quality and is ideal for effects and graphics work. If all the editing equipment is kept in the Dl digital domain, hundreds of generations of copying can be performed with little signal degradation.

VIDEO ANALOG-TO-DIGITAL (A/D) CONVERSION

Generally, a composite color signal is not a good format for a digital video system. Conversion of analog red, green, and blue (RGB) signals to digital RGB format is done by applying the digitizing process. Conversion of a composite analog signal is usually done by analog *decoding* of the signal first into its RGB components, and then digitizing each one.

It is also possible to digitize the composite signal directly using one A/D converter with a clock fast enough to leave the color subcarrier components undisturbed and then perform decoding in the digital domain to get the desired RGB format. Usually the clock is synchronized to the color subcarrier at a multiple of 3 or 4 times higher. The resulting digitized composite signal is decoded by digital processing; however, digital decoding in real time requires custom hardware to be fast enough to keep up with the signal. If such hardware is available, this is a good approach.

COMPRESSION: THE SOURCE FOR DIGITAL MULTIMEDIA

Video can be seen on the computer screen using interactive videodisc which is an excellent multimedia storage and delivery platform. However, interactive videodisc is an analog medium, not digital. We are also seeing digital full-motion video on a computer screen (full-screen) that is rivaling the analog videodisc. One thing manufacturers all share in common, however, is compression/decompression techniques. Compression/decompression is critical to digital multimedia at the desktop.

The computer operates as a digital medium. Information is made up of bits and bytes. For the computer to handle digital full-motion video, text, graphics, animation, and sound, compression is required. Table 3.2 shows uncompressed digital video storage requirements.

Window Size (in Pixels)	Frame Rate (fps)	Storage Per Min.
160 x 120	24	49MB
320 x 240	15	197MB
320 x 240	30	395MB

Table 3.2. Storage requirements for uncompressed video.

Full-motion video requires huge amounts of computer memory. Based on a screen resolution of 512 x 480, converting one analog video frame to digital data requires 750 kilobytes of storage. That is just one Frame out of the 30 per second needed to represent full-motion video. At this rate, one second of video requires 22.5 MB of storage. Of course, when you add digitized sound and graphics, for example, memory requirements are enormous. Basic computer storage cannot handle digital multimedia without compression techniques.

One second of full-motion uncompressed video can consume as much as 30MB. A single minute would use 1.8GB of storage space.

HARDWARE-BASED VIDEO COMPRESSION

Digital Video Interactive, or DVI, is Intel's scheme for digitizing and compressing multiple media for storage, editing, playback, and integration in PC and Macintosh systems. It is a proprietary product. DVI is not a compression scheme per se, but a brand name for a set of processor chips that compress media onto a digital storage device (e.g., CD-ROM) and decompress it for playback. DVI compression algorithms, to use full-motion video as an example, achieve approximately a 160:1 compression ratio (that is, about 9 MB per minute of 30 fps full-motion video) from a CD-ROM disc. This scheme has allowed applications developers to pack 72 minutes of full-motion video in a storage space of 650 MB. Although video is the most exciting breakthrough with the compression technology, DVI will also digitize, compress, and play back a variety of media.

Compression ratio represents the size of the original image divided by the size of the compressed image.

COMPRESSION SCHEMES

Following is a list of the most common compression schemes.

- Moving Pictures Experts Group (MPEG) is developing a compression chip for full-motion video and associated audio compression on digital storage media. First-generation MPEG chips, called MPEG1, promise real-time compression and decompression of VHS-quality full-motion video. Compression ratios are expected to be as high as 200:1. The chip will also define the synchronization and decoding of audio.

- The MPEG1 version is designed to create TV-quality, full-motion video. However, development is already underway for two updated versions of the MPEG1 standard. MPEG2 is intended as an interim TV standard with resolution somewhere between NTSC/PAL and the new High Definition Television (HDTV) standard. MPEG3's target is HDTV, which is the FCC's defined standard for commercial television in the future.

- The P x 64 standard has been developed for video-teleconferencing systems that incorporate video, graphics, audio, or other types of information for two-way real-time communications over low-data-rate switched digital networks. The standard calls for data rate transmission of multiples of 64 Kbps up to 2048 Mbps (thus the P x 64 name) with compression ratios of up to 500:1. Although it may seem unnecessary to even mention P x 64 because it is a specification for video-teleconferencing, this standard will allow open transmission between different codec (compression/decompression) manufacturers. When digital multimedia video-teleconferencing is common at the desktop, it is the P x 64 standard that will have brought it there.

- As with MPEG, the International Standards Organization has proposed a worldwide standard color or gray-scale still-image compression solution for storage on digital

> The compression ratio represents the size of the original image divided by the size of the compressed image—that is, how much the data are actually compressed.

media. This standard was developed by the Joint Photo graphic Experts Group. JPEG can achieve compression ratios as high as 100:1; however, these images are of low quality. Best results compression of JPEG fall between 8:1 and 75:1. One of JPEGs most significant features is that it allows for user-selectable compression ratios, which means that users can choose monitor resolution. Another advantage is that the JPEG compression/decompression algorithms can be embodied in software to allow for software-only compression and decompression of images. However, the time to compress and decom press is considerably slower, and image quality suffers.

• In search of a solution to the limited play time, Time Warner Inc. and Toshiba Corporation are developing a new standard for digital videodisc machines. The digital videodiscs, which look like audio compact discs, are designed to play 270 minutes of video. The new discs are likely to become an important medium for computer data storage and could eventually replace CD-ROM discs. The Toshiba-Time Warner system features a double-sided disc with 4.8 gigabytes of storage—enough for 135 minutes of movies—per side.

• The Sony-Philips system uses a single-sided disc capable of storing 135 minutes of motion pictures with a 3.7-gigabyte storage capacity. The storage gap could be closed through "dual-layer" technology proposed by Sony, in which an optical pickup would read picture and sound data recorded in two layers on the same side of the disc.

> QuickTime includes four major compression schemes: Photo Compressor (JPEG), Video Compressor, Animation Compressor, and Graphic Compressor.

SOFTWARE-BASED VIDEO COMPRESSION

QuickTime is an extension to Apple's latest Macintosh operating system, System 7+. QuickTime handles real-time synchronization of video, animation, graphics, and sound on Macintosh, Windows, and interactive television platforms. The compression/decompression scheme, which conforms to the JPEG format, is code-named Road Pizza. Road Pizza will perform compression/decompression based on software-only algorithms, therefore making the purchase of separate hardware unnecessary. Still-image compression comes in ratios from 10:1 to 25:1. Moving video compression allows ranges from 5:1 to 25:1 with a frame rate of 15 fps. Thirty frames per second (fps) are displayed at 320 x 240 pixels on most 68030- and 68040-based Macintosh computers and 30 fps at 640 x 480 on Power Macintosh computers. In a Windows environment, QuickTime for Windows supports Cinepack, which plays video up to 320 x 240 pixels at up to 30 fps, depending on the type of processor.

QuickTime is important in digital multimedia for many reasons. First, it is included with all System 7+ computers. Second, it ensures a consistent architecture for applications that manipulate and deal with images and sound. Third, because it is a software-only solution, no additional hardware is necessary. Storage will be relatively easy—a floppy or hard disk is all that is required. Finally, QuickTime for Windows provides cross-compatibility among QuickTime-developed products.

INDEO VIDEO TECHNOLOGY

Developed by Intel Architecture Labs in 1992, Indeo video technology is Intel's video recording and playback software technology. Indeo provides PC users with a format for recording digital video. More specifically, Indeo is a family of software compression techniques that together form a compressor/decompressor (codec) used for recording and compressing video data.

Indeo name is short for Intel Video Technology.

Indeo is an ingredient technology licensed free of charge to software application developers, CD-ROM publishers, operating system vendors, computer OEMs, as well as graphics hardware manufacturers who, in turn, include its technology within their products. PC users find Indeo technology already built into the multimedia extensions of operating systems such as Microsoft's Video for Windows, IBM's OS/2 Multimedia Presentation Manager, and Apple's QuickTime for the Macintosh and QuickTime for Windows.

Indeo offers PC users more than a family of techniques for compressing and decompressing video data. Indeo also incorporates the following features to help make recording, playing, or distributing digital video applications on a PC easy and affordable. Indeo's capabilities include:

- Real-time, one-step capture and compression

- Scalable playback

- Software-only playback

- Cross-platform compatibility

Indeo has a unique feature that allows video to be captured and compressed in one step (real-time). Running on a video capture board, such as the Intel Smart Video Recorder, Indeo video compresses a one-minute video clip from 50MB to 9MB and stores it on an average-sized hard disk. The video recorder can capture and compress video in window sizes up to 320 x 240 pixels and at speeds of up to 15 frames per second.

640 x 480 pixels = full screen
320 x 240 pixels = 1/4 screen
10 x 120 pixels = 1/16 screen

The highest quality frame rate possible is 30 fps. This appears completely fluid to the human eye and is the rate used in television. Motion pictures use 24 fps, but 10-15 fps is considered acceptable quality motion. Images will appear "jerky" if the frame rate goes below 10 fps. Users can, however, make tradeoffs between the frame rate and window size, depending on which aspect is more important for their application. With the addition of an i750 video processor-based board, the same file can be played back with 320 x 240 resolution at 30fps (Table 3.3).

Indeo allows any Intel 486 SX or higher CPU-based PC to play back video clips without requiring special hardware or software. This feature helps to reduce the cost of using video.

Files captured with Indeo technology include video-player software (also called the run-time player), which can be freely distributed. Because no extra multimedia software or hardware must be purchased, playing back prerecorded clips is essentially free.

Processor	160 x 120 Pixels	320 x 240 Pixels	640 x 480 Pixels
i486 SX-25	30 fps	12 fps	2 fps
i486 DX-66	30 fps	28 fps	10 fps
i750	30 fps	30 fps	

Table 3.3. Video playback performance by microprocessor.

FRACTALS

Fractals are part of a relatively new science of geometry. Classical geometry is useful for describing objects with geometric shapes, such as straight lines, squares, and triangles. Fractal geometry, on the other hand, describes natural objects, such as clouds, trees, and mountains. Fractal image compression can produce compression ratios of up to 10,000:1.

To compress images, the process begins with an image and then finds a code that can describe it in terms of fractals, called *iterated function system* (IFS) codes. The codes are built up into a library of codes and are manipulated by adding the proper parameters to represent an actual image.

To view the image, the user runs the IFS codes through a random iteration algorithm to generate the image. The fractal transformation compression process is called POEM. Currently, Iterated Systems is offering a "floppy book" as an example of the fractal compression scheme. The floppy book disk contains 100 pages of full-screen 24-bit images and text. The 1.44 MB disc holds the equivalent of 77 MB of data. POEM floppy books can also contain two minutes of compressed video, digitized sound, and ASCII text. The floppy books need no special hardware to view and are simply a plug-and-play solution. At this point, fractals may be a breakthrough software compression solution for digital multimedia at the desktop.

IBM is busy developing software-only compression algorithms as well. The computer giant has already displayed its scheme displays motion sequences (stills were captured one screen at a time to develop motion) in about 1/4 screen windows without requiring additional cards or decompression hardware. Frame rate is estimated at between 10 and 15 fps.

Broadcast-quality video is the ultimate information gas-guzzler, requiring almost 1 MB per frame in uncompressed form. If digital video is going to speed along the information highways, it will have to get many more miles per gallon. There are four things you can do to reduce this glut of data. You can reduce the number of pixels that represent the picture (reduce the size); you can show fewer pictures per second; you can reduce the number of colors (bit-depth) per pixel; or you can compress the data. Even when you have tried the first three measures, to some extent you will still need to compress the data to achieve a data rate that is low enough to squeeze through existing pipelines.

The challenge for multimedia developers, meanwhile, is deciding which of the many competing codec algorithms they should use. For CD-ROM applications, codecs that can decompress video without special hardware are attractive since the potential audience is much larger. This is why most video on CD-ROM is compressed with software, such as SuperMac's Cinepak (the most popular codec) and Intel's Indeo. These codecs can achieve a full 30-fps rate for 160 x 120 pixel, 16-bit-color pictures, and typically 15 fps at 320 by 240. But today's codec conundrum is far more than a battle between Cinepak and Indeo. The industry-standard codec for compressing movies, MPEG, has moved out of the committees and into the marketplace. MPEG1, the Motion Picture Experts Group version designed for CD-ROM, can achieve 320 x 240 pixels at 30 fps played back on boards such as Sigma Design Reel Magic board for the PC (marketed by Radius for the Macintosh), which zooms the image to full-screen.

> A bus is a circuit that provides the pathway for the transfer of information between two or more devices.

On fast Pentium and PowerPC machines equipped with higher-bandwidth local buses, Cinepak and Indeo movies can display 320 x 240 pixels at up to 30 fps. They can be blown up to approximately a 640 x 480 pixel display on a full screen using new graphics accelerator boards that include video zoom circuitry. The quality is still not as good as MPEG, but it is getting closer, and it is a lot cheaper for encoding and playback.

VIDEO FORMATS

Videotapes come in different widths to fit various videotape machines. Every tape machine can work with only one width of tape. There are four primary formats:

3/4-inch U-matic. The original Sony 3/4-inch "U-matic" format, introduced in the early 1970s. It was designated U-matic because the threading path of the tape resembled the letter U. In this system, as with all cassette formats, two open reels are enclosed in a cassette. During record and play a mechanical device in the VTR opens the tape housing, and little metal fingers thread the tape. The early 3/4-inch VTRs lacked features such as fast scan and freeze frame, and the first crude editing interface was not introduced for several years, but by the end of the 1970s the use of 3/4-inch tape for video production in corporations and educational institutions was well established.

Many variations and improvements have been made to the original 3/4-inch VTR during its long tenure as the reigning small format. The original 3/4-inch format, although ideal for simple industrial production and video instruction, was not quite good enough to satisfy the many on-air broadcasters who were looking for a replacement for the 16mm film they used in news gathering. A broadcast-quality version, the 3/4-inch BVU (broadcast video U-matic), was introduced and is still widely used by broadcasters for news production. It is compatible with standard 3/4-inch but has better mechanical stability and picture resolution. The latest version, designed for industrial users, is called SP. All versions of 3/4-inch U-matic remain composite and compatible with all other 3/4-inch equipment.

1/2-inch VHS. Another popular video format found in most colleges, most public schools, many industrial media centers, a few commercial TV production shops, and many U.S. homes. VHS includes tracks for composite video and stereo hi-fi audio. VHS resolution is 240 lines.

In 1987, JVC introduced S-VHS format. It uses the same size cassettes as VHS but with better tape formulation. At about 400-line resolution, S-VHS yields better signal-to-noise ratio. It also provides the ability to record high-fidelity audio onto the video tracks. S-VHS machines can play VHS tapes, but VHS machines cannot play S-VHS tapes.

The 1/2-inch VHS-C minicassette format is gaining popularity among home users. The cassette is smaller and uses an adapter for playback on regular VHS machine.

VHS tapes offer three record/play speeds yielding 2, 4, or 6 hours of playing time. A tape recorded at the 6-hour speed must be played at the 6-hour speed. A VHS 2- 4- 6- machine will play all three speeds. Recording at the slow speeds (4 or 6 hours) will result in loss of video and audio quality. Also, many industrial-grade editing units will not playback 4- or 6-hour recorded tapes.

Sony Corporation introduced 1/2-inch Beta, which yielded better audiovisual quality. Because Sony tightly controlled the licensing of the Beta standard, and partially because VHS was the first to offer movie-length recordings on a single cassette with acceptable quality, VHS format won the market share.

8mm. In 1985 8mm video was introduced as the smallest tape width and cassette size to date, making it popular for lightweight camcorders. 8mm is approximately 1/4" wide. The drawback of relatively small surface area of the tape is offset by the use of metal-particle tape capable of retaining much higher signal

> A more widely used tape-head arrangement is the helical-scan format. The tape head rotates across the tape at an angle.

levels. The tape also provides enough room for the video heads to record PCM (pluse code modulation—encoding technique) audio tracks rivaling the quality of audio CDs.

Hi8. Sony introduced the Hi8 format in 1989 as an improvement to 8mm. The resolution increased to more than 400 lines, and color improved as well. Hi8 can also record time code discretely. Hi8 decks can play 8mm tapes, but 8mm decks cannot play Hi8 tapes.

Betacam SP. The second generation version of Sony's Betacam format has become quite popular in the high-end industrial and low-end broadcast markets because it employs a form of component video on 1/2" tape and does not downgrade bandwidth and color quality via the color-under method. Betacam SP can use standard oxide tape formulations, and performance can be improved with metal-particle tape. Two longitudinal audio tracks supplement FM encoding of hi-fi audio into the video tracks.

M-II. The M-II format is the second generation version of the M-format originally introduced by Matsushita and RCA and is a direct competitor of Betacam SP. M-II does not use color under and employs special metal-particle tape exclusively to record its component video signal. It also features full-range FM audio encoding in parallel with the two longitudinal audio tracks.

1-inch Type C. This format is used by U.S. commercial broadcasters and others who require the highest technical quality. It is the only remaining composite 1-inch Type C video format. This format combines color and black-and-white information into one composite recording. The oldest of the still-used broadcast formats, 1-inch C, is the open-reel helical scan format that gradually replaced the original open reel standard, 2-inch quad, in the 1970s. Newer, smaller, and better formats are in use, but the fact that l-inch has been the broadcast standard for more than fifteen years will probably ensure its use for a few more years. The 1-inch VTRs are obviously too large for most on-location shooting, but the format is still

Format	Number of Acceptable Generations
VHS, Beta III	1
3/4 U-Matic	2-3
3/4 U-Matic, S-VHS	3
3/4 U-Matic-SP	3-4
C	5
Betacam, M	6
MII	7
Digital	20+

used in post-production editing. One-inch type C videotape is probably the last open-reel, composite video recording format that will be used widely.

Which format should you use for an interactive multimedia production? Depends on the company you are using for videodisc mastering and duplication, you should determine the video format. Most companies require 3/4-inch U-matic (professional), 1-inch Type C, or D-2. However, other formats can be transferred to this format prior to the videodisc mastering process. For detailed information on mastering tapes, see Chapter 6.

COLOR VIDEO

Four basic elements constitute the color video signal: the luminance or brightness (white) values within the picture, and the three chrominance or color values (red, green, and blue). These four elements combine to create the color signal in several different ways. Composite video integrates both luminance and chrominance portions of the signal and thus can be transmitted from point to point along one wire.

Another type of color recording is called Y/C, which is used to record the video signal in VHS, S-VHS, 8mm and Hi8 recordings.

RGB is another type of video signal that provides a separate channel for output from computers. This type of signal is of extremely high quality, and in many cases carries even more information than a component signal. However, to record the output of a computer, the RGB signal moves with its accompanying luminance signal into a converter, where its information is transformed into a composite signal.

TYPES OF CAMERA

There are many different kinds of video cameras available, and they vary considerably in purpose, price, and performance characteristics.

LARGE STUDIO CAMERAS

These cameras have every operational feature available. Until 1988 all studio cameras have used pickup tubes. The tubes are primarily Plumbicons and Staticons, and Newvicons have been introduced into a few designs. These cameras are mounted on massive pedestals with every facility for smooth operation. They employ a variety of Hexible lens systems and a large viewfinder. To permit rapid verification of the operating condition and to facilitate adjustments, automatic setup systems are quite common.

SMALL STUDIO-OUTSIDE BROADCAST TYPES

Small studio-outside broadcast cameras are more compact, but still employ multisensor imaging configurations. They have either three Saticons or Plumbicons tubes format. These cameras are used in the TV studio for everyday news and commentary programs, and for sports coverage in outside broadcasts. In the latter application they must be capable of accepting the most exotic wide-range focal-length lenses.

ELECTRONIC NEWS GATHERING (ENG)

The ENG camera evolved into a most practical camera. Mobility comparable to that of a 16mm motion picture camera was considered essential. Many configurations were tried. Among those initially were very lightweight camera heads with separate processing packs on the operator's back or on a belt. This design gave superior image stability and allowed for a light enough weight to achieve adequate performance.

ELECTRONIC FIELD PRODUCTION (EFP)

Electronic Field Production is the highest-quality shoulder or light tripod video camera. They are similar to the ENG cameras, but they have the added flexibility of remote control of the setup conditions which permits the matching several cameras and artistic control of the camera output. The requirements for electronic field production are stricter than those for electronic news gathering.

UTILITY CAMERAS

A large market exists for cameras that have the basic features of broadcast cameras at minimum cost. They are used by broadcasters for throwaway operations, such as low-priority and high-risk news. The enhancements of S-VHS and D2 recording formats, together with higher-resolution solid-state cameras, produce results that surpass those of stripped-down broadcast designs.

STILL VIDEO CAMERA

When Sony introduced the still video camera in 1981, its developers believed that it had many advantages over the conventional film camera. Its pictures can be viewed immediately on a TV screen, and its signals can be transmitted to a distant point over a telephone line. They suggested that it would be widely used by the press and broadcast stations. At least two factors have prohibited the realization of these goals. First, the price of most still video cameras has remained too high for the consumer market. Second, its picture resolution is somewhat lower than that of a film picture.

TUBE OR CHIP?

There are two types of video cameras, those that use tubes as an imaging or pickup device and those that use chips called *charge-coupled devices,* or CCDs (Figure 3.1). In the tube camera the light falls on the face of the pickup tube which electronically scans the subject and generates a varying voltage analogous to the light and dark areas of the picture. In the CCD camera light-sensitive silicon chips contain many thousands of tiny pixels, or sensors, that generate voltages when light reflected from the scene falls on them.

Figure 3.1. A digital 3CCD (charged-couple divice) camera. The CCD camera has a great number of image-sensing elements that transfer an optical image into many spots carrying an electric charge. These charges are temporarily stored and then translated line by line into a video signals (courtesy of Panasonic).

CCDs are 1/2-inch microchips arrayed with 380,000 photo-sensitive diodes. The diodes generate an electronic charge proportional to the light intensity that strikes them. The charges are scanned, converted to electronic signals that represent the scene, and sent to the recorder.

The better cameras have less image lag, less susceptibility to burning caused by bright light, and less noise in low-light situations. The chip cameras are better suited for location use because they weigh less and a smaller amount of battery power is required to operate the camera on location. Tubes, like light bulbs, have filaments that must light up to effect the discharge of electrons in the tube. Chips do not. The chip camera uses a smaller, less expensive battery, and it will last longer before it must be recharged.

The chip camera also requires less engineering setup and regular maintenance than does a tube camera. With a three-tube camera, a task called *registration* must be performed daily. Registration means aligning the red and blue pickup tubes with the green tube so that the camera sees the image from each tube in perfect alignment. An out-of-registration three-tube camera (with one tube for each primary color) will have a red or blue outline around the image. The three-chip camera will hold its factory-preset registration for a long time, which translates into less worry on location.

Today, the lighter weight and lower maintenance of chip cameras have already made them the first choice in television, school instruction, and corporate production.

THE ZOOM LENS

The zoom lens has been more precisely called a vari-focal lens. Its focal length can be varied by moving one or more of its lens elements along the lens axis. At the same time, the image may be maintained in focus by either mechanical or optical means.

Although the zoom lens was first introduced in professional movie cameras around 1930, it did not play a role in 16mm cameras until the Zoomar lens was introduced in 1946. The first applications to television were in the early 1950s, when zoom lenses were made for use with image Orthicons in broadcast TV cameras. By the late 1950s they were being made for broadcast TV cameras that used Vidicons.

A zoom lens consists of three optical modules. The front module may consist of a negative lens followed by two or three positive lenses. Moving from left to right, it is followed by a module, called a variator, which is moved along the axis to change the zoom ratio either manually or by a motor drive. The latter provides "power" zoom from wide angle to tele-photo. To the right of the variator is the third module, a positive lens group, which is separated by focus and light control elements. One of these is a half-mirror prism, which is in the autofocus chain. The other is the iris, which is controlled to regulate the amount of light reaching the image-pickup device

(CCD or tube). Overall, the final module in the zoom lens is a positive lens group, usually referred to as the rear lens. In a typical zoom lens for broadcast TV cameras, 18 or more lens elements may be found. In a typical lens for consumer TV cameras, there are 13 separate lens elements in the complete structure.

The zoom lens is not only one of the heaviest parts of consumer video cameras and camcorders, but also one of the most important in obtaining a high-quality picture. To satisfy the requirement for high resolution and high sensitivity, a bright zoom lens should be as large as possible in diameter while remaining consistent with other requirements. It should also be as lightweight as possible.

> The zoom lens combines the characteristics of lenses of different fixed focal lengths. At a wide setting, the zoom acts as a wide-angle lens. When zoomed in, it acts as anarrow-angle lens.

Full-featured video cameras and camcorders usually have switch positions for manual and autofocus and sometimes for "one-shot" focus. In the manual position, focusing is accomplished by adjusting a focusing ring on the lens barrier. One-shot provides for momentary use of autofocus during manual focusing. Many manufacturers recommend that autofocus not be used on the following subjects and scenes:

- subjects with very glossy or shiny surfaces (such as the exterior of automobiles);

- subjects with very little or no reflection (such as black clothes, black hair, and water surface);

- scenes having a strong contrast between the right and left halves of the screen;

- subjects with an object in front of them (such as animals in a cage).

A useful focusing variant in the manual position is macro–focusing. With the focus selector set to manual, the zooming lever is rotated to the wide-angle position. Then this lever is pulled out and rotated into the macro range for close-up shots. Figure 3.2. illustrates a zoom lens.

Figure 3.2. A zoom lens (courtesy of Canon).

Various systems have been developed for video cameras and camcorders to provide automatic focusing. A compact mechanism that provides adequate image-resolving power is desirable. The systems most widely used employ the infrared method, the TTL Piezo method, and the through camera lens (TCL) phase-differential method.

CAMERA-MOUNTING EQUIPMENT

The camera-mounting device controls the steadiness of the image. A camera can be mounted on a tripod or hand-held. The camera-mounting option or options that you use will depend on the type of production you are doing. For many productions, you will need a sturdy tripod. Most of the better–quality ones are supplied with separate heads and legs. Most common is the fluid-head tripod with tilt and pan controls, friction adjustment, and level indicator; these are often equipped with a quick-release plate for instant camera mounting. The fluid-head tripod allows smooth operation and movement.

The tripod legs are either aluminum or wood, with a lever to adjust the height of each. The ends of the legs terminate in a point that can be stuck into the ground or fitted into a rubber foot for floor or pavement.

You may attach accessory wheels to attach to the tripod, or you can attach the tripod securely to an audiovisual cart with heavy tape. If you need a noise-free dolly you might borrow an electric golf cart or use a wheelchair. Also, you could shoot from the sunroof of a car using the camera on tripod set up inside the car.

CONTROL TRACK

Control track refers to a pulse recorded on one track of the videotape. Because the pulse, which is created during an assemble recording, marks each revolution of the record drum and the beginning of each frame, it is called the *frame pulse*. The control track could be called the "electronic sprocket holes of video," because its purpose is to act as a guide for the playback of the video signal.

because the pulses on the control track are recorded in evenly–spaced intervals at each revolution of the recording drum, the playback machine must maintain the same relationship to play the signal properly. If the spacing of the control-track pulses is altered, the picture will roll, or be out of sync, until the spacing becomes even again.

All video formats use different but similar control-track signals. Some of the newer video machines are even capable of playing back video that has a damaged or different control track.

TAPE RECORDING AND EDITING

Two basic types of video recording are used: assemble and insert.

ASSEMBLE RECORDING

Assemble recording erases everything on the tape from the starting point, replacing it with the new picture, audio, and control track. One disadvantage of this method is that it is not very helpful if you want to record audio from a source other than your picture. It is, however, a very effective way to make a direct copy of another videotape or to record a control track in preparation for an insert-editing session. A second disadvantage of the assemble method of recording is that sometimes the control-track pulses at the edit can occur either earlier or later than the old control-track pulses. This difference in spacing might cause the picture to break up or roll. Most newer machines have the ability to lock to the previous control track, producing a stable assemble edit.

INSERT RECORDING

Insert recording offers the advantage of clean editing and the option of performing audio-only or video-only edits. The editor can replace video, audio, or both without disturbing the tape's control track. Most often a videotape is blank when purchased, so before an insert recording can be made, the tape must have a control track recorded on it. To do this, a recording is made for the length of the videotape; this recording lays down a continuous, unbroken control track.

The assemble recording is usually a black picture that has a time code on it but no audio. This black and coded tape is used as a record tape for insert recordings. Therefore, when buying a record tape from a professional editing house, you will usually find that it already has the control track and time code on it. Insert recording is the method used by most professional editing companies.

An assemble recording erases everything—all video, audio, and control track—and replaces it with totally new signals. An insert recording replaces only those tracks (video or audio) selected.

EDITING

Insert edit means to place an edit between two other edits or to erase part of a previously recorded edit by inserting a new edit. An assemble recording erases all signals on a tape and records new signals on it. Assembly refers to an on-line editing session using either an edit log or a computer-generated edit decision list (EDL); assembly is accomplished using insert recordings. To auto assemble means to have the computer editor automatically perform a series of edits in an EDL list.

FRAMES AND FIELDS

Recorded video signals are rather complex and thus are tightly structured. The standard unit of video is a *frame*. Similar to film, motion video is created by displaying progressive frames at a rate fast enough for the human eye and brain to perceive continuous motion. Standard broadcast video in the United States, the rest of North America, and certain other countries records and displays approximately 30 frames per second (29.97 frames to be exact). However, a frame of video is composed of two *fields*. These are recorded adjacent to each other on videotape and are interlaced during the playback process to display a full frame of video.

Blank videotape has no frames, fields, or control track.

The basic means by which video images are recorded and displayed is a *scanning* process. When a video image is recorded by most cameras, a beam of electrons sweeps across the recording surface in a progressive series of lines. NTSC video, the North American standard, defines a frame as containing 525 scan lines: Each field therefore contains 262.5 lines. One of the two fields in each frame contains the odd-numbered scan lines, and the other contains the even-numbered scan lines. Thus, when they are interlaced, they create a full frame.

RANDOM-ACCESS EDITING

The limitation of linearity in videotape editing is an annoying reality to many producers. Today, new systems using up-to-date computers and hardware are totally accepted by the post-production industry. Random-access editors are employed in the film industry, the commercial arena, broadcast television, and the non-broadcast video industry. The speed with which changes can be effected and the relatively easy output of a clean, accurate EDL has brought random-access editing from the research and development stages right to mainstream postproduction use. In addition to allowing editorial changes to be made quickly, random-access editors virtually eliminate the time consumed by shuttling tapes back and forth to each edit.

Editing videotape is a linear process. Each edit is recorded onto a record tape, thereby occupying a firmly defined space on that tape. To change the length of any edit, the edits following must be recorded one by one, linearly. A random-access system is not constrained by this linearity. Because each edit is only a preview, a change in an edit is immediately taken into account by the system. The edits following are instantaneously adjusted to accommodate the previous edit's change.

> Various random-access editing systems may operate differently, but their goal and ultimate impact are the same: to foster more creative and efficient editing by minimizing obtrusive technology and making the process truly interactive.

The random-access editor only previews what all the edits of the show will look like. Conventional editing systems can only preview one edit at a time. When a random-access editing session is over, a recording of the show is often made for viewing.

There are three types of random-access editing systems. One type uses multiple videotape playbacks and thus is referred to as a tape-based random-access editor. The second type of system uses multiple videodisc copies. This disc-based random-access editor requires fewer playback sources than the tape-based system because videodiscs can locate a specific frame within seconds. The third system uses digitized computer video as its playback source. By transferring videotape or disc images directly onto a computer hard disk, these digitized computer images are accessed within the computer itself. All three systems are able to find and preview any sequence of edits in real time, eliminating the need to record anything until the segment or show has been completely edited.

Most random-access systems do not require extensive time code manipulation. Rather, they operate via relatively intuitive icon- and cursor-based computer screen interfaces that are easy to learn and use. Real-time picture displays and dynamic graphic diagrams of the work in progress facilitate visualization and decision making, as opposed to traditional reliance upon representative time code numbers. Extensive preview functions and system memory result in a very fluid editing environment that encourages experimentation and changes. Initial editing decisions are not permanent and can easily be corrected or abandoned. All successful random-access editing systems maintain accurate, clean EDLs in their memories.

> Random-access editing is unlike traditional tape editing. Search and preview times are dramatically reduced or virtually eliminated.

Computer technology is developing at an explosive rate. Tremendous processing power and memory in particular are becoming increasingly cost effective. This technology will continue to be applied to video production and postproduction to meet the needs of the growing visual media industries. The read/write videodisc, for example, is now a reality. Where once source material was permanently written to disc, now that source material can be erased or edited. Although these discs are currently expensive, the price is expected to drop. Digital video has improved greatly and will continue to do so. Eventually (by the end of the century), broadcast video may be on-line edited entirely within the desktop environment, including effects and graphics.

NONLINEAR EDITING

The process of video postproduction is undergoing rapid and widespread changes. Digital nonlinear editing becomes a viable means of editing even the most footage-intensive feature film. This technology is slowly dominating all facets of video postproduction. Over a dozen corporate players in the nonlinear editing world have recently announced breakthroughs in image quality. Many claim that their improved video output performance is good enough to broadcast.

Of course, this improvement comes at significant cost. Some "all-in-one" nonlinear editing systems claim "release quality." Their total system costs vary from $20,000 at the "industrial-quality" S-VHS level to over $75,000 for the "high-end" Betacam-quality level. This section covers a brief description of few nonlinear editing systems.

MEDIA 100

Media 100 is a digital system that can be output at broadcast quality—including video effects, motion effects, graphics, titles, animations, QuickTime movies, and mixed audio. Media 100 is fully compatible with standard Macintosh components. The all-digital architecture eliminates the problem of degradation between generations associated with analog systems. Its software allows users to add effects, titles and graphics, and mix sound—all in a real-time.

Media 100 takes video production from the realm of proprietary equipment and consoles to the Macintosh screen.

With Media 100, users can create animation one frame at a time and bring animation directly into the system and view it in real time. In addition, users can edit animation with frame accuracy and sync, add video, create effects, and mix up to four tracks of audio. Figure 3.3 shows the Media 100 nonlinear editing system.

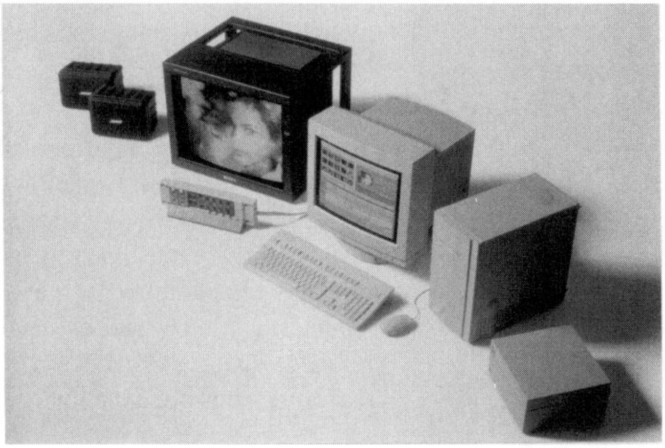

Figure 3.3. Media 100 editing system.

AVID PRO MEDIA SUITE

Avid Media Suite Pro provides a digital nonlinear editing solution from desktop to broadcast for corporate, education, small business, healthcare and government markets with prices starting at less than $15,000.

Media Suite Pro for the Macintosh allows users to produce videos, lets users print finished programs directly to videotape, in real time, or use the EDL option to bring their programs to an on-line suite for finishing. The software provides numerous digital effects, including motion control and user-definable picture-in-picture.

Media Suite Pro for Windows, like Media Suite Pro for the Macintosh, is a complete desktop video solution for professionals in the corporate, education, training, marketing communications and government fields to create videotapes directly from their Windows platforms. A robust and intuitive tool, Media Suite Pro for Windows uses the same cut/copy/paste video, sound, graphics animations and titles found in word processors.

Programs created with Media Suite can be recorded, edited, and played at full-size, full-motion, as well as recorded directly from computer onto videotape in real time, incorporating any combination of video, audio, graphics and animations.

Media Suite offers a programmable video effects including dissolves, wipes, pushes, squeezes, page turns, flips, etc., chroma key overlay and importing/exporting capabilities for animation. It can import other media, including QuickTime movies, PICT files, Photo CD files and various audio file types.

OTHER NONLINEAR EDITING SYSTEMS

There are other alternatives for both Amiga- and Macintosh-based systems. NewTek has produced the Video Toaster Flyer for the Amiga and Adobe Systems has developed Premiere for the Macintosh. Adobe Premiere is also available for Windows.

ADOBE PREMIERE

Adobe Premiere is a nonlinear video editing software for Macintosh and Windows users. Premiere works with QuickTime movies and special effects transitions to create a series of edits, all from the Macintosh computer. Like most competing nonlinear editors, Premiere uses the time-line approach with separate audio and video tracks.

As with other nonlinear editing systems, video must first be digitized into the computer's hard disk. With Premiere, you can create a sequence of scenes to be edited with transitions, plac them into the video time line, along with respective audio tracks in their time lines, and select appropriate transition effects between sequential video clips.

A nonlinear video editing needs real-time playback of video sources from computer hard drives. This requires video compression boards for the record and playback cycles. Radius Video Vision Studio system, which includes video interface card, JPEG compression daughter card, connector panel for external video and audio connections, and software controls is capable of compressing and decompressing Macintosh video at 60 fields per second, full frame, at 640 x 480 resolution, and at 24-bit quality. Compression boards from other manufacturers are also available.

VIDEO TOASTER FLYER

NewTek, the maker of Video Toaster for the Amiga, has intreduced a new system called the Video Toaster Flyer (VTF). The VTF is a new Toaster hardware peripheral card that works with any existing Toaster. NewTek claims that the Toaster Flyer system delivers broadcast-quality video Also, it is capable of professional D2 video quality at its highest possible level, Betacam quality at the middle level, and S-VHS quality at the baseline level.

The Video Toaster offers real-time effects. Most of the compression standards in use have some form of digital artifacts which make the compressed video look unnatural. NewTek developed Video Toaster Adaptive Statistical Coding (VTASC), NewTek's own proprietary compression technique. VTASC is claimed to achieve significant compression benefits without the digital artifacts so prominent on other compression standards such as JPEG and MPEG. With VTASC, it is possible to achieve three levels of broadcast quality: D2, Betacam, and S-VHS.

NewTek defines "broadcast quality" as a video signal that has at least a 50dB video signal-to-noise ratio and a chrominance bandwidth specification of at least 1.5 mHz at the low end of its quality scale.

The Toaster now supports digital audio editing when used with the Toaster Flyer. Every video clip digitized into Video Flyer's hard drives also carries its respective stereo audio clip. The audio is CD quality and is stored uncompressed. A special digital signal-processor chip provides for additional multi-channel audio mixing features. Figure 3.4 illustrates Video Toaster Flyer editing system.

Figure 3.4. Video Toaster Flyer editing system.

With nonlinear editing, new methods and equipment would replace the common setup of linked video effects machines, character generators, and edit controllers. In nonlinear editing, you will first need to transfer all your desired video source tapes to a computer hard drive that is fast and has a large capacity (one gigabyte or more). Editing is then performed directly from the computer's hard drive.

The process is liberating because scene selections, previews, and edits can be made instantly. Scenes are played back in real time, on the fly, with considerable saving's in edit time. The possibility of videotape wear and tear is also eliminated. Digital random-access video editing carries with it another big plus—the virtual elimination of generation loss in the editing process.

Chapter 4

Video Production

Production is the most visible stage of multimedia development. Production includes all in-studio and on-location activities directly related to the recording of audio and video, from preparing the set and lighting it to rehearsing and directing the talent and technical crew. During the production stage you will attempt to translate the results of preproduction planning, research, and writing into the visual language of video. Although the time spent in actual production is small, it is guaranteed to provide the most demanding yet rewarding times in the entire project.

On location you will finally become the director, but before you travel to your location to begin work, you will want to be certain that everything is in place so you can concentrate on directing the talent and crew. Whether your production is a one-minute commercial or a five-minute informational project, the activities of production are basically the same.

Rehearsal is an important step in the directing process. When you rehearse, you'll find out how a carefully planned combination of script, location, and personnel can come together as television. Rehearsal is practicing the script. Ideally, everyone in the cast and crew should know exactly what your intentions are and what they must do to execute your ideas. The process of rehearsal, or predirecting, will give you confidence on location and in studio as you begin to get your vision onto videotape.

LIGHTING

You may use lighting to get a technically acceptable image or you may use it to set the scene and create a mood. In informational video, getting an acceptable image of an interview subject may require only one or two lighting instruments bounced off the ceiling of an office. You may even be able to use existing light. In drama, lighting is more important because it must be used to suggest moods, set the time and place, or fill in or override shadows. If you are doing a drama, you will probably need twice as many lights as for an informational production.

Video lighting must satisfy two basic requirements: technical and aesthetic considerations. These two requirements introduce several problems and challenges for electronic imaging. The primary responsibility of the lighting person is to simultaneously control the science and the art of lighting to produce the desired effect.

Cameras require light. Without adequate illumination a video camera cannot produce a high-quality image. Light intensity requirements vary from one camera to another depending on the camera design and the type of image reproduction device used (chip or tube).

Although a light meter is used to measure light intensity, one should depend on a correctly adjusted video monitor for aesthetic judgments. In order to achieve an artistic effect, you must be capable of controlling a variety of lighting instruments and a light meter while simultaneously evaluating the results on a video monitor display. There is a difference in the way a scene appears to the eye and how it will look on camera because the human eye perceives the qualities of light differently from the way a camera registers that light.

The video image has only two dimensions: height and width. The third dimension, depth, is made possible through the illusions of creative staging, lighting, and camera angles. Arranging and controlling the different lighting instruments makes it possible to alter or to establish depth and separation. Camera placement, lens aperture, and focal length also contribute to the creation of the third dimension.

Texture, size, shape, and the importance of an object can also be influenced to a large extent by light. Shadows and highlights convey the size and shape of an object and can reveal distance. Sets and props are usually lit to convey the tone or atmosphere of a scene. Because the human eye is attracted to brightly illuminated areas, the point of visual interest in a picture can be emphasized through selective lighting and subject placement. A lighting balance must be established and careful consideration given to the placement of lighting instruments, cameras, talent, and supporting scene elements.

Each production will have its own unique lighting problems and needs. For instance, you may not have the time to survey a location site or be given access to it and consequently you may encounter unexpected artificial or natural lighting problems requiring considerable time to correct. Conversely, studio lighting is more easily managed because all filming takes place in a controlled environment. Regardless of the production site, you must understand several lighting characteristics: color temperature, direction of light, and contrast ratio.

THE NATURE OF LIGHT

A number of scientists have spent their lives trying to figure out what light is. It is fairly obvious that light is energy of some kind—it supports all life on earth and, furthermore, is easily changed into heat, a measurable form of energy.

One theory concerning the nature of light is that light seems to be a wave phenomenon. According to this theory, the wave is an action under the influence of some kind of energy. All energy that is free to move in a straight line (light, heat, radio waves, and so on) can be thought of as moving in waves, even though it may not actually move this way. Using various measuring devices we can attribute wavelengths to each form of radiant energy. Whether or not energy actually moves this way, the wavelength theory has proved to be extremely useful. Radiant energy is produced, transmitted, or reflected by a primary or secondary energy source and is free to travel through space.

The wavelengths of most types of radiant energy make up what is called the *electromagnetic spectrum*. A spectrum is an orderly display ranging from one point to another. The energies are called electromagnetic because they all seem to relate to both electricity and magnetism.

Visible Color Wavelengths in Nanometers	
violet	380 to 450 nm
blue	450 to 490 nm
green	490 to 560 nm
yellow	560 to 590 nm
orange	590 to 630 nm
red	630 to 760 nm

On a typical chart of this spectrum you will find cosmic rays, gamma rays, X rays, ultraviolet light, visible light, infrared rays, short Hertzian waves, radio waves, and long electrical oscillations. The wavelengths of these energies range from about one trillionth of a centimeter (cosmic rays) to about 620 miles (long electrical oscillations).

Visible light fits about midway in the electromagnetic spectrum, each color having its own short spectrum of wavelengths. Together, the colors of light make up "white" light, which sunlight approximates very well. In the order in which they occur on the electromagnetic spectrum, the colors are violet, blue, green, yellow, orange, red, and deep red, with wavelength ranging from about 400 to 700 nanometers. Because a nanometer is 1/10,000,000 of a centimeter, you can see we are working with very short distances. Even so, science has determined wavelengths quite accurately. Electromagnetic radiation with wavelengths just greater than 700 nm is known as infrared radiation. At the opposite end of the visible spectrum is ultraviolet radiation, with wavelengths just below 400 nm. Figure 4.1 shows the whole electromagnetic spectrum. Of course, the color perceptions merge gradually into one another with changing wavelength, and both ends fade into darkness.

Another theory—that light is some kind of an attenuated substance—is called the corpuscular theory. According to this idea, light contains minute particles (corpuscles) known as *photons*. In a vacuum, these photons apparently travel at the rate of 186,000 miles per second, but they are slowed down somewhat in air and quite a bit more in glass. This slowdown is what makes photographic lenses possible. If light strikes glass at an angle, its slowdown is accompanied by a deviation from its path—it is bent, so to speak—and this deviation makes it possible to use it to form images. The deviation varies according to the color of the light, with violet and blue being deviated the most and red and deep red the least. It was this phenomenon that led to Sir Isaac Newton's discovery that the sun's "white" light is made of many colors.

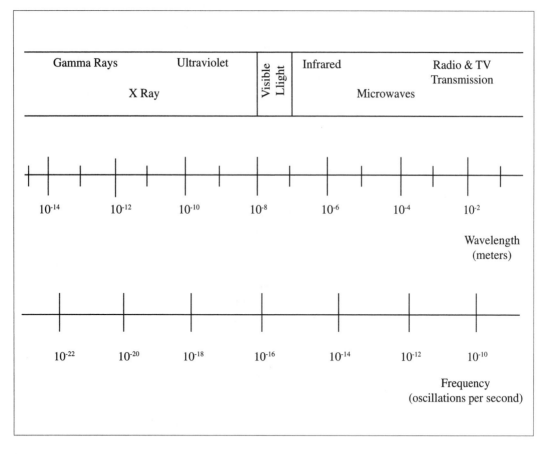

Figure 4.1. Electromagnetic spectrum.

TEMPERATURE OF COLOR

Light sources vary between artificial and natural light. These distinct sources of illumination produce wavelengths of different colors. The quality of color in a light source is known as *color temperature*, and the Kelvin (K) temperature scale is used to measure color gradients.

A Kelvin is named after the British physicist W. T. Kelvin, who constructed the Kelvin scale.

Although most visible light appears white to the eye, an electronic video system interprets that same light according to color temperature. Only after the camera is adjusted to a nominal 3200°K and the white balanced will colors appear normal. For example, viewing bluish daylight at noon (5600°K) from a window mixed with interior reddish incandescent (2800°K) or greenish fluorescent (4500°K) lamps can be accurately interpreted by the human eye through a remarkable occurrence known as *approximate color consistency*. This mental adjustment makes it possible for the eye to adjust to subtle color temperature variations and see an object as it truly exists. A video camera cannot adjust in this way to mixed color temperature and, as a result, color reproduction will be inaccurate.

The ideal situation would be to maintain consistent color temperature for all production work, but the nature of video production makes this impractical. In order to achieve color balance, video cameras are fitted with selectable built-in filters that correct the wavelengths of incoming light to the 3200°K range. Some camera models provide two basic filters to balance light: one for 3200°K tungsten-halogen lamps (this is really not a filter but clear glass) and another for the 5600°K range of normal daylight. More expensive cameras have four filters of more critical and precise color balancing under a wider range of conditions. Filters provide only gross correction. Additionally, a white balance adjustment must be made to set the primary colors in a perceptually correct relation to one another.

Because it is often necessary to shoot in offices or factories that have high-color-temperature fluorescent lighting, a

Color Temperature	
Tungsten bulb	
for home use	2800°K
Tungsten bulb	
for photography	3200°K
Daylight,	
early or late	3200°K
Fluorescent,	
warm white	3500°K
Fluorescent,	
white	4500°K
Fotoflood	5000°K
Daylight,	
midday	5500°K
Daylight,	
hazy or foggy	7000°K

4500°K filter is usually included. Another typical choice is a 7500°K-rated filter for shooting outside on a cloudy or overcast day. Although specific degrees Kelvin are used for these examples, it should be noted that all are approximate. Because fluorescent instruments are pulse light, they have an "apparent" Kelvin temperature. For instance, depending on the type of fluorescent tubes used, the apparent color temperature might range anywhere from 3500 to 6500°K. Likewise, depending on the time of day, weather conditions, and proportion of direct and reflected light, exterior color temperatures might range from 4500 to 25000°K.

As a consequence, colors shot at midday will not match colors shot in late afternoon because of changing light conditions. The best solution is to shoot consecutive scenes within the same time period. Because such continuity is not always possible, supplemental lighting and reflectors are sometimes used in addition to filters and gels to modify or compensate for color quality.

DIRECTION OF LIGHT

One way to understand how the direction of light affects our surroundings is to consider a familiar source of light: the sun. Sunlight's direction is overhead, changing position and altitude throughout the day. On a clear day the sun produces brilliant illumination and shadows with distinct borders. Depending on the object it strikes, sunlight is absorbed into, transmitted through, or reflected off the object's surface. Because of the sun's movement, the appearance of exterior objects and structures are affected through changing shadows, scenic contrast, and specific features of the objects. Because light travels in a straight line, it creates shadows on the opposite side of the object it strikes. The light should come from the direction that produces the best illumination for a scene. A high noon sun generally creates objectionable facial shadows, especially under the eyes and chin. Likewise, buildings are not as pleasing at midday because of excessive brightness resulting in washed-out highlights and lost detail in dark shadow areas.

Reflectors and halogen-metal-iodide (HMI) lamps help soften shadows and restore some highlights and dimensional qualities.

In a studio or other indoor production setting, you must be mindful of the relationship of subject to light. Shooting with grid or floor-stand instruments provides the flexibility to move the source and direction of illumination. This advantage over the uncontrollable sun is offset by the multiple shadows created by the several instruments required for illumination.

Most people are accustomed to sunlight with its single shadow. The key light source simulates the intensity and direction characteristics of sunlight. Additional light sources required to balance or fill in some shadows created by the key light are positioned in a way that creates multidirectional shadows.

CONTRAST

Extremes of contrast between the darkest and brightest parts of a scene are to be avoided for the video medium. The nature of an electronically produced image creates a limited contrast range. Tonal values for a color video camera should be maintained within a maximum 40:1 contrast range in order to maintain color response in shadow and highlight areas. This relationship means the brightest object in a scene should not be more than 40 times brighter than the darkest object. Technical personnel prefer to balance cameras using a grayscale with a 20:1 contrast ratio. By comparison, motion picture film has a contrast ratio of approximately 100:1. Due to the video camera's reduced contrast-handling capability, video images produced under low illumination do not reproduce accurately. Exceeding the 40:1 contrast ratio creates excessive brightness that, in turn, reduces definition.

| Contrast enhances the communicating power of your image. |

A routine video contrast problem occurs when an individual wears a white shirt or blouse. White clothing reflects approximately 90 percent of the light striking it. The average Caucasian skin reflects approximately 30 percent.

Reducing the video level in response to highly reflective clothing causes the face to become dark. Increasing the video level to compensate for the dark skin results in the clothing "blooming" (a halo around the edges). To avoid this problem, the on-camera talent should wear clothing that reflects less than 60 percent of the available light.

MEASURING LIGHT

Light intensity is measured in footcandles (fc) using a footcandle meter. A *footcandle* is the amount of light produced by a candle one foot in height striking a vertical surface at a distance of one foot. For most three-tube, prism optic color cameras, 125 to 200 fc are satisfactory for good reproduction. Charge-coupled-device (CCD) cameras are generally more sensitive to light than tube cameras. Some manufacturers advertise CCD cameras that function with as little as 1 fc.

A light meter measures the brightness of a light or a scene and gives a readout in footcandles or lux.

Although most light meters measure the intensity of light by footcandles, some manufacturers' equipment specification sheets use a European metric unit of measurement called a *lux*. Ten lux is approximately equal to one footcandle (10 lux = 0.93 fc).

STUDIO LIGHTING

Most video producers do not have access to a multiple-camera television production studio with a separate control room. In most instances one camcorder is used for production. In these cases converted rooms are sometimes suitable for studio work, which includes standup presentations, discussions, or graphic card insertions.

Hanging lighting instruments overhead increases camera mobility because there are no obstacles created by light stands or power cables on the studio floor. Floor lights can be added as needed for supplemental illumination, mobility, and quick adjustment.

A video production studio usually includes a suspended light grid system from which lighting instruments are hung. A fixed grid consists of a cross matrix of 2-inch diameter pipes, called battens, connected within one or 2 feet of the ceiling and covering all production areas.

Flexibility in positioning and adjusting suspended lighting instruments is essential for a fixed grid. Some instrument hangers are attached directly to the grid by a C clamp. Several vertically adjustable hangers are available for adjusting the operating height of lighting instruments. It is necessary to position some instruments at varying heights for different lighting requirements. The least complicated type of hanger is a sliding pole, which can be quickly lowered but requires several feet of clearance above the grid.

LAMPS

Tungsten-halogen lamps are the standard source of illumination for color video production. Aside from its smaller size, the tungsten-halogen lamp maintains a consistent 3200°K throughout its life. An additional advantage of the tungsten-halogen lamp is its longer life expectancy.

Tungsten-halogen lamps are available in intensities ranging from 500 to 10,000 watts and are applicable for all types of instruments. It is important not to touch the lamp envelope with the hands when replacing a lamp because oily fingerprints and skin salt can cause the quartz envelope to devitrify (crystallize), which in turn creates premature lamp failure. Lamp manufacturers provide a protective piece of paper or foam with which to handle double-ended lamps and a plastic covering for bayonet or mogul-mounted bulbs. A contaminated lamp should be wiped with a soft cloth and alcohol prior to use to prevent damage. It is a good idea to keep a pair of heat-resistant gloves available to protect the hands from serious burns when handling hot instruments or removing burned-out lamps.

Figure 4.2 shows different types of light.

Multi-barndoor light.

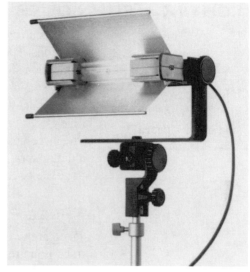

Quartz-halogen light.

Hand-held light.

Camera-mounted light.

Figure 4.2. Types of light. Courtesy of Lowel-Light Manufacturing, Inc.

LIGHTING TECHNIQUES

> It is better to place one light about 45° to the side of the camera.

There is no specific formula that will work for all lighting situations. The variables associated with light and differing production situations are too numerous to permit an exact rule. The best approach to video lighting includes following a few basic techniques and then spending a considerable amount of time observing the illumination created by each light source. The three-point formula approach is a good starting place, although practical experience and experimentation will prove to be the greatest influence on the completed lighting plan.

THREE-POINT LIGHTING

There are three basic types of instrument functions in the three-point formula to lighting: (1) key light, (2) back light, and (3) fill light. The arrangement of these lights is determined by camera placement and shot angles of the subject. If the subject remains stationary, the lighting plan is relatively simple as compared to that needed for talent movement on the set. Additionally, multiple-camera coverage compounds the lighting design. Talent movement and multiple-camera shooting tend to require flat lighting because of the need to cover all the action.

> The key light produces a contrast—directional illumination that creates deep facial and background shadows.

Before setting any instruments, the director should establish talent and set separation. The talent should be physically separated by 8 to 10 feet from any set wall to reduce shadows on the background and provide depth.

Following the three-point lighting technique, the first instrument set is the key light, which is the main source of illumination. Its illumination quality is harsh, creating distinct shadows. A 1000-watt Fresnel instrument focused between spot and flood and located between 25° and 40° on either side of the camera-subject axis is a starting point. As the primary light source, the key fixture is positioned high on the grid or floor stand with a 30° to 45° vertical angle. Moving the key instrument within the given horizontal and vertical parameters will provide the flexibility needed to enhance the appearance of the talent. One result of key light is a small shadow on one side of the nose. Moving the instrument toward the camera–subject axis will reduce the nose shadow and at the same time introduce flat lighting. Likewise, a 45° vertical angle will contribute to a deep eye shadow and reduce the chin shadow to create a flatter appearance. Continual compromises must be made and understood when an instrument is adjusted.

The back light is the second instrument established. The illusion of a third dimension is created largely through back lighting. A 500- or 650-watt Fresnel instrument located immediately behind the talent and at a 45° vertical angle produces illumination around the shoulders and highlights the hair. This enhances space between the talent and background, giving depth to the picture.

> The back light produces a rim effect, separating the talent from the background, highlighting the hair, and adding a third dimension illusion.

The intensity of the back light is dependent on the talent's hair and clothing. A blonde person wearing medium-tone clothing requires less light than a person with dark hair dressed in medium-tone clothing. It is important that barndoors (Figure 4.2) be used on all back lights to restrict such things as light reflection from a bald head and camera lens flare. It is best to start with the back light beam spread at the wide position and adjust as necessary to avoid hot spots on the hair.

The final instrument placed is the fill light, which is intended to balance the key light by softening facial shadows. A fill instrument is a 1000-watt scoop or broadlight (floodlight) set to produce soft, evenly distributed illumination. The fill instrument is located opposite the key light between 25° and 40° from the camera-subject axis.

> In contrast to the key and back lights, the fill instrument produces a soft illumination designed to balance hard shadows created by the key light.

Most video programs involve lighting people. The appearance of the actors is certainly affected by lighting. Remember, facial shadows are not to be totally eliminated or the lighting becomes very flat. Learning to control the shadows and soften their appearance is the objective. Background lights are usually required to illuminate the background and add to the contrast range and depth of the scene. Scoops are satisfactory for this purpose because of their soft illumination. Diffusers attached to the instruments will reduce intensity, thus maintaining a lower light level that helps establish depth between the brighter foreground subject and background wall. Background lighting can also reveal shape, form, and texture associated with a set. Figure 4.3 illustrates different lighting techniques.

Key light.

Fill light.

Back light.

Figure 4.3. Different lighting techniques.

TIME CODE

SMPTE time code, developed by the Society of Motion Picture and Television Engineers, can label and find any section of a videotape by hour, minute, second, and frame.

The development of time code made frame-accurate, repeatable video editing possible. *Time code* is a labeling system that specifically identifies video frames and audio signals by referencing a 24-hour clock. Each video frame is identified by an eight-digit number in the format hours, minutes, seconds, and frames. Time code enables each frame to be identified and accessed for editing or reference. The time code is digitally encoded in videotape in one of several places, generally on one of the audio tracks (called longitudinal time code) or in the vertical interval portion of the video signal (called vertical interval time code, abbreviated VITC).

In concept, time code is very similar to the edge numbers found on film. It is an arbitrary number assigned to each frame of video. Time code is arbitrary because the important portion of the tape is not the number but the picture the code identifies. When recorded properly, time code is synchronized to the beginning of each frame.

Time-code recording originates with a time-code generator. Time code should not be copied from tape to tape in an edit because time code is a digital signal that degrades with a straight transfer, and tape noise can render the code useless. Time code is regenerated by feeding the original time code signal into a regenerator, which creates a clean new signal that can be recorded onto the same tape.

The time code must be in exact sync with the video, thus the generator must be locked to the record deck or a common reference signal. Recording unlocked time code will result in nonsynchronous code, meaning that the code for one field will fall across two separate video fields, thus making the code impossible to edit.

It is generally cheaper to rent a time-code generator and record the code during the production. This method also allows the producer to record identical time code on multiple videotape recorders (VTRs) during complex camera setups.

SWITCHER EFFECTS

A videotape machine can only record. A switcher creates effects such as wipes, dissolves, and keys. The purpose of a switcher is to mix many sources of video into a single video signal, to which the record machine cuts. The number of video signals that the switcher can access is determined by the number of inputs into the switcher. For instance, a switcher could be mixing sources such as a tape machine, a camera, a digital effects generator, a character generator, a color bar generator, or a safe-title generator.

The switcher can create background colors and matte colors but not video images. The video images that the switcher mixes always come from some source other than the switcher itself. A magazine picture, for instance, must be transferred to video by a camera before the switcher can deal with it.

> A safe-title generator is a white box placed in a monitor to indicate the acceptable areas where titles can be placed and still be seen on a home television. Since a portion of the video picture is not visible on many home receivers, this equipment sets boundaries for title placement.

A switcher can be a tiny box with only a few inputs, or it can be six feet long and require two operators. In addition, some switchers have a built-in computer that allows one to program the effects; others must be operated by hand. However it is used, the switcher's purpose is the same: to mix sources of video into one signal.

Wipes. A wipe is a transition from one picture to another using some sort of pattern, such as a vertical bar, that moves across the screen. The pattern reveals the new picture as the old one is wiped away. Some switchers have options concerning these wipe patterns. The edges of the wipe can be hard or soft, or the wipe can have a colored border. A very soft-edged wipe almost looks like a dissolve. Wipes come in many shapes and sizes, from stars to squares to diamonds, but not all switchers produce the same patterns. With some switchers, these wipe shapes can also be modulated or electronically distorted.

Dissolves. A dissolve is a fade from one source to another. A dissolve to or from black or a dissolve to a key is usually called a fade.

All switchers can create wipes, dissolves, and keys. Although these effects might seem limited, many larger switchers offer the operator hundreds of ways to use them.

Keys. A key is an electronic hole cut into a picture and filled with video source. One example of a key is the credit sequence at the end of a television show. The switcher cuts a hole for the words using a video source (a character generator videotape or artwork) and then fills the hole with the video signal.

EXTERNAL EFFECTS

The second type of effect is the external effect that is created when another machine's video is fed into the switcher. External effects are often used in conjunction with switcher effects.

Character Generators. Character generators create video words. Most of these machines offer several fonts (boldface, roman, italic, and so on) from which to choose. In the more expensive models, words can be manipulated in much the same way they are manipulated with a digital effects machine. Character generators can also create designs or capture images from camera source and manipulate or store those images on floppy disk. The character generator's signal is often keyed over the video sources.

Slow-Motion Devices. These can range from the newer videotape playback machines to a metal disk that stores video information and plays it back at different speeds. Slow motion is a generic term that indicates an alteration of the original speed of a moving image. Each slow-motion device has its own limitations as to the speed variation in both forward and reverse.

COMPUTER DIGITAL EFFECTS

The computer digital effect can be broken down into two categories: digital video effects, which are created by a digital-effects generator, and computer-generated graphics. In the 1990s, two advances brought the microcomputer into the video postproduction world. The Apple Macintosh with its impressive capabilities and NewTek's Video Toaster, platformed on an Amiga computer, have opened effects to everyone. In Chapter 3, Media 100 and Avid Media Suite Pro Macintosh-mediated editing systems, have been discussed.

> One of the most effective uses of the digital video effect is to build a story from still pictures.

Digital Video Effects. The digital video effect is accomplished by taking any existing video source (video image, a moving shot, a still shot from a camera, a wipe, or another effect created by a switcher) and manipulating its position within the video frame. The devices that produce it can flip a picture upside down or reverse the image.

SHOTS

A system of visual devices is used in video to communicate intentions, attitudes, and information. Specific types of shots, angles, and camera movements show time, space, distance, and mood and communicate the content of a story and the feelings of a character to an audience.

The individual shot is the smallest, simplest unit in the video language. A shot begins when the camera operator rolls the tape and continues until the tape is stopped. Some shots are short and involve no camera movement; others are long and complex with plenty of motion. A shot cannot always stand alone; it usually takes on meaning in connection with other shots that are logically grouped.

THE ESTABLISHING SHOT

> The establishing shot does not have to be the first shot in a show. It can be a sense of the broader surroundings of the main character, subject, or topic.

The *establishing shot,* or ES, is sometimes referred to as a long shot (LS) or wide angle shot (WS). It shows as much as possible of a scene or location in a single shot. Often the first shot in a show or a scene, the establishing shot gives the viewer a perspective on the total location where a story or action will take place. An establishing shot may also be used for transitions between scenes or locations and as background for opening and closing credits. Figure 4.4 illustrates an example of an establishing shot that would be appropriate for "A Day in the Life of Americans" program.

Figure 4.4. An establishing shot for a program entitled "A Day in the Life of Americans."

Proper composition is often difficult in an establishing shot. Generally you will want to show the complete object or group of objects or the largest possible area centered within the frame. For a well-composed shot of a building, for example, try not to cut off the sides or the top; in fact, allow plenty of space around the entire object or area you are trying to establish. On the other hand, too much space on one side of the subject can make it appear to be pushed out of the picture. Such a composition could send an unintended message. For an establishing shot of a building you might also create a sense of depth by including the walkway or driveway leading to the building in the foreground of the frame.

Long shot

THE MEDIUM SHOT

The *medium shot* is a midrange shot that guides the viewer to see something specific the director has selected. The content or scope of the medium shot, or MS, often depends on the establishing shot that preceded it or the close-up that may follow. Like the establishing shot, the medium shot must have a purpose. For a conversation between two people, a medium shot may be a tightly composed shot featuring the people but excluding the background surrounding them. A medium shot is often used to make the transition between an establishing shot and a close-up seem less abrupt. In some informational programs, a medium shot of one person about to be interviewed is often used with a voiceover introduction.

Composition of the medium shot is often easier than the establishing shot because the subject or area may be smaller and easier to define. Maintain correct *headroom,* an ample space between the top of the frame and the top of the subject's head. Because many camera viewfinders see more of the image than a typical television, the top of the head shot may disappear on some television sets. Always compose each frame looser than you think is necessary; but if you are composing a medium shot of two people, move the subjects closer together if there is too much wasted space between them. Figure 4.5 shows examples of medium shots.

Figure 4.5. Examples of medium shots.

THE CLOSE-UP

The close-up is a shot in which a single person or object fills the entire frame. Some close-ups are neutral in that they add little extra meaning to the shot, while others convey a special meaning. Close-ups range from the medium close-up (MCU), a head-and-shoulders shot, often used to present news reporters and government leaders in a neutral setting, to the tight close-up (TCU) and the extreme close-up (ECU). Figure 4.6 shows TCU and MCU shots.

Figure 4.6.a. An example of a TCU shot.

Figure 4.6.b. An example of a MCU shot.

The type of close-up you select, more than any other type of shot, can send a specific message to an audience. In drama, when the main character has just been given devastating news by another character, his or her reaction is often communicated in an extreme close-up.

When composing the close-up, look for both a clear representation of the subject of the shot and for balance within the frame. You should think of your shots as a group working together to set a mood, tell a story, or communicate content clearly. Think about what you are trying to present first and then plan the visuals to support it.

CAMERA ANGLE

The angle from which the camera shoots is another important aspect of videotaping. In some scripts the writer uses terms such as *angle up* (low, shooting up to a character) or *angle down* (high, shooting down) to denote the camera position. A neutral angle is accomplished by placing the camera lens at about the eye level with the subject. An angle that is neutral adds no extra meaning and is typically used to present straightforward information, as in an interview. A less-than-neutral angle is often used to give a specific meaning to the shot. Camera angles can be used to tell an audience how to perceive a particular character or situation.

MOVEMENT

Movement includes movement of the entire camera and its mounting, movement of the camera on a stationary mounting device, and movement of the characters within the frame of a stationary camera. A camera movement must have a purpose that relates your story.

The entire camera and mounting can be moved by a dolly, crane, wheelchair, audiovisual cart, or a person holding the camera. When the entire camera and its mounting move, the movement can take the form of a dolly, truck, or arc. A *dolly* is an in-and-out movement of the entire camera on its mounting. To dolly in you push toward the subject; to dolly out you pull back. A *truck* is a side-to-side movement; you can truck right and truck left. Combining a dolly and a truck causes the camera to move in an *arc*. A dolly, truck, or arc is usually performed using the widest-angle camera lens available to minimize the jerkiness caused by wheels rolling over a bumpy surface and focus problems caused by a rapidly changing depth of field.

> When you use pan or tilt, begin on something significant to the story and end on something just as important. For greater flexibility when editing, always begin and end pans and tilts with a stationary shot.

A tripod with a movable head is normally used for movement from a fixed mounting, but in some cases the camera is hand-held. The most common forms of moving the camera on a fixed mounting are the *pan* and *tilt*. An internal movement of the camera's actual lens elements is known as the *zoom*.

When the area to be shown is too large for a single stationary shot, or if a connection must be made between several persons, places, or objects, you can use a pan or tilt. A pan is a side-to-side movement, and a tilt is an up-and-down movement.

The zoom lens allows you to get a range of shots from wide angle to close-up without moving the camera. It does this, however, in a manner that may introduce some visual compromises such as compressing objects or altering the depth of field in a way that requires constant attention to the focus. The zoom is probably the most overused camera movement as well as the most useful. Many zooms are unnecessary and can actually make the viewer uneasy. As with all other camera movements, the zoom should be used for a purpose and begin and end on something related to the content of a show.

The final form of movement involves people or objects moving from one part of the frame to another while the camera remains stationary. This motion must be well rehearsed. The talent must know exactly when to enter the frame, perform an action, and exit the same frame, all while the tape is rolling.

ON LOCATION

When confronted with the task of producing a program that will be shot on location away from home base—or maybe in a town that is not even on the map—the video director will find that planning is a necessity.

IDENTIFY THE LOCATION

The first and most important stage in any production includes identifying location, the site specifics, and production requirements. Depending on the type of production, there are various elements present for most location shoots. The following considerations should be examined:

Specific location: The location will be dictated by the need to shoot at a particular building or plant, or to shoot a particular person at the person's home or office. The script may specify a location.

Type of location: The script will specify a type of location, such as "an emergency room at a major city hospital" or perhaps "a majestic mountain with a river and major highway in the foreground."

Nonspecific location: The script will be more general, calling for a city street scene or busy restaurant, or a house in a middle-class, suburban setting.

When the script specifies a particular location, first obtain permission to shoot there. If the location is a high-profile site, call the local film commission to ask whether permission must be obtained to shoot at that location.

When the script calls for a more general location, such as a hospital or mall, the Yellow Pages is often a good reference to identify these types of locations. Then call the public relations director or communications coordinator to get permission to shoot at the site.

For those locations that are more difficult to identify or that have specific script requirements (such as the majestic mountain with a river and highway in the foreground), use your location search network. This network includes anyone from the geographical region. It also includes the following:

- State and city film commissions. Many film commissions have local area production directories, location photographs and listings of user-friendly locations.

- State or local tourist information offices.

- Local town council or police department. People within these organizations should be happy to supply you with the information you need.

- Local production companies or freelance production personnel.

SITE SURVEY

The next step is to perform a site survey. Budget parameters will always dictate the ability to do a site survey before the production. If the budget does not allow for a prior site survey or there are time constraints, have a location scout or production assistant at the location conduct the survey. The following are some important instructions that you should give the site surveyor:

> Establish requirements for liability insurance coverage.

- Shoot stills and video of the location.

- Identify hours of entry, parking facilities, ease of access to the building, any special security clearances or requirements, and sound quality (is it quiet or noisy?).

- Determine the dimensions of the site. Use a tape measure if distances are critical. Sketch the layout of the interior/exterior, mark window locations and power outlets, and note the direction of buildings in relation to the sun.

> Select and prepare a location that will suit both the script and the budget.

- Check climatic conditions and weather forecast for the site: temperature, wind, rain, snow conditions, water temperature at a beach/lake, times of sunrise/sunset, and the months in which the leaves turn during autumn.

- Determine whether police will be required for crowd control, road closure, or access to public property.

- List available hotel accommodations.

- Estimate the distance and travel time from the airport and hotel to the shoot location.

CREW AND EQUIPMENT

The next stage is to find equipment, crew, and talent. Identify what equipment and crew will be acquired at the location. Depending on the type, size, and location of the shoot, finding a good source of local equipment and crew can range from easy to nearly impossible. Several resources are readily available to help you:

- Film commissions.

- Local production and rental companies.

- Crewing services.

- Crew fax services.

- Production directories—there are many types available.

- Professional associations.

When talking with an unknown crew, try to obtain as much information about the crew as possible, including references and experience. Always check the references. Following is more important information to establish before the shoot:

- How much will the crew/equipment cost, and what is included?

- What is considered a base day, and what is the overtime charge?

- What are the payment terms and conditions?

- Do they have transportation, and is it included in their rate?

- How far are the crew members from the location, and will they pick you up at the hotel?

HOTEL/TRAVEL ARRANGEMENTS

Now that the shoot is organized, the final items to arrange are travel and accommodations. Be sure to book all accommodations well ahead of time, especially if there will be a large contingent of crew and talent. In remote areas, consider alternative methods of accommodation when hotels are not available, for example, private homes or trailers. However, always let the crew members know ahead of time that they may not be staying in a hotel. The following are some basic guidelines for arranging travel:

- Check whether there are direct flights to the area and the frequency of the flights. Remember that many remote areas may only have a few flights a week.

- Determine driving distance to the location and how long the journey will take.

- Find out whether there are rental cars/vans available at the airport. Remember to book well in advance of the shoot.

- If you are flying with equipment, especially on small commuter aircraft, notify the airline ahead of time that you will have excess baggage and estimate how much you will have. Be prepared to pay excess baggage charges. Domestic airlines normally allow each passenger two carry-on bags and two pieces of checked baggage.

No matter what size your production budget may be, shooting on location or in a region you are unfamiliar with will always provide some risk. However, if you do thorough production planning, check the references you are given, and use your location search network, you will at the least minimize the chances of problems on the shoot.

ON-LOCATION AUDIO

If you plan to do the audio yourself, there are four areas that demand your attention:

- Acoustical

- Electrical

• Radio-frequency interference (RF)

• Performance

Before you can address any of them, however, you first need to have a good monitoring system. Inexpensive headphones that do not give a full or accurate frequency response can hide problems which will then appear only when you are in the editing suite. If the camera, deck, or mixer does not have enough power to feed the headphones at a level loud enough to allow you to hear what is going on, spend the extra money for a battery/AC headphone amp.

> Always monitor the audio as it is being recorded.

Monitor the audio from a source as close to the recorder as possible: From the recorder is good; from the recorder off the playback head is better. Not all recorders offer the ability to monitor the playback head while the machine is recording. You may also find it disconcerting to hear the delay that listening off the playback head produces while recording on analog decks, but it will allow you to instantly hear any tape dropouts or other flaws.

In addition to airplanes, traffic, pearl necklaces clacking on a lavaliere mike, and change or keys jingling in a pocket, acoustical problems also include camera motor noise, clothing that rubs against a poorly positioned body mike, a loose mike cable that slaps against a mike boom, farm animals, and someone in the next room who produces noise.

Electrical problems can be purely electrical or electromechanical, such as an intermittent cable connection, inexpensive audio cables that crackle when moved, ungrounded or improperly grounded audio or power connections, or audio equipment plugged into the same branch from which a lighting system draws power. Dead batteries and batteries with corroded connections also fit here.

RF culprits include any nearby high-power radio transmitters close enough to get into a mike circuit or a wireless mike. Just because your wireless mikes work well at the studio does not mean they will not cause problems when you try to use them on location. In most metropolitan areas there is a frequency coordinator who has a list of all frequencies in use in that area. Check the phone book for the local office of the SBE (Society of Broadcast Engineers), or contact the engineering department of one of the larger local radio or TV stations to find out what frequencies are available.

Performance problems may result from anything performers do. You may have to suggest that a performer not move in certain ways if that movement results in noise from a body mike. Even the smallest stone scraping between a shoe and pavement can sound immensely loud when transmitted via a boom-mounted shotgun mike from above.

Most professional talent are trained to speak at consistent levels. However, you may find that their sentences trail off at the end, requiring a retake. Nonprofessional performers can be much more difficult to record. The energy levels of their speech patterns may vary widely. Directing them may be successful, but it may make them too self-conscious. If this happens, you will have to reduce the record level so their peaks will not distort, or use a limiter or compressor. Performance problems also occur if performers turn away from the mike while delivering lines. Lost lines can be prevented if the scene is blocked properly and the sound person knows where the talent will be.

> Sweep the area with a broom, change shoes, glue some thin foam to the shoe soles and/or request that performers try not to slide their feet when moving.

ON-LOCATION LIGHTING

It is good practice to carry as many portable lighting instruments as possible when producing a field assignment because circumstances will vary depending on shooting location, time, and available electrical power. For these reasons it is wise to also consider battery-powered instruments and reflectors. There are many battery-powered instruments available that are lightweight and attach to a camera; others may be hand-held. Such lights cannot do much more than boost illumination levels for improved video contrast indoors and fill in shadows created by excessive contrasts outdoors. For daylight use, a bluish dichroic filter must be used with 3200°K lamps to correct color temperature.

However, battery-operated instruments are not a panacea for remote lighting problems. One of their major drawbacks is that they have a limited period. The amount of time they can be used without recharging is influenced by lamp voltage and wattage, battery type and size, and ambient temperature; but it can be as long as two hours. Several disadvantages of battery-operated instruments are a lack of light control, the need to carry additional battery packs or belts, the recharging equipment needed for extended field production, and the relatively high cost compared with conventional lighting systems. Nevertheless, they do have obvious advantages, and if you have the budget, they are frequently a good investment.

> When combined, the key, back, fill, and set background illumination should produce a video picture that is balanced in contrast and light intensity.

A portable light kit is a better alternative to a battery-powered instrument when creative lighting control and significantly more intensity is desired. Basic kits usually include three or four relatively weightless instruments, light-mounting stands, light control accessories, and a carrying case. Less expensive kits have lenseless reflector instruments with fixed-focus lamps and intensities varying from 500 to 1000 watts. More expensive kits include additional instruments with greater intensity, variable-beam focus control, and caster stands.

On-location lighting situations may require accessories such as rotatable four-leaf barndoors and scrims for precise light control; compact, collapsible stands that extend to a height of 6 or 8 feet; and a heavy-duty carrying case.

Kit lights have standard three-prong (grounded) electrical connectors, which are satisfactory for most applications. It is good practice to include several three-prong to two-prong adapters in a kit for those situations where three-prong connectors will not work, although grounded plugs should be used whenever possible. In addition, one or more 50- and 100-foot extension cords should be included.

One of the most versatile light-restricting attachments for spotlights is the barndoor. Available with either two- or four-door control, barndoors are hinged flaps that can be positioned to restrict the height and width of the lamp output. By opening and closing the flaps and rotating the entire barndoor assembly, the beam can be shaped to fit a given dimension and angle.

REHEARSALS

For many extensive productions, especially dramas, you will want to have some rehearsals prior to coming into the studio. Studio time is too precious to start from scratch with basic blocking. Using a rehearsal hall, an empty studio, a warehouse, or a living room, you can begin working with talent. Specific areas can be measured off and marked with masking tape or furniture to represent major staging areas. Documentaries and educational programs can benefit from having early rehearsals where the director and talent can work together.

> Rehearse and walk the actors through each scene carefully and rehearse them before taping.

One of the first rehearsal techniques you will conduct from the studio floor will be a walkthrough rehearsal. This might be either a talent walkthrough or a technical walkthrough. In this walkthrough rehearsal, you will explain major camera moves, audio placement, scene changes, and special effects. In many instances, the walkthrough is a combination, taking both the talent and crew through an abbreviated version of the production.

Full rehearsals are usually conducted with the director calling shots. The first camera rehearsal usually is a start-and-stop rehearsal. In this approach, you interrupt the rehearsal every time there is a major problem, correct the trouble, and then continue the rehearsal.

Another approach to the first camera rehearsal is the uninterrupted runthrough. In this approach, the director attempts to get through the entire production with a minimum of interruptions.

Finally, there is the dress rehearsal. Theoretically, this is the final rehearsal—a complete, uninterrupted, full-scale rehearsal after all of the problems have been straightened out.

GETTING READY

In any kind of production, you should plan on holding one or more production conferences involving different production members (such as set designer, art director, lighting technician).

You must now make sure that all of the preproduction elements are properly requested and constructed. If any special costumes or props have to be ordered or fabricated, they are initiated. All graphics have to be ordered and produced. Any special effects will have to be arranged. Music and other soundtrack selections must be chosen and/or ordered.

During this preproduction process, many production elements cannot proceed until other items are taken care of first. Everything, therefore, must be scheduled days and weeks in advance. To protect yourself, you should leave a few extra days' protection here and there throughout the schedule.

> Learn how the equipment works as a system before going on location.

Prepare your script with specific markings and instructions, including written instructions for key positions on the production crew—camera shot sheets, audio instructions, and so forth. You should direct the setup and test all cameras, VTRs, and microphones. Prepare and plan lighting. Exterior shots may use existing light, or maybe your show is a drama that calls for a certain style of lighting. Make sure to plan and execute the lighting design for your location.

Chapter 5
Sound Technology

The sound in a video program is just as important as its picture; audio and video must always reinforce each other and the content of the story. The language of location audio includes the sense of presence when the dialogue and picture are synchronized, the ambient sound that exists at every location, and the use of indigenous sounds to define and add realism to a location. The quality of your sound recordings will only be as good as your equipment. So if you want professional-level sound, you should plan to use professional-level equipment.

Although well-recorded synchronous audio is important, theme music, narration, sound effects, and naturally occurring environmental sounds can add much to the overall presentation of a production. In some productions, the addition of music or other audio could interfere with the development of the characters or the visual presentation of the story. In a typical informational video, however, where much of the content is in the audio track, the use of music, narration, and natural sounds may be needed both to reinforce the content and to make the presentation more interesting.

TYPES OF AUDIO

There are two types of audio in every production. You already have audio that was recorded simultaneously with the video on location using a microphone. This is called *synchronous audio*. Examples include the dialogue of the actors in a drama, the voice of an interview subject in an informational show, and the music of a live band. Much of this audio will remain synchronized with its video throughout the editing process. *Nonsynchronous* audio is sound that is not recorded with accompanying video, sound not necessarily recorded on location, or sound that can stand alone without video. It is sometimes called *wild sound* because it is not tied to the picture. Nonsynchronous audio includes voiceover narration, music, sound effects, and natural or ambient sound. It is added during postproduction.

> Music and sound can keep your audience tuned in and focused.

The soundtrack can carry three types of audio information:

Words, whether a written narration or the quotes of interviewed authorities.

Sound effects, the aural details of a place, object, or event. Sound effects add another dimension to the production of a subject: they take you "on location." The sound of a wren singing, for instance, conveys as much information about the bird as does a picture.

Music, a more subtle, affective form of communication, is used to influence a listener's mood, usually by emphasizing visual action. Music can also be used to maintain a listener's attention during breaks in narration.

When narration is backed by the impact of sound effects and music, sound becomes a powerful instrument of persuasion. Given the power of sound, you should strive to produce a professional sound track. Initially this means attending to your sound recording equipment and techniques.

DIGITAL AUDIO FUNDAMENTALS

Sound is an integral part of video, therefore, we need to look at techniques to bring sound into the computer. Digital audio calls for many of the same considerations as digital video, but there is at least one aspect that makes audio more difficult than video. Audio has to be a continuous signal with no blanking intervals or other structural features that could make the signal easier to handle. Furthermore, there is no such thing as a still frame in audio. In video, if things get ahead of us, we can always display a still frame while the processing catches up—and if it is not too long, the viewer may not even notice. In audio we can never stop—to do so will cause an abrupt loss of information and a loss of synchronism (or *lip-sync*) with the video.

> The sample rate defines the reproducible bandwidth of the encoded signal. A sample rate greater than 40 KHz is required to reproduce the audible range of frequencies.

There are some applications for realistic audio without realistic video. Real audio is so effective—and so unexpected with a computer—that it will find use as a help medium, as a background environment medium (music, motor sounds, and so on), or simply as a feature in itself, such as using it for a telephone receiving and answering medium.

Natural sounds are analog—minute pressure variations in the atmosphere that we can pick up with various kinds of pressure-to-electrical transducers. Of course such a transducer made specifically for sound pickup is a *microphone.* It is tailored to the frequency range and the pressure values that relate to the audibility characteristics of the human ear. The microphone produces an analog electrical signal that is as precisely as possible a replica of the pressure variations in the air surrounding the microphone.

A full range of equipment is available for storing, processing, and reproducing analog audio signals. Even more so than video, audio technology is mature and available for a wide range of applications and price/performance levels. Audio equipment can be categorized into the same groupings we used for video—broadcast, professional, and consumer. You are probably already familiar with much of the equipment available. The audio production industry has many clients—more than video. There are audio record, tape, and compact disc producers; film makers; television; business; education; and industry. All of these are looking for much the same service from audio production equipment.

Audio production is done with microphones and tape recorders. Audio recorders for production usually have only one or two tracks on magnetic tape. Video recorders also record audio of course, but in many broadcast-level or professional-level productions, the audio will be recorded separately and go through separate postproduction. Only at the end of the process will the audio and video be combined on the same tape.

> You can store as much as 16 hours of speech-quality sound on the same CD that only carries about 70 minutes of CD-quality music.

There are large facilities available for audio postproduction in most major cities around the world. In these studios, audio from many sources may be equalized, effects may be inserted, and the sources combined (mixed) into the tracks that will be used by the final application. Typically, an audio postproduction house will work with many parallel tracks on magnetic tape—24-track machines using 2-inch-wide tape are common. Separate mix tracks for music, dialogue, and effects will be developed, and a final mix of these to the output tracks will be done. If the output tracks are in stereo, positioning of sound sources in the stereo field will be accomplished during the various mixes. Audio postproduction is an art in itself and commands a lot of the attention of a producer because the audio is a crucial part in conveying the message intended by the audio-video material being produced.

Just as in the broadcast-level video business, there is a trend in audio production and postproduction to go to digital equipment. Products for digital recording of audio are on the market at broadcast-level performance and prices. The motivation is the same as for video: unlimited generations of recording. In the audio business there is already a digital medium for distribution of audio to consumers—the compact disc—and this also has been a major motivation for the audio production industry to convert everything to digital.

To bring real sounds into the personal computer environment, we first must convert the analog audio to digital using an A/D converter (unless we have captured the audio on one of the new digital tape systems—then we face only a format conversion process). The A/D process is exactly the same as we discussed for video—sampling and quantizing–however, the frequencies and the precision are quite different. For audio, where the maximum bandwidth is 20 kHz, sampling rates need to be around 44–50 kHz. This is slow compared to the MHz rates required by video, but that is partially offset by the need to have many more bits per sample. In video, we talked about 46 dB signal-to-noise (S/N) ratio as being good, but that number is terrible for audio. Audio S/N ratio needs to be above 70 dB for noise not to be heard in normal listening, and when the considerations of the production process are included, S/N ratios in the 90 dB range become necessary. Therefore the standard of audio digitizing is to use 16 bits per sample. This gives a theoretical S/N ratio of about 96 dB.

> *Sampling* is a process whereby a section of digital audio representing a sonic event, acoustic or electro-acoustic, is stored on disk or into memory.
>
> *Quantizing* is a process of assigning discrete numerical values to digitally sampled sections of a waveform.

AUDIO COMPRESSION

Quantizing 16-bit digital audio is normally done with *linear* PCM, where each step of quantization has equal size. This is the format used with the audio compact disc. However, with fewer than 16 bits per sample, other strategies are worthwhile. Quantization noise occurs at low signal levels because the quantization steps become a large fraction of the signal amplitude.

For even more compression of audio, one can use *differential* PCM or DPCM. In this scheme, the quantizer codes the *difference* between adjacent samples instead of the samples themselves. Because most of the time the difference between samples will not be as large as the samples themselves, fewer bits can be used for coding. If adjacent audio samples tend to be similar in amplitude, then DPCM will work well.

> Compression can be accomplished with either hardware or software.

A further improvement is to make the DPCM system *adaptive.* In this system, called ADPCM, the scale factor of the difference bits is changed by a strategy that is sensitive to the signal level or degree of high-frequency content. This means that when the signal is small, the difference bits will control small steps of amplitude, but if the signal becomes large, the range of voltage represented by the difference bits also become large. The information for control of the scale factor is also contained in the stream of difference bits, so that the decoder for ADPCM can find out how to control the scale factor when playing back the sound. Dedicated integrated circuits are available to do some of the ADPCM algorithms; already one has been standardized in the telephone industry by the CCITT (Consultative Committee for International Telephone and Telegraph). This algorithm is intended for telephone speech and operates at 32 kbits per second, using ADPCM at 4 bits per sample and with a sampling rate of 8,000 per second. It provides very satisfactory speech at telephone-quality levels and is suitable for use on personal computers. Higher quality sound can be achieved with a similar 4-bit-per-sample ADPCM system simply by increasing the sampling rate and therefore the system bandwidth.

TIME AUDIO

Audio must play continuously and cannot be interrupted. To a computer, this means that audio is a real-time operation and must have a high priority compared to other things going on in the computer. Many personal computer operating systems do not provide for real-time operations, and therefore audio on these computers must have a path around the operating system. To keep the audio playing while more data is being fetched usually requires that the audio hardware contains *buffering* on its data input.

Buffering in the audio hardware will allow us to fetch audio data in blocks large enough so that there will always be audio data stored ahead in the audio hardware, and therefore the computer will not run out of data during the longest possible disk access. Usually the rest of the applications (video and computer functions) can be designed so that an access longer than several seconds is never required without an interrupt. Because the audio data rate is, on the average, quite low (4,000 to about 16,000 bytes per second), and it is not too much to ask the audio hardware to have 16 KB of memory on board, we can buffer up to four seconds of audio to cover disk accesses. (The capability to do buffering is a key advantage of digital systems over analog systems.)

One disadvantage to buffering is that it implies some delay in starting because we must fill up the buffer before we begin playing audio. There also can be a delay in making a change to any audio that is playing if the change also has to go through the buffering. A good system will have a strategy for getting around that, so that the audio hardware can respond instantly when necessary.

SYNTHETIC DIGITAL AUDIO AND THE MUSIC INDUSTRY

A tremendous amount of technology has been developed for creating synthetic sounds digitally. The main thrust of this work has been the music equipment business. Electronic musical instruments began as keyboard devices using analog technology. These instruments were known as *synthesizers,* which combined a keyboard controller with analog sound generators. As digital technology became available, synthesizers became digital. Today, however, the controller and the sound generation have become separated, and we have digital sound generators that can be controlled by any kind of player interface. If you are a wind instrumentalist, you can get an electronic controller that is played the same as your clarinet, or if you prefer to play guitar, there are electronic controllers that play like guitars—in either case, the sound generation is electronic.

The key to this flexibility is the *Music Instrument Digital Interface* (MIDI), which is a digital bus specification for connecting musical devices and music controllers. A *bus* is a channel of a group of related buttons on a switcher. Essentially all professional electronic music equipment today has a MIDI interface on it. There are keyboards that do nothing but send out MIDI signals as you play, and there are music modules that can respond to MIDI signals and make almost any kind of sound imaginable. There are also instruments that combine controller and sound generation, but even these have MIDI so that they may be combined with other instruments to produce layers of sound.

One kind of sound generator that is gaining acceptance in the music industry is the *sampler.* This instrument samples and stores real sounds and then plays them back with pitch change. For example, in the simplest case you can sample one note from a piano, and then the sampler will let you play from its own or another MIDI keyboard as if you had all the notes from a piano. Of course, the pitch-change algorithms used in these instruments introduce approximation errors when you sample just one note and then try to make an entire keyboard from it. However, the more elaborate samplers are set up so that the pitch-change algorithm only needs to sample a few notes to create a realistic range of sounds.

MIDI systems embrace personal computers. There are MIDI interface boards for microcomputers and a host of software that performs all kinds of functions. For example, the microcomputer can function as a multitrack recorder, which records MIDI commands from many instruments in parallel. If these are played simultaneously by the computer, you can essentially play an entire orchestra from the microcomputer. At the same time the computer can edit the data to make changes or corrections, it can adjust the timing or the tuning, rearrange the measures—you name it. We have essentially a word processor for music. With samplers, the mass storage of the computer can hold samples, and the microcomputer can function as a sample librarian.

> An alternative way to keep music files short is to use MIDI instead of digital audio.

MIDI is an alternate route to digital audio. With a microcomputer connected to a suitable bank of MIDI sound generators, you can produce high quality music of any style, and with far less data than any audio compression of real audio data could ever deliver.

CHOOSING A MICROPHONE

The most important piece of equipment you will need is a microphone. You may need a tape recorder and an audio mixer. Choosing the right microphone for a video shoot is easy if you understand how microphones work and the advantages and disadvantages of the various types. By becoming familiar with microphones in general, you can make an intelligent choice for your shoot. The two most popular types of microphone capsules for video work are the dynamic and the condenser.

DYNAMIC MICROPHONE

The dynamic, or moving coil, microphone is a pressure-operated device consisting of a tightly wrapped coil of fine wire that is attached to a delicate movable diaphragm. This coil is suspended within a permanently charged magnetic field. When a sound wave hits the diaphragm, the diaphragm and the connected coil are displaced in proportion to the intensity of the oncoming wavefront. By this displacement, the coil is made to cut across the many fixed lines of magnetic flux supplied by the permanent magnet, thereby inducing an electrical current into the wires of the coil. This becomes the analogous electrical output of the microphone. The dynamic microphone does not require a battery—an important distinction on location, where the lack of a replacement battery can stop an entire day of production.

> Dynamic microphones lack the fidelity of the condenser microphone but are good enough for most video use.

CONDENSER MICROPHONE

The condenser microphone operates according to an electrostatic principle rather than the electromagnetic principle governing the functioning of the dynamic and ribbon microphones. The head, or capsule, of a condenser microphone consists of two very thin plates (often on the order of 0.001 inch): one movable (diaphragm) and one fixed (backplate). These two plates form an electrical device known as a *capacitor* (also known as a *condenser*, and hence the name condenser microphone). A capacitor is capable of storing an electric charge. The condenser microphone requires a battery.

DIRECTIONAL PATTERN

All microphones fall into one of three polar (directional) pattern categories: omnidirectional (also called nondirectional), unidirectional (also called directional), and bidirectional. As its name implies, the omnidirectional microphone picks up sound from all sides. It has little discrimination as far as the angle of pickup is concerned. One advantage of the omnimicrophone is that the talent does not have to pay much attention to being on axis. That is, staying in front of the microphone is not critical. Because the omni will pick up sound from the sides and rear as well as from the front, it can be useful when working with nonprofessional talent. However, it will also pick up sounds that you may not want on your videotape—studio background noise, cameras being moved, traffic sounds during an outdoor shoot. This is where a unidirectional microphone would be a good choice.

The unidirectional microphone picks up primarily from the front of the microphone. This is not to say that it will completely ignore sounds that are not directly in front of the microphone. It will still pick up off-axis sounds, but at a reduced level. This would certainly help in a situation where you have no control over the noise, such as an outdoor shoot. But staying on-axis of the microphone becomes a consideration.

There are various categories of unidirectional microphones, including cardioid, supercardioid, hypercardioid, and shotgun. These variations describe the shape or width of the polar pattern of the microphone, with cardioid being the widest at

> An omnidirectional microphone can hear in all directions, a unidirectional microphone can hear only in front of it, and a bidirectional microphone can hear in two directions: front and back.

about 132°, and the shotgun, which is narrowest, about 60°. Obviously, the narrower the pattern, the more off-axis rejection of unwanted sound, and the more critical the aiming of the microphone becomes.

The bidirectional microphone picks up sound from both the front and rear in equal measure. Because there is only one diaphragm involved, the sound picked up from the rear of the microphone is out of phase with the sound picked up from the front of the microphone. Bidirectional microphones are normally used in recording studios for large orchestra sessions and have not found much use in video work. There is an application for stereo microphones that uses bidirectional capsules. Figure 5.1 illustrates microphone pickup patterns.

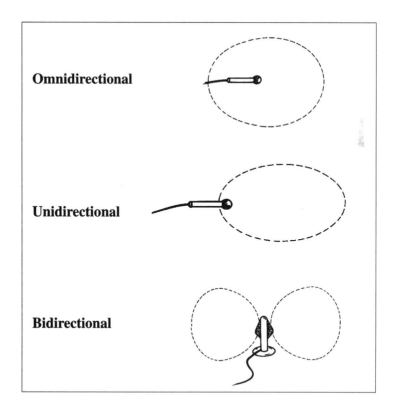

Figure 5.1. Microphone pickup patterns.

Just as there is a variety of polar patterns (microphone's directional sensitivity), there is a variety of microphone types that use those patterns for different applications. Let's look at some of the more popular types and their uses for videotaping.

**The Cardioid
Microphone Pickup
Pattern**

The cardioid pattern
allows the talent to
work at a greater
distance from the
microphone without
having the mike pick
up too many room
echoes.

THE LAVALIERE MICROPHONE

The lavaliere microphone is popular for use in video today. You hear it every night on the news and in some cases you may even see it. The lavaliere is an attempt to get good sound while minimizing the visual presence of the microphone in the picture. Most lavalieres are omnidirectional, because an omni is the smallest way to build a microphone. Although a good lavaliere will give you good audio, there are some things that need to be taken into account when you use one.

The most important thing to consider is the polar pattern of the lavaliere microphone. The smallest lavalieres available are omnidirectional. This makes the talent's job of staying on-axis easy, especially when the lavaliere is attached to the talent. Minor head swivels do not noticeably affect the audio quality. But just as the talent has no problem staying on-axis, extraneous sound from the surrounding area has no problem staying on-axis either. The omnidirectional lavaliere will pick up unwanted sounds just as easily as it will the talent. In a controlled indoor environment, this is usually not a problem. But take the same lavaliere outside and the noise can make the audio track unusable.

There are directional lavalieres available today, but they also have their considerations. The most noticeable is their size. In order to make a microphone directional, a rear entry must be added to the housing so that sound can reach the back of the diaphragm. This translates directly into a larger housing for the microphone capsule. Although not as large as a hand-held microphone, a unidirectional lavaliere is noticeably larger than a comparable omnidirectional one.

Windscreens for lavaliere microphones are a must on an outdoor shoot. Even a soft breeze can cause the audio track to sound as if it were recorded in a wind tunnel. The culprit is turbulence caused when the wind hits the grille or case of the microphone. The sharper the edges, the more turbulence; the more turbulence, the more noise.

A good windscreen helps break up the flow of air around the microphone and reduce the turbulence. It works best when fitted loosely around the grille of the microphone. A windscreen that has been jammed down on a microphone only serves to close off some of the normal path the audio would take to get to the diaphragm. The end result is attenuated high frequencies and not much wind protection.

THE HAND-HELD MICROPHONE

The hand-held microphone comes in many shapes and in both omnidirectional and unidirectional versions. The hand-held microphone serves to give good frequency response, good handling noise characteristics, and the widest choice of sounds. Because the space is available, a good shock mount system is incorporated in most hand-held microphones. This prevents the handling noise from becoming too objectionable.

The Hypercardioid Microphone Pickup Pattern

A hypercardioid microphone is more sensitive in one direction than a cardioid. It is a cross between unidirectional and cardioid.

Just holding a microphone or dragging its cable can cause low-frequency noise to be transmitted to the cartridge. A good shock mount system minimizes these noises. The same polar characteristics that were mentioned in the lavaliere section also apply to the hand-held microphone: An omni will pick up sounds from all angles; a unidirectional will discriminate in favor of the sounds arriving from the front of the microphone. Hand-held microphones also offer tighter pickup patterns than do most directional lavalieres.

A standard unidirectional microphone is cardioid. In fact, most people use the two terms interchangeably. Supercardioid and hypercardioid microphones have even tighter patterns and reject even more background noise than a cardioid. This allows a cleaner audio track with less ambient noise. The drawback is the smaller pickup area with which the talent has to work.

As the pattern gets narrower, the working angle of the microphone gets narrower, and the closer to the center the talent has to stay. If the talent strays too far off-axis, the microphone will assume that the talent is part of the background noise and attenuate them accordingly.

THE SHOTGUN MICROPHONE

**Shotgun Microphone
Pickup Pattern**

Shotgun microphones are a version of unidirectional microphones that have an extremely tight pattern. Although they seem to reach farther than a normal cardioid microphone, the truth is that they reject background noise better than a cardioid and can pick out sounds at a greater distance while ignoring the general noise around the shoot. As such, they have a narrow working angle, and staying on-axis is critical. The closer the talent is to the shotgun microphone, the more attention you must pay to microphone placement. In the world of shotgun microphones, the rule of thumb is that the longer the microphone, the more directional it will be: A short shotgun will not be as directional as a long shotgun. Today's shotgun microphones use a combination of cartridge tuning and interference tube tuning to achieve a smooth frequency response and polar pattern. The compromises of the tuning factors dictate what the microphone will sound like and how it will behave.

In drama productions, a shotgun or similar directional microphone is mounted on a long arm called a *boom* and held over the head of the actors. Sometimes this same microphone can be hand-held and placed just to the right or left of the frame, out of the picture. If your production calls for a directional microphone, you'll need a *boom operator* to point the microphone at the person speaking. Using a boom can be troublesome; you must not only keep it out of the picture but avoid letting its shadow fall across the actors or the background. Also, depending on the noise level of your chosen location and the voice level of the actors, you may not be able to get a boom-mounted microphone close enough to get good sound.

Up to this point, we have talked exclusively about wired microphones. Wired microphones are cost-effective and microphone cable is relatively cheap, but there are times when the talent simply cannot be tied to the camera or recorder. The obvious answer is the wireless microphone.

THE WIRELESS MICROPHONE

The wireless microphone offers the user the freedom to move about the studio or location without tripping over the microphone cable. The microphone cable has been replaced by an RF link. This may sound like the ideal situation for all shoots, but the wireless microphone is not without its own set of constraints.

When choosing a wireless microphone system, make sure that the mike is transmitting on an unoccupied frequency in your area. Otherwise, you may pick up commercial FM radio broadcasts, walkie-talkie conversations, or other interference.

In general, any microphone may be used with a wireless transmitter. The two most popular types are the hand-held and the lavaliere. Most wireless microphone manufacturers offer a version of each in their product lines. However, a body pack transmitter can be made to accommodate almost any microphone simply by using the right cable. Shotgun microphone, hand-held, lavaliere, headset—all can be turned into wireless units with the proper connecting cable. But, in addition to the acoustic cautions above, the wireless world brings with it a new set of factors that must be taken into account. The most important of these is frequency selection.

As the airwaves get more crowded each day, finding a frequency that is not in use is at best more art than science. A frequency that works well in the studio may not work at all on location. One solution would be to carry RF units set for different frequencies. This would allow the backup units to be used in case of a frequency problem. But frequency coordination is only one of the wireless concerns. RF, like audio, cannot be seen and is hard to pinpoint. A signal that you might expect to go directly from the transmitter to the receiver could very well do just that. It could also bounce off the light rails in a studio, or even the camera bodies. The reflected signal would arrive at the antenna a split second later and a dropout would result. The best thing to do is to follow the same rules of use that you would with wired microphones.

Keep the transmission path as short and as obstacle-free as possible—you wouldn't give the talent a 500-foot microphone cable when 25 feet would do. Keep the antennas where they can see each other. Putting the transmitting or receiving antenna where it is out of sight may look nice, but it will adversely affect the operation of the wireless microphone. Anything that gets between the transmitting and receiving antennas adds to the possibility of a dropout. This includes sets, cameras, lights, and people.

When done right, wireless can allow the talent the freedom to move about without the fear of cable entanglement. It can also allow the production team the freedom to move about with the same ease.

SPECIAL-PURPOSE MICROPHONES

There always comes a time when you need a special microphone. Although another microphone might be rigged to partially cover the need, special-purpose microphones have their place in the video world.

The parabolic microphone is attached at the focal point of a large parabolic reflector.

Parabolic microphones are one breed of special-purpose microphone. Used primarily for sporting events, they allow the audio to zero in on a player or particular area of the playing field. A parabolic microphone works in much the same way that a satellite dish works: It concentrates the acoustic energy at the focal point of the parabola, which is where the microphone is mounted.

Although a shotgun will give good directivity and wide frequency response, the parabolic microphone is even more directional, but at the expense of frequency response. The low-end response of a parabolic microphone is limited by the diameter of the parabolic dish. The larger the dish, the lower the frequency. Because most parabolic mikes are hand-held, a small dish is used. Response below 300Hz is minimal. A larger dish would yield a better low end, but holding and steering the dish would be a problem. A windy day would make matters worse.

Microphones that are hidden from view are another category of special-purpose microphones. Hiding microphones falls into the same category as hiding wireless antennas. It may look good on camera, but the audio suffers accordingly. As with RF, anything that comes between the microphone and the signal that you are trying to pick up only serves to degrade the audio signal.

Microphones have successfully been hidden in plants, sets, desks, walls, and on the talent, but most of those installations have taken a lot of trial and error to get the right positioning and equalization. There are microphones that are designed to be mounted at or near a reflecting surface, and they work well if mounted properly. However, taking a standard hand-held or lavaliere microphone and putting it on a reflective surface destroys the high-frequency response. Surface-mount microphones take this into account and plan for it in the design. Using a microphone that was designed for the purpose makes the job much easier.

STEREO MICROPHONES

Stereo can add much to your video production but only if it is done right. Adding another channel to your video complicates things tenfold. If there is a chance of mono playback, then mono compatibility is a major concern. Simply folding the stereo back to mono by summing the channels can lead to strange-sounding results. Sound effects and music or dialogue can disappear if mono compatibility is not checked in production.

One of the cleanest ways to do stereo audio is to use an M-S stereo microphone. This arrangement uses two microphone capsules in a common housing. The M (mid) capsule is a unidirectional capsule that faces forward, like the lens of your camera. The S (side) capsule is a bidirectional unit that faces

Stereo Microphone

left and right. The output of the two capsules is added together through a matrix in the microphone that gives you left and right sound images.

The big advantage to the M-S technique is that it is fully monocompatible. Summing the left and right channels gives you just what the M capsule was picking up, as if it were a mono microphone. It is also easy to use because all capsules and electronics are housed in a common microphone. Other methods of doing stereo use multiple microphones and are not fully monocompatible.

Music and sound effects work well in stereo and add realism to the production. Stereo dialogue, however, is highly distracting and can ruin an otherwise good presentation.

TAPE RECORDERS

You can choose among three different types of tape recorders—cassette recorders, portable reel-to-reel recorders, and studio recorders. Each type has advantages and disadvantages that you must consider when making a choice.

Cassette recorders. Many of the cassette recorders on the market today record and play back sound with the fidelity of reel-to-reel recorders. Cassette recorders are highly practical if you are recording interviews as part of your preliminary research. Their compact size and ease of operation make them ideal for situations where the emphasis is on gathering information.

> Most tape recorders have three heads: erase, record, and playback.

Portable reel-to-reel recorders. These can be used for almost any sound recording assignment. If necessary, they can even be used to record sound in a studio.

With tape recorders, as with almost all other products, you usually get what you pay for. So, in general, the more you spend for a portable reel-to-reel recorder, the more sophistication you will receive. This is particularly true with such features as the tape transport mechanism, the pre-amplification components, options used for recording lip-synchronized film sequences, and so forth.

Most portable tape recorders use five-inch and seven-inch reels of tape—enough for 20 to 45 minutes of taping at a speed of 7-1/2 inches per second (ips).

Studio recorders are highly sophisticated and extremely costly. Unless you are equipping a sound studio, you will not be in the market for this type of equipment, which is best used to full advantage by a professional sound-recording engineer.

The factors that make studio equipment so expensive are its reliability and durability, as well as a far superior signal-to-noise ratio, low distortion, and wide range of capabilities. For example, the output from numerous microphones can be fed into these units, allowing the recording system to tape a single narrator or a 200-member choral group. Instead of adjusting the recorder with a few knobs and dials on the unit itself, the sound engineers sit at a mixing console, where they control dozens of equipment functions through an array of switches, potentiometers (pots), and meters.

In general, you should buy the best possible recorder offering the features you are most likely to use. Do not buy features or options you will not use. On the other hand, do not cut corners on the basic unit itself.

You will record sound in one of two places: in a sound studio or "on location." Each situation places slightly different requirements on you.

WORKING IN A STUDIO

A sound studio is a room designed and constructed specially for recording and mixing sound. When constructed properly, the studio is isolated from external sounds that might interfere with recording. The recording area itself should be acoustically balanced, neither too flat nor too tinny and sharp, with little echo or reverberation present.

You will use a sound studio to record the narration for your production (with the exception of segments recorded on location), to record music and library sound effects, and to mix the various elements into a final soundtrack.

> A sound studio is a room designed and constructed specifically for recording and mixing sound.

When you are recording narration at a studio, the sound engineer will assume responsibility for the quality of the recording. Your job at this time is to direct the narrator. This means attending to such factors as the following.

DELIVERY

Should the script be read with a solemn, serious delivery, a lighthearted delivery, a straightforward, matter-of-fact, businesslike delivery, or the urgent delivery of a newscaster? You must make that decision, then communicate it to your narrator. Because discussions of delivery usually involve subjective interpretations, the narrator, especially if he or she is a professional, will want to rehearse several times to find and refine the proper delivery. By all means take advantage of these practice runs. If the narrator does not suggest a few trial readings, you make the suggestion. It is better to refine the delivery before recording begins, rather than after, when repeated starts and stops threaten the overall quality of the recording.

PACE

The pace of narration can be quick and urgent, suggesting matters of immediate concern; leisurely and casual, suggesting friends discussing a matter of common concern; or crisp and businesslike, suggesting matters that are to be dealt with in a matter-of-fact manner. Once again, you make that decision, then communicate it to your narrator.

During the recording session, your ear is the standard against which to judge the narrator's delivery. You know what "sound" you want in the narration, so if the narrator is not producing that sound, stop the recording session and let him or her know. But do not limit your comments to criticism—offer suggestions for improving the delivery to meet your standards. Do not be hesitant about offering suggestions or constructive criticism.

MUSIC

Sound track can be recorded in one of two ways. If you are recording an original composition, the experience of your recording engineer becomes critical. Recording music involves greater problems and considerations than recording voices, so the studio you hire for this assignment should have experience in mixing and recording musical arrangements. Music played from published compositions is copyrighted and requires that you obtain permission to use it. You may also have to pay a royalty fee.

An easier way to record music, of course, is from a record produced and legally cleared for public use. This approach avoids problems arising from possible infringement of copyright laws. If, on the other hand, you want to use music from an album or record produced for retail sale, you must ask the record company, the recording artist, and the publishing company for permission to use the music. If they agree to your planned use of the music, they will give you written permission. Do not use the music without written permission from the copyright owner. Allow enough time to obtain these permissions.

SELECTING A NARRATOR

Although you may narrate your own show or ask someone in your organization to do the job, the results are rarely as satisfactory as those achieved with a narrator. The diction of inexperienced narrators is not usually as clear as that of professionals and their voices do not carry the same tone of authority.

If you do not know any professional narrators, ask the recording studio to recommend someone, or try a radio station.

RECORDING NARRATION

Give the narrator a double- or triple-spaced copy of the script, but do not include the visuals. Mark any passages you want emphasized. Spell out all numbers (that is, nineteen ninety-five, not 1995) and put in phonetic spelling of all terms. Make sure all paragraphs begin and end on the same page so the announcer will be able to change pages during the pause between paragraphs. If you want the announcer to pause at certain points, indicate the length of the pause by counting out the seconds in the script (one thousand, two thousand, and so on). Make identically marked copies of the narrator's version of the script for yourself and the recording engineer. Give the narrator a copy of the script a day or two before the recording session. On the day of the session, ask the narrator to read through the script so you can suggest any necessary changes in emphasis. The technician can use this rehearsal to arrange the microphone and set the recording level.

When mistakes occur, have the narrator back up to the beginning of the last paragraph after each mistake and then keep going. Make a note of each restart in your script so the engineer can edit mistakes out later. If the narrator makes several attempts at a section, note all of them and indicate which one you liked best.

SELECTING MUSIC

It is recommended that you limit your use of music to short compositions at the beginning and end of the production.

Most instructional presentations include at least a few minutes of music. Music can enhance a production when it is carefully chosen to appeal to the audience and to match the style of the show. However, like printed materials and photographs, music is covered by copyright laws and must not be used without permission. There are collections of music that have been specifically produced for use without requiring copyright permission. These types of music are developed with particular themes. Instead of the 10 or 12 songs found on most record albums, they contain dozens of short selections designed to introduce, bridge sections of, or end a production.

WORKING ON LOCATION

If you are recording sound on location instead of in a studio, you have additional problems to deal with, foremost of which is ambient sound. Usually, however, if you use an appropriate microphone and a little common sense, you can minimize the problem. Two suggestions will help make your recording job easier.

- Do not record your narration in a normally noisy location. Unless your intention is to prove the sophistication of your sound-recording techniques and equipment, do not go looking for problems to solve.

- Do not overlook obvious sources of unwanted sound. And when you find them, eliminate them. Before you begin a recording session, look around your site for people, objects, or events that are likely to ruin a take. If you are recording in an office, for example, beware of telephones. Have a secretary, receptionist, or operator intercept all calls headed for your recording site. If you eliminate possible interruptions ahead of time, you will not be bothered by them later.

The best equipment to use when recording narration on location is a portable reel-to-reel recorder such as one of those mentioned earlier in this chapter. Use a cardioid microphone if you want to pick up some ambient sound from the location; use a shotgun mike if you want to eliminate as much peripheral noise as possible.

> Not all background sound is music. Street sounds, machines, sirens, motors, gunfire—all can be background to your dialogue.

Location recording usually involves working with three sources of sound: wild sound, spoken words, and sound effects.

Wild sound or *ambient noise* is everywhere. Noise from traffic, airplanes, jackhammers, thunder, rain, people shouting, and so on, creates problem for on-location audio production. Even though unwanted sound is always present, in producing audio it must be brought within tolerable levels so that it does not interfere with desired sound.

The words will be spoken either by your narrator or by the subject of an interview. Working with a narrator on location is no different than working with one in a studio. You have to supply instruction, direction, and encouragement.

Recording an interview, however, presents a different set of problems to solve. First you have to judge the suitability of the person you want to interview. Then you must ask the questions and direct the recording session.

Choosing the right person for an interview requires editorial judgment on your part. You have to judge whether the person is worth recording. If your subject's words merely repeat a commonplace fact or opinion, perhaps you would be better off having your narrator quote or paraphrase the person. If, on the other hand, your subject offers new, controversial, highly opinionated, or emphatically spoken information, you will probably want to record his or her words.

Preparing for an interview means thinking out the order and phrasing of your questions. Unless you have hours of tape or film to devote to a single interview, the worst interviewing technique you can use is to ask a broad, open-ended question. This leads to a rambling answer—and an ineffective sound track.

PRODUCING THE SOUND TRACK

Often you can hear the music and effects you want when you look at your visual images. And you may feel more comfortable when you have a sound track against which to plot your visual images. In a very real sense, the music and effects help you "see" how images should be developed.

Let sound and visuals influence each other. One way multimedia producers do this is to create a rough sound track—or "scratch track"—to use as the basis for visual planning and programming. They edit their scratch track until it sounds right for the show. Then they select and program their visuals as if creating the choreography for a dance. Once the union of sound and visuals feels right, the final sound track is mixed.

There are three major advantages to producing a scratch track.

1. The sound track will help you determine the mood or feeling of visuals, or the entire presentation. Naturally, the visual style and programming should be in harmony with this mood.

2. The music used in your sound track influences the pacing of your presentation. So your scratch track will help you pinpoint the time you need to complete a sequence or an entire presentation.

3. Producing a scratch track is particularly useful if a sound track is to be an involved, multitrack mix. A complex 10-track mix—with multiple voices, music, and a variety of sound effects—is difficult and costly to change just to add or delete a few seconds from a visual image.

USING MUSIC AND SOUND EFFECTS

Although your narrator's voice may form the core of your sound track, music and sound effects animate that core and give it color. This makes the selection and use of the right music and sound effects extremely important.

> The sound track will help you determine the mood or feeling of a sequence or of the entire program.

People starting their first multimedia production often ask when to use music and sound effects. Unfortunately, there's no set formula to follow. Some presentations work best when music and effects are present throughout the whole show, coming up and receding between narrated segments. In contrast, we have all seen presentations with continuous musical backgrounds that bring to mind the monotonous sound tracks from training films of the 1950s. Still other productions work best when music and effects are restricted to opening and closing sequences, where they act as punctuation to set the tone, or function like an exclamation point. Unfortunately, this approach is too often used as a way out when, in fact, the production cries out for more "color."

Each production is unique in this sense, and the type and amount of music and effects used must be determined on an individual basis, depending upon the audience, the objective, the tone of the message, and even the location and environment in which the production will be used.

By using separate tracks for music segments and sound effects, a sound mixer can control their respective levels in relation to the voice track. Once you have laid down all music sequences and sound effects with your voice track, you are ready for the final mix. Once you have locked in your timing, you can come back with any changes and do the final mix. You can plot that final mix either by means of notations in the margin of your script or on a separate mix-down chart, if the mix is to be relatively involved. The most effective method is to plot the changes in music or effects against a time frame. With various pieces of music and sound effects on separate tracks, you'll be able to adjust levels, change fade points and, in effect, create whatever total impression you want your final sound track to convey.

> The music used in your sound track influences the pacing of your program.

Above all, keep in mind the fact that you—as the producer—must represent the client in judging what sounds right. You will be the one responsible for the final outcome. So make certain your final mix is exactly what you want. A good sound engineer can be very creative and can offer many useful suggestions that might improve the final result. You are familiar with the objectives of your multimedia production. You know what kind of effect that sound track has to have on your audience. So you are the one who must direct the final mix. And if you are not satisfied with the results of the first attempt at a mix, do not hesitate to tell your engineer what you want changed. It is not uncommon to make two or three passes at a final mix before the right one is achieved.

SOUND EFFECTS

Sound effects can add greatly to the realism and impact of certain kinds of productions; however, the cost of including them can be substantial. Unlike music segments, which can be used sparingly in a production, sound effects should be mixed through the entire sound track—the way they are in motion-picture production. A few sound effects may not accomplish this objective. On the other hand, adding sound effects to an entire sound track can be time-consuming. Each new location in your production will require a different background sound.

MIXING NARRATION AND MUSIC

After you have chosen your music, figured out how you want to use it, and recorded the narration, the mix takes place. Although you can just tag music onto the beginning and end of the narration, it will blend better and sound more polished if it is actually combined with the narration. When you are ready to mix the narration, music, and sound effects, give the recording engineer a copy of the script with all the inserts clearly marked. If you want the music to begin 15 seconds before the narration begins and fade out after the first minute, indicate that in your script.

> Choose a power amplifier that will give sufficient force and impact to the audio portion of the presentation.

The basic element of the sound system for a multimedia production is the tape deck, and the number of makes and models available is staggering. They range from simple cassette units with or without built-in synchronization capabilities to elaborate solid-state eight-track units. Although some of these new cassette decks are finding increased application among multimedia producers, most still rely on solid-state reel-to-reel equipment.

Some producers, when putting together a complex sound track for a sophisticated production, take advantage of eight-track decks. This equipment enables them to isolate and play back specific parts of their sound track.

MIXER

A mixer accepts signals from various sources, allows each signal to be individually adjusted for loudness, and sends this combination to a recording device. As with all production equipment, you can have small, medium-sized, and enormous mixers that can do basic, moderate, and miraculous tasks.

MIXER'S OUTPUTS

The mixer's output sends the combined signals to the recording device. Just as each microphone's volume is adjustable with a knob on the mixer, the volume of the signal the mixer sends out is also adjustable with the *master* volume control. Usually this knob is a different color, shape, or size from the rest. The mixer may have several outputs. Although one output from a mixer is all that is needed, the others are there to permit flexibility in setting up and using the audio system. The mixer's outputs are the following:

MIKE OUT or MIKE LEVEL OUT is an audio output that has a tiny signal like a microphone, thus it can be plugged into the MIKE IN of a recording device.

LINE OUT or AUX OUT or AUDIO OUT is a medium-sized signal destined to go to a recorder LINE IN or AUX IN.

The microphones and other things feed into the mixer and get combined. The audio signal could be fed to the recorder and monitored either on the recorder's speaker (if it has one), or on headphones plugged into the recorder. What happens if you get no sound? Is it the recorder's fault? The mixer's fault? The mike's fault? If the mixer has a meter and the meter wiggles when someone speaks into the microphone, the mixer and mike are most likely working. If you can plug headphones into the HEADPHONE jack on the mixer to monitor the input, you can make sure that the mixer and mike are working well.

MIXING SOUND

There are some basic techniques that can help in mixing sound:

SEGUE

Segue (pronounced "SEG-way") is a smooth change from one sound to another. For instance, the sounds of traffic can be smoothly replaced with music. The traffic's volume control is lowered at the same time that the music's volume control is being raised. This is often done between two pieces of music—as one finishes, the other is being faded up.

Some segues prepare the listener for things to come, like faint traffic noise before we enter the street or the sound of windshield wipers before the actors begin to speak in the car on a rainy night.

VOICEOVER

Voiceover is when the music fades down just before the first words are heard. The music becomes subordinate to the speech and is played under it. This is a music under. Sometimes you have to decide whether to fade the music out entirely when the action starts or to hold the background throughout the scene.

One guide to proper volume setting can be your VU meter. If your narration makes your needle huddle around 0 dB (the 100 percent mark on the scale), the background should wiggle the needle about -8 dB (about 40 percent on the scale). If you only have a nonprofessional record level meter, the narration should wiggle the needle just below the red and the background should wiggle it one-fourth to one-third of its range. These are just generalities. Some musical selections are inherently more obtrusive than others.

When all the microphones are turned on at the same time, you hear not only the sound of the one person speaking but also the breathing and shuffling of the others in the background. You also get the hollow echo of the speaker as his or her voice is picked up on everybody else's microphone. To avoid this, turn down all the inactive mikes, allowing only the speaker's mike to be live. This is easy to do in a scripted production like a newscast or a play, but it is difficult to do in a free discussion. One partial solution may be to lower the mike level by a third or a half the inactive microphone volumes, raising it after the person begins speaking. Although the person's first words may be weak, they will be audible and will soon be up to full volume.

AUDIO TRACKS ON VIDEO

All videotapes have two audio tracks. You can record on channel 1 (track 1) or channel 2 (track 2). Upon playback, you have the choice of listening to channel 1, channel 2, or a mixture of both by flipping the audio monitor selector from CH-1 to CH-2 or to MIX. If your VCR is equipped to record on both tracks at once, then record both channels. That way no one can switch to the wrong channel. If recording on only one of the two channels, make channel 2 the main one (that is almost the standard channel).

The microphone serves as the basic input, collecting sounds and converting them into a form that can be manipulated. The choice of the specific microphone to use should take into consideration the type of generating element the microphone has, its pickup pattern, its frequency response, and other performance characteristics.

The audio console is designed to process the audio input. Several inputs can be mixed and routed through the output section to recorders or to a transmitter. Volume levels and balance can be checked with various monitoring devices, including VU meters, LED displays, cue speakers, loudspeakers, and earphones.

To produce an effective audio, you must consider the requirements for good communication, and the possibilities and limitations of the technology. These factors affect decisions made during preproduction planning, preproduction technical preparation, production, and postproduction.

Chapter 6

Videodisc Technology

Mastering and duplication of the videodisc are processes handled almost entirely by your mastering facility. Once you have prepared the pre-master tape in the postproduction facility, the process is in the hands of the mastering facility—but you should pay close attention to several parts of this process to ensure that the disc will perform as expected.

In addition to the program postproduction requirements, the videotape (source tape) must be subjected to a pre-mastering process to ensure that it will be usable for making a videodisc master.

THE LASER PICKUP SYSTEM

The laser beam modulations are recorded on the photosensitive surface of the master disc. This process is basically reversed in the playback system: the pickup laser beam is modulated by the signal recorded on the disc and this modulated laser beam is converted back to an electrical composite audio/video signal for playback.

The microscopic pits representing the recorded signal must be tracked with unerring precision by the laser/optical playback system, requiring the utmost in mechanical and optical precision. Four independent and extremely accurate servo systems are required to perform this task— the focus servo, the tracking servo, the slider servo, and the disc speed servo system.

The focus servo is essential for maintaining perfect pinpoint focus of the laser beam on the disc surface. Even if there are slight warps in the disc or irregularities in its surface, the focus servo will react immediately to maintain perfect focus at all times.

The tracking servo compensates for any eccentric motion of the signal track. This can be caused by a slightly off-center disc hole, a sloppy fit of the disc on the player's spindle, or irregularities in the drive mechanism. Once again, this servo system must respond with absolute precision to ensure that the laser beam spot does not leave the signal track.

As the signal track spirals from the center of the disc outward, the entire laser pickup mechanism must follow it, just as a phonograph cartridge follows a record's groove. This is the job of the slider servo.

The precision and stability of disc rotation are just as important to accurate signal pickup as the other factors discussed above. The disc speed servo rotates the disc at the precise speed required for signal pickup. The speed of the disc must remain perfectly constant for CAV discs, and it must be varied at a precisely determined rate in order to play back long-playing CLV discs.

The laser beam reflected from the signal track is modulated by the signal pits. This modulated laser beam is then routed through a sophisticated optical system to a photodiode matrix that not only converts the laser light signal to an electronic signal for processing by the playback circuitry but also derives the servo signals to be fed back to the four servo systems.

VIDEODISC FEATURES

A videodisc is either 8" or 12" in diameter. There are about 14 billion pits of information recorded on one side, arranged in a spiral. One ring of the spiral is called a *track*, and there are 54,000 tracks per side.

Videodiscs allow data and video images to be encoded on a plastic disc that can be read by a low-power laser beam. Following is a general reference to interactive videodisc production, providing an overview of the technical information and specifications for the process of interactive videodisc mastering and replication. Some of the information has already been presented in Chapter 1.

The audio/video information is recorded on the disc in form of tiny "pits" measuring a mere 0.4 micron across and 0.1 micron deep. The signal track is recorded in a spiral from inside to the outside of the disc, and the distance between each section of track on the disc is approximately 1.6 microns. Figure 6.1 shows the videodisc construction.

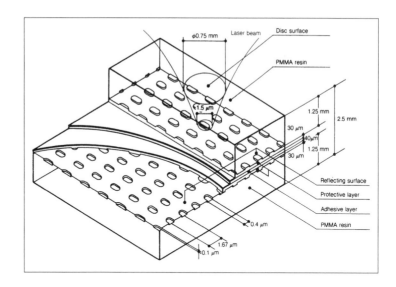

Figure 6.1. Videodisc construction.

DISC FORMATS

Videodiscs can be mastered in two formats: Constant Angular Velocity (CAV) and Constant Linear Velocity (CLV). The format you select depends on the applications for your program, the length of your program, and the specific capabilities of the disc player you choose as part of your program delivery system. Videodiscs have spiral tracks and play from the inside track to the outside track. Figure 6.2 shows the videodisc tracks.

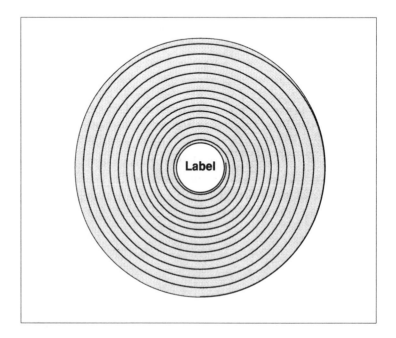

Figure 6.2. Videodisc tracks.

CAV DISC

The interactive-play CAV disc format gives you the broadest range of program capability, including still/freeze frame, step frame, slow/fast motion, scan/search by frame or chapter, autostops, and dual channel or stereo audio. The CAV disc format allows for nonlinear play, which means that the information on the disc can be read in any sequence. Standard play is up to 30 minutes per side for 12-inch CAV and 14 minutes for 8-inch CAV.

Each track on a CAV disc contains two video fields that make one complete video frame. A CAV disc holds a maximum of 54,000 frames per side. Rotating at a constant rate of 1,800 revolutions per minute (rpm), the CAV disc achieves the NTSC standard of 30 frames per second (fps). The vertical interval appears as a wedge-shaped section on a CAV disc. It holds data such as the vertical timing signal and frame number (Figure 6.3a).

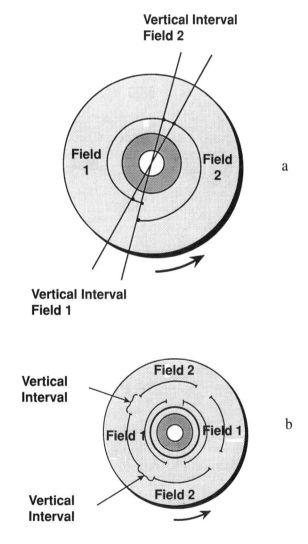

Figure 6.3. Videodisc tracks: a. CAV disc format and b. CLV disc format.

CLV DISC

The most significant advantage of extended-play CLV format is that it doubles the play time to 60 minutes per side in the 12-inch format and 20 minutes in the 8-inch format. Program capability on the disc itself is limited to scan, chapter search, and dual-channel or stereo audio. However, continuing technology advances in disc players (commercial players in particular) allow a broader range of program activity controlled by the end user. The specific level of interaction possible in CLV disc format depends on the capabilities of the player you choose.

CAV discs can be read in any sequence and provide up to 30 minutes of play time per side.

The CLV format allows information to be read linearly either forward or reverse and provides up to 60 minutes of play time per side.

Each video frame on a CLV disc is also made up of two video fields, but the number of frames per track varies from 1 in the innermost track to approximately 3 at the outermost track. The increased number of frames per track provides twice the amount of play time available in CAV format, but the degree of user interactivity is limited (see Figure 6.3b).

To compensate for the increased number of frames per track and constant read speed, the CLV rpm ranges from 1,800 rpm on the innermost track to approximately 600 on the outermost track. The location of the interval that holds the vertical timing signals and frame address varies in the CLV format. In CLV, the address of the frame is encoded in elapsed play time: hours, minutes, seconds, frames. Table 6.1 shows play features by disc format.

CHAPTER NUMBERS

Chapter numbers allow you to designate divisions of the program, much like a book. Chapters can be accessed in both CAV and CLV formats through the player's search feature. In the CAV format, the player typically freezes (still frames) when it searches to a chapter. In the CLV format, the player usually resumes play when it searches to a chapter. Not all players can accurately search to the very first frame of a chapter. This is especially true in the CLV format, where a 30-frame window (one second of black) between chapters is recommended to avoid playback of the end of the previous chapter.

Play Features	12" CAV	12" CLV
30 minutes of play time per side	Yes	No
60 minutes of play time per side	No	Yes
Autostops	Yes	No
Dual channel/stereo audio/digital	Yes	Yes
Fast motion	Yes	No
Linear play	Yes	Yes
Nonlinear play	Yes	Yes
Scan	Yes	Yes
Search by frame number	Yes	No
Search by elapsed time	No	Yes
Search by chapter	Yes	Yes
Slow motion	Yes	No
Step frame	Yes	No
Still/freeze frame	Yes	No

Table 6.1. Play features for CAV and CLV discs.

A maximum of 80 chapters may be used on a videodisc. If you choose to use any chapter numbers in your program, then all program frames must be organized by chapter. Chapters can be numbered 0 through 79 and increase numerically one increment at a time from the beginning of the tape (1, 2, 3, and so on). Your postproduction personnel will indicate the number of the first chapter and the location of all subsequent chapters.

Chapter numbers will be encoded during the videodisc mastering process. To ensure reliable playback, manufacturers recommend that each chapter contain at least 30 video frames.

PLAY FEATURES

The play features of videodiscs include still frame, freeze frame, step frame, and slow motion, as well as special search features. In the CAV videodisc format, all play features are available. In the CLV format, disc scan, chapter scan and search, search by elapsed time, and dual channel/stereo audio/ digital audio are always available. The additional play features may be possible with a CLV videodisc depending on the capability of the particular player used (see Table 6.1).

AUTOSTOP

Autostop codes (also called picture stops or still codes) automatically stop the player on the encoded framers during playback. This function allows the videodisc designer to integrate motion and still sequences.

DUAL CHANNEL/STEREO AUDIO/DIGITAL AUDIO

The two analog audio channels available on videodisc may be used in a variety of ways. The audio may be encoded as mono, stereo, or dual independent. In stereo, the two channels are meant to be played simultaneously. In dual independent, the two channels are independent. Typical uses of dual channel include bilingual programs. Not all videodisc players are capable of playing digital audio.

FAST MOTION

Some players can create the effect of fast motion, up to two or three times normal speed. In fast motion, the player will read one frame and then skip the next one or two frames. Fast motion may be played in either forward or reverse.

SCAN

In scan, the player skips over several tracks at a time, displaying only a fraction of the frames it passes. Scanning can be done in forward or reverse.

SEARCH

The videodisc is available in both NTSC and PAL systems. An NTSC TV screen has a 525-line scan system, scanned in 1/30 second. One second of video in NTSC system uses 30 frames. A PAL TV screen has a 625-line scan system, scanned in 1/25 second. One second of video in PAL system uses 25 frames.

The search function allows the operator to go to a specific frame or chapter. The operator enters the number of the frame or chapter desired. When the enter key is pressed, the player goes to the location and will freeze-frame at the location.

A player that searches by frame will read the frame address code on each disc frame. This code is located in the vertical interval of the dominant field of the frame. The frame number may be displayed on some player models.

Because of the quick accessibility with frame searches, the information on the disc can be read in sequences other than the one in which it was recorded. This is called nonlinear play.

SLOW MOTION

The slow-motion function allows the operator to view the disc at a speed of less than 30 frames per second. Slow motion may be played in either forward or reverse.

STEP FRAME

When the step-frame function is used, the player will step forward or in reverse, playing each frame over a specific number of times before going to the next frame.

Different viewing rates are selected by the operator. Typically, the speeds can be varied from one frame per second to one frame every five seconds.

STILL FRAME/FREEZE FRAME

Still frame refers to a nonmoving sequence of video frames. This sequence may be text, art, or still photographs. If a video sequence is only one frame in duration, it is called a single-frame edit. Freeze frame refers to freezing a video frame during a motion sequence.

In CAV format, a videodisc player can create still pictures from any of the 54,000 frames by replaying the same frames on the disc. Unlike videotape, where jogging over the tape frame will cause tape wear, videodisc frames can be reread indefinitely with no wear to the disc.

FLICKER

A video frame is made up of two interlacing fields, one following 1/60 second behind the other. One field contains the odd-numbered lines that create half of the picture. The second field contains the even-numbered lines that create the other half of the picture. In most uses of videotape, it matters very little whether field 1 leads field 2 or vice versa. The constant, uninterrupted alternation of the fields creates a smooth flow from picture to picture. But videodisc players can be instructed to interrupt motion sequences and continuously reread a single frame. When the videodisc player stops on a frame containing fields recorded from different pictures, flicker or jitter is created on the television screen.

To avoid flicker caused by mismatched video fields in the videodisc program, know which field is dominant on the master tape. The only way to avoid mismatched fields is to determine the correct field dominance at all edit points. This is done by observing the order of the video fields during edits and transfers.

FIELD DOMINANCE

Determining the field dominance throughout your master tape is a concern only if you are using still frames or freeze frames in your program. Still frames that have been mastered with incorrect field dominance will appear to flicker during playback.

Videotape can be field 1 dominant or field 2 dominant. In a field 1 dominant tape, the first half of the video image is in field 1 and the second half in field 2. In a field 2 dominant tape, the reverse is true.

On a videodisc, the address code is placed in the vertical interval of the dominant field. The address code tells a disc player where on the continuous spiral of tracks to begin its still-frame rotation. When you still-frame a disc, the player plays a single track, steps back, and plays it again, thirty times per second.

> Field dominance is defined as a determination of which field (the odd or the even) is used first when a videodisc player creates a still frame from two video fields.

Field dominance changes can occur on the videotape for a number of reasons. If you transferred film to tape through a 3/2 pulldown (see p. 182 for an explanation of this process) you will have field dominance changes. If your source footage was edited on more than one set of equipment, you will likely have field dominance changes. Contact professionals (such as 3M or Pioneer) to obtain procedures for determining field dominance.

> Caution: Using the videotape recorder in the still-frame mode for a long period of time can degrade the tape. If you have many edit points to check for field dominance, it is advisable to use a dub of the master tape.

All that remains then is to apply labels and package the finished discs in album sleeves and shrinkwrap. Most disc makers provide for standard packaging or custom-designed labels and sleeves at extra cost.

As an extra service, disc makers will provide check discs that may be used for testing program logic (flow of the interactive program) in a Level II or Level III system.

PROGRAMMING INTERACTIVE DISCS (LEVEL II)

As stated earlier, an interactive disc permits a highly effective level of communication between user and disc and also between discs. At the simplest level, the viewer can use a remote control unit to conduct a dialog in question-and-answer format. Or a computer can be used to select and display video data automatically. The computer program responds to the user's input and controls the player accordingly. Random access of this nature can provide instant retrieval of information from an extremely large amount of storable data, and two-way communication is also possible

Basic functions and random access capabilities can be programmed to follow a predetermined procedure. The videodisc mastering manufacturers use two methods of programming:

Manual Programming. This method utilizes a special player with a built-in microcomputer. Programming is carried out using a remote control unit. This is a flexible, easily altered method that can be used, for example, to arrange sections of an instructional program in the sequence most suitable to the level of the user.

Digital Program Dump. A disc that has a program prerecorded on it is known as a *programmed* or *Level II* disc. When the disc is loaded into a videodisc player, the program is "dumped" into the player's microprocessor, which then plays the video material in the order specified by the program. It is possible to modify or change the program for flexibility in playback. For instance, the disc can respond in various ways to answers from questions, or have program material changed to suit different events or display situations. The digital program dump disc is extremely useful in video displays, sales promotions, and educational applications.

SOURCE TAPE SPECIFICATIONS

Generally, source tapes submitted for mastering and replication should meet the following specifications:

Original-source program material must be transferred to video tape. Program material must first be submitted on D-2 composite; one-inch type C composite; Betacam SP; or 3/4-inch professional NTSC 525-line, 60Hz videotape. D-2 and one-inch master tapes result in discs with noticeably better image resolution than discs mastered from 3/4-inch professional master tapes.

You may submit both sides of a two-sided program on the same master tape. If this is done, all of the same specifications must be followed exactly as if you were submitting the two sides on separate master tapes. Time code must be continuous (nonstop) and contiguous (without break) through both programs.

TIME CODE

A SMPTE non-drop frame time code should placed on the time code track (Channel 3 audio). It must be unique and sync-locked (hardware setting mode required to ouput synchronized component video to other video devices and systems). The code must be contiguous and always increasing, beginning with the color bars and running through the lead-out.

Nondrop frame time code is not time-accurate. One hour of indicated nondrop frame time code actually requires one hour and 3.6 seconds of play time (error of 0.03 frame per second).

SETUP

Plan to include at least two minutes of standard NTSC color bars followed by at least 40 seconds of video black before the program begins. During the color bars there should be at least one minute of 1 KHz tone at 0 VU on each audio channel containing program audio. The video 40 seconds prior to the program material will be the source video for the lead-in portion of the disc. Audio must be off during this lead-in portion. If Dolby A encoding is used, the "Dolby tone" should be used rather than the 1 KHz tone. If Dolby SR encoding is used there should be 30 seconds of standard tone and 1 minute and 30 seconds of "Dolby Noise." Figure 6.4 illustrates the tape setup format.

Dolby A is an encoding / decoding scheme to enhance the analog audio playback.

Dolby SR gives audio playback qualities usually associated with digital recording methods.

VIDEO

The maximum instantaneous peak of the video signal (luminance and chrominance) must not exceed 110 IRE, with the working maximum level considered 100 IRE (International Radio Engineers, a measurement unit for measuring video signals' brightness). Also, chrominance saturation should not exceed 100 percent or 110 IRE, whichever occurs first. In addition, the chroma level must not exceed 100 percent modulation.

Tape Leader	NTSC Standard Color Bars	Audio Disabled Video Black Disc Lead-In	Active Program Material			Video Black Disc Lead-Out	Tape Trailer
			Optional Black for Digital Dumps	Optional Black for Digital Dumps	Optional Black for Digital Dumps		
	120 Sec.	40 Sec.		30 Minutes - CAV 60 Minutes - CLV		30 Sec.	

Figure 6.4. Format for video tapes to be used in videodisc mastering. SMPTE time code must be present from the begining of color bars through the end of video black.

AUDIO

> It is recommended that a first dub production master tape be submitted to ensure the most consistent playback possible.

Audio channels are either monaural, dual-independent, or stereo. Audio channels for both stereo and mono channels must be in phase, with levels not exceeding 0 VU as read on a standard ballistics VU meter. Instantaneous peak levels exceeding +8dB above the 1 KHz 0 VU reference tones will be compressed/limited.

TAPE CHECK-IN

When the master-making company receives your input tape (preferably a protection master, which is a first dub of the edit master), the technicians check the tape to verify that the information submitted on the company's postproduction forms matches what is on the tape.

> To ensure a clean ending to your production, include a minimum of 30 seconds of video black with no audio at the end of the active program.

The technicians check four major elements:

- Do the active program's start and end times (SAP—start of active program, and EAP—end of active program) submitted in SMPTE time code on the form match the tape?

- Is the field dominance identified on the form the same as the tape?

- Is the audio in phase and do the format and routing specified on the form match the tape?

- Is the time code continuous and error-free?

If this is the first time your program is being mastered, frame accuracy refers to the accurate placement of frame 1 at the point you identified as the start of active program (SAP) as well as the use of correct field dominance. One way to ensure the correct placement of frame 1 is to use a frame 0 slate on your tape. This slate is not recorded in the active program portion of the videodisc and is used only to indicate that the following frame will be frame 1 on the disc.

After your tape has passed check-in and frame accuracy has been determined (if needed), it is ready for mastering. Mastering begins with the synchronization of the tape playback videotape recorder and the laser beam recorder (LBR).

Once this step is accomplished, the tape is played back through the mastering equipment, where laser disc codes are added to the vertical interval. This combination of information is then sent to the LBR where it is encoded on the glass master by the laser. After several more process steps, a stamper is made from the glass master. This stamper is the reverse image of the glass master and is used during replication to stamp the encoded information onto the videodiscs. The discs are then tested, labeled, and packaged for delivery.

THE PRE-MASTERING PROCESS

The pre-master tape should be inspected for overall quality. Close attention to line dropouts, audio levels, quality, and other technical aspects of the tape is necessary to ensure that the disc will play back properly. A poor-quality tape will not be improved in the mastering process. If the tape is found to be out of conformance with the stated specifications, it should be corrected by the pre-mastering facility prior to submission to the disc maker. This will save a great deal of time in avoiding having tapes or discs returned with flaws.

> When you submit the tape for mastering, the mastering company will ask you to indicate the Start of Active Program (SAP) and End of Active Program (EAP) in SMPTE time code. SAP is the first frame of the active program and EAP the last frame. The higher the level of interaction you are using, the more critical frame accuracy becomes.

The pre-master tape, made to the disc maker's specifications, is sent to the mastering facility. The procedures are quite involved and require a great deal of equipment and technical expertise. All of the necessary details will be handled by the disc maker.

The videotape will be inspected to ensure that it meets the mastering facility's technical specifications. It will not be inspected for program content or design error. The production quality and content is the responsibility of the program producer.

After the tape has passed inspection, it is placed on a videotape machine for playback. The signal from this videotape is fed to a videodisc master recorder inside a "clean room"—an environment that is free from dust and other foreign matter—because of the small size of the pits recorded on the master disc.

CREATING THE MASTER TAPE

The quality of your videodisc program depends on the quality of your master videotape. The videodisc mastering and replication processes in themselves cannot improve the quality of your program. To help you create the highest quality tape and, therefore, the highest quality videodisc, we have included the following technical information and master tape specifications.

VIDEOTAPE SOURCES

The videodisc will be simply a copy of the master tape. To achieve a high quality program, the best approach is to use the highest quality videotape you can afford. All upper-end, professional tape formats produce discs of virtually equal video quality, but the lower-end professional, industrial, and consumer market tape formats do not.

Regardless of the video formats of your source footage, the master tape you submit for videodisc mastering must meet two format standards. First, it must conform to the U.S. NTSC RS-170A composite video broadcast standard. Second, the master tape must be one of the following three formats:

1. 3/4-inch U-matic (professional)

2. One-inch Type C

3. D-2

The wide variety of source video formats (Betacam SP, SVHS, D-1, D-2, and so on) may complicate the transfer of source material to the master tape because they do not all meet the NTSC RS-170A format. General advice is to use a common sync processor when possible and to check your final product for unwanted format transfer errors. Specifically, you should be aware that some consumer tape formats do not deliver a true NTSC RS-170A signal and that tapes made in areas other than North America and Japan very likely do not conform to NTSC standards. Tapes made in countries that use PAL or SECAM television transmission standards must be converted to NTSC before they are transferred to the master tape.

> The quality of your videodisc program depends on the quality of the master tape you submit for videodisc mastering and replication.

The point in the production process at which you transfer source video to NTSC RS-170A composite video is up to you. You may choose to shoot and edit all your source footage on Betacam SP and dub it over to D-2 or one-inch Type C tape.

One final consideration in transferring source video to the master tape is how accurately you want the videodisc frame number to match the master tape numbers. If you want a particular video content to occur at a specific frame on the disc, it is up to your postproduction facility to put it in the right place on the tape.

OTHER MEDIA

Film is definitely a preferred source medium for those who can afford it. The high resolution of film is what video is striving to match with enhancements like HDTV and improved NTSC. And if your program includes freeze frames, using film as the source medium is the only way to guarantee that freeze frames are completely jitter-free.

Film may be transferred directly to tape when the film was shot at 30 fps or when there are no real time constraints in your videodisc program. However, if the film was shot at 24 fps or your program has real time constraints, then the film needs to be converted to the 30 fps speed of videotape through an intermediate step called *3/2 pulldown*.

What are real-time constraints? Transferring a filmed movie to a videodisc provides a good example. An hourlong movie shot at 24 fps and transferred directly to videotape (which plays at 30 fps) would be compressed to 48 minutes. The viewed motion and audio would be correspondingly faster than the film version. Clearly, that viewing experience would not be acceptable. Something has to be done so the film can be played at 24 fps and yet transfer to videotape playing at 30 fps. Somehow 6 extra video frames (12 fields) per second have to be generated. The solution is 3/2 pulldown.

The 3/2 pulldown process scans the first frame of film into three fields of video and the next frame of film into two fields of video. The film frame video contents are repeated either 3 times or 2 times on the videotape. If you refer to Figure 6.5, you can see the 3/2 pulldown process. The 3/2 pulldown also causes the field dominance of the tape to change after a film frame is repeated 3 times. However, this will not be a problem as long as you accurately identify the location of the 3/2 sequence on the tape.

Recently, Toshiba and Time Warner Company announced a plan to produce a double-sided CD-ROM capable of holding 270 minutes of video to compete with the Sony-Philips single-sided 135-minute CD-ROM.

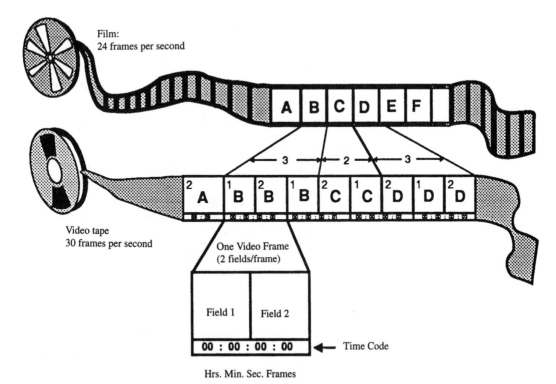

Figure 6.5. Sequence of film frames and video fields resulting from 3/2 pulldown.

Slides, *microfilm*, *microfiche*, or *electronically generated graphics* can be transferred in three ways.

- Transferred via a camera or multiplexer

- Transferred to motion picture film, then to videotape (transfer at 30 frames per second)

- Transferred to video tape in real time using digital frame storage editing.

COST AND TURNAROUND TIME

The following tables show an example of cost and turnaround time for mastering and replication of a videodisc. The manufacturers apply additional cost for other services such as verification of the master, media, and programming; storage; or labeling. This is an approximate pricing.

Check tapes, in either a 3/4 or 1/2-inch format, are also available from the disc makers. The check tape is a copy of the edited master with a visible time code window that includes SMPTE time code, picture numbers, chapter numbers, and field indicators. It is useful to the program developers in order to check the video content against the program design and complete coding for the application. This is essential in the development of Level II or III discs and saves the cost of a second check disc because the tape is considerably less expensive.

Table 6.2 shows mastering and replication cost and turnaround time, Figure 6.6 demonstrates a videodisc production checklist, and Figure 6.7 displays a typical videodisc production form.

Mastering

Turnaround time	CAV Level I & III (per side)	CAT Level II (per side)	CLV (per side)
8 days	$1,800	$2,500	$2,300
5 days	$2,600	$3,300	$3,000
3 days	$3,100	$3,700	$3,400
1 day	$4,000	$5,000	$4,300
Same day	$6,000	$7,000	$6,500

Prices are for both 12" and 8" formats.

Replication

Quantity per Master	1 side	2 sides
1–49	$18.00	$23.00
50–399	$14.00	$19.00
400–699	$12.00	$17.00
700–999	$10.00	$15.00
1,000 +	$8.50	$13.50

Additional Editing Services

Multi Audio	$125 per side
On-Line Editing	$300 per hour
Time Code Restripping	$125 per hour
Charactor Generation	$125 per hour

Note: These are approximate prices. For current prices, contact videodisc manufacturers.

Table 6.2. Approximate costs and turnaround time for videodisc mastering and replication.

√	**Planning/ Production**	√	**Postproduction**	√	**Mastering/ Programming**
	Develop the objectives		Edit video and audio		Schedule for mastering and replication
	Define your audience		Develop computer graphics		Check standards and compatibilities
	Develop the plan and budget		Produce/obtain sound effects and music		Create videodisc master
	Write the script		Determine action points (chapter starts, autostop)		Replicate the discs
	Evaluate the resources		Create the master tape		Develop the program for interactivity
	Develop a flowchart		Schedule tape transfer		
	Create storyboards of visual and audio sequences		Develop transfer specifications		
	Evaluate and revise		Create pre-master copy		
	Shoot the program				
	Estimate: 45 percent of time and budget		*Estimate: 40 percent of time and budget*		*Estimate: 15 percent of time and budget*

Figure 6.6. Videodisc production checklist.

Videodisc Order Form

☐ CAV ☐ 12" ☐ New
☐ CLV ☐ 8" ☐ Reorder
☐ Level II (Digital Dumps)

For Internal Use Only	
Log No.	Date

Customer Information

Charge To:

Ship To:

Contact Person

Phone Number   Fax Number

Purchase Order Number

Please attach purchase order (credit approved) or check.

☐ Taxable ☐ *Exempt Exempt No. _____

*New Customers must complete Tax Exemption Certificate and return with Order Form.

Order Detail

Mastering and Replication Production:

Requested Turnaround: ☐ Standard ☐ 5 Days ☐ 3 Days ☐ 1 Day ☐ Same Day

Quantity of Replicas: Advance Copies _____ Production Run _____

Alpha Disc Production:

Requested Turnaround: ☐ 5 Days ☐ 3 Days ☐ 1 Day **Quantity** _____

Date Tapes will arrive _____

Ship Disc Order Via: (FOB Menomonie) ☐ UPS (Surface) ☐ Air (Express Service)

Express Company _____   Account No. _____

Special Services (Please see published price sheet for additional charges)

Storage: Glass Master and Tape ▶ ☐ 6 Months ☐ 12 Months ☐ Tape Only Storage - 12 Months

☐ Frame Accuracy Check to a Previous Program

If no storage is requested your master tape(s) will be returned to the address below 30 days after completion of your order.

Ship Via: ☐ UPS ☐ Air Collect Acct# _____

Return Tape(s) Company Name   Address   City, State, Zip

Label & Packaging Information

Labels: a. ☐ Standard b. ☐ Custom c. ☐ Custom Generic

If Custom or Custom Generic: ☐ Artwork due _____ (3 wk lead) ☐ Customer supplied labels _____

Jackets: a. ☐ Standard b. ☐ Custom c. ☐ Custom Generic

If Custom or Custom Generic: ☐ Artwork due _____ (6 wk lead) ☐ Customer supplied jackets _____

Artwork contact _____   Phone _____

Disc Labeling: Opposite side labeling (standard) will be used unless advised otherwise.

Side 1 Program title (as it is to appear on label):

Side 2 Program title (as it is to appear on label):

Line 1: Max. 35 characters and spaces

Line 1: Max. 35 characters and spaces

Line 2: Max. 27 characters and spaces

Line 2: Max. 27 characters and spaces

Line 3: Max. 22 characters and spaces

Line 3: Max. 22 characters and spaces

Miscellaneous

Additional Information:

Ship Tape(s) and Forms: To assist us with scheduling please send purchase order or check, signed and completed order form (retain customer copy), 2 weeks before tape(s) and production detail forms to:

SEE REVERSE SIDE FOR IMPORTANT ADDITIONAL TERMS AND CONDITIONS, AS PART OF THIS AGREEMENT, INCLUDING DISCLAIMER OF WARRANTIES AND LIABILITIES.

Authorized Signature   Date

Title

By signing this agreement, customer acknowledges that he/she has read and understood all the terms and conditions of this agreement.

Fig. 6.7. A typical videodisc production form.

Chapter 7
HyperCard for Interactivity

HyperCard program can help you create interactive presentations using still images, motion sequences, and sound stored on videodiscs. Use HyperCard program, a Macintosh, a videodisc player, and a monitor to access, organize, and control the images and sounds of your multimedia presentation.

HyperCard is a multifunction program. On one level, you can approach HyperCard as an information retrieval system that you use primarily to look up specific data in applications developed by others. On another level, you can approach it as a development system that allows you to create your *own* information-based applications. In either approach, you will encounter the metaphor that HyperCard uses—that of a *card* and of a group of related cards combined into a *stack*.

Most often, each electronic file card in a particular HyperCard stack follows the same presentation, thereby standardizing the layout of the information it contains. This is analogous to any paper card file you use, whether it be the card catalog at the library, a Rolodex file at the office, or a stack of 3" x 5" cards for a research paper. In HyperCard, each screen of information on your Macintosh represents a single card in a particular stack of cards. Regardless of the way in which the information (including text and graphics) is presented on the screen, the basic unit that you view and work with at all times is one card out of a stack of related cards.

HYPERCARD FEATURES

HyperCard allows you to design a card form for your stack, similar in many ways to a database input form. On this card form, you can arrange fields for storing each item of text data that you wish to maintain in the card file (stack). However, as stated earlier, HyperCard restricts the layout of the input form to the basic file card format. Despite this limitation, you still have a great deal of freedom when designing card forms, because the HyperCard "form" can consist of almost any layout that your Macintosh can display in a single-screen view.

HYPERCARD AS A DATABASE PROGRAM

Database programs make you declare the type of data entry that a field can contain. At the most basic level, these programs differentiate between fields that contain character strings (text) and those that contain numbers. The basis of this division is that number fields can be calculated and character fields cannot. Depending upon the program in question, it may further differentiate number-type fields into those that contain special numbers representing dates and times and the logical values of true or false (1 and 0), and those that carry standard values.

> A *field* is a rectangular area on a card where you can type and edit text.

When setting up fields in HyperCard, you do not have to declare the type of data that they can carry beforehand. This is because HyperCard stores *all* field entries of the card as *text* (character strings). It does not matter whether you enter *500* or *Five Hundred* in the field—both are treated as text. Although this presents somewhat of a problem when you wish to perform calculations between fields in a card, it eliminates the step of designating the field type and makes it much easier and faster to locate information in the HyperCard stack.

HYPERCARD AS A PAINT PROGRAM

It is also important to note that a card created in HyperCard is not restricted to displaying only text fields. HyperCard contains its own paint program with which you can design graphics that can be displayed along with text fields or alone.

You can also incorporate graphics generated with other graphics programs such as MacDraw or MacPaint, the Adobe Illustrator, GraphicWorks, and the like. With HyperCard you can generate sounds in cards, including musical notes, that were created in HyperCard or with a standalone program such as ConverWare + or MusicWorks, or speech generated with a program such as MacinTalk.

HYPERCARD AS A LINKING PROGRAM

HyperCard also allows you to link information stored in different cards, whether in the same stack (file) or another stack. However, when you create links in HyperCard, they are direct links, quite unlike those created in a relational database system. A HyperCard link takes you right to the new card and displays whatever information that card contains. As a result of the direct links that HyperCard maintains, it is ideally suited to different types of applications than those to which relational database management systems are put. In fact, it is this ability to establish links between any card in the same or in a different stack that makes HyperCard so flexible when it comes to creating information storage and retrieval systems. To understand how this is so, let's consider how linking works in HyperCard.

HyperCard uses buttons to activate the links between cards. When you click on a particular button, the script associated with that button is activated. Quite often, the button script simply instructs HyperCard to take you to a new card in the same stack or a different stack (Figure 7.1).

Because HyperCard makes it so easy to move to cards in the same or a different stack, it allows you to relate information in a free-form manner, similar to the manner in which we think.

ADVANTAGES OF HYPERCARD

The great promise of HyperCard is that it will enable users to build the information-based applications that meet their unique needs without requiring them to submit to the rigorous

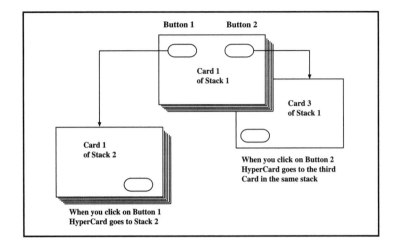

Figure 7.1. Clicking on Button 1 takes you to the first card in a second stack, clicking on Button 2 takes you to the third card in the same stack.

structure demanded by database management programs. In practical terms, this means that the only real limitations to designing HyperCard applications reside in its fixed-card format and the limits of the user's imagination. The major strengths of HyperCard:

- HyperCard allows users to build a flexible information retrieval system that does not constrain the user into one way of looking at the information it contains.

- The system can include text and nontext information (both graphics and sound).

- Applications can be designed and executed quickly and do not require a background in or previous exposure to programming.

- Applications can be easily modified to meet new requirements.

- Applications can be designed for any subject matter, whether for business, academic, or home requirements.

- Videodiscs can be played using HyperCard buttons.

HYPERCARD ORGANIZATION

The HyperCard program is organized into five distinct user levels, referred to as User Preferences (Figure 7.2):

- Browsing

- Typing

- Painting

- Authoring

- Scripting

In practice, the five user levels naturally combine into three modes of working in HyperCard:

- Browsing/Typing

- Painting/Authoring

- Scripting

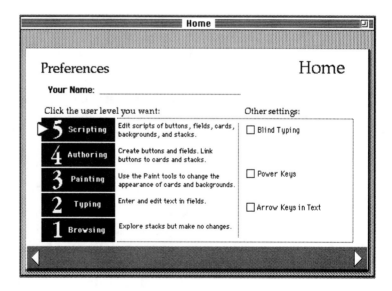

Figure 7.2. *User Preferences* dialog box.

To use HyperCard in Browsing/Typing mode, set the User Preference level to Typing. To use HyperCard in Painting/ Authoring mode, set the User Preference level to Authoring. To program in HyperCard with HyperTalk, set the User Preference level to Scripting.

THE BROWSING LEVEL

When you set the User Preference level to Browsing, you can only use HyperCard to perform browsing operations, which include viewing cards in the stack, locating specific information in cards, and jumping to linked cards. You keep the level set to Browsing if you are using stackware that does not require any updating, and information is intended to be absorbed in the same way as when printed in a book.

THE TYPING LEVEL

Set the User Preference level to Typing if you are using a stack that does require routine editing, such as the Address Stack supplied with HyperCard. Typing mode allows you to perform all of HyperCard's editing functions, which include adding and deleting cards in the stack, filling out fields in new cards, and changing data in existing cards.

When the level is set to Typing, you can perform not only all of these editing functions but also all of the browsing functions. The Typing level, then, is used whenever you need not only to find information in a stack but also to modify the information it contains.

THE PAINTING LEVEL

When you set the User Preference level to Painting, you can use HyperCard's built-in painting program to add, delete, and modify graphic elements in the cards in the stack. If you have used MacPaint or SuperPaint, you will find HyperCard's painting tools quite familiar. You will need to set the User Preference level to Painting only when you are designing new card forms or making modifications to existing ones.

THE AUTHORING LEVEL

HyperCard uses the term *authoring* to mean designing and implementing an application of any kind that involves designing card forms and linking stacks. At the Authoring level, you can use the painting tools as well as set up links between cards (a function that is not available when the level is set at Painting). If you are an instructor, you may think of authoring in the more specialized sense of CAI (computer-aided instruction) or CBT (computer-based training), where the application is most often a lesson delivered by the computer. Although you can certainly use HyperCard to create such applications, this cannot be done from the Authoring level alone. To create real CAI or CBT lessons with HyperCard requires knowledge and use of HyperTalk in the Scripting level.

THE SCRIPTING LEVEL

When you set the User Preference level to Scripting, you have complete access to HyperTalk, an English-like programming language included in the product. Note that you do not have to learn how to use HyperTalk in order to create your own stackware in HyperCard. However, the applications you create solely from the Authoring level will be limited, for without HyperTalk you can do no more than set up direct links between cards.

Although the first applications you create in HyperCard may not require any "programming" beyond linking information stored in different cards, you will undoubtedly soon come up with applications that can benefit from the use of simple HyperTalk scripts.

Even if you have never had any exposure to programming languages, you should have no trouble mastering the basics of HyperTalk. The language uses a syntax close to that of English, making it easy to read and, therefore, to understand. If you are a programmer, or have had some exposure to programming languages (either on the Macintosh or another computer), you will also find HyperTalk easy to learn.

In HyperCard, you use HyperTalk to create short scripts (programming), executed only when links established in the stack are activated (or when you enter a command statement directly), that control just the working of a small part of the application. This means that you do not use HyperTalk to create a monolithic program to run your stackware. Rather, you use it just to set up limited actions between components of the stack.

As a result of the way scripting is used in HyperCard, you will find it much easier not only to design procedures but also to debug the scripts you create in HyperTalk. So too this system of limited control makes it a great deal easier to add new features to the application or modify existing ones.

COMPONENTS OF HYPERCARD

THE HOME STACK

As soon as HyperCard is loaded into the computer's memory, the Home Stack is displayed on your screen (Figure 7.3). This is the place from which you normally begin a session with HyperCard (if you do not see the Home Stack, you need to copy this stack onto your startup disk). The Home Card is really the first card in a Home Stack. The Home Stack is automatically opened when HyperCard is loaded. In HyperCard terms, Home Cards normally contain many buttons. A click of a particular button sets in motion the necessary actions to open and display the stack that is "linked" to that button.

TOOLBOX

Before explaining a HyperCard component, you should be familiar with the *Tools* menu. Place the pointer on the *Tools* menu, click, and hold the mouse button. A Toolbox appears (Figure 7.4), and you will see the following tools:

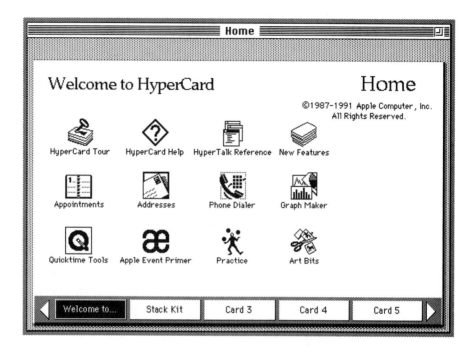

Figure 7.3. The Home Card.

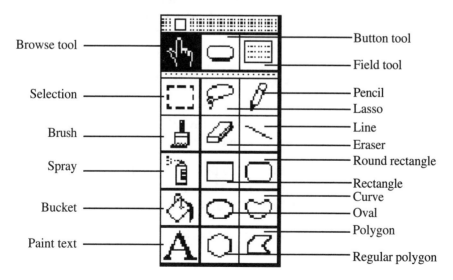

Figure 7.4. The Toolbox with the various tools.

- The Browse tool (a pointing hand) is used to maneuver around the card and stack. Also, it is used to when typing text in a Field.

- The Button tool (a rounded-rectangle button) is used to select, modify, and script a button.

- The Field tool (the rectangle) is used to select, modify, and script a field.

- The Paint tools (the 15 items in the bottom section) are used to draw, paint, and modify objects on a card.

For easy access, the *Tool* menu can be placed anywhere on the screen. To do this, select the *Tool* menu from the menu bar, and, with the mouse button depressed, drag the Toolbox and move the outline to the desired location on the screen. Release the button when you have the Toolbox at its new location. To hide the Toolbox, place the pointer on the small close box at the upper left of the Toolbox, and click the mouse button.

FIELD

A field is an area on a card that can contain text. Each card may have more than one field. Fields can be different sizes and shapes. Also, fields can contain type in different styles, fonts, and point sizes. To create a field:

1. Select the Field tool from the Toolbox in the *Tools* menu.

2. Select *New Field* from the *Object* menu. A shimmering box appears on the middle of the card.

If you wish to change the size of the field, place the pointer on the shimmering line, click and hold the mouse button, and drag the field to desired size (Figure 7.5).

To type text on the field, select the Browse tool from the Toolbox, click the I-beam cursor on the field, and type.

If you decide to move a field:

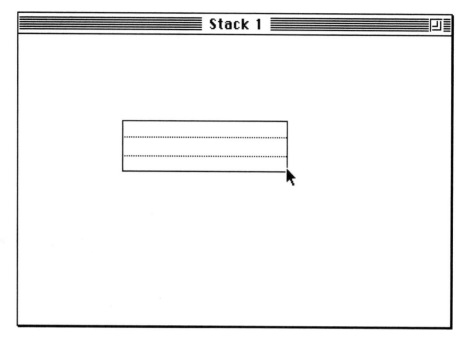

Figure 7.5. Resizing a field.

1. Select the Field tool from the Toolbox in the *Tools* menu.

2. Click the pointer anywhere on the field by pressing the mouse button and drag the field to the desired place.

BUTTON

This is an area on a card that may be clicked with the mouse button to initiate a specific action that has been programmed in a HyperTalk script. A button is often represented by an icon but can also have many other forms, shapes, and sizes. To create a button:

1. Select the Button tool from the Toolbox in the *Tools* menu.

2. Select *New Button* from the *Object* menu. A shimmering box appears in the middle of the screen with the name "New Button."

To change the size of the button, place the pointer on the shimmering line, click and hold the mouse button, and drag the button to the desired size.

To place an icon in the button:

1. Select the Button tool from the Toolbox in the *Tools* menu.

2. Place the pointer on the button and double-click the mouse button. The dialog box for the button displays on the screen (Figure 7.6).

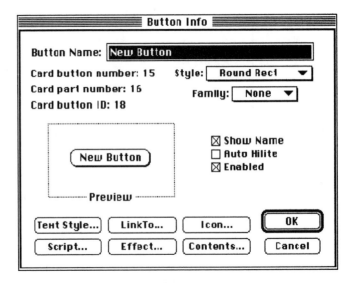

Figure 7.6. *New button* dialog box.

3. Click on the *Icon* button. The icon options appear on the screen (Figure 7.7). Use the scroll bar to see more icon options.

4. Select an appropriate icon with the pointer and click OK. The icon appears on the button. Sometimes you may need to readjust the size of the button.

To move a button:

1. Select the Button tool from the Toolbox in the *Tools* menu.

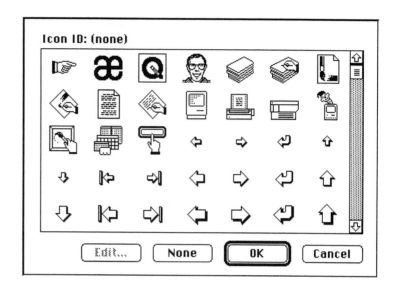

Figure 7.7. Button icons.

2. Click the pointer anywhere on the button by pressing the mouse button and drag the button to the desired place.

BUTTON STYLES

There are several button styles that you can use when creating a button.

Transparent Buttons. The transparent button style is invisible to the browser—it does not show the button's name or icon. There are no borders or even any cursor indication that a transparent button exists on the screen. There are many instances in which a transparent button is the ideal choice.

Opaque Buttons. An opaque button appears to the browser as a rectangle that doesn't let any objects behind it show through. This button style requires the Show Name attribute to be checked.

Rectangle Buttons. By selecting the rectangle button type, you instruct the button to show itself clearly to the browser with a single line border around the rectangle defining the area of the button. Because the area inside the border is opaque, no graphics or text fields beneath the layer of that button will show through. Therefore, this button style is usually best suited for those that show the button name.

Shadow Buttons. A shadow button is just like a rectangle button, but HyperCard draws a drop shadow to the right and below the rectangle. Shadow buttons may be useful only for larger buttons.

Round-Rectangle Buttons. The round-rectangle style draws a shadowed round rectangle inside the rectangular area of the button. This button style will look familiar to most Macintosh users, because it and versions like to it are used commonly in dialog boxes. Buttons that show the button name look particularly appealing in this button style. Round-rectangle buttons are also opaque and observe the same layering properties as opaque, rectangle, and shadow buttons.

Radio Buttons. Radio buttons are usually grouped together in sets of two or more. They should behave in a way that lets only one button in the group be engaged—set with a black center dot—at a time. Hence its derivation from push-button-model car radios.

Button Highlighting. The *Button Info* dialog box presents two choices to let you control the *hilite* properties of a button: Auto Hilite and (for background buttons only) Shared Hilite. When Auto Hilite is turned on, buttons (other than the check box and radio buttons) invert their pixel colors (white turns black and vice versa) when they are selected. This is similar to the way buttons in the Finder react when you click once on them to select them. Highlighting is a good method of offering feedback to users that they are clicking on the desired button and that the button is responding to their click.

Instant Link Scripts. The *Link To...* button in the *Button Info* dialog box allows you to establish a link for the button. Click on the *Link To...* button, which displays a small window with instructions to navigate your way to the card to which you wish to link.

Effect. In working with some HyperCard stacks, you may have been enamored by the visual effects that occurred when navigating from card to card. Click on the *Effect* button and you will see the *Visual effect* dialog box appear on the screen (Figure 7.8).

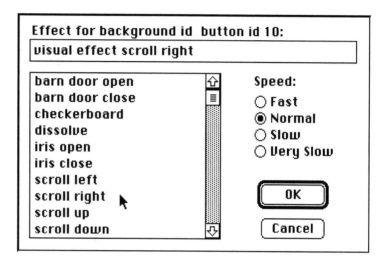

Fig. 7.8. *Visual effect* dialog box.

Although you can type the visual effect into the long field at the top of the dialog box, there is an easier way to construct the visual effect line for the button's script. In the scrolling field is a list of the basic visual effects available in HyperCard. Click on any effect, and the visual effect command appears in the field across the top.

Additionally, you can adjust the speed of the visual effect with the radio buttons at the right of the dialog box. As you select a speed, its modifier is added to the visual effect command line.

CREATING A NEW STACK

A HyperCard stack consists of cards. Each card may include field(s), button(s), and graphic(s) (Figure 7.9).

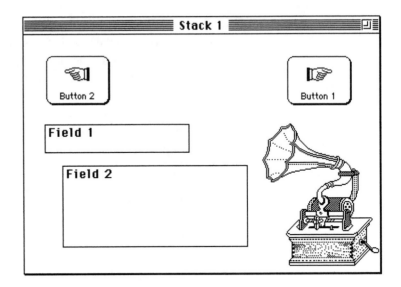

Figure 7.9. Elements of a card.

HyperCard

To create a HyperCard stack, you must have the HyperCard program and the Home Stack residing in the same folder. To start HyperCard, click twice on the HyperCard program icon. After the program begins, make sure the menu bar at the top of the screen is visible (the bar that contains *File, Edit,* and so on). If the menu bar is not showing, press the Command key and the Space Bar at the same time. This is a toggle switch that will show the menu bar if it is hiding or hide the menu bar if it is showing. It is a very useful command, because many stacks automatically hide the menu bar when they open.

To start a new stack:

1. Select *New Stack* from the *File* menu. The New Stack window appears.

2. Fill in a new stack name and click on *New*. For this example, type in *Videodisc Buttons* for the stack's name (Figure 7.10).

Before creating buttons and fields, you should check that you are at the correct UserLevel. The UserLevel determines the

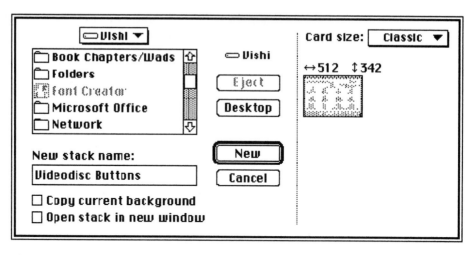

Figure 7.10. *New stack* dialog box.

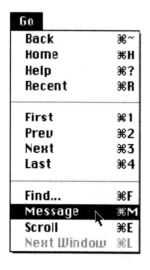

amount of changes the user is allowed to make and it ranges from level 1 (Browsing—does not allow any changes) to level 5 (Scripting—allows full creation, deletion, and modification). To perform this task, follow these steps:

1. Choose the *Go* menu and select *Message*. This will bring up a small window (called a *message box)* on the bottom of the screen. The message box is used to communicate directly with the HyperCard program.

2. Type in *set UserLevel to 5* and press Return (Figure 7.11). This action places you at level 5 and provides access to the full range of HyperCard's capabilities.

SETTING UP THE BACKGROUND CARD

At the most basic level, a stack has a background card. The background card includes those text fields, graphic images, and buttons that are shared by all of the cards in a stack. Many stacks have only one background that is shared by all of the cards in it. However, it is possible, and sometimes desirable, for a stack to have multiple backgrounds. In such a case, some of the cards may use one background and others may use a different background structure.

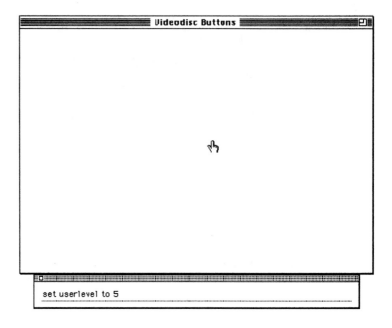

Figure 7.11. Setting up the user level.

For the purpose of this practice exercise, the following fields will be placed on the background card: Name, Address, Phone Number, Emergency Number, and Comments. The following buttons will be placed on the background card: Add New Student, Find Student, Go To Next Card, and Go To Previous Card. To set up the background card follow these steps:

1. Select *Background* from the *Edit* menu.

2. From the *Objects* menu select *New Field*. A field will appear on the screen.

3. To move the field, place the pointer anywhere on the field, click and hold the mouse button, and move the field to the upper-left-hand corner of the card.

4. Resize the field by placing the pointer on the lower-right corner of the field, click and hold the mouse button, and drag the field boundary downward to enlarge the field (Figure 7.12).

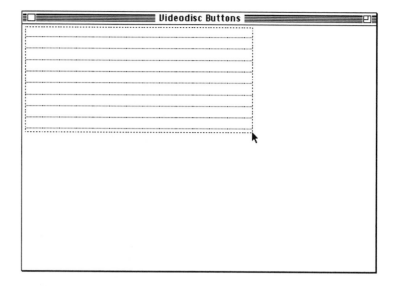

Figure 7.12. Resizing a field.

5. Double-click on the field for the field information dialog box. Type `Title` in the text box (Figure 7.13).

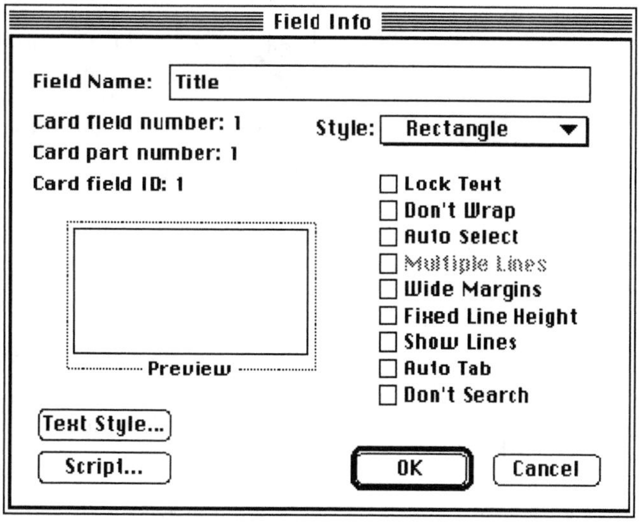

Figure 7.13. Field dialog box.

6. Select the *Auto Tab* box for easy typing. When *Auto Tab* is selected, you can move easily from field to field by pressing the tab key.

7. Select *Shadow* from the *Style* section. This option adds a drop-shadow-box effect to the field.

If you wish to change the type fonts, type style, or type size, click on Text Styles button. The *Text Properties* dialog box displays on the screen (Figure 7.14). Select a new value and click OK. For the purpose of this exercise, select *Helvetica*, *Bold*, and *42*, and then click OK.

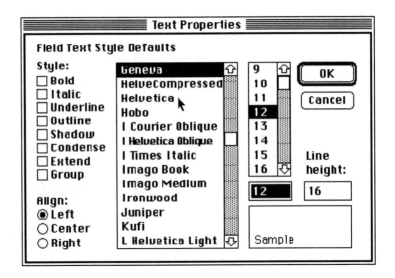

Figure 7.14. *Text Properties* dialog box.

CREATING BUTTONS

To make the stack automated and enable the user move around the stack easily, you should create four buttons as follows: Go to next card, Go to previous card, Go Home, and Quit.

Normally, a new card is added to a stack by selecting the *New Card* option from the *Edit* menu. This procedure should be repeated each time you need to add a new card. By creating a button on the background card, you can automate the task.

To create a button to move to the next card, follow these steps:

1. Select *New Button* from the *Objects* menu. The New Button shimmering box appears on the screen.

2. Position the pointer anywhere on the button, click and hold the mouse button, and move the button to the lower right of the card.

3. Double-click on the button. The *Button* dialog box will appear (Figure 7.15).

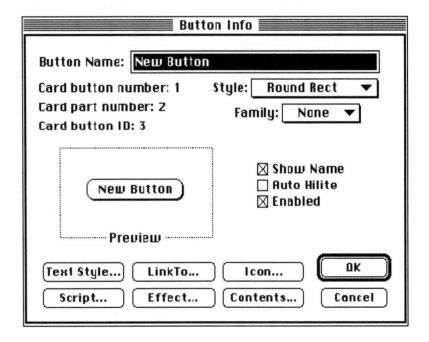

Figure 7.15. *Button* dialog box.

4. Type: Next Card. The New Button name will be replaced.

5. Click on the box next to *Show Name* to deselect the option.

6. Select *Transparent* from the *Style* option to make the button's border transparent.

7. Click on the *Icon* button. The icon options will display on the screen. Click on the arrow icon pointing to right.

8. Click OK. The icon appears on the button. You may need to resize the button.

To make the button automated:

1. Double-click on the button. Click on the *Script* button. The *Script* dialog box will display (Figure 7.16).

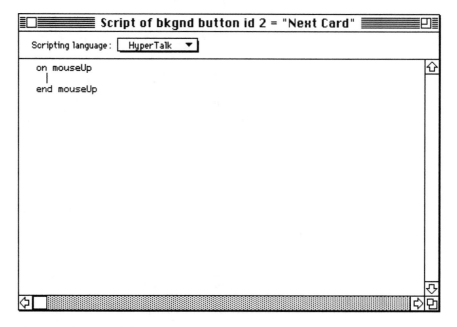

Figure 7.16. *Script* dialog box.

2. Between the two script's *message handlers*: "on mouseUp" and "end MouseUp," type:

```
go to next card
```

3. Click on the close box located on the upper-left corner of the script box. *Save changes to button* dialog box will appear.

4. Click on the *Yes* button to save the script.

To create a button to go to a previous card, follow these steps:

1. Select *New Button* from the *Objects* menu. The New Button shimmering box will appear on the screen.

2. Position the pointer anywhere on the button, click and hold the mouse button, and move the button to the lower right of the card, beside the "Next Card" button.

3. Double-click on the button. The *Button* dialog box will appear.

4. Type: `Previous Card`. The New Button name will be replaced.

5. Click on the box next to *Show Name* to deselect the option.

6. Select *Transparent* from the *Style* option to make the button's border transparent.

7. Click on the *Icon* button. The icon option will display on the screen. Click on the arrow icon pointing to left.

8. Click OK. The icon appears on the button. You may need to resize the button.

To make the button automated:

1. Double-click on the button. Click on the *Script* button. The *Script* dialog box will display.

2. Between the two script's *message handlers*: "on mouseUp" and "end MouseUp," type:

   ```
   go to previous card
   ```

3. Click on the close box located on the upper-left corner of the script box.

4. Click on the *Yes* button to save the script.

To create a button to go to Home Card, follow these steps:

1. Select *New Button* from the *Objects* menu. The New Button shimmering box appears on the screen.

2. Position the pointer anywhere on the button, click and hold the mouse button, and move the button to the lower left of the card.

3. Double-click on the button. The *Button* dialog box will appear.

4. Type: `Home Card`. The New Button name will be replaced.

5. Click on the box next to *Show Name* to deselect the option.

6. Select *Transparent* from the *Style* option to make the button's border transparent.

7. Click on the *Icon* button. The icon option will display on the screen. Click on one of the home icons.

8. Click OK. The icon appears on the button. You may need to resize the button.

To make the button automated:

1. Double-click on the button. Click on the *Script* button. The *Script* dialog box displays.

2. Between the two script's *message handlers*: "on mouseUp" and "end MouseUp," type:

   ```
   go home
   ```

3. Click on the close box located on the upper-left corner of the script box.

4. Click on the *Yes* button to save the script.

To create a button to quit the HyperCard program, follow these steps:

1. Select *New Button* from the *Objects* menu. The New Button shimmering box appears on the screen.

2. Position the pointer anywhere on the button, click and hold the mouse button, and move the button to the lower left of the card, beside the "Home Card" button.

3. Double-click on the button. The *Button* dialog box will appear.

4. Type: Quit. The New Button name will be replaced.

5. Click on the box next to *Show Name* to deselect the option.

6. Select *Transparent* from the *Style* option to make the button's border transparent.

7. If you wish to change the type font, type style, or type size, click on Text Styles button. The *Text Properties* dialog box will display on the screen. Select *Chicago*, *Bold*, and *16*, then click OK.

To make the button automated:

1. Double-click on the button. Click on the *Script* button. The *Script* dialog box will display.

2. Between the two script's *message handlers*: "on mouseUp" and "end MouseUp," type:

```
ask "Are you sure?"
if it is "Yes" then
domenu "Quit HyperCard"
else
beep 1
end if
```

3. Click on the close box located in the upper-left corner of the script box.

4. Click on the *Yes* button to save the script.

ADDING A PICTURE TO A CARD

HyperCard program includes a stack called *Art Bits,* which can be accessed from the Home Card. The Art Bits stack contains several categories (Figure 7.17).

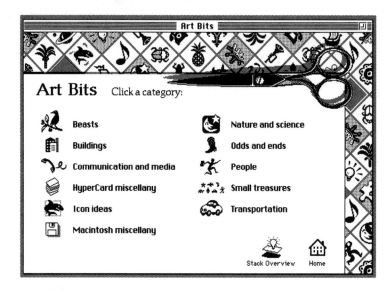

Figure 7.17. Art Bit categories.

Each category offers many different graphics that can be placed on any card. Follow these steps to transfer a graphic from the Art Bits Stack to a card in the *Videodisc Buttons* Stack:

1. Select *Open Stack* from the *File* menu.

2. Select *Art Bits* from the *HyperCard Program* dialog box.

3. Select the *Communications and Media* category.

4. Click on the right arrow to reach page 3.

5. From the *Tools* menu, select the Lasso tool.

6. Place the Lasso tool above the videodisc, click the mouse, hold, and draw a line around the picture (Figure 7.18).

Figure 7.18. Picture selected from Art Bits using the Lasso tool.

7. Release the mouse button; the picture starts shimmering.

8. Select *Copy Picture* from the *Edit* menu.

9. Open the *Videodisc Buttons* Stack by selecting *Open Stack* from the *File* menu. The stack opens the first card.

10. Select *Paste Picture* from the *Edit* menu. The picture appears on the card (Figure 7.19).

11. Place the pointer anywhere on the picture, click and hold the mouse button, and drag the picture to the desired place.

To reposition the picture after it is placed on the card:

1. Select the Lasso tool from the *Tools* menu.

Figure 7.19. Completed background card with graphic.

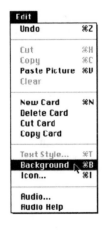

2. Draw a line around the picture. This procedure will not affect any background item.

3. Select *Cut Picture* from the *Edit* menu. The picture disappears.

4. Select *Paste Picture* from the *Edit* menu. The picture reappears on the card.

5. Position the pointer on the picture, click and hold the mouse button, and drag the picture to the desired place.

At this time, the background card is completed. Select *Background* from the *Edit* menu to go to the first card. Now you are ready to add videodisc basic operation buttons.

VIDEODISC BASIC OPERATION BUTTONS

This portion of the chapter offers ideas that you can use in creating your own HyperCard buttons for controlling the basic operations of a videodisc player. Using the following instructions, you should be able to create buttons to initialize player, play forward, play reverse, stop video, still video, fast forward, fast reverse, play audio channel 1, play audio channel 2, play stereo, mute, eject/park disc, play slow forward, and play slow reverse.

The procedure for creating buttons is the same for all of the buttons. However, the script part is different from one button to another. The common procedure for creating buttons is as follows:

1. Select *New Button* from the *Objects* menu. The New Button shimmering box appears on the screen.

2. Position the pointer anywhere on the button, click and hold the mouse button, and move the button to the desired place on the card.

3. Double-click on the button. The *Button* dialog box will appear.

4. Type a name based on the button function (for example, Play Forward, Stop Video, Audio 1, and so on). The New Button name will be replaced.

5. Click on the box next to *Show Name* to deselect the option.

6. Select *Standard* from the *Style* option. You may select *Radio Button* for audio buttons.

7. Click OK. You may need to resize the button.

WRITING SCRIPT

To write the script for the Initialize Player button, follow these steps:

1. Double-click on the button and select *Script*. The *Script* dialog box will appear.

2. Between the two script's *message handlers*: "on mouseUp" and "end MouseUp," type:

```
video "init"
```

3. Click on the close box located on the upper-left corner of the script box.

4. Click on the *Yes* button to save the script.

To write the script for the Play Forward button, follow these steps:

1. Double-click on the button and select *Script*. The *Script* dialog box will appear.

2. Between the two script's *message handlers*: "on mouseUp" and "end MouseUp," type:

```
video "play"
```

3. Click on the close box located on the upper left corner of the script box.

4. Click on the *Yes* button to save the script.

To write the script for the Play Reverse button, follow these steps:

1. Double-click on the button and select *Script*. The *Script* dialog box will appear.

2. Between the two script's *message handlers*: "on mouseUp" and "end MouseUp," type:

```
video "play", "reverse"
```

3. Click on the close box located on the upper-left corner of the script box.

4. Click on the *Yes* button to save the script.

To write the script for the Video Stop button, follow these steps:

1. Double-click on the button and select *Script*. The *Script* dialog box will appear.

2. Between the two script's *message handlers*: "on mouseUp" and "end MouseUp," type:

   ```
   video "stop"
   ```

3. Click on the close box located on the upper-left corner of the script box.

4. Click on the *Yes* button to save the script.

To write the script for the Still Video button, follow these steps:

1. Double-click on the button and select *Script*. The *Script* dialog box will appear.

2. Between the two script's *message handlers*: "on mouseUp" and "end MouseUp," type:

   ```
   video "still"
   ```

3. Click on the close box located on the upper left corner of the script box.

4. Click on the *Yes* button to save the script.

To write the script for the Fast Forward button, follow these steps:

1. Double-click on the button and select *Script*. The *Script* dialog box will appear.

2. Between the two script's *message handlers*: "on mouseUp" and "end MouseUp," type:

   ```
   video "fast"
   ```

3. Click on the close box located on the upper-left corner of the script box.

4. Click on the *Yes* button to save the script.

To write the script for the Fast Reverse button, follow these steps:

1. Double-click on the button and select *Script*. The *Script* dialog box will appear.

2. Between the two script's *message handlers*: "on mouseUp" and "end MouseUp," type:

```
video "fast", "reverse"
```

3. Click on the close box located on the upper-left corner of the script box.

4. Click on the *Yes* button to save the script.

To write the script for the Play Audio Channel 1 button, follow these steps:

1. Double-click on the button and select *Script*. The *Script* dialog box will appear.

2. Between the two script's *message handlers*: "on mouseUp" and "end MouseUp," type:

```
video sound, 1

set hilite of button "audio 1" to true

set hilite of button "audio 2" to false

set hilite of button "Stereo On" to
  false

set hilite of button "Mute" to false
```

3. Click on the close box located on the upper-left corner of the script box.

4. Click on the *Yes* button to save the script.

To write the script for the Play Audio Channel 2 button, follow these steps:

1. Double-click on the button and select *Script*. The *Script* dialog box will appear.

2. Between the two script's *message handlers*: "on mouseUp" and "end MouseUp," type:

```
video sound, 2

set hilite of button "audio 2" to true

set hilite of button "audio 1" to false

set hilite of button "Stereo On" to
  false

set hilite of button "Mute" to false
```

3. Click on the close box located on the upper-left corner of the script box.

4. Click on the *Yes* button to save the script.

To write the script for the Stereo On button, follow these steps:

1. Double-click on the button and select *Script*. The *Script* dialog box will appear.

2. Between the two script's *message handlers*: "on mouseUp" and "end MouseUp," type:

```
video sound, on

set hilite of button "audio 1" to false

set hilite of button "audio 2" to false

set hilite of button "Stereo On" to true

set hilite of button "Mute" to false
```

3. Click on the close box located on the upper left corner of the script box.

4. Click on the *Yes* button to save the script.

To write the script for the Mute button, follow these steps:

1. Double-click on the button and select *Script*. The *Script* dialog box will appear.

2. Between the two script's *message handlers*: "on mouseUp" and "end MouseUp," type:

```
video sound, off

set hilite of button "audio 1" to false

set hilite of button "audio 2" to false

set hilite of me to true

set hilite of button "Stereo On" to
  false
```

3. Click on the close box located on the upper-left corner of the script box.

4. Click on the *Yes* button to save the script.

To write the script for the Eject/Park Disc button, follow these steps:

1. Double-click on the button and select *Script*. The *Script* dialog box will appear.

2. Between the two script's *message handlers*: "on mouseUp" and "end MouseUp," type:

```
video "eject"
```

3. Click on the close box located on the upper left corner of the script box.

4. Click on the *Yes* button to save the script.

To write the script for the Slow Forward button, follow these steps:

1. Double-click on the button and select *Script*. The *Script* dialog box will appear.

2. Between the two script's *message handlers*: "on mouseUp" and "end MouseUp," type:

```
video "slow"
```

3. Click on the close box located on the upper-left corner of the script box.

4. Click on the *Yes* button to save the script.

To write the script for the Slow Reverse button, follow these steps:

1. Double-click on the button and select *Script*. The *Script* dialog box will appear.

2. Between the two script's *message handlers*: "on mouseUp" and "end MouseUp," type:

```
video "slow", "reverse"
```

3. Click on the close box located on the upper-left corner of the script box.

4. Click on the *Yes* button to save the script.

When finished, your Videodisc Basic Operation card should look like Figure 7.20.

Figure 7.20. Completed Videodisc Basic Operation Buttons card.

Chapter 8
Creating Interactivity

The HyperCard stack supplies a set of videodisc drivers and resources that allow your Macintosh to talk to a videodisc player.

To control a videodisc player, in addition to the HyperCard program and commands, you will need XCMD and XFCN drivers for the videodisc player. In order to transmit your HyperCard videodisc commands to your videodisc player, special XCMD and XFCN resources must be installed in your Home Stack or in your presentation stack. These XCMDs and XFCNs are not part of HyperCard and cannot be copied and pasted into your stacks as you would copy and paste text and graphics.

The pre-produced videodisc controllers already include these drivers, but if you are creating your own videodisc controller, you should obtain the XCMD and XFCN drivers from Apple Computer, Inc., 20525 Mariani Avenue, Cupertino, California 95014.

GETTING STARTED

Before you start, you should make sure that hardware is properly connected and software is appropriately installed and is communicating with hardware. You need to check the following points to successfully run a videodisc player and develop a HyperCard videodisc stack:

- Is a power cord securely plugged into each piece of hardware?

- Does the player show video on the television monitor?

- Is each cable securely plugged in?

- Are you using the cable that matches your videodisc player?

- Are the DIP switches on the videodisc player set correctly? Refer to the videodisc player manual for proper DIP switch settings.

- Are you using the right Macintosh System and Finder version?

- Is HyperCard software present on your system?

- Are XCMD and XFCN drivers installed on your HyperCard program?

- Is a videodisc in the videodisc player?

- Is the correct side of the videodisc up?

- Is the videodisc player set for the right model (such as Pioneer 4200 or Sony 2000)?

- Have you set the HyperCard user level to Scripting (level 5)?

- Do you understand how to use the basic elements and functions of HyperCard (refer to Chapter 7)?

- Do you understand at least basic scripting in the HyperCard programming language, HyperTalk?

To control a videodisc presentation, you may be able to buy a pre-produced HyperCard stack such as Apple Videodisc Toolkit or Voyager Videodisc Toolkit. If no pre-produced HyperCard stack suits your needs, you should produce your own HyperCard stack to control your multimedia presentation. Figures 8.1 and 8.2 show examples of pre-produced HyperCard stacks.

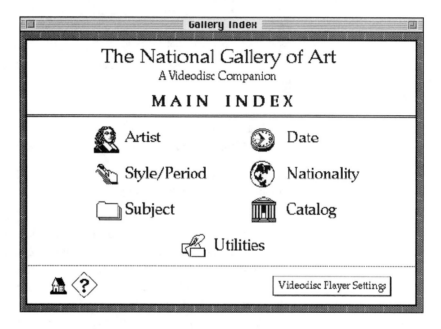

Figure 8.1. HyperCard stack main menu for the National Gallery of Art videodisc.

The following HyperCard videodisc commands work with all currently available versions of HyperCard, but as always, it is recommended that you use the most recent release. These commands are a collection of XCMDs, HyperTalk code, and examples. The HyperCard videodisc commands allow a HyperCard stack to control a videodisc player. It uses a simple, high-level set of commands designed to be much like HyperTalk.

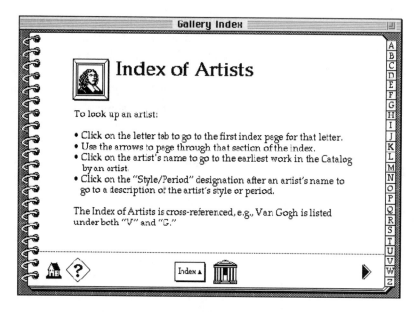

Figure 8.2. Index of artists on the National Gallery of Art videodisc. Artists are indexed alphabetically.

HyperCard does not have built-in facilities for controlling the Macintosh serial port. However, there are some serial port add-ons, such as XCMD (external commands, or ex-commands) and XFCN (external functions, or ex-functions), written in Macintosh programming language (such as Pascal, C, or 68000 assembly language) available from outside sources. XCMD or XFCN can be attached to the HyperCard application or a stack with a resource editor such as ResEdit. The resource type of an external command is "XCMD," and the resource type of an external function is "XFCN." The Apple Programmer and Developer Association (APDA) offers a set of external resources for reading and writing data through either the modem or printer ports. External commands and functions are essentially vocabulary words that you add to HyperTalk so that your stacks can do something that HyperTalk cannot provide.

For CAV discs, these commands provide facilities for displaying a single frame from the disc, playing a sequence of frames at a variety of speeds, returning to the current frame number, and turning on and off player functions such as audio channels, picture, and frame number display. The videodisc commands also work with CLV discs.

The videodisc control commands can be used in HyperTalk script (between the HyperTalk handlers: `on mouseUp` and `end mouseUp`), conditional statements in a handler (for example, `if...then`), or by typing them in HyperCard's message box.

Before using the videodisc commands, you must set the type of player being used with the `setVideoPlayer` command and reset the serial port and player with a "`controlVideo reset`" command. A list of available players for the `setVideoPlayer` command is obtained with the `videoPlayers()` function. The `playVideo`, `searchVideo`, `stepVideo`, and `scanVideo` commands can be used to selectively display single frames or sequences of frames. The `controlVideo`, `blankVideo`, and `videoFramesPerSecond` commands modify these operations and control other aspects of the player. The current frame number can be found using the `videoFrame()` function. If player-specific commands need to be issued, the `sendVideo` command can be used.

HyperCard Videodisc Commands

The following is a list of commands and features for developing an interactive videodisc presentation.

- **blankVideo**
  Summary: Blank the display during the next search.

Turns off the picture on the video monitor for the next `playVideo`, `searchVideo`, or `stepVideo` command.

A sample script follows:

```
on mouseUp
blankVideo — turn off the video image while going to the
start frame
playVideo 1000,1500 — play the videodisc from frame
1000 to frame 1500
end mouseUp
```

This command should be executed immediately before a
`searchVideo` or `playVideo` command in order to blank
the display during the search. It applies only to the next
`searchVideo` or `playVideo` executed.

Most players will automatically blank the display with searching for more than a few frames. Therefore, this command is
seldom needed.

- **`controlVideo <keyword1,keyword2,...>`**
  Summary: Issue a videodisc control command.

Controls one or more functions of the videodisc player. The
parameter list is arbitrarily large and consists of a series of
keywords. The following keywords are recognized:

`init` or `reset`	Stop and reset the player.
`eject` or `reject`	Eject the disc from the player (some players merely spin down the disc and do not actually eject it).
`stereoOn`	Turn on both audio channels.
`audio1On`	Turn on audio channel 1 only.
`audio2On`	Turn on audio channel 2 only.
`audioOff`	Turn off both audio channels.
`pictureOn`	Turn on the video output.
`pictureOff`	Turn off the video output.
`framesOn`	Turn on the display of frame numbers.
`framesOff`	Turn off the display of frame numbers.

`modemPort`	Use the modem port to communicate with the player.
`printerPort`	Use the printer port to communicate with the player.

Note that LocalTalk networks, E-mail packages, CDEVS, INITs, and other software that initialize the printer port at boot time will not always give up control unless you remove the software from the startup disk and reboot the computer. Therefore simply plugging in cables to control the videodisc player and sending a `controlVideo printerPort` command may not allow control of the player through that port. It is usually easiest to use the modem port.

`port<n>`	Use port number n — 1 is the modem port, 2 is the printer port.
`baud<n>`	Use baud rate n. The baud rate can currently be 600, 1200, 1800, 2400, 3600, 4800, 7200, 9600, 19,200, or 57,600.
`defaultComm`	Set the default communications parameters for this player, including baud rate, data bits, stop bits, and parity.
`frameMode`	Subsequent `playVideo` and `searchVideo` commands use frame number rather than chapter numbers. This is the default mode, and the gobal variable `videoMode` is empty while `frameMode` is chosen.
`chapterMode`	Subsequent `playVideo` and `searchVideo` commands use chapter numbers rather than frame numbers.

Other: Anything not recognized by the `controlVideo` command as a keyword will be passed on to the `SPortConfiguration` command, which configures the serial port. An example of `ControlVideo` command is the following:

```
on mouseUp
controlVideo
pictureOn,framesOn,stereoOn,chapterMode
```
— show the image on the video monitor, display frame num
bers, turn on both audio channels, and search and play by
chapter number (rather than frame)
```
end mouseUp
```

This command handles most of the configuration management
for the XCMDs, the player, and the serial port. It takes a list of
keywords, each of which selects some action or configuration:

- **HMSToTicks()**
  Summary: Converts from hour-minute-seconds to ticks.

Converts the string (hours, minutes, seconds) to sixtieths of a
second (ticks) and returns the result.

HMSToTicks(010503) — converts 1 hour, 5 minutes, 3 seconds into
ticks and returns the result 234180 (234180 sixtieths of a second)

- **playVideo <first,last>**
  Summary: Play a sequence of frames on the disc.

Plays the videodisc from the first frame specified to the last
frame specified. Enter the first frame to play, or here to play
from wherever the disc is currently playing. Then enter the last
frame to play, or lastFrame to play to the end of the disc.

If first is omitted or is here, play begins wherever the player
is when the command is issued (in other words, no search is
done first) until the specified last frame.

The last frame of the disc can be specified by last. If the
second argument is omitted, last is assumed. If last is
less than first the sequence is played in reverse. If last
is 0, 1 or lastFrame, continuous play (forward or backward) through the videodisc is assumed.

If a blankVideo command was issued since the last

`playVideo`, `searchVideo`, or `stepVideo` command, the picture will be turned off during the search to the first frame. If a `videoFramesPerSecond` command was issued since the last `playVideo` command, the speed specified in the `videoFramesPerSecond` command will be used. To play from frame 1,500 to frame 2,500:

```
on openCard
playVideo 1500,2500 — when the user arrives at this
card (when the OpenCard message is sent) play the video
disc starting at frame 1500 and stop play at frame 2500
end openCard
```

Players vary in their response to commands to play backward. See the Video Tips stack for more detail on this. To play backward regardless of what player is used, numbers should be used for both the `first` and `last` parameters. For example:

```
on mouseUp
playVideo 1000,500 — will play the videodisc back
ward 500 frames
end mouseUp
```

```
on mouseUp
playVideo videoFrame(),500 — will obtain the cur-
rent frame number then play forward or backward to the last frame
specified
end mouseUp
```

- **scanVideo <forward | backward>**
  Summary: Scan very quickly through the disc.

Scans forward if the argument is `forward`, or backward if it is `backward`.

```
on mouseDown
```

```
scanVideo backward — tells the player to scan back-
ward once
repeat until the mouse is up
— check to see if the command needs to be issued again
— to continue scanning
if the result is not "only once" then
scanVideo backward
end repeat
stopVideo — stop scanning when the mouse is released
end mouseDown
```

This command works slightly differently in different players. In some, scanning continues until another command is issued; in others, the `scanVideo` command must be continually reissued to continue scanning. For consistent behavior across players the command should be used as shown in the example above.

- **searchVideo <frame>**
  Summary: Search to the specified frame on the disc.

Searches across the videodisc and shows the specified frame.

If a `blankVideo` command was issued before the `searchVideo` command, the video picture is turned off during the search to the specified frame.

```
on mouseUp
searchVideo 25543 — find and show frame number 25543
of the videodisc
end mouseUp
```

- **sendVideo <command,param>**
  Summary: Send a low level command to the player.

This command allows implementation of instructions specific

to a given player. Players have different command sets, for example, some use one-letter commands or hex codes; others use ASCII strings to direct their activity. See the Video Tips stack for specifics on the players supported by this kit.

The `sendVideo` command sends the command to the player and waits for an acknowledgment from the player that the command has been accepted or completed. The second parameter is optional additional information required for some players.

```
on mouseUp
sendVideo "PL" — sends a play command to the Pioneer
4200
end mouseUp
```

> Not every feature of the players presented here is supported. Various players handle commands in different ways. See the manufacturer's specifications for details on some of these behaviors.

- **`setVideoPlayer <"type of player">`**
  Summary: set the type of player being used.

Sets the type of video player being used. The names of players can be found in the "Select a Player" dialog box or by using the name of the player-specific XFCN. You can use the following players:

```
None (no player connected)
Sony 1500 or S1500
Sony 2000 or S2000
Pioneer 4200 or P4200
Pioneer 6000A or P6000A
Pioneer 6010A or P6010A
Hitachi 9550 or H9550

on mouseUp
setVideoPlayer "Sony 1500" — set the player type
to Sony 1500
end mouseUp
```

- **stepVideo <number of frames,count>**
  Summary: Step a number frames, and do it "count" times.

Steps the specified number of frames, and repeats the operation `count` times. If the number of frames parameter is a positive integer, the player steps forward. If the number is negative, the player steps backward.

```
on mouseDown
repeat until the mouse is up
stepVideo -1 — step backwards 1 frame at a time until the
mouse is released
end repeat
end mouseUp
```

- **stopVideo**
  Summary: Goes to still mode.

Stops the videodisc.

```
on mouseUp
stopVideo — stops the videodisc player where it is
end mouseUp
```

- **ticksToHMS()**
  Summary: Converts from ticks to hour-minute-seconds.

Converts the argument (a number of sixtieths of a second) to hours-minutes-seconds (HHMMSS) format.

`ticksToHMS(1200)` — converts 1200 ticks into hours-minutes-seconds and returns the result 000020 (00 hours, 00 minutes, 20 seconds)

- **videoChapter()**
  Summary: Returns the number of the chapter being shown.

Returns the chapter number the player is currently showing.

```
on mouseUp
videoChapter() — returns the number of the videodisc
chapter being shown by the player
end mouseUp
```

- **`videoFrame()`**
  Summary: Returns the number of the frame number being shown.

Returns the frame number the player is currently displaying.

```
on mouseUp
put videoFrame() — put the number of the current video-
disc frame into the message box
end mouseUp
```

- **`videoFramesPerSecond <speed>`**
  Summary: Set the speed for the next play Video command.

Sets the speed in frames per second for the next `playVideo` command. Standard speed is 30 frames per second, and at other speeds sound is usually shut off. Players usually can only play specific speeds, so arbitrary choices (for example, `videoFramesPerSecond 26`) may not work. Use the `videoSpeeds` function to get a list of frame speeds available for the currently connected player.

Instead of a number, the parameter for frame speed can be one of the following keywords: `slowest`, `slower`, `slow`, `normal`, `fast`, `faster`, or `fastest`. These speeds are not necessarily the same on all players. It is generally best to use the keywords because they are always translated to a speed the player can actually play.

```
on mouseUp
videoFramesPerSecond 15 — set the player speed to
15 frames per second
playVideo here, lastframe — play the videodisc
from here until the end
end mouseUp
```

Some players have a very wide range of speeds available (for instance, about 120 for the Pioneer 4200). In such cases the `videoSpeeds` function will return a range of some, but not all, available speeds. If a specific speed is required, use the `sendVideo` command and see the manufacturer's technical documentation.

- **videoPlayers()**

  Summary: Returns a list of available player types.

Returns a comma-separated list of available XFCNs for video players. This is useful for making sure a driver is available for the videodisc player connected to the Macintosh. The list returned can be used to let the user select a player. Any of the items in the list returned can be used as the parameter to setVideoPlayer.

```
on mouseUp
put videoPlayers() into the List — put a list
of drivers into a variable
repeat with i = 1 to the number of
items in the List
put item i of the List & return into
line i of card field "Players"
end repeat — put the available drivers into a list in a field
end mouseUp
```

- **videoSpeeds()**

  Summary: Returns a list of speeds the selected player type can play.

Returns a comma-separated list of available frames-per-second speeds for the currently connected videodisc player. If a specific frame speed is desired, this function will tell whether the player supports it.

```
on openCard — when the user arrives at this card in the stack
get videoSpeeds() — return a list of available videodisc
player speeds
if it contains "3" then
videoFramesPerSecond 3 — play at 3 frames/second
else videoFramesPerSecond slower — play at
almost the slowest speed possible for the currently connected
player
playVideo 3000,4500 — play from frame 3000 to 4500
at the chosen speed
end openCard
```

- **videoStatus()**
  Summary: Returns the status of the player.

Returns a comma-separated list of keywords describing the current status of the player. The items appear in the following order: MODE, DISC TYPE, DISC SIZE, DISC SIDE.

MODE

noAnswer	This command attempts to communicate with the player were unsuccessful; the player must be disconnected or turned off.
park	The disc is parked or ejected.
still	The disc is displaying a still frame.
play	The disc is playing.

DISC TYPE

CLV	A CLV type disc is in the player.
CAV	A CAV type disc is in the player.

DISC SIZE

disc8inch	An eight-inch disc is in the player.
disc12inch	A twelve-inch disc is in the player.

DISC SIDE

side1	The disc in the player is on side one.
side2	The disc in the player is on side two.

Not all players can respond to this command. If the player cannot provide a particular item, its place is returned empty. If the player cannot tell the disc side, only three items are returned. Handlers can test for this by checking the number of items returned by the function. If the player cannot provide any status information the function returns the single keyword notImplemented.

```
on openStack — when the user opens this stack
get videoStatus() — return current videodisc player
status
if item 2 is "CLV" then — what kind of disc
is in the player
answer "Are you sure you have the right
disc?"
exit openStack — if it's a CLV disk, don't search to the
frame number
else searchVideo 2300 — show frame 2300 on the
video monitor
end if
end openStack
```

- **videoVersion()**
  Summary: Returns the version of the video disc drivers.

Returns the current version number of the video XCMDs and XFCNs as two comma-separated items: the first item is the version of the XCMDs for the commands (for example, `playVideo`, `stopVideo`, `searchVideo`). The second item is the version of the currently selected player XFCN (for example, Pioneer 4200).

```
on openStack — when the user opens this stack
get videoVersion() — return the version of installed
video XCMDs and XFCNs
if last word of item 1 of it > 2.0 then —
what version of the toolkit is this?
searchVideo 212 — find and show the frame
else
answer "The video control software is
old." with "Okay" or "Cancel"
if it is "Okay" then searchVideo 212 — find
and show the frame
else exit openStack — don't play the videodisc
end if
end openStack
```

- **`waitForPlayVideo`**
  Summary: Waits for the last `playVideo` to finish.

Waits for the current playing sequence (`playVideo`) to complete, then performs a new action. Because this command locks out user interruptions (except the aborting with Command-period) it should be used sparingly. It is also wise to set the cursor on the Macintosh screen to tell the user to wait for the sequence to complete.

```
on mouseUp
set cursor to 4 — the watch cursor, so people will know
to wait
playVideo 20000,24000 — play from the current frame
to frame 24000
waitForPlayVideo — wait until it's done playing
answer "Would you like to see that
again?" with "Yes" or "No"
if it is "Yes" then playVideo
20000,24000
else exit mouseUp
end mouseUp
```

- **`<name of the player XFCN>(cmd,parameters)`**
  Summary: Implements player's XFCN by name.

Helps implement functions for a particular player by accessing a specific player XFCN by name. The first item in parentheses is a command name. Most of the keywords duplicate the standard commands and functions listed in this document and take the same parameters. These are useful when one wishes to bypass the first layer of XCMDs and control the videodisc player directly or create a stack with handlers to work with specific videodisc players. Here are the currently implemented keywords for this command:

Command	Function
chapter	Same as `videoChapter()`
control	Same as `controlVideo`
fps	Same as `videoFramesPerSecond`
frame	Same as `videoFrame()`
name	Returns a long name for the player (for example, "Pioneer 4200" for the XFCN named vidDrvrP4200). The name for the driver XFCNs supplied with this kits are `vidDrvrH9550` — Hitachi 9550 `vidDrvrP4200` — Pioneer 4200 `vidDrvrP6000A` — Pioneer 6000A and 6010A `vidDrvrS1500` — Sony 1500 `vidDrvrS2000` — Sony 2000
play	Same as `playVideo`
scan	Same as `scanVideo`
search	Same as `searchVideo`
send	Same as `sendVideo`
step	Same as `stepVideo`
speeds	Same as `videoSpeeds()`
status	Same as `videoStatus()`
stop	Same as `stopVideo`
version	Returns the second item from `videoVersion()`

```
on mouseUp
vidDrvrS2000(play,1345,7500)  — sends the Play
command along with start and end frame numbers to the Sony
2000 driver XFCN
end mouseUp
```

THE VOYAGER VIDEOSTACK

The Voyager VideoStack includes four HyperCard stacks. Open the stack named Voyager VideoStack and click anywhere on the "stack" of video monitors to go to the Main Index.

Before using the tools in The Voyager VideoStack to control a videodisc player, you must set the player type, baud rate, and serial port for your hardware configuration. The Voyager VideoStack supports 36 different videodisc player models. It can control a player from either serial port—modem or printer—at your choice of five transmission speeds ("baud rates"). You can also control two players, using both ports.

The Voyager VideoStack includes a number of tools you can use to create your own interactive videodisc programs. The tools are organized into the following parts, accessible from the Main Index (Figure 8.3).

Video Script Installer. This function automatically installs video software commands into any HyperCard stack.

Video Buttons. These cards provide more than 50 buttons that control different videodisc functions and can be pasted into your own HyperCard stacks (Figure 8.4).

Video Controllers. Use these ready-made remote controls for both CAV and CLV videodiscs. You can use the Button Maker palette to create buttons within your own stacks that control video.

Event Maker. You can define video events (such as "play from frame 25 to frame 100 with audio track 1 only") and create a button that activates that event.

Slide Tray. Frame numbers (with optional descriptions) can be loaded into a list. Frames can be played back manually or automatically from the list.

Overlay. With various Pioneer and Sony players, you can create text that will appear on the video monitor (and buttons for your own stacks to display that text).

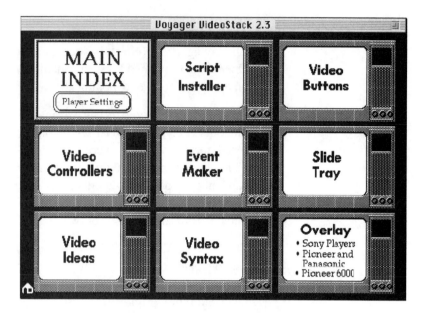

Figure 8.3. The Voyager VideoStack Main Index.

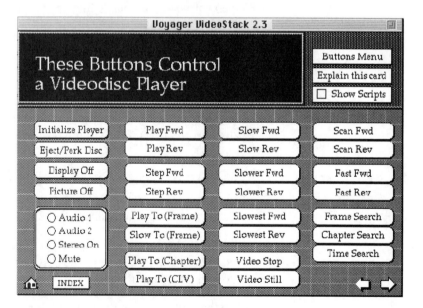

Figure 8.4. The Voyager VideoStack video buttons.

Video Ideas. Voyager's scripting ideas and examples can be used in your own interactive video programs.

Video Syntax. This function provides a full explanation of the HyperTalk video commands supported by The Voyager VideoStack.

Video Syncrasies. Gathers together player-specific tips and information into a single section.

VIDEODISC SETTINGS

The Player Settings button on the Main Index takes you to the Voyager Videodisc Settings Stack to check or change the player type, baud rate, and serial port. The Voyager Videodisc Settings Stack displays the current settings. Click and hold the mouse button over the name of the setting you want to change to open a pop-up menu of choices. Drag the mouse pointer over your selection and release the mouse button. When you are through, click the bent arrow to return to the Main Index of The Voyager VideoStack.

SERIAL PORT

Your videodisc player can be connected to either the modem or the printer port of your Macintosh. Choose the setting for the port to which you have connected the cable between the Macintosh and the videodisc player. Always specify which serial port before setting or changing the player type or baud rate. To use the printer port, you must first disable AppleTalk through the Chooser.

PLAYER TYPE

The following player types and players are supported:

Players with RS-232 interface:

Hitachi	Hitachi 9500, 9550, 9600
PanasonicPlayer	Panasonic LS-150

PhilipsPlayer	Philips VP406 (PAL)
PioneerPlayer	Pioneer 2200, 2400, 4100 (PAL), 4200, 4400, 8000
PioneerLDV6000	Pioneer 6000, 6000A, 601 OA
SonyPlayer	Sony 1000A,1200,1450,1500, 1500 (PAL),1550, 2000, 3600, MDP-1100

Players without RS-232 interface:

These players require "The Box to Connect a Consumer videodisc Player to a Macintosh." Set the baud rate to 4800.

PlayerSetl	Pioneer 900, 2000, 4000, LDA1, LDW1
PlayerSet2	Pioneer 1010,1030, 2070, 3030, 3070
PlayerSet3	Pioneer 700, 900; Magnavox 8040

PUTTING A STACK "IN USE"

The Voyager Videodisc Settings Stack (part of The Voyager VideoStack package) supplies a set of video drivers and resources that allow your Macintosh to talk to a videodisc player. You do not need to install the drivers in every stack; all you have to do is install a script in your stacks that puts the Voyager Videodisc Settings Stack "in use." Putting a stack "in use" allows your stacks to use all the resources in the specified stack.

When you set the serial port, player type, and baud rate in the Voyager Videodisc Settings Stack, the settings are utilized in every stack that uses the Voyager Videodisc Settings Stack's resources. If the video drivers are changed or upgraded, you only need to replace the Voyager Videodisc Settings Stack, and all the stacks that use it will have access to the changes.

You can make your stacks use the Voyager Videodisc Settings Stack by adding the following line of HyperTalk code to the script of a stack that's intended to control a videodisc player:

```
start using stack "Voyager Videodisc
Settings"
```

The preceding HyperCard commands can be incorporated into the Voyager Videodisc Toolkit Stack.

USING BARCODES FOR INTERACTIVITY

Multimedia technology platforms is dynamic, captivating, and instructionally profitable. In appropriate settings, using the barcode reader to control an interactive videodisc (IVD) is a very powerful yet simple solution. The best applications of a barcode/IVD setup are for presentations and self-paced tutorials. As a presentation device, barcode/IVD facilitates effective use of interactive videodisc material supplemented by lecture. For example, during a lecture on anatomy, the teacher could use IVD to show the beating of a human heart or an animation of the flow of blood.

As a self-paced tutorial this technology is nonintimidating to students and draws on the best attributes of written text and IVD. Textbooks can contain barcodes directing students to view portions of videodisc before or after reading text material. Testing can be done by having a barcode access still or motion images such as microscopic slides.

Reading Barcodes

The barcode reader works much like the scanners seen in grocery stores that read UPC codes. An infrared beam "sees" the code and translates it to information that the computer or videodisc player can use. Depending on the type and model of the barcode reader, using the barcode reader is relatively simple. The reader can be used as a wireless remote control device to control the videodisc player or in a direct link using a wire that plugs into the reader at the send end and to an input jack on the IVD. If you are using the reader in remote control mode, the barcode must be 'sent' to the videodisc player.

MAKING YOUR OWN BARCODES

There are many programs available for creating barcodes. For example, the HyperCard stack "Bar-n-Coder," available from Pioneer, is a very easy to use intuitive package. In creating barcodes, always use the "descriptive words" option to describe the commands and include frame numbers if appropriate to identify barcodes once they are created. Barcodes all look basically the same and, as they become more numerous, it is very easy to lose track of which one is which.

The barcode reader "reads" the barcodes and translates that information into a command for the videodisc player. The barcode is usually in printed form. The barcode reader translates it into electronic form.

The Bar-n-Coder program allows you to control a videodisc or player from the computer by the use of an on-screen control panel. The buttons for PLAY, PAUSE, STOP, and so forth will control the videodisc player allowing you to find the section or frame you need. This is a very helpful tool in choosing the appropriate place to begin or end each section, or to preview any portion of the videodisc. To take advantage of this capability, connect the videodisc player to the computer and then choose WITH PLAYER at the opening dialogue box in Bar-n-Coder.

CONVERTING AN EXISTING PROGRAM

Changing a computer-based IVD interface to the barcode system is possible. To do this you should have the frame numbers used in the existing computer program available. If the program is written in HyperCard or similar programs, you can usually find the numbers in the script of the button or card that is associated with the video segment. Write down the frame numbers that the program used. If you cannot access the frame numbers you can find out what the frame numbers should be and press the display button on the videodisc player to see the frame numbers for that particular segment.

Pioneer Barcode Reader

EXPANDING BAR-N-CODER CAPABILITIES

One of the drawbacks to this program is the limited number of barcodes that can be created before new barcodes overwrite old ones. The limit is 12 for printing on regular paper and only

4 if printing on labels. This is fine if you intend to print your barcodes immediately. However, if you are planning to use them in a word processing document your options are limited to the following:

1. Physically cut and paste the barcodes into your document.

2. Print them on adhesive labels and put the labels on your document.

Sometimes, we need to place barcodes directly into word processing documents. However, Bar-n-Coder does not have the capability of exporting directly to other applications. In addition, the barcodes are bitmapped into the current Bar-n-Coder card and cannot be selected as an object to be copied and pasted. Therefore, if you wish to use electronic copy-and-paste techniques, you must have some knowledge of how HyperCard stacks work.

To use electronic copy-and-paste techniques, use the following steps:

A. You may increase the number of barcodes that the program can contain by adding to the Bar-n-Coder Stack.

1. Copy the card that stores the codes (on paper or labels).

2. Move to the card previous to the card that stores the codes. To do this, use *Previous Card* under the *Edit* menu.

3. Paste the copied card as an extra card in the stack. You can then add 12 more codes to the new card.

Unfortunately, Bar-n-Coder does not know that you have added this card. Consequently, when you transfer your new barcode to paper, the program will automatically go to the card with 12 barcodes on it so that you may check your work. You must use the *Previous Card* and *Next Card* commands from the *Edit* menu to check to see if the new barcode has been sent.

B. To copy and paste to other documents, use the following procedure:

1. To copy and paste to a word processing document, it is easier to design a document first, including all the descriptive information. Then you will be able to add the barcodes one at a time. To copy and paste from the Bar-n-Coder Stack to a word processing document (such as one created with Microsoft Word):

   a. Click on the *Tools* menu in HyperCard.

   b. Drag the Toolbox to the window so that it is available to you.

   c. Choose either the lasso or the dashed square to select the barcode to copy. The dashed square works well because you must be consistent in how much white space you are cutting out surrounding the barcode.

   d. Copy the desired barcode. Choose your word processing document. Then paste the barcode in the appropriate place.

Your barcode descriptions and frame numbers will not be copied with the barcode. These are HyperCard fields and will not transfer with the copy function. You must therefore keep track of which barcode you are copying and label it accordingly.

Copying the barcode from the stack must be done in a consistent style because the white space around the barcode is also copied.

To copy and paste to another HyperCard stack that you have previously used as the interface for your videodisc, print the stack to facilitate recall of the video segments. Barcodes may be transferred into this stack. However, the background must be white for approximately one-half inch surrounding the barcode. A pattern background will interfere with the barcode reader's ability to interpret the code and will not allow confirmation that the code has been read.

Many publishing companies have already incorporated videodiscs and barcodes with their textbooks. On the left of this page, there is an example of barcodes for an accounting textbook.

Using a barcode reader is a simple, effective means of controlling existing videodiscs for presentations or individual study. Using a barcode reader is less complex and cumbersome than controlling the program from a computer. The reader also allows for more versatile control than using a videodisc remote control. It is low cost, easy to use, easy to modify, and very reliable. Figure 8.5 shows the Pioneer LaserBarcode commands.

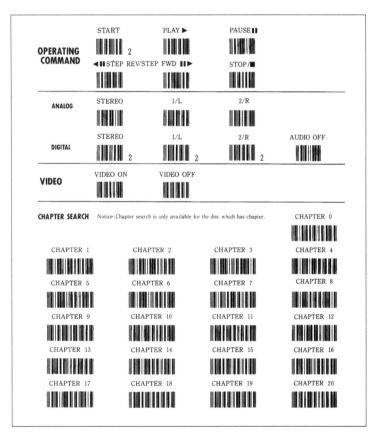

Figure 8.5. Example of videodisc barcode commands.

Appendixes

Appendix A

Multimedia Resources

MAGAZINES/JOURNALS/NEWSLETTERS

Advanced Imaging. Monthly coverage of all facets of imaging, including video. Free.
PTN Publishing
445 Broad Hollow Rd.
Melville, NY 11747
(516) 845-2700

AmigaWorld. Amiga gets short shrift most of the time. But it's a great multimedia platform. Monthly.
AmigaWorld
P.O. Box 595
Mt. Morris, IL 61054
(800) 827-0877

AVC Presentation. A monthly magazine geared to those involved in visual communications. Free.
PTN Publishing
445 Broad Hollow Rd.
Melville, NY 11747
(516) 845-2700

Boardwatch. Actually directed to on-line users of bulletin boards, but a good source of information.
5970 South Vivian Street
Littleton, CO 80127
(800) 933-6038

Business Publishing. Specifically for those interested in corporate publishing. Information on desktop publishing and electronic delivery. Monthly.
Hitchcock Publishing Co.
191 S. Gary Ave.
Carol Stream IL 60188
(800) 234-0733,
(708) 665-1000

CD-I World. CD-I magazine on paper and disc. Bimonthly.
Parker Taylor & Company Inc.
49 Bayview, Suite 200
Camden, ME 04843
(207) 236-8524

CD-ROM Professional. Covering the CD-ROM and optical-publishing industries. Monthly.
Pemberton Press, Inc.
11 Tannery Lane
Weston, CT 06883
(203) 227-8466

CD-ROM World. Information on new titles and techniques in the ever-expanding world of CD-ROM. Monthly.
Meckler Corporation
11 Ferry Lane West
Westport, CT 06880
(203) 226-6967

Computer Pictures. Graphics publication. Bimonthly.
Montage Publishing, Inc.
Knowledge Industries Publications, Inc.
701 Westchester Avenue
White Plains, NY 10604
(914) 328-9157

Consumer Multimedia Report. Oriented toward games, interactive video, and so on. Monthly.
Warren Publishing Inc.
2115 Ward Ct. NW
Washington, DC 20037
(202) 872-9200

Digital Media. A Seybold publication providing the usual high level of Seybold insight. Monthly.
Seybold Publications
428 E. Baltimore Pike
P.O. Box 644
Media, PA 19063
(215) 565-2480

Digital Publishing Business. Newsletter published for Optical Publishing Association members.
Optical Publishing Association
P.O. Box 21268
Columbus, OH 43221
(614) 442-8805

Digital Technology Report. Report on digital publishing in the consumer arena. Biweekly.
Digital Technology Report
102-30 67th Avenue
Forest Hills, NY 11375
(718) 997-1581

Digital Video. Magazine published by IDG. Very much oriented toward experts. Bimonthly.
TechMedia Publishing
80 Elm Street
Peterborough, NH 03458
(603) 924-0100

Information Today. Magazine about information resources. Monthly.
Learned Information Inc.
143 Old Marlton Pike
Medford, NJ 08055
(609) 654-6266

The Interactive Engineer. Publication about CD-I software engineering. Free.
Philips Interactive Media of America
11050 Santa Monica Boulevard
Los Angeles, CA 90025
(310) 444-6519

Information Standards Quarterly. A National Information Standards Organization (NISO). Quarterly.
National Information Standards Organization (NISO)
P.O. Box 1056
Bethesda, MD 20827
(301) 975-2814

The International CD-ROM Report. Report on what's new and what's not in CD-ROMs. Bimonthly.
Innotech
110 Silver Star Blvd., Unit #107
Scarborough, Ontario M1V 5A2
Canada
(416) 321-3838

Link-Up. A newspaper for users of on-line services and CD-ROM. Encompasses information of interest to business people, educators, and private individuals. Bimonthly.
Learned Information Inc.
143 Old Marlton Pike
Medford, NJ 08055
(609) 654-6266

Multimedia Business Report. Covers interactive CDs, on-line services, audiotex, software interactive television, video games, integrated learning systems. Published 24 times a year.
SIMBA Information, Inc.
P.O. Box 7430
Wilton, CT 06897
(203) 834-0033

Multimedia/CD Publisher. Newsletter with a multimedia publisher's orientation.
Meckler Publishing
11 Ferry Lane
Westport, CT 06880
(203) 226-6967

Multimedia Networking Newsletter. Specifically deals with the issues of networked multimedia. Published monthly.
Publications Research Group
P.O. Box 765
North Adams, MA 01247
(413) 664-6185

Multimedia Review. Academic-oriented journal. Quarterly.
Meckler Publishing
11 Ferry Lane
Westport, CT 06880
(203) 226-6967

Multimedia Monitor. Filled with the latest news.
Future Systems Inc.
P.O. Box 26
Falls Church, VA 22040
(703) 241-1799; (703) 532-0529 (fax)

Multimedia Week. An executive report on business opportunities in the multimedia marketplace.
Phillips Business Information, Inc.
7811 Montrose Rd.
Potomac, MD 20854
(301) 424-3338

Nautilus. Published on CD-ROM. Provides the latest news and also provides demos of the latest products in the field.
Nautilus
Metatec Corporation
7001 Discovery Blvd.
Dublin, OH 43017
(800) 637-3472
(614) 766-3165

Multimedia: Nuts and Bolts. CD-ROM journal that covers new products, technology, applications, "how-to," trends, and case histories. Quarterly.
Multimedia: Nuts and Bolts
115 Bloomingdale Lane
Woodbridge, Ontario L4L 6X8
Canada
(800) 363-3227

New Media. Covers information about new technology.
Hypermedia Communications Inc.
901 Mariner's Island Blvd, Suite 365
San Mateo, CA 94404
(415) 573-5170

New Media News. A publication for Boston Computer Society members.
Boston Computer Society
One Kendall Sq., Bldg 100
Cambridge, MA 02139
(617) 252-0600

Online & CDROM Review. An international journal of information sciences concentrating on on-line and optical information sources, systems, and services. Published every two months.
Learned Information Ltd.
Woodside, Hinksey Hill
Oxford OX1 5AU
United Kingdom
44 (0) 865 730275

PC Presentations/Productions Magazine. Focuses on the use of PC technology for better business presentations and on the use of products to get the job done.
PCPP Magazine
Pisces Publishing Group
417 Bridgeport Aveune
Devon, CT 06460
(203) 877-1927

Ultimedia Solutions. Concentrates on the case histories of multimedia uses. Bimonthly. Free.
IBM Multimedia Solutions
4111 Northside Parkway
#HO4L1
Atlanta, GA 30327
(404) 238-3455

Virtual Reality Report Magazine. A must-have, if you're into VR.
Meckler Corporation
11 Ferry Lane West
Westport, CT 06880
(203) 226-6967

Wolf World. Covering multimedia issues relevant to PC sound card users. Available both in paper and electronic format on CompuServe via GO WESTPOINT. Monthly.
Westpoint Creative
Delta House
264 Monkmoor Road
Shrewsbury SY2 5ST
United Kingdom
44 (0) 743 248590

PROFESSIONAL
ORGANIZATIONS

ACM (Association for Computing Machinery)
11 West 42nd Street
New York, NY 10026
(212) 869-7440

Electronic Artists Group
P.O. Box 580783
Memphis, MN 55458
(612) 331-4289

IICS (International Interactive Communications Society)
P.O. Box 1862
Lake Oswego, OR 97035
(503) 649-2065

IMA (Interactive Multimedia Association)
3 Church Circle, Suite 800
Annapolis, MO 20401
(410) 626-1380

IMA (International MIDI Association)
5316 West 57th Street
Los Angeles, CA 90056
(213) 649-6434

ITVA (International Television Association)
6311 North O'Connor Road DB51
Irving, TX 75039
(214) 869-1112

NCGA (National Computer Graphics Association)
2722 Merrilee Drive, Suite 200
Fairfax, VA 22031
(800) 225-6242

Optical Publishing Association
7001 Discovery Blvd. #205
Dublin, OH 43017
(614) 793-9660

SMPTE (Society of Motion Picture and Television Engineers)
595 West Hartsdale Avenue
White Plains, NY 10607
(914) 761-1100

Software Publishers Association
1730 M St. NW Suite 700
Washington, DC 20036
(202) 452-1600

ANIMATION

ADDmotion
Mac
Motion Works Inc.
1020 Mainland St., Suite 130
Vancouver, British Columbia, Canada V6B2T4
(604) 685-9975

Animator Pro
PC
Autodesk, Inc.
2320 Marinship Way
Sausalito, CA 94965
(415) 332-2344

Animation Stand
Mac
Linker Systems
13612 Onkayha Circle
Irvine, CA 92720
(714) 552-1904

Animation Studio
PC
Walt Disney Computer Software Co., Inc.
500 S. Buena Vista Street
Burbank, CA 91521
(818) 567-5340

Animation Works Interactive
PC
Gold Disk, Inc.
385 Van Ness, Suite 110
Torrance, CA 90501
(310) 320-5080

Cinemation
Mac
Vividus Corp.
651 Kendall Avenue
Palo Alto, CA 94306
(415) 494-2111

Creative Toonz 2D CEL
PC
Softimage Inc.
660 Newton-Yardley Rd., Suite 202
Newton, PA 18940
(215) 860-5525

Cyberspace Developer Kit.
PC
Autodesk, Inc.
2320 Marinship Way
Sausalito, CA 94965
(415) 332-2344

Deluxe Animation
PC
Electronic Arts
1820 Gateway Drive
San Mateo, CA 94404
(415) 571-7171

Deluxe Paint
PC, Amiga
Electronic Arts
1820 Gateway Drive
San Mateo, CA 94404
(415) 571-7171

Director
Mac
MacroMedia, Inc.
600 Townsend
San Francisco, CA 94103
(415) 442-0200

Grasp
PC
Paul Mace Software
400 Williamson Way
Ashland, OR 97520
(800) 523-0258

Liberty
UNIX-based
Softimage Inc.
660 Newton-Yardley Rd., Suite 202
Newton, PA 18940
(215) 860-5525

On the Air
Mac
Meyer Software
616 Continental Road
Hatboro, PA 19040
(800) 643-2286

PC Animate Plus
PC
Brown Wagh Publishing
130-D Knowles Drive
Los Gatos, CA 95030
(408) 378-3838

Photorealism
Mac
Strata
2 W. Saint George Blvd., Suite 2100
St. George, UT 84770
(801) 628-5218

PROmotion
Mac
Motion Works Inc.
1020 Mainland St., Suite 130
Vancouver, British Columbia, Canada V6B2T4
(604) 685-9975

3D Studio
PC
Autodesk, Inc.
2320 Marinship Way
Sausalito, CA 94965
(415) 332-2344

IMAGE PROCESSING

SOFTWARE

Adobe PhotoShop
Mac, PC
Adobe Systems, Inc.
1585 Charleston Road
Mountain View, CA 94039
(415) 961-4400

Adobe PhotoStyler
PC
Adobe Systems, Inc.
1585 Charleston Road
Mountain View, CA 94039
(415) 961-4400

Color It!
Mac
MicroFrontier, Inc.
3401 101st Street, Suite E
Des Moines, IA 50322
(800) 388-8109

Color Studio
Mac
Fractal Design Corporation
335 Spreckels Drive, Suite F
Aptos, CA 95003
(408) 688-3800

Halo Desktop Imager
PC
Media Cybernetics
5201 Great America Parkway, Suite 3102
Santa Clara, CA 95054
(408) 562-6076

PhotoFinish
PC
ZSoft Corporation
450 Franklin Road, Suite 100
Marietta, GA 30067
(404) 428-0008

Picture Publisher
PC
Micrografx, Inc.
1303 Arapaho
Richardson TX 75081
(800) 272-3728

Gallery Effects
PC, Mac
Adobe Systems, Inc.
1585 Charleston Road
Mountain View, CA 94039
(415) 961-4400

CLIP ART/BACKGROUNDS

Adobe Collector's Edition: Textures and Patterns
Mac, PC
Adobe Systems, Inc.
1585 Charleston Road
Mountain View, CA 94039
(415) 961-4400

ArtRoom CD
PC, Mac
Image Club Graphics
Suite 5, 1902 11th Street
SE Calgary, Alberta, Canada T2G3G2
(800) 661-9410

Background and Clip Art Collections
Mac
Educorp
7434 Trade Street
San Diego, CA 92121
(619) 536-9999

Backgrounds for Multimedia
Mac
Art Beats
P.O. Box 1287
Myrtle Creek, OR 97457
(800) 444-9392

Chinese Clip Art
Mac
Pacific Rim Connections
3030 Atwater Drive
Burlingame, CA 94010
(415) 697-9439

Design Clips
PC
LetterSpace
338 E. 53rd Street, #2C
New York, NY 10022
(212) 935-4130

Designer's Club Collection
PC, Mac
Dynamic Graphics, Inc.
6000 N. Forest Park Drive
Peoria, IL 61614
(800) 255-4800

Dover Clip Art Collection CD
PC, Mac
Aide Publishing Inc.
6520 Edenvale Blvd., Suite 118
Eden Prairie, MN 55346
(612) 934-2024

EduClip Images
Mac
Teach Yourself By Computer Software, Inc.
34 N. Monroe Avenue
Rochester, NY 14618
(716) 381-5450

EPS Clip Art
PC, Mac
3G Graphics, Inc.
114 Second Avenue South, Suite 104
Edmonds, WA 90202
(206) 774-3518

EPS Clip Art Collections
PC, Mac
T/Maker Company
1390 Villa Street
Mountain View, CA 94041
(415) 962-0195

Japanese Clip Art
Mac
Qualitas Trading Co.
6907 Norfolk Road
Berkeley, CA 94705
(415) 848-8080

MacKids Kolor Klips
Mac
Nordic Software, Inc.
917 Carlos Drive
Lincoln, NE 68505
(402) 488-5086

Medical Clip Art
PC, Mac
TechPool Studios
1463 Warrenville Center
Cleveland, OH 44121
(800) 777-8930

Native American Art Collection
Mac
Grafx Associates
P.O. Box 12811
Tucson, AZ 85732
(800) 628-2149

Power Backgrounds
Mac
California Clip Art
17951 Sky Park Circle, Suite E
Irvine, CA 92714
(714) 250-0495

ProArt
Mac
Multi-Ad Services, Inc.
1720 W. Detweiller Drive
Peoria, IL 61615
(800) 447-1950

Vivid Impressions
PC, Mac
Cassady & Green, Inc.
P.O. Box 223779
Carmel, CA 93922
(800) 359-4920

Wraptures
Mac
Form and Function
1595 17th Avenue
San Francisco, CA 94122

Appendix B

Glossary

A

A/B. Editings creating an edited result by combining inputs from two or more sources.

A/B roll edit. Two source VTRs are operated under video and time code sync, under the direction of an edit controller. This is one production method for creating special effects from prerecorded source material by means of dissolves, wipes, and so on.

Access time. The time required to retrieve video information during edit or assembly.

ActionMedia. An Intel trademark for a video capture card that uses the firm's Digital Video Interactive (DVI) technology.

Action point. A point on the master tape where an action is to be initiated. Action points are identified by SMPTE time code. Action points may be the placement of an autostop, field dominance changes, the beginning of a new chapter number, or any combination of the three.

Active lines. The number of horizontal sweeps across the screen in a video display that represent picture information rather than those used for timing or data. In the standard 525-line NTSC system, there are about 490 active lines.

Active switcher. Uses power and thus can alter the signal passing through it.

Active Program. The area on the videodisc that contains user accessible video and audio.

Adaptive differential pulse code modulation (ADPCM). A type of digital encoding used for audio signals that continuously alters the meaning of the codes to best represent the range of the signal.

A/D converter. A circuit or unit that produces digital codes corresponding to a sample or series of samples of an analog input.

Additive color mixing. Producing colors by mixing colors of light rather than by mixing pigments. If the additive primary colors are mixed in equal proportions, the result is white.

Additive synthesis. In the creation of sound by computers or electronic instruments, creating a composite waveform by summing the signals from multiple sources.

Address lines. Serial or parallel lines used exclusively for transfer or communication of address information with a memory device.

Alpha channel. In video and computer graphics, an extra signal, bit or set of bits used to control special effects such as transparency and overlay.

Analog audio. The two audio channels on the videodisc that are from an analog source and recorded in an analog format. These are the standard audio channels in the videodisc format.

Analog video. A signal that represents video image information directly by changes in signal size or timing.

Animation. A video or film sequence that provides the illusion of motion by presenting a succession of slightly different drawn or artificially constructed images.

Anti-alias. To smooth over sharp or small jagged edges to create more pleasing images or reduce the effects of limitations in signal capture or storage.

Aspect ratio. The ratio of the width to the height of an image. Standard VGA screens for the PC or external screens for the Macintosh are 640:480 or 4:3, as is broadcast television.

Assemble. Referring to editing, a style in which sequences are placed one after another without a continuing reference signal. While requiring less preparation than insert editing (which places sequences on top of an existing image), the result is likely to have small errors in timing.

Assemble mode A. A sequential assembly of the edit list. This assembly will continue in automatic mode until all edits have been assembled or until the first event with an unassigned reel number is found.

Assemble mode B. In this mode, the auto-assemble process continues as long as there are reels from which to record. This mode is also known as "checkerboard" assembly. The system in many cases is more efficient in this mode.

Asymmetrical compression. As applied to video or audio data, methods for squeezing the data for storage or transmission that take a different (usually larger) amount of time or resources to compress the data than to decompress it.

ATR. Abbreviation for audio tape recorder.

Attenuate. To reduce the level of a signal, especially to do so deliberately to fit the level of a signal to the needs of an input.

Authoring system. (1) The hardware and software used to create a multimedia project, but not necessarily needed for playback. (2) A programming environment designed to help users create computer-aided instruction (CAI) lessons.

Auto-assemble. Generation of an edited master by a video or audio for video edit controller using an existing edit decision list.

Autostop. Part of the address code that will cause a CAV disc to automatically stop and still-frame on a given frame of video. Also called a picture stop.

AU or auxiliary. A channel through which a video device (video camera, film chain, and so on) may be connected to a video edit controller.

B

Back time. Calculation of a tape in-point by finding the out-point and subtracting the duration of the edit.

BCD. Abbreviation for binary coded decimal.

Binary data. Information encoded as a series of two-state levels, usually referred to as high and low or logical 1 and logical zero.

Bitmapped. Referring to video displays and other graphic output, a system where each possible dot of the display is controlled independently by one or more corresponding bits in memory.

Black burst. Provides the synchronizing signals for the system to lock onto and thus stabilize the VTRs; also known as color black, crystal sync, and edit black.

Boolean. (1) Refers to the system of logic that deals only in true and false values plus the combinations made up of those values and the operators "and," "or," and "not." (2) A variable that can only take on a true or false value.

Broadband. A communications link that provides a large enough bandwidth (range of frequencies) to accommodate several independent channels.

Browser. A program, system, or mode that helps the user look through a body of information. Most commonly, browsers show some kind of overview or summary, allowing the user to zoom in for a more detailed view.

Buyout music. Music that is sold with a license that permits it to be used in specified types of productions without further royalty payments.

C

Caddy. A plastic carrier used with many popular CD-ROM drives to hold the disc while it is inserted in the drive and to protect the disc while it is not in use.

Capstan servo. An electronic circuit that controls capstan speed with enough stability so that video information can be read in correct sequence by the magnetic video heads.

CD-DA. An abbreviation for Compact Disc Digital Audio, the standard format for compact discs and players used for mass-market music applications.

CD-I. An abbreviation for Compact Disc Digital Interactive, a standard for CDs containing combinations of sound, images, and computer instructions and for players specially constructed for these discs. Also known as Green Book for the document that defines the format.

CD-PROM. A proposed acronym (pronounced see-dee-promm) for Compact Disc Programmable ReadOnly Memory, proposed term for optical discs that can be written on by special recorders and read back on any standard CD-ROM reader.

CD-ROM. An acronym (pronounced see-dee-romm) for Compact Disc read-only memory, a type of optical data disc that uses the same basic technology as the popular CD audio discs to store computer data. Although the standard CD-ROM drive can only read data (the data is permanently stamped on the disc during manufacturing), discs are inexpensive to make and each can hold up to about 600 megabytes of data.

Channel. A communications line.

Chapter. The portion of address code that marks an area of frames with a common chapter number.

Chrominance (chroma). The color component of a signal or image.

Chroma key. A color-based video matting (overlay) system that drops all areas of a selected color (usually blue) out of the foreground image and substitutes instead the corresponding areas of a second image.

Chyron. A popular brand of video character generators. The name is often used loosely in the video industry to indicate any character generator or the resulting lettering.

CMYK. A color model based on the cyan (C), magenta (M), yellow (Y), and black (K) inks used in color printing. The first three inks are used to form all the available colors using subtractive color mixing, while the black is used to change tones or define edges.

Coaxial cable (coax). A type of wire that surrounds a central conductor with an insulating layer and a foil shield or wire braid. This arrangement provides high bandwidth and good protection against signal interference or radiation.

Color bars. A standard video test signal that uses blocks of solid colors made up of the three primary colors and their combinations. The most commonly used version was developed by the Society of Motion Picture and Television Engineers (SMPTF) and is consequently called "SMPTE bars."

Color framing. An action during the start-up of the play mode on videotape playback that ensures that the tape playback is in sync with the house reference to the correct color field (1 or 3 and 2 or 4). This allows for a greater degree of accuracy for the horizontal position of the playback video.

Color model. A method of representing the color of colored items, usually by their components as specified along at least three dimensions. Common models include RGB (using red, green, and blue light), HLS (hue, lightness, and saturation), HSV (hue, saturation, and value) and CYMK (using the common printing colors of cyan, yellow, magenta, and black).

Compact disc (CD). An optical disc developed by Sony and Philips for distributing music and other information.

Compact disc interactive (CD-I). A standard both for CDs containing combinations of sound, images, and computer instructions and for players specially constructed for these discs.

Compact video. The original name of the video compression method developed by SuperMac now called CinePak.

Component. (1) Referring to video signals, a format that keeps color and brightness (luminance) information as two or more separate signals rather than combining them in one composite signal. Popular component formats include Betacam, MII, D-1, and SVHS (2). In the Apple operating system, a software object that provides services to clients.

Component video. Video that has two or more components that make the complete picture signal. For example, RGB (pure component) and Y/C.

Composite. (1) As applied to video, a signal that contains more than one type of information, such as picture and timing, or monochrome and color. (2) In image-creation software and systems, several items that are treated together as one object or given one name.

Composite video. Video that has all picture elements combined into one signal.

Compression. The translation of data to a more compact form for storage or transmission (after which it can be restored to normal form).

Constant angular velocity (CAV). Disc format is based on one frame per rotation maintaining a constant rotation speed (1800 rpm). CAV format has a 30-minute capacity per side and allows for the full range of interaction options.

Constant linear velocity (CLV). Disc format is based on the disc rotation slowing down as the program

proceeds (1800 to 600 rpm). CLV format has a 60-minute capacity per side and allows for reduced interactive options.

Control track. (1) On many video recording formats, a separate track that carries pulses used to set the timing and align the tape with the recording and playback heads. (2) A simple type of video positioning that relies on counting pulses on the tape rather than reading.

Courseware. Originally the term referred to the software containing actual lesson material for computerized instructional systems. Now, the term is often used more generically for educational software, audiovisual aids, and sometimes even textbooks.

CPU. Abbreviation for central processing unit.

Cut. The instantaneous transition from one information source to another. (2) As applied to video editing, a system that can create a finished piece from separate clips. (3) The usual contrast is with "on-line" systems.

D

Data lines. Serial or parallel lines used exclusively to transfer data in binary, ASCII, or other encoded form.

Decimate. To throw out selected portions of a signal to reduce the amount that has to be encoded or compressed. Decimation is the most common form of subsampling.

Device driver. A special section of computer code that translates the more general commands from an operating system or user programs into the exact code needed by a specific peripheral device.

Device-independent bitmap (DIB). A Microsoft Windows format for 256-color bitmapped graphics.

Digital audio. Two audio channels on the videodisc that are recorded using digital input signal. Requires a disc player capable of digital-to-analog conversion.

Digital compositing. Combining images in digital form rather than as analog signals. Digital compositing allows all the features of computer image processing to be applied to video or graphic arts images.

Digital dump. A digital program placed on the videodisc that certain disc players (level II) recognize and place in an internal microprocessor to control disc playback. The initial dump has to be placed starting at frame 1 of the disc. The initial dump and all other dumps that follow it are placed on the disc audio channel 2 and use a frequency shift scheme of 5 kHz or less.

Digital signal processor (DSP). A specialized computer chip designed to perform speedy and complex operations on signals representing wave-forms. Most DSPs include some type of parallel processing capability.

Digital-to-analog converter (DAC). A circuit or module that changes a digital value to a corresponding continuous signal such as a current or voltage.

Digital video. Signals that represent moving pictures (with or without sound) as a series of number values rather than as a smoothly varying signal.

Digital video interactive (DVI). A set of hardware and software products for compressing and decom-pressing video images sold by Intel Corp. The system offers both a real-time form (RTV) offering near-VHS quality and a more detailed version (PLV) that requires more extensive processing.

Dissolve. An edit transition where one source of video or audio fades out while at the same time another source fades in.

Dissolve or lap-dissolve. One picture melts into another. Actually, as one camera's picture is being faded out, another is being simultaneously faded in.

Dither. To place small dots of black, white, or color in an area of an image to soften an edge, to visually smooth a jagged line, or to simulate a shade or tone.

DMA. An abbreviation for "direct memory access," the transfer of data to and from memory without routing through the central processing unit (CPU) chip.

D-1. A format for recording component video signals (in which color and brightness information are carried on separate signals) in digital form developed by SMPTE.

Dolby A. A tape audio encoding/decoding scheme to enhance the analog audio playback of off-tape audio. Encoding is done during the recording of the master tape audio and decoding is done during tape playback.

Dolby SR. The latest analog audio encoding/decoding process from Dolby. Dolby SR gives audio playback qualities usually associated with digital recording methods. Encoding is done during the recording of the master tape and decoding is done during tape playback.

Downsampling. To reduce the amount of data in a file or stream by selecting only parts of the original information.

Drop frame. A type of time code for video sequences that periodically skips a code to take into account the small difference between the nominal 60 frames per second (fps) and actual 59.57 fps rate of NTSC-format video. Over an hour, 108 codes are dropped.

Dropouts. Small bits of missing picture information, usually caused by physical imperfections in the surface of the videotape.

D-2. A format for recording composite video signals (in which color and brightness information are carried with the same signal) in digital form developed by SMPTE.

Dual independent audio. Audio where the separate audio signals are not meant to be listened to together. Hence, dual and independent of each other.

Dub. To make a copy of a video or audio sequence or program.

E

Edit. Any point on a videotape where the audio or video information has been added to, replaced, or otherwise altered from its original form.

Edit controller. Device that is central to the modern electronic video edit in that it provides both memory and control functions (it often takes the form of a microprocessor or computerized device). The central unit is able to extend limited or complete control over the peripheral devices involved within the video or audio-for-video process.

Edit list (edit decision list, or EDL). A record of all the edit decisions to be made in creating a video program; takes the form of a printed copy, paper tape, or floppy disk and is used to automatically assemble the program.

Edited master (EM). The final edited videotape with continuous program material and time code from beginning to end.

Edit points (edit-in, edit-out). The beginning and ending points of a selected event within a program being assembled on magnetic tape.

Effects switcher. An electronic switcher that includes the generation control and coordination of special effects.

8-bit sound. Sound boards and other digital sound systems that record or play back sound using 8 bits of resolution for each digital sample. The result is fidelity slightly better than normal AM radio.

End of active program (EAP). The SMPTE time code on the master tape that corresponds to the last frame or end of your disc program.

Envelope. Referring to sound or video signals, the shape of the waveform that makes up a sound. Two notes of the same basic pitch will sound very different if they have different envelopes.

Event number. A number assigned by the editor to each edit that is recorded in the EDL.

Extended code. Part of the address code that carries additional disc operating information. Called extended because it was mandated several years after the initial laser disc specifications were published.

Extended graphics architecture (XGA). A video display standard introduced by IBM in 1990 that provides users 256 colors at 1024 by 768 pixels or 65 thousand colors at 640 by 480 pixels. The original IBM version only supported interlaced displays.

External key. Another key effect in which one camera decides which parts of two other cameras' pictures will be shown. That camera makes its decision depending on whether it sees black or white (or in color situations blue or lack of blue).

Extrude. A video effect that seemingly gives three dimensions to a two-dimensional object by generating solid objects outward from two-dimensional lines and shapes.

F

Fade. A smooth change from black to the desired picture or vice versa. Generally, a FADE IN starts the show (a blank screen changes to a picture) while a FADE OUT follows the show's end (the picture turns blank). Sometimes a FADE OUT followed by a FADE IN is used to denote passage of time or the change from one scene to another.

Fall motion video (FMV). Video presented at the standard frame rate (number of images per second) normally used for broadcasting in that area. In the U.S. and Japan, FMV is usually 30 frames per second, while in Europe it's 25 frames per second.

Field. (1) In NTSC system, one-half of a complete video scanning cycle, or 1/60 second. (2) One-fourth of a complete video scanning cycle, or 1/50 second (PAL/SECAM).

Field rate. The number of fields transmitted per second.

Fidelity. Closeness of the received signal to the original. In most audio and video formats, there is a trade-off between fidelity and maximum storage capacity.

Field dominance. The first field of any two field combinations that make up a complete video frame.

Field dominance flicker. Picture flicker caused when two fields from different video frames are combined to make a video frame.

Field master. The raw, original program footage on videotape containing original time-of-day and shoot time code identification and, where applicable, original field audio (also known as a source master).

Fill. (1) In video production, a supplementary light used to soften shadows and bring out the background missed by the key light. (2) In graphics, a color occupying a defined area to place color or pattern.

Filter. (1) A partially transparent material that passes (or blocks) light of a particular color or orientation. (2) An electronic circuit or unit that passes (or blocks) signals of a particular type or frequency.

Flash digitizer. A device that turns an analog signal such as a video input into digital form through a rapid direct parallel process instead of through a longer sequential process. Flash digitizers are used in some video frame grabbers for fast image conversions.

Flat. (1) As applied to images in general, ones with low contrast. (2) As applied to the shading of objects in image creation software, shading that uses a uniform color and brightness for each polygon (small region) rather than varying the shading at edges or across the polygon.

Flicker. (1) Perceived rapid variations in image brightness caused by insufficiently rapid screen refresh rates. (2) Rapid variations in an interlaced image caused by differences in the image presented in each field.

Flying erase head. An erase head that rotates along with the recording heads in a helical scan video recorder and consequently can erase a single video line at a time. This allows new segments to be added after previously recorded segments without a visible glitch between them.

FM synthesis. A method of creating sounds or musical tones by directly manipulating the frequency (number of cycles per second) of the audio signal. Most simple computer music systems use this method.

Frame. (1) A complete video image (which in an interlaced system such as the NTSC format used for television is made of 2 fields). (2) In computerized instruction, usually taken as the material shown at one time on screen. But with greater use of animation and interactive screens, the term is also used to mean a logical sequence of images treated as a unit in the instructional design.

Frame address. Indicates the location of a video frame for use in controlling the program. In CAV, the frame address is a number. In CLV, the frame address is in elapsed time from the start of active program (hours, minutes, seconds).

Frame accurate. Video editing, record, and playback systems that can locate and act on video images exactly at a specified single picture image. Most professional video equipment is frame accurate, but consumer products can find only approximate locations.

Frame buffer. (1) An area of memory used to hold a complete video image. (2) A video adapter that includes enough memory to hold an entire image.

Frame grabber. A circuit or card that can capture and digitize a single video frame.

Frame rate. For a video image or movie, the number of complete images shown per second.

Freeze frame. A frame of video on a disc that was meant to be viewed in the play mode but the user has decided to view it in the still mode.

G

General MIDI. A standard configuration for MIDI digital music systems that assigns popular instruments and sounds to specific channels.

Generation. For an image or copy, the number of reproduction steps from the original (which is the first generation). In general, higher generation numbers are likely to be less sharp.

Gen-lock. This device allows a videotape player's picture to be mixed with the camera's pictures. Sometimes built into the switcher, this mechanism uses the sync to synchronize the cameras much like the sync generator does. With all machines synchronized electronically, they can be switched, faded, wiped, and keyed cleanly without glitches or other visual disturbances.

Green book. An informal name for the standard developed by Sony and Philips for CD-I discs and players.

H

High definition TV (HDTV). There are several different proposed schemes all aiming at increased resolution video. The videodisc format is not capable of recording HDTV signals.

Hi8 (Sony trademark). A variation on the 8mm videotape format that adds extended fidelity for the luminance (brightness) detail and separated video (S-video) outputs.

High sierra format (HSF). A format for (CD-ROM discs that can be read on different types of computers.

Hybrid. For a CD-ROM, one that contains tracks in more than one format.

Hypermedia. A system or document that presents multiple pathways that the user can select and follow, rather than simply follow from beginning to end. It may include text, graphics, sound, and other types of data.

Hypertext. A system or document that provides multiple pathways through a collection of text that the user can select and follow, rather than simply presenting material from beginning to end.

I

Indeo. Intel's trademark for products that apply the firm's DVI technology to desktop and digital video systems.

Initialization. System startup, or setting of equipment switches and circuits to their beginning positions and values.

Insert edit. Type of edit in which new video material is inserted into existing material already recorded on the master tape (or into black), with the capability of returning to the existing video. No new time code or control track is recorded.

Interactive Multimedia Association (IMA). A trade association of producers of interactive multimedia equipment headquartered in Arlington, Virginia.

Interactive video. (1) The integration of video and computer technologies in which a video program (moving pictures and voice tracks) and computer programs run together so that the user's choices or actions affect the program outcome. (2) The linking of a videodisc or videotape player to a computer, allowing selections from the video program to be shown under computer control.

Interactivity. The ability of a user to quickly and easily manipulate and respond to a video disc program.

Interfield flicker. Flicker in still-frame video playback caused by the difference in subject position on two fields that make up a video frame.

Intelligent interface. A sophisticated microprocessor-based controller of VTRs and ATRs and switchers.

Interlock. To run sound and picture together in perfect sync from separate film and/or tape transports.

Interlaced. For video signals and displays, ones that paint each image in two passes (fields) down the screen, with the first pass carrying the odd lines and the second the even lines. This reduces bandwidth for transmitted video, but causes flicker in computer graphics.

International Interactive Communications Society (IICS). An organization of producers of interactive multimedia projects headquartered in Washington, D.C.

Interpolated frames. In the MPEG standard for encoding video signals, a single video image recreated by the received based on applying averaging or smoothing operations to preceding and following frames.

Intraframe compression. Methods for reducing the size of a video stream or file that make use of the information within each frame but not the similarities between successive frames.

ISO 9660. A standard format adopted by the International Standards Organization for CD-ROM discs intended for use with diverse computer systems. Most drives now come with software to read ISO 9660 discs.

J

Jewel box. The clear hard plastic case that many CDs come in.

Jog. In a video editing system, to change position in a video clip by a single frame or small number of frames.

JPEG. (1) An acronym (pronounced jaypegg) for "Joint Photographic Experts Group," an industry committee that developed a compression standard originally intended for still images. (2) More informally, the compression standard developed by that group.

Jukebox. An optical or magnetic storage unit that holds multiple discs that can be selected and automatically loaded into the player.

K

Key. (1) In an animation sequence or video edit, short for keyframe (an image used as a starting, ending, or reference point). (2) In lighting for video, film, or photography, short for keylight, the principal (and usually brightest) light illuminating the main subject. (3) To switch between two or more video sources, based on a control signal. (4) The control signal used to switch between two or more video sources. (5) An image whose color or brightness at each point is used to determine the switching between two or more video signals.

Keyframe. In animation or video editing, an image used as a starting, ending, or reference point.

Kinescope recording. Made by photographing the display of a television monitor with a motion picture camera.

L

LaserDisc. A trademark of Pioneer Electronics for its line of videodiscs and players.

LaserVision. Any video disc that conforms to the IICS LaserVision standards.

Lead-in. The portion of the videodisc before the active program. It corresponds to the video black portion of the master tape.

Lead-out. The portion of the videodisc after the active program. The lead-out code will cause the disc player to either recycle or stop, depending on how the player is set up.

Level 1 or Level I. As applied to a videodisc system, the common industry designation for one that supports only direct controls such as start and stop, rather than complete computer-controlled interaction or programmability.

Level 2 or Level II. As applied to a videodisc system, the common industry designation for one that supports some interaction through an internal processor, but not full control by an external computer. A Level 11 system can read a data program from audio channel 2 of the videodisc but can't normally record user responses.

Level 3 or Level III. As applied to a videodisc system, the common industry designation for one that supports interactive use, computes connections, and records user responses. Macintosh computer-controlled systems are usually configured as Level III systems.

Linear audio. A method of recording audio on videotape that uses a separate track along the length of the tape. This method generally provides lower fidelity but allows the audio to be edited separately from the video.

Linear editing. Video editing methods where you have to shuttle the tape back and forth to get from a clip at the beginning of the source reel to one at the end.

Line-in. An input on an audio or video system that expects a preamplifier-level signal.

Line level. In audio connections, a signal that ranges up to approximately 1 volt for full signal. This is likely to be the output of a preamplifier rather than the direct signal from a microphone.

Line-out. An output on an audio or video system that provides a preamplifier level signal for connection to other equipment.

Linear play. A section of video that is to start at point A and play to point X without interruption.

Link. (1) A connection between nodes or items of information in a hypermedia system. (2) A connection between network nodes.

Log mode. A standard function available on broadcast-quality VTRs equipped with dynamic tracking (DT). In this mode, the VTR may be moving in fast forward, fast reverse, slow forward, or slow reverse, or be in stop frame, and the picture can be viewed.

Longitudinal time code (LTC). A time signal placed in one of the tracks that run the length of a videotape. On some recorders, one of the audio tracks must be used for the LTC, while others provide a special time code track. The code is normally the SMPTE Time Code. LTC can only be read while the tape is moving.

Loop through. On a video on MIDI connection, an output connector that provides the signal received on a corresponding input.

Lossey compression. Compression methods that produce files that decompress to provide only an approximate copy of the original data. These approaches usually provide larger compression ratios than lossless methods and are used primarily for images or sounds where every bit of data isn't essential to provide a useful representation.

Lossless compression. Compression methods that produce files that decompress to provide an exact copy of the original data. These approaches usually provide smaller compression ratios than lossey methods and are used primarily for programs or text files where every bit of data is essential.

Luminance. The brightness or intensity of an image or signal, particularly the brightness without regard to color.

Luminance bandwidth. The range of frequency representing brightness (and therefore the amount of shape detail) that a system can record or transmit. In many video formats, it is greater than the chroma (color) bandwidth.

Luminance key. A signal used to switch between two or more video images based on the brightness (luminance) of a signal.

M

Mastering. The process of making a glass master from which replicas can be made.

Match-frame edit. An edit by which a scene already recorded on the master is continued with no apparent interruption; performed by setting the record and source in-points equal to their respective out-points for the scene that is to be extended.

Media control interface (MCI). A platform-independent set of commands and structures that define how a program can interact with multimedia devices and resources. It was defined by Microsoft as part of the firm's multimedia specification.

Mike level or microphone level. A high-sensitivity audio input intended for low signal-strength inputs such as those provided by microphones rather than the more powerful signals provided by amplifiers.

Mono audio. Audio on one channel only.

Morph. (1) To change one image into another by moving corresponding elements rather than by cross-fading. (2) A graphics program published by Gryphon Software in both Mac and Windows versions that produces such changes.

Motion blur. A blending or streaking effect deliberately added to images to simulate the appearance of moving objects.

Motion choreography. In animation and computer graphics, determining the displacement (change in position) of each object over time.

Motion video. The type of video image produced by a camera rather than still video, animation, or computer graphics.

MPEG. (1) An acronym (pronounced emm-pegg) for Moving Pictures Experts Group, an industry committee that is developing a set of compression standards for moving images that use interframe compression (frame differencing) as well as compression within frames. (2) Informally the first standard developed by the group.

MPEG 1. A form of the MPEG compression method optimized for data rates in the 1 to 1.5 megabit/second range, such as the transfer rate of CD-ROM drives and T-1 communications links.

MPEG 2 or MPEG II. A form of the MPEG compression method optimized for data rates above 8 megabit/sec rate and intended for applications such as broadcast video and medical imaging.

Multimedia Extensions. A set of routines and specifications for running multimedia programs with Microsoft Corporation's Windows 3.0 operating environment. Their functions were absorbed into Windows 3.1.

Multimedia Windows. An informal term for Microsoft's Windows operating environment along with the company's Multimedia Extensions running on the appropriate hardware.

MultiSpin. A trademark of NEC Technologies for the firm's line of dual-speed CD-ROM drives that transfer data at both 150 KB/s (kilobytes per second) and 300 KB. The first model was introduced in 1992.

MultiSync. A registered trademark of NEC Technologies, Inc. for the firm's line of monitors designed to work with a wide range of video input frequencies and formats.

N

Narrowcast. (1) To aim a program at a small but defined portion of the potential audience. (2) A program so aimed.

National Television Standards Committee. A common misnomer for the National Television Systems committee (NTSC), the industry group that formulated the standards for American (U.S.) color television.

Noninterlaced. Said of video systems that create images by painting each horizontal line across the screen in succession rather than painting alternate sets of lines in two sweeps down the screen (which is called interlaced scan). Also called progressive scan.

Nondrop mode. A system for time code recording that retains all frame numbers in chronological order.

Nonlinear editing. Video editing methods that record the source clips on hard disk, allowing you to jump directly to any clip without having to shuttle through any clips.

NTSC format. A system of coding color information for television transmission, used primarily in the United States and Japan and formulated by the National Television Standards Committee in the early 1950s.

O

Off-line. (1) As applied to video editing, a system than can only make an edit decision list (EDL) or simple edits (recordings) such as cuts, rather than one that can perform a full range of editing and video effects. (2) To edit a program using such a system.

Off-line editing preparation. That is done to produce an edit decision list, which is later used in the auto-assemble on-line process. A videotape (sometimes called a work tape) may be produced as a by-product of off-line editing.

On-line. (1) As applied to video editing, a complete system that can perform edits (make recordings) and add special effects.

Overlay. To show one video image positioned on top of another. To overlay two video signals, they must be synchronized to the same timing signal (gen-locked), especially in video images, to show text on top of a picture.

Oversampling. To read data at a higher rate than normal to produce more accurate values or to make it easier to filter the results.

Overscan. For a video system, a mode in which the image is made slightly larger than the face of the screen, ensuring that the image fills the whole screen. This is the normal mode for television-style video, but most computer systems use underscan instead.

Optical memory disc recorder (OMDR). Another version of the "one off" non-Laser Disc videodisc recording format.

Open-ended edit. An edit without a defined out-point. The system will record until the record or stop button is depressed.

P

PAL (phase alternation by line). The color television standard used primarily in Europe. Based on 25 frames per second and 625 scan lines per frame.

Pan. (1) In video and film, to rotate the camera horizontally. (2) In computer graphics, to move in a specified direction along the plane of an image, maintaining the same scale and orientation. (3) In a MIDI (computerized music) system, a controller that shifts the position of a voice between the right and left stereo channels.

Passive switcher. A push-button device that simply selects which of several video signals is to be shown. It consumes no power and is merely a switch specially designed for video.

Pickup. (1) A nonacoustic transducer intended to emit an electronic signal corresponding to the sound produced by a musical instrument. (2) In video or film production, a shot or sequence recorded after the main sequence and used in editing either to add interest during editing or to cover flaws.

PICT. The standard file format used to paste images between Macintosh applications using Clipboard.

Picture depth. The amount of storage allocated per picture element, usually expressed either in bits or in the number of colors (or shades) that can be represented by that number of bits. Common values include 1-bit (black and white), and 24-bit (millions of colors).

Picture element (pixel). The smallest part of a picture that can be addressed or changed in a digital image.

Pose short. For postproduction, the steps in producing a film, video, or multimedia project that take place after any live filming or construction of the images.

Posterize. To transform an image to a more stark form by rounding all tonal values to a small number of possible values.

Pre-master. In the production of a compact disc, record, or videodisc, to format the data into the special logical configuration needed on the master. This might include adding error correction and location information on digital recordings.

Preroll. The physical rolling back of both the record and source videotapes to a tape location preceding the edit cut-in point in time. This allows for both VTRs to be synchronized for control and time code functions in advance of the actual edit.

Processor audio. Sound, music, or speech created by data that has been routed through or created in the normal digital pathways of a computer system and played back under the control of the computer, rather than sound that is merely encoded in digital format for playback using standard digital-to-analog circuits.

Progressive scan. Video systems that create images by painting each horizontal line across the screen in succession rather than painting alternate acts of lines in two sweeps down the screen (which is called interlaced scan).

Public access. (1) Referring to public or private television and radio systems, the provision of time for independent program producers to air their work. Many cable TV systems are required to provide a certain level of public access as part of their franchise agreements. (2) Referring to multimedia systems, ones intended for use by the general public or by a wide variety of customers or visitors. Most feature touchscreens or other simple inputs.

Pulse code modulation (PCM). The representation of analog signals as discrete pulses of digital information.

Q

QuickTime (QT). (1) Apple Computer's architecture for working with time-based data types such as sounds and video. (2) The extension program for the Macintosh Operating System used to add the ability to work with time-based media. (3) Used loosely for the QuickTime Movie Format, a data format defined by Apple Computer for digital presentations that can include sound, animation, and video images.

R

Random access. The ability to retrieve video, audio, or data from any point on a tape, disk, or solid-state memory device.

Ray tracing. A technique for creating graphic images by calculating where each ray (small point) of light that reaches the viewer would have come from and what objects would have altered it.

RCA connector. The common connector used for most back-panel audio connections and for some types of video. It uses relatively low-cost push-on male and female connectors consisting of an inner connector within a concentric ring about 8 mm in diameter that forms the outer connector. Also commonly called a 'phone connector" because of its frequent use on phonographs.

Real time. Actual elapsed time.

Refresh rate. The number of times per second that a video display system redraws the image on screen. Rates below about 75 images per second can cause flicker, depending on the image size, lighting, and image content.

Rehearse. During editing, to see what the results of an edit step would look like without actually recording the result. Also called "preview" on most systems.

Replication. The process of copying a glass master on to many plastic replicas.

RGB. (1) As applied to video systems, short for red, green, and blue, three color signals that can between them create a complete video image. Most computer graphics systems use this tricolor approach. Most computers now use analog RGB, which allows the color signals to take on a continuous range of values. (2) As a color model, a method of representing all colors as the combination of red, green, and blue light that would create that color.

RGB analog. A characterization of video systems that work with video signals carried on three signal lines in continuous (analog) form. This is the type of video used by the IBM VGA video system, the Apple Macintosh 11 line, and by most other high-end personal computers.

S

Safe area. In a video image, the portion that will be visible after transmission and reception on the average receiver or monitor. The outer 10 percent to 20 percent of the image is usually considered unsafe because it may be hidden behind a bezel (frame) on the receiver.

Sampled sound. Sound that has been captured in digital form from an acoustic or electrical waveform rather than synthesized (created) by a computer system.

Scan. Scan has two definitions. First, it is the process of creating a video frame. In NTSC a video frame is composed of 525 scan lines, 262-1/2 in each field. Second, it is a method of going from point A to point B on a disc. A videodisc scan is equivalent to fast forward on a tape player.

Scan line. One of the horizontal sweeps across the screen that make up a video image.

Scanning frequency. (1) Usually meaning the horizontal scanning frequency, the number of horizontal sweeps across the screen per second used to form a video image. (2) The vertical scanning frequency; the number of sweeps down the screen used to form a video image.

Score. (1) The written form of a piece of music. (2) The process of writing down a composition in a form suitable for reading and playing. (3) In MacroMedia's animation programs, the diagrammatic representation of an animation sequence (a movie).

Search. The method used to get from one section of a disc to another quickly and accurately. Searches may be keyed on frame, time, or chapter. Video playback is usually blanked during the search.

Seek time. The time required to locate specific data on a disc. On average it includes the time necessary to move the read head to the correct track and the time for the disc to rotate half the way around.

Serial VTR. A videotape recorder (VTR) that can be controlled over a single-channel control wire such as the normal RS-232 or RS-422 connections used between computers and modems.

Sequencer. (1) A computer or controller that issues instructions to programmable musical instruments. (2) Software that lets the user compose and edit music.

Servo motor. An electromechanical control device using an external reference.

Shot. A single continuous run of film or tape.

Simulator. The equipment used to simulate a disc (for program development) or to simulate a condition (for example, a flight simulator) with the videodisc supplying the video.

16-bit. An add-on hoard that can exchange 16 bits of data at a time with the computer's processor or memory. However, for a sound, video, or other I/O board this does not necessarily mean it uses 16 bits of data for each pixel or sample.

16-bit color. Display systems that allocate 5 bits of memory each for red and blue components of each pixel and 6 bits to the green hues. Such an arrangement can show more than 32,000 different colors at a time.

16-bit sound. Audio that is created or digitized using 16 bits of information (and thus over 64,000 levels) for each sample. This is the standard used for audio compact discs.

SMPTE. An abbreviation for Society of Motion Picture and Television Engineers, a group that, among its other efforts, defined a time-coding system used on almost all professional videotape and film. SMPTE is based in White Plains, NY.

Special-effects generator. A device that makes special effects such as fades or wipes.

Split edit. A type of edit transition where either the audio or the video of the source is delayed (not recorded) for a given period of time.

Standards conversion. Needed when a tape in one standard must be converted for use in a different standard. After conversion, a 30 minute program remains 30 minutes long but the number of frames will change and the video motion will be averaged over several fields.

Standard MIDI File (SMF). A format for placing the data from a MIDI data stream in a file that can be used with many music applications.

Start of active program (SAP). The SMPTE time on the master tape that corresponds to the beginning (frame 1) of the videodisc program.

Status code. Part of the extended address code that conveys additional disc operation parameters (disc side, disc size, and so on).

Step time. In MIDI recording, recording event by event for later playback at full speed instead of recording at full (real-time) speed.

Stereo audio. Audio on two channels that are relative to each other and will be listened to simultaneously.

Storyboard. (1) To produce a set of images representing the flow of a video or film project. (2) A mounted collection of images produced for that purpose.

Subsample. To throw out selected portions of a signal to reduce the amount that has to be encoded or compressed. It is a usual step in most types of lossey compression. The most common technique is decimation.

Sustained transfer rate. For a CD-ROM disc, the number of bytes per second the drive can supply when reading a clip much longer than its built-in buffer.

S-video. Short for separated video, formats such as S-VHS and Hi8 that keep the brightness and color (luminance and chroma) as separate signals. Also called Y/C video.

Switcher. Device used for performing simple switching (on/off) functions, transpositions, or, in complete devices, coordination of special effects.

Switcher/fader. A switcher that can do a FADE or a DISSOLVE between two or more cameras.

Synchronization. The precise coincidence of two signals, pulses, or events.

Symmetrical compression. As applied to video or audio data, methods for squeezing the data for storage or transmission that take an equal amount of time and resources to compress the data as to decompress it.

Sync. As applied to video signals, the portion of the signal or a separate signal that carries the overall timing information.

Sync generator. A box of electronics that generates the signals we affectionately call *sync*. Its signals go to the cameras and perhaps to some of the other video equipment in the studio. This device is sometimes built into the switcher.

Synthesized sound. Sound that is created based on a series of parameters rather than replayed from recorded samples.

Synthesizer. (1) A musical instrument, module, or circuit that creates and shapes sounds electronically according to changable settings. Along with providing a choice of such basic sound qualities as pitch, loudness, and duration, most synthesizers allow the user to alter the tonal qualities of each note. (2) Particularly, a module or instrument that responds to MIDI commands and produces the requested audio output.

T

Take or cut. An abrupt change from one camera's picture to another. If camera 1 is on and you "TAKE 2," camera 2's picture will appear in the blink of an eye.

Timebase corrector (TBS). A unit that resets the timing portion of a video signal to the standard values for a specified video format. TBCs are often used to clean up the output from computer video boards or videocassette recorders (VCRs) before broadcast or further recording.

Time code. (1) In video production, an electronic marking of elapsed time placed on a tape to facilitate editing. (2) Specifically, the SMPTE time signals as defined by the Society of Motion Picture and Television Engineers. The code consists of 4 sets of numbers representing hour, minute, second, and frame.

Time code generator. A signal generator designed to generate and transmit SMPTE time code.

Time code reader. A counter designed to read and display SMPTE time code.

Title. In publishing, a single volume or set of volumes sold as a set under the same name. Often used in discussions of the number of titles available in different electronic formats.

Track. The name given to the row of pits that convey the signal on a videodisc, usually in reference to a single rotation.

True color. (1) Color systems in which the color information in the image is used directly to create the output color rather than as an index to a table of colors in a palette. (2) Color systems that have enough available colors to make the choices seem continuous to the human eye. In most cases, this is considered to be 24-bit color (about 16 million available colors).

24-bit color. Video systems that allocate 24 bits of data to each point in an image. Usually, the bits are allocated as 8 bits each for the three additive primary colors (red, green, and blue). That provides up to 16.8 million color, possibilities.

U

UHF. (1) Short for "ultra-high frequency," the radio frequency from 300 to 3,000 MHz. (2) Also used more specifically to indicate the TV broadcast band located in this range. In the United States, UHF channels 14 through 83 occupy the range from 470 MH2 to 890 MHz.

Ultimedia. IBM's brand name for its multimedia hardware and software products. It is supposed to suggest "the ultimate in multimedia."

U-matic. A trademark for Sony Corporation's 5/4-inch video systems, including tape, recorders, and players. The first U-matic units were delivered in 1971. It is a composite format, with moderate resolution.

Unbalanced. Signal channels in which the information is carried as the signal on a single wire referenced to ground.

Underscan. As applied to video images, set to fill less than the full screen (and thus making the edges of the image visible). Although the normal mode for computer images, this mode is used in traditional video only for checking signal quality.

User code. Part of the extended address code that is user selectable and placed in the lead-in portion of the disc. Its most common use is as a disc identifier.

V

Value. When speaking of color, the degree of lightness or darkness.

Vector graphic. Images and drawings made up of lines and other geometric elements rather than out of individual dots.

Vertical blank interval (VBI). The portion of the video signal during which the picture information is suppressed at the end of the field. It is provided to allow the scanning beam in a CRT to return from the bottom to the top of the picture. In the standard NTSC video format, it includes the first 21 horizontal lines of each field.

Vertical interval. That portion of the TV signal between the active picture scan lines. On the videodisc, the vertical interval contains vertical sync, address code, and test signals.

Vertical interval switching. Changing between two video signals during the vertical blanking interval at the end of a scan down the screen so that there is no visible glitch in the output signal.

Vertical interval time code (VITC). A digital time signal placed in a portion of the video signal normally used for the interval between images. Once recorded, it cannot be changed or edited without rerecording the accompanying video signal, but it can be read in slow motion or pause modes.

VHS. An abbreviation for "Video Home System," a trademark for the 1/2-inch consumer videotape format developed by Matsushita and JVC and now widely used for consumer videotape recorders.

Videodisc. A standard format for 12- or 8-inch optical discs that carry analog video signals. Optical videodiscs are composed of plastic and a reflective coating designed to reflect light from a laser beam. The reflected light contains the information encoded onto the surface of the videodisc during the replication process and is a duplicate of the information etched onto a glass master disc during the mastering process. The information on the optical videodisc is encoded as microscopic pits pressed in a spiral configuration onto the disc surface. Each 360 degree rotation of the spiral is called a track. The laser beam strikes the pits and is reflected to a mirror and onto a decoder within the videodisc player. The decoder reads the data and converts them through complex logic and video circuitry into the correct video format for viewing. Because the pits are layered beneath a protective surface, the videodisc is immune to dust and superficial scratches. Information may be encoded on both sides of the videodisc. These discs are also sometimes called laserdiscs.

Video Electronics Standards Association (VESA). An industry trade group formed to codify the software interface to advanced video cards and now active as well in the definition of one type of local bus.

Videographic. Loosely speaking, a term for computer video systems and subsystems that produce signals compatible with standard noncomputer video. In the United States, this usually means units that support output in the NTSC format.

Video overlay. (1) The combining of two or more video signals to get one resulting video output. (2) In particular, the placement of computer-generated video over standard video, including the placement of lettering (titles) by dedicated titling systems. Video overlay requires special hardware (including a unit called a gen-lock) to synchronize the input video signals.

Video RAM (VRAM). Memory chips or systems engineered for use with video displays, particularly those built with dual data ports to allow the video information to be read out without interfering with reading and writing of data through the primary port. (2) A section of main memory used to store data for display.

Video server. A computer or program that delivers video sequences over a network.

Videotext. A text-based information service that distributes information over video links or displays the information on a video display. Videotext services can be distributed through cable or any other television system, or by sending signals over telephone lines to a computer that can draw the images locally.

Video wall. A large display made up of multiple monitors with synchronized programming.

VU meter (volume unit meter). An indicator of audio signal strength. Most VU meters are set to indicate 0 dB as the maximum undistorted signal level, with markings that show a red zone for levels above that.

W

Walkthrough. (1) In film and video production, a rehearsal done without cameras. (2) A simulated trip through a computerized architectural model, especially one where the viewer can interactively navigate a path through the model.

Waveform monitor. A video test instrument that shows the shape of the video signal graphed over a selected interval of time rather than the video picture itself.

White balance. The adjustment of a camera so that a white object will produce the correct signal for white. Most consumer video cameras have automatic white-balance circuits.

White level. In a video signal, the signal level corresponding the brightest possible white value. Because of the way the signal is encoded, in most video formats it is actually the minimum voltage.

Wipe. An edit transition where one video signal replaces another video signal on the screen in some predetermined pattern.

Wipe or split screen or corner import. A final picture made up from a section of one camera's picture and a section of another. A wipe is the process of moving this split across the screen, thus replacing one picture with another. A vertical wipe moves up or down, splitting the screen horizontally, while a horizontal wipe moves left or right, dividing the screen vertically. A vertical and a horizontal split screen can be combined on screen (good for showing a close-up and an overall view simultaneously).

Wipe code. A two- or three-digit numeric code used to identify a wipe pattern.

WORM. Write Once Read Many.

X

XA. Short for "Extended Architecture," an addition to the format for CD-ROM optical data discs that adds provisions for storing and playing back interleaved sound and graphics.

XCMD. The resource type of an *external command.* HyperCard external commands are attached to the HyperCard application with resource editors such as ResEdit.

XFCN. The resource type of an *external function.* HyperCard external function commands are attached to the HyperCard application with resource editors such as ResEdit.

Y

Y/C. A type of component video signal found in S-VHS, Hi-8mm, and 3/4" SP video formats that separates a signal's brightness (luminance) and color (chrominance) information to maintain better picture quality. This is an intermediate step in image resolution between standard video (composite) and component video.

Z

Zero frame dissolve. A dissolve with a duration of zero frames, equivalent to a cut; a technique used to synchronize two source machines so that manual audio or video transitions can be made between them.

Zoom. (1) To change the size of the area selected for viewing or display to provide either a more detailed view or more of an overview. (2) For a camera shot to change the magnification of the lens and thus change the width of the shot and its apparent closeness.

Appendix C

Bibliography

Barron, Ann and Orwig, Gary. (1993). *New Technologies for Education*. Englewood, CO: Libraries Unlimited.

Bergman, Robert and Moore, Thomas. (1990). *Managing Interactive Video/Multimedia Projects*. Englewood Cliffs, NJ: Educational Technology Publications.

Borras, Isabel. (1993). Developing and Assessing "Practicing Spoken French": A Multimedia Program for Improving Speaking Skills. *Educational Technology, Research and Development*, April, 91–103.

Bowers, Dennis and Tsai, Chia. (1990). HyperCard in Educational Research: An Introduction and Case Study. *Educational Technology,* February, 19–24.

Burtness, Larry. (1989). A Look at IBM LinkWay. *Hyperlink Magazine*, May/June, 25–30.

Collins, James W. (1989). Texas Teachers Add New Technology to Classroom Instruction. *T.H.E. Journal*, September, 52–54.

Dana, Ann and Megeau, Theresa. (1989). Hypermedia, Hapermania. *Teaching and Computers*, October, 16–17.

Electronic Learning. (1990). Q & A with Fred D'Ignazio. *Electronic Learning*, Special Supplement on Multimedia. January, 6–7.

Fiderio, Janet. (1988). A Grand Vision. *Byte*, October, 237–244.

Fontana, Lynn, et al. (1993). Multimedia: A Gateway to Higher–Order Thinking Skills. *ERIC Document* ED 362165.

Jonassen, David H. (1989). *Hypertext/Hypermedia*. Englewood Cliffs, NJ: Educational Technology Publications.

Jones, Loretta L. and Smith, Stanley G. (1989). Light, Camera, Reaction! The Interactive Videodisc: A Tool for Teaching Chemistry. *T.H.E. Journal*, March, 78-85.

Jones, Pam. (1989). What Multimedia Means to Learning. *T.H.E. Journal*, Macintosh Special Issue (annual), 16–18.

Keathly, David. (1989). Discovery Through Interactive Technology. *T.H.E. Journal*, October, 91–93.

Marchionini, Gary. (1988). Hypermedia and Learning: Freedom and Chaos. *Educational Technology,* November, 8–12. Also look through *Educational Technology Special Issue: Hypermedia,* November 1988.

McCarthy, Robert. (1989). Multimedia: What the Excitement's All About. Electronic Learning, June, 26–31.

Mendrinos, Roxanne. (1990). CD-ROM: A Technology that Is Steadily Entering School Libraries and Classrooms. *Electronic Learning,* January, 34–36.

Meskill, Clara. (1993). ESL and Multimedia: A Study of the Dynamics of Paired Student Discourse. *System*, August, 323–341.

Morariu, Janis. (1988). Hypermedia in Instruction and Training. *Educational Technology*, November, 17–20.

Nielsen, Jakob. (1990). *Hypertext and Hypermedia.* Boston, MA: Academic Press.

Nummikoski, Marita and Smith, Woody. (1993). Multimedia in Russian Classrooms. *ERIC Document* ED 360881.

Phillipo, John. (1988). Videodisc's Impact on the Changing Needs of the Learner. *Electronic Learning*, October, 50–52.

Phillipo, John. (1989). CD-ROM: A New Research and Study Skills Tool for the Classroom. *Electronic Learning*, June, 40–41.

Pina, Anthony and Savenye, Wilhelmina. (1992). Beyond Computer Literacy: How Can Teacher Educators Help Teachers Use Interactive Multimedia? *ERIC Document* ED 343567.

Pioneer Electronic Corporation. (1987). *Videodisc/ LaserVision System Guide Book.* Pioneer Electronic Corporation.

Sprayberry, Roslyn. (1993). Using Multimedia to Improve the Aural Proficiency of High School Students of Spanish. *ERIC Document* ED 358735.

Waters, Tom. (1989). Hypermedia. *Discover*, June, 72–76.

Wohler, Janet (1992). The Multimedia Language Lab. *Media and Methods*, January–February, 36 ff.

Index

P9-BZR-850

ROSELLE PUBLIC LIBRARY

WITHDRAWN

3 3012 00170 5694

DEMCO

Broadway Books
New York

ROSELLE PUBLIC LIBRARY DISTRICT
40 SOUTH PARK STREET
ROSELLE, IL 60172
(630) 529-1641

Christmas 101

Celebrate the Holiday Season—
from Christmas to New Year's

Rick Rodgers

BROADWAY

CHRISTMAS 101. Copyright © 1999 by Rick Rodgers. All rights reserved. Printed in the United States of America. No part of this book may be reproduced or transmitted in any form or by any means, electronic or mechanical, including photocopying, recording, or by any information storage and retrieval system, without written permission from the publisher. For information address Broadway Books, a division of Random House, Inc., 1540 Broadway, New York, NY 10036.

Broadway Books titles may be purchased for business or promotional use or for special sales. For information, please write to: Special Markets Department, Random House, Inc., 1540 Broadway, New York, NY 10036.

BROADWAY BOOKS and its logo, a letter B bisected on the diagonal, are trademarks of Broadway Books, a division of Random House, Inc.

Library of Congress Cataloging-in-Publication Data
Rodgers, Rick, 1953–
    Christmas 101 : celebrate the holiday season, from Christmas to
New Year's / Rick Rodgers. — 1st ed.
        p.   cm.
    ISBN 0-7679-0399-4   (pbk.)
    1. Christmas cookery.   I. Title.   II. Title: Christmas one
hundred one.
TX739.2.C45R63   1999
641.5′68—dc21   99-31151
                                                        CIP

FIRST EDITION

Designed by Sam Potts

99 00 01 02 03 10 9 8 7 6 5 4 3 2 1

 Contents

Roasts, Birds, and Other Main Courses 42

The Groaning Board

Side Dishes and Stuffings 63

From Cranberries to Black-Eyed Peas

Festive Breads 77

Comfort and Joy

Candies 90

Visions of Sugarplums

Cookies 100

The Christmas Cookie Jar

Desserts 131

Oh, Bring Me a Figgy Pudding . . .

Acknowledgments

The holidays bring especially wonderful memories of my family. My parents, Dick and Eleanor Rodgers, play a big part in all of my books, because they taught my brothers and me how to cook in the first place. And in a holiday book where generosity and warmth of spirit are celebrated, this terrific couple deserves to be up front and center.

Diane Kniss, as always, stuck by me through countless dozens of cookies, mountains of candy, and yet another batch of turkey recipes. Celebrating Christmas outside of its season was fun, but even more so with Diane around.

Thanks to the friends and family who supplied recipes, Vicki Caparulo, Marie Intaschi, Ron Marten, Mary-Lynn Mondich, Grigg K. Murdoch, and Howard Shepherdson, and to Kelly Volpe for testing recipes.

A special thanks to the cooking schools around the country who allow me the chance to interact with my students: Sur La Table (Kirkland, WA, San Francisco, Berkeley, Los Gatos, Newport Beach, and Santa Monica, CA, and Dallas, TX), Adventures in Cooking (Wayne, NJ), Draegers' Culinary Centers (Menlo Park and San Mateo, CA), The Silo (New Milford, CT), Classic Recipes (Westfield, NJ), Cook 'n' Tell (Colts Neck, NJ), Central Market (San Antonio and Austin, TX), Rice Epicurean (Houston, TX), Gelson's Market (Calabasas, CA), Kroger's Market (Alpharetta and Peachtree City, GA), and Dierberg's School of Cooking (St. Louis, MO area).

Everyone at Broadway Books makes the publishing process as much fun as decorating a Christmas tree; bit by bit, it gets done, and when it's finished, you hope it is something to admire. First, thanks to my friend and editor (or is she my editor and friend?) Harriet Bell, who saw value in my idea for a holiday cookbook that taught the basics. Hats off to Alexis Levenson who cheerfully fields my questions and problems. The amazingly talented Roberto de Vicq de Cumptich designed the charming cover, and Sam Potts provided the festive interior design. Special thanks to Sonia Greenbaum, my hard-working copy editor, and the Publicity Ladies, Caitlin Connelly and her assistant, Lisa Bullaro. A toast of Grand Marnier to Susan Ginsburg, my agent, with whom I have been sharing holiday goodies for almost twenty years, and her assistant, Ann Stowell.

Finally, a note of deep appreciation and thanks to Patrick Fisher, who has come home to goose dinners in the middle of July and still has a sense of humor. And to his office associates, who gleefully helped us eat through all of those cookies and candies.

Introduction

*I*t's no secret. I love the holidays. Now, Thanksgiving is great, but I have to admit that it has one flaw—it's only one day long. Luckily, it makes up for this slight deficiency by being the start of the long Christmas and New Year's holiday season. The day after Thanksgiving, as soon as I set the turkey soup on to simmer, I inaugurate the next six weeks of partying. It's quite a whirlwind, but I revel in every second.

In my cooking classes, where many of my students are young people who want to start their own holiday traditions, I hear the same questions over and over again. How can I have a big holiday cocktail party that I will enjoy as much as my guests? How do I get my kitchen together to bake a big batch of cookies? What's a great Christmas dinner menu and how can it be organized to get all the food on the table at once? But most of all, I hear a sad story of regret: They never got that recipe for their favorite cookie from Grandma, and now they live a life of regret. (I hope that they find it in this collection.)

As in *Thanksgiving 101,* where I concentrated on how to deal with that holiday's demands and pleasures, I want to share my tips on how to have a hassle-free, fun, and delicious Christmas season. You can do it! It boils down to one word: organization.

When I was catering, we often had two or three parties on the same day. But busy as I was, I never allowed business to get in the way of my own personal Christmas festivities. I always found the time to bake my own cookies, make food gifts, send out cards, and put up the tree. How? I baked cookies before the holiday rush began and froze them. I made food gifts that improved with aging, like flavored vinegars. I bought Christmas cards the first week they appeared in stores, and addressed them on lazy October afternoons or while trapped on long airplane flights between coast-to-coast cooking classes. And how did I put up the tree? I threw an annual tree trimming. I would much rather make a buffet meal (of easy, never-fail recipes that I've included in this book) for my friends than fret over hanging the ornaments.

Too many people think of these recipes as strictly holiday fare. O.K.—maybe you don't want to serve fruitcake at a Fourth of July bash, but there are plenty of other dishes here to use for year-round entertaining. Everyone should have a recipe for a great baked ham or a roast tenderloin for buffets. The appetizers in this book would be welcome at any party. And the tips on how to turn out dozens of cookies without stress will come in handy whenever you have a cookie craving.

It is not the goal of this book to be a complete holiday cookbook—to include all of the traditional Christmas and New Year's foods cooked around the world would take volumes. The recipes are for my favorite holiday foods in time-tested versions that I have served to catering clients, cooking class students, and friends for years. Some recipes are labeled "101." These are basic recipes that I explain in depth, just as if you were taking one of my cooking classes. Also, I am fascinated with how our culinary traditions developed. In the sections entitled "It Wouldn't Be the Holidays Without . . ." you'll find out why we eat the things we do during the holidays.

This is also a somewhat personal book, as I have been influenced by the recipes and traditions of my family and friends. If you have a family favorite that isn't included here, I hope it motivates you to get the recipe from your elders and start your own holiday collection. Don't be one of those people who regret not getting Aunt Zelda's cookie recipe! Ask her. That is the only way these wonderful traditions are passed along.

Making a List and Checking It Twice

*O*rganization is a skill I developed as a caterer. The holiday season was our busiest time. We catered every kind of party from corporate cocktail bashes, to celebrity-studded open houses, to tree trimmings (once a hostess insisted that the children decorate cookies to hang on the tree—nice idea, but what a mess!), to elegant sit-down dinners. We often had two or three parties on the same day, so each one had to be organized to the last frilled toothpick. Lists saved the day.

No matter what kind of party you are giving, a series of lists will help you breeze through the process. Every time you mark a chore off the list, you will get a rewarding sense of accomplishment. And if you look at a list and feel overwhelmed, pick up the phone and get a friend to give you a hand! Here are the lists that I use again and again.

- Guest List: If you are having a large holiday season party, send out invitations as early as possible, no later than three weeks beforehand. Very often, guests will receive multiple invitations for the same evening, so get your claim in first. The most popular dates seem to fall on the two weekends before Christmas. (The weekend before Christmas, many prospective guests are already traveling to visit their families.) We usually give our holiday party the week between Christmas and New Year's, or sometimes even up to Epiphany, on January 6. This avoids the usual holiday party snafu, and we get a lot more acceptances. If necessary, send maps to the party with the invitations so you don't have to spend time on the phone giving directions the afternoon of the event.

Plan on making follow-up calls to get an accurate guest count. Lately, even with an RSVP, people just aren't very good about confirming invitations.

- Grocery Lists: For every large party, be it a buffet, cocktail gathering, or dinner party, make at least three grocery lists and a beverage list. This way you're not stuck doing a huge amount of shopping at the last minute. Also, try to shop during off hours. Especially during the last couple of holiday season weekends, it is usually less crowded at the supermarket on Friday night at 10 P.M. than on early Saturday morning. When you write down your grocery items, organize them by category so you don't have to retrace your steps because you forgot something across the store.

The first grocery list is for nonperishable items that can be purchased two to three weeks ahead of the party. This includes candles, coffee filters, guest towels and soap, camera film, paper towels, aluminum foil, plastic wrap, bathroom tissues, and other incidentals. Buy coffee and freeze it. As I will be doing a lot of baking, I buy flour, sugar (granulated, brown, and confectioners'), eggs, vanilla, ground cinnamon, active dry yeast, and other common baking ingredients to have on hand. This way, if I have some time and the mood strikes, I don't have to go running out for staples—I just preheat the oven and stir up some dough.

The second grocery list is for a few days before the party and is more specific. Buy all the produce that will keep for a week (like onions, potatoes, garlic, lemons, and limes), dairy items (cheese, cream, and milk, and more butter and eggs if you need them), and canned goods. If necessary, order special ingredients like prime grade meat, fresh goose, seafood, or caviar. Call the bakery to reserve rolls, cookies, cakes, and pies (if you aren't baking them yourself).

The last grocery list is for the day before the party. Now you will need to get the meats, seafood, produce items, and ice that you'll need. I usually buy my produce at a greengrocer—it's less crowded and the quality is higher than many supermarkets.

Holiday recipes call for the very best ingredients. Baked goods, in particular, require high-quality candied fruits, nuts, and chocolate. If you need to mail-order ingredients, or make a detour to a specialty shop, write a separate list for them. For example, I have a favorite shop that makes wonderful hard candies and sells great candied fruit and another that provides me with perfect walnut halves—they're out of my way, but if I anticipate what I need, I can stop by when in their neighborhoods.

The beverage list includes all drinks, alcoholic

or not. If you live in a state that sells liquor in grocery stores, put it with the second list. Otherwise, don't forget to include nonalcoholic drinks and mixers on your first grocery list. And don't forget to add drink garnishes like cinnamon sticks or whole nutmegs.

- Prep Lists: There are a lot of cooking chores that can be done well ahead of time. Look at your menu for potential freezable items. I am not a big "freezer person," but I do freeze a few quarts of homemade stock.

Many cookie crusts need to be chilled for a few hours or overnight before rolling out. This can actually be a boon, as it allows a window of opportunity to bake other cookies that don't need prechilling.

Be realistic about how much time it will take for you to make something. Only you know how fast you can roll out and decorate cookie dough. And schedule in cleaning time. It is much easier to clean as you go along than to wait until the dishes are piled so high you can't stand it anymore.

- Utensil Lists: When I was a beginning cook, I was pretty enthusiastic and very often jumped into a recipe before checking to be sure if I had the right utensils or serving dishes. Sometimes the recipe turned out, and sometimes . . . not. The same thing happened when I designed an overly ambitious menu, and found myself trying to make a sauce in a skillet because all of the saucepans were already filled.

Make a list of all the pots, pans, basters, roasting racks, coffeemakers, and baking dishes you'll need to make the food for your party. If you're baking cookies, take stock of your cookie cutters, decorating bags and tips, and cookie sheets (you can never have too many of these during the holiday baking season). I have tried to use pots and pans found in typical kitchens, but if a recipe calls for something out of the ordinary, it says so in the headnote. You may have to go to a kitchenware shop or a mail-order source for a couple of items, but then you will have them for future holiday celebrations.

- Tableware List: At the top of the list is a healthy supply of large, self-sealing plastic bags to store cookies and other baked goods. When I throw a party, I use them to store food in the refrigerator instead of bowls, which take up too much refrigerator space.

Check that you have all the serving dishes and utensils you need for your party. Many items are probably stored away, so take them out and wash them. To keep all of these bowls and platters straight, list what food goes in what dish. If silver has to be polished or linens washed and pressed, schedule those jobs well ahead of time.

If you don't have enough china and silver, purchase high-quality disposable plates and utensils at a party-supply shop. Buy the good stuff—you really don't want your plate to collapse under the weight of the food. A few years ago, I bought inexpensive dishes and flatware at a restaurant supply shop, and they have paid for themselves many times over. Sure, you don't have to wash the disposable stuff, but my ecological conscience tells me that it's not so hard to wash plates and forks. And at a buffet, where you sometimes balance food on your lap, a disposable plate can't hold a candle to a sturdy glass or china one. In a pinch, I'll use plastic cups (or heatproof ones for hot drinks), but I still prefer my stash of cheap restaurant-quality glassware and coffee mugs. You can always borrow what you need from family or friends, or rent them. Most rental companies have a minimum charge during the holidays. It might seem excessive, but if you factor in convenience, it may not seem so expensive after all.

For a multi-dish dinner party or buffet table, draw a "map" that shows where the serving dishes and centerpiece will go so as to be sure that everything will fit. If it doesn't, figure out where you will put the excess. At my house, I have found that I have more room if I put the plates on a sideboard, and the silverware (which has been rolled up inside the napkins) goes at the end of the buffet, so guests don't have to juggle it while filling their plates. If you are serving a crowd at a buffet, pull the table away from the wall, if necessary, so guests can serve themselves from both sides, and put two utensils in each bowl for faster service.

- The Bill of Fare: Always write out the complete menu, including beverages, and tape it in a prominent space in the kitchen to be sure that everything is served. In the fray of a big party, it is easy to forget to put something out. For a large dinner party with dishes that require final preparations, I make a timetable (see Holiday Menu Planner on page 149). I even put down "Make coffee and tea" on the timetable as a reminder.

I have also started a new tradition. A friend gave me some blank engraved menu cards. In addition to the scribbled menu in the kitchen, I now inscribe the complete menu in my best handwriting, and place it on a stand in the dining room. It's a nice touch, and my guests enjoy knowing the "official" names of the dishes. (My friend Charlie is handy with a computer, and when you go to his house for dinner, each place setting has an elegantly printed menu. Now, that's class!)

When planning a menu, be realistic about what you can prepare and store. Don't become a victim of what I call "TV-itis." That's where someone who watches television cooking shows where the chefs prepare an elaborate dish thinks he or she can pull off the same dish with the same ease. What you don't see on these shows is the crews of helpers backstage chopping and mincing and cleaning up!

A common dinner party problem is having too many side dishes that need to be heated in the oven. (Not everyone has a double oven.) To avoid an oven traffic jam, balance the baked side dishes with those that can be prepared on the stovetop. Also for a buffet, it's easy to prepare too many dishes that need refrigeration. If necessary, plan to borrow refrigerator space from a neighbor. (Occasionally, when the weather is cold, I turn my terrace into a walk-in refrigerator and chill some food outside, but that's not for all climates, and if there's a warm spell, I'm in trouble.) So be practical and design a menu that works for your kitchen and your cooking skills.

Decking the Halls

During the holidays, everyone wants his or her home to look like it came out of the pages of a glossy lifestyle magazine. But my strengths lie in the kitchen. You won't find me making papier-mâché Nativity scenes or hot-gluing Styrofoam reindeer. But if you can fit craft projects into your schedule, be my guest.

When it comes to holiday decorating, if it can't be done simply and quickly, I don't do it. One of my easiest and most effective centerpieces is a large glass bowl of red and green apples, entwined with colorful French wired ribbon. The guests can eat the apples, but there are usually some left over to turn into apple pie or applesauce later. Clementines, which are in season in December, look great in a bowl decorated with metallic gold ribbon.

A quick stop at the florist shop will give you lots of ideas. Take advantage of seasonal plants and greens: It's amazing what can be done with reasonably priced poinsettias, holly, mistletoe, and sprigs of pine. Please remember that the first three plants are poisonous, so don't use them to decorate food platters! To be safe, I don't put them anywhere near food. And if you plan to use evergreen boughs anywhere near a lighted candle, spray the greens with fire retardant (available at hobby shops and nurseries). My florist also sells me large bows of red ribbon (he calls them "church pew bows") that I wire to the stairway banister. Professionally tied and inexpensive, they look a lot better than anything I could come up with myself. If I store them properly, I can get a couple of years' use out of them.

Don't your friends comment when they walk into your home on the mouthwatering aroma of a roasting turkey or prime rib? Your house should smell delicious; it sets the scene for good food. When I am having a cocktail buffet, a lot of the cooking is done already, so there won't be enticing kitchen aromas. To compensate, I simmer a handful of spices (cinnamon sticks, allspice berries, cloves, and freshly sliced ginger) in a pot of water, allowing their scent to waft through the house. At the very least, I sprinkle room-scenting oil on a few light bulbs (the heat of the bulb warms the oil and disperses the scent). You'll find a selection of room-scenting oils at bathware shops, such as Crabtree & Evelyn. Many of these oils are designed specifically for the holidays and have evergreen or spice scents. Scented bayberry candles also do the trick. My own taste runs to the spicy or herbaceous—I don't like anything too sweet.

The lighting of your party location is important. Strings of twinkle lights are festive, but test the lights before you hang them and replace any bulbs as needed. Use lots of candles to give the room a glow. Make sure to use dripless candles. I have seen plenty of furniture ruined by a lava flow of dyed hot wax. One of my catering clients always replaced a few of the light bulbs in her lamps with soft-pink bulbs. She claimed it not only made the room more romantic, but it made everyone look fabulous, too. She was right.

Even Santa Has Elves

The upside of having a big holiday party is enjoying the company of your friends in your festive, seasonally decorated home. The downside is cleaning the house and putting up the decorations. Make a list of all the chores, from cleaning the windows to taking the Christmas decoration boxes out of storage.

I also firmly believe in letting friends help out. When I bake cookies, it is usually with my friend Diane by my side. With four hands, we can really crank out a stack of cookies. However, I have learned for myself that potlucks don't work because my buddies rarely bring what they were asked to bring. ("I really tried to get to the bakery and pick up the cake you asked for, but Santa twisted his ankle when he came down the chimney, and we had to take him to the emergency room, so I bought this bottle of wine instead.") What I really need is someone to come over the night before a party and keep me company while I cook. Of course, they are asked to chop an onion or two or wash a few dishes during the visit, but it really helps me keep things under control.

But whenever I need serious help, I dig into my pockets to pay for it. When I budget my holiday bash, I hire a maid service to come in a day or two before to vacuum, dust, and do all the other mundane cleaning that I just can't find the time to do. If you don't want to call a maid service from the phone book, check with your local college to see if they have a temporary employment office, or hire a neighbor's kid.

If you are really pressed for time, remember the dictum I learned from Peg Bracken (the original "I Hate to Cook" lady) a long time ago: Clean the bathroom really well and be sure to shine the faucets. If the bathroom faucets sparkle, everyone will think you're a great housekeeper. If you use enough candles and turn the lights low enough, they'll never see the dust in the living room.

If you're having a large party, try to budget a wait staff. For a party of thirty or less, you'll only need one person, but what a help that can be. Your waitron (a nonspecific-gender term that my friends and I invented when we were waiters and waitresses ourselves) can help answer the door, hang coats, pick up dirty glasses and dishes, warm things up, make drinks, keep the kitchen tidy, and do other little things that keep you from enjoying your guests. It is money well spent. Make another list of the duties you expect them to perform. I live in the New York area, where people are used to seeing wait staff at parties. If you feel it is a little pretentious, why not hire someone familiar, like that neighbor's kid (just be sure they're over drinking age if you expect them to handle alcohol). I hate having to face a dirty house after a party. My Christmas gift to myself is waking up after a big party to a clean house.

Appetizers, Snacks, and Beverages

'Tis the Season to Party

$\mathcal{I}$t's the holiday season, and that means lots of parties—especially big cocktail parties. Be it the "let's have everyone in the office over for a drink" get-together to the New Year's Eve bash, I will throw a Yuletide cocktail party at the drop of a paper hat. As a caterer, I have learned some pretty specific rules about what makes a good one. First of all, a good party is one that the host actually attends. To be specific, he is *not* buried in the kitchen, heating up little itty-bitty appetizers, arranging them artistically on platters.

In my catering days, I was paid handsomely to create intricate hors d'oeuvres, but my days of piping goat cheese into snow peas are over. If you hire a caterer with a full service staff, then you can relax with your friends while the help is working in the kitchen and passing those doggone hors d'oeuvres. But if you're making and serving the food yourself, you'd better take a different approach.

Prepare lots of easy-to-make appetizers with bold flavors that go well with beverages, whether they're cocktails, beer, wine, or nonalcoholic drinks. Choose make-ahead recipes that can be easily multiplied into larger quantities. Banish any food that must be passed—especially hot appetizers that are only good if they are served warm from the oven. Serve big bowls of wonderfully tasty food to which people can help themselves: warm dips, savory spreads, spiced nuts, smooth-and-nutty cheese balls, crunchy snacks like my Santa Fe Crunch, flaky cheese straws, slow cookers filled with meatballs.

Fill out the menu with a baked ham or roast turkey, an overflowing basket of fresh rolls, and condiments like honey mustard and mango chutney, so the guests can make their own sandwiches. Serve one or two salads, something substantial like Tortellini Antipasto Salad, and another salad on the light side, such as Real Ambrosia. To cut down on washing plates, make desserts that can be eaten out of hand, like homemade cookies or gingerbread. With this kind of a menu, all you need to do is fill up bowls and replenish platters every now and then.

Take a similar approach with the bar. You can be a bartender or a host. It's one thing to put out a few bottles of liquor and mixers and let your guests make their own drinks. It's another to pull out the blender, just in case someone wants a Margarita. (Once they hear that blender going, you may be making Margaritas all night.)

Holiday parties should have holiday drinks. Always serve at least one seasonal beverage, like ice-cold eggnog or warm mulled wine, and make that the evening's specialty of the house. (I love Christmastime beverages so much, I usually make one cold and one warm drink.) Because you are legally responsible for your guests' alcoholic intake, pay as much attention to your nonalcoholic beverages as the liquor. So designated drivers don't feel left out, make the nonalcoholic Cider Wassail, or serve chilled sparkling cider in champagne glasses.

A lot of wine and champagne is poured during the holiday season. For a large party, it isn't easy to find someplace to chill a case or two. The worst place is in the refrigerator, because the bottles just take up too much room. Many kitchenware shops and hardware stores have large attractive copper or galvanized tubs that will hold plenty of bottles. If you like to give parties, these tubs are a very good investment, and can also be used in the summertime to hold beer at your barbecue. In a pinch, I have lined the champagne's cardboard cases with heavy-duty garbage bags, replaced the bottles in the cases, and filled them with ice. Place the ice-filled boxes someplace like an auxiliary sink or bathtub, where they can drip without causing a dangerous puddle. Don't forget to order and pick up plenty of ice.

There are a few cocktail party logistics that are commonly overlooked and should be addressed.

- Be sure you have enough space to hang coats. You may have to rent or borrow a coat rack.

- If parking might be a problem, talk to your neighbors before the party to see if you can work out a solution. (If you ask really nicely or bring them a box of your homemade cookies, they might let you use some of their parking area.)

- Remove all of the furniture you can from the main gathering rooms, or at least rearrange it so the room can accommodate more people. Guests expect to stand at a cocktail party, and they can circulate more easily if they aren't tripping over the ottoman.

- Buy lots of cocktail napkins—you'll need some for the appetizers, and extra as coasters. Don't let your guests look all over for napkins, or you'll end up with ring marks on your tables.

- Keep the phone number of a taxi or car service handy, and use it to send any overindulgent, driving friends home in style.

Brie and Wild Mushroom Fondue Dip

Makes about 12 appetizer servings

Make Ahead: The fondue can be prepared up to 1 day ahead, cooled, covered, and refrigerated. Reheat in a double boiler over simmering water, stirring often.

Everyone loves fondue. A regular fondue pot is a nice utensil when you're serving fondue for dinner, but a slow cooker or electric fondue pot is the best way to serve this hot dip at a party. (The alcohol burner in a conventional fondue pot burns the cheese mixture on the bottom if the fondue isn't stirred often.) That being said, you can't lose with this new-wave fondue. Instead of bread (b-o-r-i-n-g), offer a more colorful, filling spread of vegetables and cooked meats for dipping. You don't need to provide fondue forks, as long as the pieces of food are big enough to hold on to.

- *All of the components for this dish can be prepared ahead of time, but heat the fondue just before the guests arrive.*

- *It is important to use a crisp, acidic, dry white wine when making fondue. A chemical reaction between the wine's acid and the cheese proteins allows the cheese to melt more smoothly. Most fondue recipes also include vinegar or lemon juice to ensure additional acid. Semidry, soft wines (such as Riesling or even some Chardonnays) don't contain enough acid.*

- *Asparagus and broccoli will have a better texture and color if parcooked until crisp-tender. Trim the asparagus, discarding the woody stems. Cut the broccoli into florets, discarding the thick stems (or save them for another use, if desired). Cook the vegetables separately in a pot of lightly salted boiling water until crisp-tender, 3 to 5 minutes, depending on the thickness of the spears. Rinse under cold running water. Pat dry with paper towels. Wrap separately in dry paper towels and store in self-sealing plastic bags in the refrigerator for up to 1 day.*

• *The amount of cornstarch needed to thicken the fondue depends on the brand of Brie. If the fondue seems a little thin after it comes to a simmer, sprinkle 1 tablespoon of cornstarch over 2 tablespoons of water and stir to dissolve. Gradually stir the dissolved cornstarch into the simmering fondue until it reaches the desired consistency.*

Fondue

1½ ounces dried porcini mushrooms, quickly
  rinsed under cold water

2 tablespoons unsalted butter

12 ounces shiitake mushrooms, stems discarded,
  rinsed and finely chopped

3 tablespoons chopped shallots

1½ cups dry white wine, such as Sauvignon Blanc
  or Pinot Grigio

1½ tablespoons white wine vinegar

1½ pounds ripe Brie, well chilled, rind trimmed
  and discarded, cut into small cubes (about
  3 cups)

3 tablespoons cornstarch

Freshly milled black pepper

Dipping Ingredients

Cooked chicken breast cubes

Cooked medium shrimp, peeled and deveined,
  with the tail segment left on

Parcooked asparagus spears

Parcooked broccoli florets

Cooked small new potatoes

Raw mushroom caps

Baguettes, cut on the diagonal into long,
  ¼-inch thick ovals

1. In a small bowl, cover the dried mushrooms with 1½ cups boiling water. Let stand until the mushrooms soften, about 20 minutes. Lift the mushrooms out of the soaking water, rinse to remove any grit, and finely chop. Set the chopped mushrooms aside. Strain the soaking water through a wire sieve lined with wet paper towels and set aside.

2. In a large saucepan, heat the butter over medium heat. Add the chopped shiitakes and cook, stirring often, until softened, about 5 minutes. Add the shallots and cook until softened, about 1 minute. Add the reserved porcini mushrooms and their soaking liquid and increase the heat to high. Cook until the liquid evaporates, about 7 minutes.

3. Stir in the wine and vinegar, and bring to a simmer over medium heat. In a large bowl, toss the Brie with the cornstarch. In three additions, add the cheese to the saucepan, stirring constantly until the first batch is almost completely melted before adding another. Using a whisk, briskly whisk the last addition until smooth. Allow the fondue to come to a bare simmer, but do not boil. Season with pepper to taste. Transfer to a 2-quart mini–slow cooker or electric fondue pot on low and keep warm. Serve with the dipping ingredients, occasionally stirring the fondue. (The fondue can be prepared up to 1 day ahead, cooled, covered, and refrigerated. Reheat in a double boiler over simmering water, stirring often.)

 ## Caesar Dip with Crudités

Makes about 12 appetizer servings

Make Ahead: The dip can be prepared up to 3 days ahead, covered, and refrigerated. The vegetables can be prepared up to 1 day ahead, wrapped in moist paper towels, stored in self-sealing plastic bags, and refrigerated.

Thick, cheesy Caesar salad dressing seemed a natural to turn into a dip. But when I was researching the original dressing recipe, I found out a fascinating fact. Caesar salad was originally served with uncut romaine lettuce hearts because it was meant to be eaten with the fingers! This dip is just as good with other vegetables. If you wish, serve it with Garlic Crostini, too. They'll remind you of the croutons served on Caesar salad.

Dip

1 cup mayonnaise
½ cup sour cream
½ cup freshly grated Parmesan or
   pecorino romano cheese
1 tablespoon fresh lemon juice
½ teaspoon anchovy paste
1 garlic clove, crushed through a press

Crudités

Assorted fresh vegetables, such as romaine lettuce
   hearts separated into leaves, carrot, celery, and
   cucumber sticks, mushroom caps, and cherry
   tomatoes, and Garlic Crostini (page 13),
   for dipping

1. To make the dip, mix all the ingredients in a medium bowl. Cover and chill for at least 1 hour before serving. (The dip can be prepared up to 3 days before serving.)
2. To serve, transfer the dip to a serving bowl and serve with the vegetables.

 ## Sicilian Caponata with Garlic Crostini

Makes about 16 appetizer servings

Make Ahead: The caponata can be prepared 3 days ahead. The toasts can be prepared up to 8 hours ahead.

There are many ways to make caponata, the Sicilian vegetable spread, but the recipe should always include the capers that give the dish its name. It partners effortlessly with just about any cracker or bread. I make Garlic Crostini because I like the crunch, but untoasted bread is fine, too. Leftover caponata can be tossed with spaghetti for a quick supper (bring the caponata to room temperature so it doesn't cool the hot pasta).

Caponata

1 large eggplant, cut into ¾-inch cubes
Salt
½ cup extra virgin olive oil, approximately
1 large onion, chopped
3 medium carrots, chopped into ½-inch
   pieces
3 medium celery ribs, chopped into ½-inch
   pieces
2 medium zucchini, cut into ½-inch pieces
1 large red bell pepper, cored, seeded, and
   cut into ½-inch pieces
3 garlic cloves, minced
One 28-ounce can tomatoes in juice,
   chopped, juices reserved
2 tablespoons red wine vinegar
2 tablespoons sugar
1 teaspoon dried basil
½ teaspoon dried oregano
½ teaspoon dried thyme
¼ teaspoon crushed hot red pepper

½ cup pitted, chopped Mediterranean black
  or green olives (or use both)
3 tablespoons capers, drained, rinsed, and
  chopped, if large

Garlic Crostini
2 loaves baguette-shaped French or Italian bread,
  sliced ¼ inch thick
⅓ cup extra virgin olive oil
2 garlic cloves, crushed

⅓ cup pine nuts (optional)

1. To make the caponata, toss the eggplant with 1 tablespoon salt in a colander. Let stand in a sink to drain off the bitter juices, about 1 hour. Rinse very well, then pat dry with paper towels.

2. Meanwhile, in a large, heavy-bottomed pot, heat 3 tablespoons of the oil over medium heat. Add the onion, carrots, celery, zucchini, and bell pepper and cook, stirring often, until the vegetables are softened, about 10 minutes. Stir in the garlic and cook for 2 minutes. Add the tomatoes with their juices, the vinegar, sugar, basil, oregano, thyme, and crushed red pepper. Bring to a simmer and remove from the heat.

3. Meanwhile, in a large nonstick skillet, heat the remaining 5 tablespoons oil over medium-high heat until very hot but not smoking. Add the eggplant and cook, turning occasionally, until browned, about 6 minutes, adding more oil if needed. Stir into the tomato sauce.

4. Bring the vegetables to a simmer over medium heat. Reduce the heat to medium-low and simmer, uncovered, stirring occasionally, until the vegetables are very tender, about 30 minutes. During the last 5 minutes, stir in the olives and capers. Remove from the heat and cool completely. (The caponata can be prepared up to 3 days ahead, covered with plastic wrap, and refrigerated. Remove from the refrigerator 1 hour before serving.) Season with salt.

5. To make the crostini, position the racks in the center and top third of the oven and preheat to 400°F. In a small saucepan, heat the oil and crushed garlic over low heat just until bubbles surround the garlic, about 5 minutes; do not brown the garlic. Remove from the heat and let stand for 10 minutes. Using a slotted spoon, discard the garlic.

6. Arrange the sliced bread on baking sheets. Brush the bread with the garlic oil. Bake, switching the position of the baking sheets from top to bottom and back to front halfway through the baking time, until the toasts are golden brown, about 10 minutes. Cool on the baking sheets. (The toasts can be prepared up to 8 hours ahead, stored in a paper bag. Do not store in a plastic bag, which will soften the toasts.)

7. To serve, transfer the caponata to a serving bowl and sprinkle with the pine nuts, if desired. Serve with the crostini.

 ## Stilton and Walnut Ball

Makes 12 to 16 appetizer servings

Make Ahead: The cheese ball can be prepared up to 5 days ahead.

Cheese balls aren't supposed to be classy, just delicious, but this one has a very sophisticated combination of flavors. It goes well with plain water crackers, but it is also terrific spread on sliced pears.

8 ounces Stilton, or other blue cheese,
   rind removed, at room temperature
8 ounces cream cheese, at room temperature
2 tablespoons tawny port
¼ teaspoon freshly milled black pepper
1 cup walnuts, toasted and coarsely chopped
Water crackers, for serving
Cored, sliced, ripe Bosc pears, tossed
   with lemon juice to discourage browning,
   for serving

1. In a medium bowl, using a rubber spatula, mash the Stilton and cream cheese until smooth. Work in the port and pepper. Place a piece of plastic wrap on the work surface, and scrape the cheese mixture into the center of the wrap. Use the plastic wrap to form the cheese mixture into a ball (it will be soft). Refrigerate until the ball is chilled and firm, at least 4 hours or overnight.
2. To serve, unwrap the ball and roll it in the chopped nuts. Transfer to a platter and serve with the crackers and pears.

 ## Sante Fe Crunch

Makes about 18 cups, 20 appetizer servings

Make Ahead: The crunch can be prepared up to 3 days ahead, stored in an airtight container.

You will probably recognize this as an updated version of that party mix that everyone loves. It's everything a snack should be—sweet, spicy, salty, crunchy, nutty, and altogether addictive. I mean, this stuff disappears!

4 tablespoons (½ stick) unsalted butter
¼ cup Worcestershire sauce
2 tablespoons light brown sugar
2 tablespoons chili powder
1 teaspoon salt
¼ teaspoon ground red (cayenne) pepper
One 12-ounce box oven-toasted square
   corn cereal
4 cups (8 ounces) mini-pretzels
2 cups (8 ounces) dry-roasted peanuts
2 cups (8 ounces) pecans
2 cups (6 ounces) pumpkin seeds

1. Position a rack in the center of the oven and preheat to 300°F. In a small saucepan, over medium-low heat, stir the butter, Worcestershire sauce, brown sugar, chili powder, salt, and red pepper until the butter is melted.
2. In a large roasting pan (such as a turkey roaster), toss the cereal, pretzels, peanuts, pecans, and pumpkin seeds, drizzling with the butter mixture to coat.
3. Bake stirring every 15 minutes, until heated through, about 1 hour. Cool completely. (The crunch can be prepared up to 3 days ahead, stored in an airtight container.)

Spicy Cheese Straws

Makes 40 straws

Make Ahead: The straws can be prepared up to 2 days ahead, stored in an airtight container. If desired, reheat and crisp in a preheated 350°F oven, uncovered, for 5 minutes.

These elegant and flaky cheese straws are another fast-and-easy favorite. With the help of frozen puff pastry dough, you'll have beautiful appetizers in no time—at a fraction of what the local bakery charges.

One 17¼-ounce package frozen puff pastry
1½ cups (6 ounces) shredded extra-sharp
** Cheddar**
½ cup freshly grated Parmesan
2 teaspoons chili powder
1 teaspoon dried oregano
¼ teaspoon garlic powder
¼ teaspoon salt
¼ teaspoon ground red (cayenne) pepper
1 large egg white, beaten until foamy

1. Thaw the puff pastry according to the package instructions. In a medium bowl, mix the Cheddar and Parmesan, chili powder, oregano, garlic powder, salt, and red pepper. Set the cheese mixture aside.

2. Position the racks in the center and top third of the oven and preheat to 375°F. Lightly grease two baking sheets or use ungreased nonstick sheets.

3. On a lightly floured work surface, unfold one sheet of pastry dough. Dust lightly with flour and roll it into a 14 × 10-inch rectangle. Brush lightly but thoroughly with the egg white. Cut the dough in half to make two 10 × 7-inch rectangles. Sprinkle half of the cheese mixture evenly over one of the rectangles. Top with the second

rectangle, egg-white side down. Lightly roll the pin over the dough to make the cheese adhere between the layers of dough.

4. Starting on a long side, using a ruler and pizza wheel or a sharp knife, cut the dough into twenty ½-inch wide strips. Twist the strips into spirals and place them ½ inch apart on the prepared (or nonstick) baking sheets, pressing the ends of the strips onto the sheets so the spirals won't untwist during baking. Repeat with the remaining dough, egg white, and cheese mixture.

5. Bake, switching the position of the sheets halfway through baking from top to bottom and front to back, until the straws are golden brown, about 20 minutes. Let cool for about 1 minute on the sheets, then immediately transfer to wire cooling racks. Cool completely. (The straws can be prepared up to 2 days ahead, stored in an airtight container. If desired, reheat and crisp in a preheated 350°F oven, uncovered, for 5 minutes.)

Blue Cheese Straws: Delete the chili powder, oregano, garlic powder, and salt. Substitute 1½ cups (6 ounces) blue cheese, well crumbled, for the Cheddar. Substitute ½ teaspoon freshly milled black pepper for the cayenne.

Greek Mini Meatballs

Makes about 100 meatballs, 16 to 24 servings

Make Ahead: The meatballs can be refrigerated up to 2 days ahead.

Do your friends like mini-meatballs as much as mine do? These have a slightly sweet sauce with a hint of cinnamon. If you have a good butcher who can provide you with lean ground lamb (ground lamb can be quite fatty), use it instead of the ground round. If you have any doubt about the lamb's fat content, ask the butcher to grind trimmed boneless leg of lamb. The fresh mint adds not only flavor but color. If you aren't a mint fan (although it is especially delicious with lamb meatballs), use parsley or even basil.

Sauce

3 tablespoons extra virgin olive oil
1 large onion, finely chopped
1 garlic clove, minced
One 28-ounce can tomatoes in thick tomato puree, pureed in a blender or food processor
2 tablespoons light brown sugar
2 tablespoons red wine vinegar
1½ teaspoons dried oregano
¼ teaspoon ground cinnamon
¼ teaspoon crushed hot red pepper

Meatballs

3 pounds ground round (85 percent lean) or lean ground lamb
1 medium onion, grated through the large holes of a box grater
2 garlic cloves, crushed through a press
¾ cup dried bread crumbs
2 large eggs, beaten

1 tablespoon dried oregano
1 tablespoon salt
¾ teaspoon freshly milled black pepper

¼ cup chopped fresh mint or parsley, for garnish (see Note)

1. To make the sauce, heat the oil in a large Dutch oven or saucepan over medium heat. Add the onion and cook, stirring often, until golden brown, about 8 minutes. (The onions should be cooked to a golden brown to bring out their natural sugars, but do not scorch them.) Stir in the garlic and cook until fragrant, about 30 seconds. Stir in the pureed tomatoes, brown sugar, vinegar, oregano, cinnamon, and crushed red pepper. Bring to a boil and reduce the heat to medium-low. Simmer, stirring often, until slightly thickened, about 30 minutes. Set the sauce aside.

2. Meanwhile, make the meatballs. Position the racks in the center and top third of the oven and preheat to 400°F.

3. In a large bowl, combine all of the meatball ingredients until well mixed (your hands will do the best job). Occasionally rinsing your hands in water, roll level tablespoons of the meat mixture into balls. Place the meatballs on nonstick rimmed baking sheets.

4. Bake until the meatballs are cooked through (cut into one to check), switching the position of the baking sheets from top to bottom and front to back halfway through baking, about 30 minutes. Stir the meatballs into the sauce. Stir in 2 tablespoons of the mint. Transfer to a large chafing dish or electric slow cooker. Sprinkle with the remaining mint and serve with toothpicks and a small bowl to collect the used toothpicks. (The meatballs and sauce can be prepared up to 2 days ahead, cooled, covered, and refrigerated. Stir ¼ cup water into the meatballs. Cover and cook over low heat, stirring often, until heated through, about 20 minutes.)

Note: To chop herbs for garnish, prepare them as close as possible to serving time or they may discolor. Rinse the herbs under cold water, pat dry with paper towels or spin in a salad spinner, then chop. If necessary, place the herbs in a small bowl, cover with a moist paper towel, and refrigerate until ready to use.

Old-Fashioned Eggnog

Makes 3 quarts, about 12 servings

Make Ahead: Eggnog should be chilled at least 4 hours before serving, and served within 24 hours.

Indulge in one of the Yuletide's greatest pleasures, and make this heady, creamy, from-scratch eggnog. I can't imagine giving one of my Christmas parties without a big bowl of nog—and, according to the evidence, neither can my friends. One year, instead of deleting it from the menu (because everyone was moaning about expanding waistlines), I compromised by making a half-batch, which disappeared quicker than an elephant at a magician's act in Las Vegas. It's so easy to make, why buy the supermarket variety?

- *To keep the eggnog cold, place a pint of vanilla ice cream in the punch bowl. It will slowly melt, and its flavor will complement the eggnog. Or for a break with tradition, try chocolate ice cream.*

- *This eggnog contains raw eggs, which have been known to contain the bacterium salmonella. When serving it, take these precautions: Purchase fresh eggs without any signs of cracks, and wash the eggs before using them. Do not serve eggnog to people with compromised immune systems. If you prefer, serve the New Wave Eggnog on page 18, which is made with cooked eggs, a step that kills the salmonella.*

6 large eggs, separated
1¼ cups superfine sugar (see Note)
1 cup dark rum
1 cup brandy
⅓ cup bourbon
1½ quarts heavy cream
1 pint vanilla ice cream, for serving
Freshly grated nutmeg, for serving

1. In a large bowl, using a hand-held electric mixer at high speed, beat the egg yolks and the sugar until thick. Beat in the rum, brandy, and bourbon, then the cream.

2. In another large bowl, using a hand-held electric mixer at high speed, and using clean beaters, beat the egg whites until soft peaks form. Stir into the eggnog. Cover tightly with plastic wrap and refrigerate until well chilled, at least 4 hours or overnight.

3. Transfer to a punch bowl. Using scissors, cut the container away from the ice cream, keeping the ice cream intact in one piece. Place the ice cream in the eggnog. Grate the nutmeg over the eggnog and serve immediately.

Amaretto Eggnog: Delete the bourbon. Substitute 1 cup Amaretto for the brandy. Decrease the superfine sugar to 1 cup. If desired, add ¼ teaspoon almond extract. When serving, substitute toasted almond ice cream for the vanilla ice cream.

Note: To make your own superfine sugar, process regular granulated sugar, about ½ cup at a time, in a food processor or blender until finely ground. It will take 1 to 2 minutes per batch.

New Wave Eggnog

Makes about 16 servings

Make Ahead: Eggnog should be chilled at least 4 hours before serving, and served within 24 hours.

This eggnog has an even creamier texture than the old-fashioned kind made with heavy cream. The cooked egg yolks make this the nog of choice for cooks who prefer to avoid raw eggs.

4 cups half-and-half or milk
1½ cups sugar
12 large egg yolks
½ cup dark rum
½ cup brandy
¼ cup bourbon

2 cups heavy cream
1 pint high-quality vanilla ice cream
Freshly grated nutmeg, for serving

1. In a medium saucepan over medium heat, stir the half-and-half with the sugar until the sugar dissolves and the mixture is hot. In a medium bowl, whisk the egg yolks. Gradually whisk in some of the hot mixture. Return to the saucepan and cook over low heat, stirring constantly, until the mixture is thick enough to coat a spoon (a thermometer will read 180°F), about 3 minutes. Strain into another medium bowl. Cool completely. Whisk in the rum, brandy, and bourbon. Cover and refrigerate until well chilled, at least 4 hours.

2. In a chilled, medium bowl, beat the heavy cream just until stiff. Fold into the chilled custard. Pour into a punch bowl and add the ice cream. Grate the nutmeg over the eggnog, and serve chilled.

🎄 Christmas at Grandma's 🎄

Grandma Perry's Christmas Eve buffet had a menu set in stone—baked ham, cold cuts, rolls, potato salad, macaroni salad, a mountain of Auntie Gisela's cookies, and of course, eggnog and Tom and Jerry. We had a very long night ahead of us, and we needed sustenance. We could eat all we wanted, but we weren't allowed to open presents until after midnight. Auntie Helen (in our family, the great-aunts were called Auntie) always sent over a newly packed jar of salty, Portuguese lupini beans, which she learned to make when she was a little girl in Waikiki. All the kids loved these beans, which are

covered with a thin skin. To eat them, you pinch the beans out of the skin, and with practice, you can shoot the beans across the room, preferably hitting a sibling or cousin.

At midnight, we had a special ceremony. Grandma's Nativity scene on the mantelpiece would be complete except for one thing—the figure of the Christ child would be missing from the manger. At the stroke of midnight, the youngest child in the family would be allowed to place the figurine in the crèche. We would sing "Silent Night," and the present opening would begin.

Grandma Perry's Tom and Jerry

Makes 10 servings

Make Ahead: The egg mixture can be prepared up to 4 hours ahead, covered, and refrigerated. Remove from the refrigerator 1 hour before using so it isn't ice cold, or the drinks will be tepid.

This is my family's traditional holiday drink. The best way to serve Tom and Jerrys is to make them one at a time. To warm the mugs, just fill them with hot tap water and let stand for a minute, then toss out the water. You can have a heated pot of milk ready on the stove, but I usually heat the milk as needed in the microwave.

• *Tom and Jerrys can also be served as a hot punch from a Tom and Jerry bowl ((I have an antique one just like Grandma's) or a soup tureen. Tom and Jerry bowls are beautiful, but they don't keep the drink warm without some electrical help. Place the bowl on a flat-topped hot plate (not the coil-burner type) set at the lowest setting. Don't let the hot milk punch stand for more than 2 hours, or the heat may curdle the milk and eggs. If necessary, make a couple of batches. Slow cookers, even set on Low, are too hot and encourage the curdling of the milk.*

6 large eggs, separated, at room temperature
3 cups confectioners' sugar
$1/3$ cup brandy
$1/3$ cup dark rum
2 quarts milk
Freshly grated nutmeg, for serving

1. In a large bowl, using a hand-held electric mixer at high speed, beat the egg yolks and confectioners' sugar until very thick and light colored, about 2 minutes.

2. In a grease-free large bowl, using a hand-held electric mixer at high speed, beat the egg whites until soft peaks form. Stir about one-fourth of the whites into the yolk mixture to lighten, then fold in the remaining whites, allowing some of the whites to stay fluffy. (The egg mixture can be prepared up to 4 hours ahead, covered, and refrigerated. Remove from the refrigerator 1 hour before using so it isn't ice cold, or the drinks will be tepid.)

3. To serve individually, place a heaping spoonful of the egg batter into a warm mug. Add about $1/2$ tablespoon each brandy and rum. Add enough piping-hot milk to fill the mug and stir gently. Sprinkle nutmeg over the top and serve hot.

4. To serve as a punch, in a large saucepan over medium heat, heat the milk until small bubbles appear around the edges. Gradually whisk about half of the hot milk into the egg mixture. Whisk the egg mixture into the pot. Stir in the brandy and rum. Heat gently, stirring constantly, just to bring up the temperature a little bit, about 1 minute. Do not heat too much, or the eggs will start to cook and thicken the milk. Immediately transfer the mixture to a warmed Tom and Jerry bowl or soup tureen. Sprinkle nutmeg over the top and serve warm.

Small Batch Tom and Jerry: In a small bowl, whisk $1/4$ cup confectioners' sugar with 1 egg yolk until thick. In another small bowl, using a clean whisk, whisk 1 egg white until soft peaks form. Stir the egg white into the yolk mixture, leaving some of the whites fluffy. Heat 2 cups milk until hot, either on top of the stove or in a microwave oven. Spoon half of the egg yolk mixture into a warmed large coffee mug. Stir in 1 tablespoon brandy or dark rum (or a splash of both). Fill with piping-hot milk and stir gently. Top with grated nutmeg. Serve immediately. Makes 2 drinks, either to serve seconds to yourself or to share with another person.

Rockin' Around the Christmas Tree

As any cocktail party host will tell you, the right music is as important as the food and drink. At other holiday parties, you can play whatever you like. (There is no actual Thanksgiving music, with the possible exception of "Alice's Restaurant," and no one will complain if you don't play "Stars and Stripes Forever" at your Fourth of July barbecue.) But Christmas carols are a huge part of the holiday experience, and should not be passed over just because a few of them are, well, not so bouncy.

Most traditional Christmas carols will slow a party down quicker than finding the family pet drinking out of the punch bowl. When I'm opening presents on Christmas morning, I'll put on "The Messiah," but a good party needs music that swings. Here are my favorites, guaranteed to get the party moving. (P.S. These are also great albums to have around when you need some motivation to whip through some gift wrapping.) It's a big variety, but different types of music will keep things interesting. There is hardly a slow song in the bunch—and if one shows up, just push "fast forward." So, stack these babies up in the CD player, and press the "random play" button. Now, hang the mistletoe, and get down with Santa!

Identifying numbers refer to compact disks, unless stated otherwise.

A Christmas Gift for You from Phil Spector (Rhino; RNCD 70235). A classic album of Christmas pop tunes from The Ronettes, Darlene Love, The Crystals, and friends.

Christmas Jollies (Right Stuff; 7243-8-53714-2-4). Wanna disco around the Christmas tree? The Salsoul Orchestra will have the crowd putting down their cider to do the hustle.

Ella Fitzgerald Wishes You a Swinging Christmas (Verve; ASIN B00000464M). Same to you, Ella. Upbeat versions of the favorites.

Jazz Piano Christmas (Dove; no ID number; call 1-800-328-DOVE). Originally broadcast over National Public Radio, this classy collection will provide a few quieter moments to balance out the music selection. *The* record to play if you are serving only Martinis in a Manhattan apartment overlooking a snowy Central Park.

Christmas Cocktails Part One (Capitol; CDP 7243 8 52559 2 2). Before Brian Setzer, there were great bands and singers recorded in fabulous high-fidelity sound. You're in Yulesville, baby!

Christmas Cocktails Part Two (Capitol; CDP 7243 8 21457 2 1). More of the same, even cooler.

Christmas Caravan (Mammoth; 35498-0192-2). The Squirrel Nut Zippers are proponents of the retro-urban-hillbilly sound, and their original Christmas songs have plenty of twang and Tabasco.

A Broadway Christmas (Varese Sarabande; tape, VSC-5517). Various Broadway and cabaret artists croon their way through a jolly bunch of Yuletide songs from the Great White Way.

Hot Buttered Rum

Makes 8 servings

Make Ahead: The spiced butter can be prepared up to 2 weeks ahead, covered, and refrigerated. Bring to room temperature before using.

To take the chill off a cold winter's night, there is nothing like hot buttered rum. The drink is usually made with boiling hot water, but you can use cider, too. It's nice to have a batch of spiced butter ready in the refrigerator for when friends drop by. Although I have rarely had a guest say no to a hot buttered rum, if there's any of the butter left over at the end of holiday season, it's delicious simply spread on toast.

8 tablespoons (1 stick) unsalted butter,
   at room temperature
¹⁄₂ cup packed light brown sugar

¹⁄₂ teaspoon ground cinnamon
¹⁄₄ teaspoon ground nutmeg
1 cup dark rum
6 cups boiling water, approximately
Cinnamon sticks, for garnish (optional)

1. In a medium bowl, using a hand-held electric mixer at high speed, beat the butter, brown sugar, cinnamon, and nutmeg until light in color and texture, about 2 minutes. (The spiced butter can be prepared up to 2 weeks ahead, transferred to a small covered container and refrigerated. Bring to room temperature before using.)

2. For each drink, place about 1¹⁄₂ tablespoons of the spiced butter into a mug. Add 3 tablespoons rum and enough boiling water (about ³⁄₄ cup) to almost fill the mug. If desired, garnish with a cinnamon stick. Using the cinnamon stick or a spoon, stir to dissolve the butter. Serve immediately.

☆ Tom and Jerrys for Everyone ☆

Proust had his madeleines, and I have my Tom and Jerrys. This warm, soothing milk drink, not unlike a hot eggnog, has always been my favorite holiday drink, probably because it was served without fail at my Grandma Perry's Christmas Eve parties. (The children's drinks were spiked with a drop of brandy extract.) One year my uncle mixed the egg batter so stiff that he burned out the electric hand mixer. My grandmother was pretty sore—this was not the first Christmas Eve this had happened. When we opened presents, luckily, Santa had thought ahead and brought her a new mixer that year. This magic absolutely convinced me of Santa's omnipotence. Every year, I mix up a small batch for myself, turn off all the lights except for the Christmas tree, and toast Grandma and the happy memories she helped create.

Cider Wassail

Makes 2½ quarts, 16 to 20 servings

Make Ahead: The wassail is best prepared just before serving.

Here's a wassail for today's tastes. This sherry-free version is sweeter and less bitter. The roasted apples are optional, but add a touch of authenticity. For a delicious nonalcoholic hot cider, just replace the ale with more apple juice.

**2 Granny Smith apples, peeled, cored, and
    each cut into 8 wedges**
2 lemons
4 quarter-sized pieces fresh ginger
12 allspice berries
6 whole cloves
Two 3-inch cinnamon sticks
Four 12-ounce bottles pale ale
1 quart fresh apple cider
½ cup packed light brown sugar

1. Position a rack in the center of the oven and preheat to 400°F. Lightly oil a nonstick baking sheet.

2. Spread the apples on the baking sheet. Bake, turning the apple slices halfway during baking, until the apples are lightly browned and tender, about 30 minutes. Set aside.

3. Meanwhile, using a vegetable peeler, remove the zest from one lemon. Rinse and wring out a 12-inch square piece of cheesecloth. Wrap the lemon zest, ginger, allspice, cloves, and cinnamon sticks in the cheesecloth and tie with a piece of kitchen string. Cut the lemons in half and squeeze the juice from the lemons. Set the juice aside.

4. In a large nonaluminum pot, combine the ale, cider, brown sugar, lemon juice, and the spice packet. Heat, stirring occasionally, over low heat until hot but not boiling, about 30 minutes. Transfer to a slow cooker set on Low and serve hot.

Nonalcoholic Wassail: Substitute an additional quart of apple juice for the ale.

Mulled Wine with Honey and Orange

Makes 2 quarts, about 16 servings

Make Ahead: The wine is best prepared just before serving.

There's mulled wine, and then there is this recipe. To be sure that the mulled wine is at its best, there are a few tips:
- *Use a fruity but full-bodied red wine. Merlot is my first choice, but Zinfandel or Cabernet Sauvignon also works. Beaujolais, while fruity, is too thin for my taste.*
- *Buy moderately priced wine, not cheap plonk. Your mulled wine will only be as good as its ingredients.*
- *Never let mulled wine come to a boil. Let it heat very slowly over low heat so the spices and orange zest release their flavors. A slow cooker on the Low setting is ideal.*

1 large seedless orange
12 whole cloves
12 allspice berries
Two 3-inch cinnamon sticks
3 cardamom pods, crushed (optional)
One 1½-liter bottle fruity red wine, such as Merlot
1 cup honey
**⅔ cup Grand Marnier or other orange-flavored
    liqueur**

1. Using a vegetable peeler, remove the zest from the orange. Rinse and wring out a 12-inch square piece of cheesecloth. Wrap the orange zest, cloves, allspice, cinnamon sticks, and cardamom, if using, in the cheesecloth and tie with a piece of kitchen string. Cut the orange in half and squeeze the juice from the orange. Set the juice aside.

2. In a large nonaluminum pot, combine the wine, honey, Grand Marnier, orange juice, and spice packet, stirring to dissolve the honey. Heat, stirring occasionally, over low heat until hot but not boiling, about 30 minutes. Transfer to a slow cooker set on Low and serve hot.

Christmas at the Movies

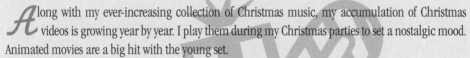

Along with my ever-increasing collection of Christmas music, my accumulation of Christmas videos is growing year by year. I play them during my Christmas parties to set a nostalgic mood. Animated movies are a big hit with the young set.

And when it's an adults-only gathering, there is always a group of grown-ups in the TV room to cheer when Kris Kringle wins his courtroom battle against Macy's or sniffle when Jimmy Stewart gathers with his family around the Christmas tree. For my holiday films, I prefer the older, black-and-white versions to any flashy, special effects—laden remakes. Here are the Christmas movies that never fail to put me in the holiday spirit.

A Charlie Brown Christmas. A little cutesy, but the Vince Girauldi soundtrack is timeless.

A Christmas Carol. The British version, starring Alistair Sim, has authentic Dickens flavor. Forget the updated version starring Bill Murray (*Scrooged*) or the musical with Albert Finney (*Scrooge*).

A Christmas Story. Just about everyone's favorite contemporary Christmas movie, with a skewed sense of humor mixed with a good dose of nostalgia. I'm a sucker for the scene where the dog eats the Christmas turkey.

Christmas in Connecticut. A sleeper from the mid-forties. Barbara Stanwyck plays a magazine food writer who can't boil water. Her unsuspecting editor invites a war hero to her country house to spend Christmas as a publicity stunt, and Barbara has to make like the perfect housemaker. Guess who falls in love with whom under the Christmas tree?

How the Grinch Stole Christmas. Boris Karloff narrates this Dr. Seuss classic for the baby boomers at the party.

It's a Wonderful Life. Before Tom Hanks, there was Jimmy Stewart to play Hollywood's Everyman. Have plenty of Kleenex handy when watching this heart-tugger.

Miracle on 34th Street. The original (with the young Natalie Wood playing the cynical little girl who doesn't believe in Santa Claus) is not only a great movie, but a lovely Christmas card to old New York.

The Nutcracker Ballet. The dancing is great, and the music isn't bad either. . . . Look for the Mikhail Barishnikov production.

It Wouldn't Be the Holidays Without . . . Champagne

Champagne is practically a synonym for celebration. When special friends get together to share a special occasion, a bottle of Champagne is usually included. During the holidays, there are many opportunities to sip a glass of bubbly, from a special holiday meal to a New Year's Eve toast. Not for nothing are caviar and Champagne a famous couple.

There are a few simple rules to buying Champagne. First, know where it comes from. Real Champagne, with its complex flavor and aroma, is made only in the Champagne region of France, not far from Paris. Even though we Americans use the word to describe any bubbling wine, the truth is, if it isn't *from* Champagne, it *isn't* real Champagne, and it must be labeled as sparkling wine. Some important names of the Champagne business include Moët & Chandon, Veuve Clicquot, and Bollinger. These are top of the line, and are worth every penny.

It is not just the grapes and the soil conditions that make Champagne special, but its painstaking, natural fermentation process. Called *méthode champenoise,* it is almost always indicated on the label. Sparkling wines made in other locations can still be made by the Champagne method. By contrast, cheap sparkling wines are injected with carbon dioxide to create the bubbles, and the results are dramatically different, to say the least.

There are less expensive, very good sparkling wines from France that are excellent bargains. (Not to be deceptive, but with their French labels, most guests will assume they are drinking the real thing.) Some of the French sparkling wines are called "blanc de blancs," which means that they are completely made from white, not red, grapes. ("Blanc de noirs," with a pink tinge, are made from red grapes.) Some Spanish sparkling wines are also good values. California makes some fine sparkling wines, many made by American divisions of European Champagne families, like Domaine Chandon.

There is only one way to buy Champagne or sparkling wine, and that is according to your budget. For a small party, go all out and buy the best you can afford. A larger event may call for some restraint. Consider the collective taste of your guest list, and if you think that a less expensive sparkling wine would be enjoyed as much as a pricey one, buy the cheaper variety. However, don't buy a very cheap sparkling wine just because you think you should have something bubbly. They just don't taste very good, and I don't care what anyone says, they can be responsible for some pretty nasty postparty hangovers.

If at all possible, serve your sparkling wine in glassware, not plastic. It makes a big difference in the tone of the party. If you don't feel like renting them, look in restaurant supply stores and price clubs and purchase a case or two. After a couple of annual parties, your initial investment will have paid off. I bought some at a postholiday sale many years ago, and have never regretted it.

It Wouldn't Be the Holidays Without . . . Christmas Punch

Alcoholic holiday beverages have their roots in pagan winter solstice celebrations, which were never abstemious affairs. Those beverages packed a punch, and their disorienting effect came to signify any heady, strong beverage.

The winter festivals lasted for a few weeks, and so did the partying. When Christianity overtook paganism, the old customs were applied to the new winter holiday, Christmas. But the pagans weren't about to trade a single-day holiday (and an alcohol-free "holy day," at that) for a monthlong party, so the tradition of the holiday season began. This eventually became the entire six-week period beginning with Advent Sunday (celebrating Christ's imminent birthday on the fourth Sunday before Christmas) and lasting until the Epiphany (also called Three Kings Day or Twelfth Night) on January 6. In fact, until the last 150 years or so, the Christmas season was abhorred by most religious leaders because it was marked by heavy drinking and general misbehavior. The Puritan movement was practically all about establishing the noncelebration of Christmas. It was only through a hard-fought campaign to bring children into the holiday and the establishment of the kindly Santa Claus in American culture that the image of the holiday began to soften. But we still love our glass of punch.

Eggnog is a close relative of the English "sack posset," a egg-and-dairy drink that could be made from a dry Spanish wine called sack, or from strong ale (also called "nog"). When the drink came over to America, the colonists substituted the more readily available rum and whiskey for sack.

Practically every northern European country has a version of *mulled wine,* where the wine is heated and flavored with spices. Most mulled wines are also fortified with liquor. For example, Swedish *glögg* is made with red wine and aquavit (talk about packing a punch!). "Mull" is an Old English word for dust, so mulled wine may mean "that which is dusted with spices."

The sugar trade was extremely important to the economy of the American colonies, and vast amounts of rum were distilled from molasses. *Hot buttered rum* became a favorite drink to chase away the winter chill.

Wassail is not just any old hot holiday beverage, but a very specific mixture of sherry and ale. The name comes from the old Anglo-Saxon greeting *was hale,* or "be hearty." It was originally topped with a garnish of toast, giving us the phrase "to drink a toast."

A number of bartenders claim the invention of the Tom and Jerry. In the 1820s, a British boxing expert wrote an immensely popular book, *Life in London, or the Days and Nights of Jerry Hawthorne and his Elegant Friend Corinthian Tom,* which many feel inspired the drink (which is not unlike a hot British posset). In America, "Professor" Jerry Thomas (who also lays disputed claim to the Martini) says that he invented the Tom and Jerry during his tenure at the El Dorado bar in San Francisco during the 1850s. Being a San Franciscan who grew up on very mildly spiked Tom and Jerrys, I'm in the Professor Thomas camp.

Salads, Soups, and Other First Courses

It Came Upon a First Course Clear

Holiday dinner parties are sumptuous affairs, usually centered around a huge roast, be it meat or fowl. For that reason, the first course, whether soup or salad, should be on the light side, or guests will quickly get overstuffed.

Because few Christmas or New Year's main courses are seafood, I often use fish or shellfish in the first course to balance the menu. If your guests include "seafood-phobes," prepare one of the salads or vegetable soups in this chapter.

The most important thing about choosing a dinner party first course is ease of preparation and serving. When serving salad, have the greens washed and ready to toss with the premade dressing. If your guests have a sweet tooth, a fruit ambrosia or Jell-O salad is the way to go. Some hearty diners would enjoy a pasta salad, and another meal opener could be a simple green salad garnished with orange slices and red onions. Also included in this chapter are salads that could do double duty on the buffet table.

Soup is an especially convenient first course because it can be made a day or so ahead of time and heated up before serving. Warm the soup tureen and soup bowls beforehand so the soup is served at its piping-hot best. Fill the tureen and bowls with hot tap water and let them stand for a few minutes. Pour out the water and dry the bowls. It's this little detail that makes the difference between hot and tepid food.

Crab Cakes on Baby Greens with Lemon Vinaigrette

Makes 10 servings

Make Ahead: The vinaigrette can be prepared up to 1 day ahead, covered, and refrigerated. The crab cakes can be prepared up to 4 hours ahead, covered, and refrigerated.

This contrast of crunchy, warm crab cakes with cool, crisp salad greens is an appetite-teasing first course that is hard to surpass. The main rule for making crab cakes is to remember that they should taste like crab, not bread crumbs. These delicious examples have just enough crumbs to hold them together. Search out the best fresh lump crabmeat available at the fish market, and don't use pasteurized or canned crab.

Lemon Vinaigrette

⅓ cup fresh lemon juice
1 tablespoon Dijon mustard
1 teaspoon sugar
½ teaspoon salt
¼ teaspoon freshly milled black pepper
1 cup olive oil
2 tablespoons minced shallots
1 teaspoon grated lemon zest

Crab Cakes

1 pound fresh lump or backfin crabmeat
¼ cup mayonnaise
¾ cup unseasoned dried bread crumbs
1 large egg, beaten
1 tablespoon chopped fresh chives
1 tablespoon Worcestershire sauce
1 tablespoon Dijon mustard

¼ teaspoon hot red pepper sauce
¼ cup vegetable oil

12 cups (about 10 ounces) mixed baby greens (mesclun)
Chopped fresh chives for garnish (optional)

1. To make the vinaigrette, combine the lemon juice, mustard, sugar, salt, and pepper in a blender. With the machine running, gradually add the oil in a slow stream. Transfer to a bowl. Stir in the shallots and lemon zest. (The vinaigrette can be prepared up to 1 day ahead, covered, and refrigerated. Blend again before using to thicken.)

2. To make the crab cakes, pick through the crabmeat to remove any cartilage or shell bits. Place in a medium bowl. Add the mayonnaise, ¼ cup of the bread crumbs, egg, chives, Worcestershire sauce, mustard, and red pepper sauce, and mix. Using a heaping tablespoon of crab mixture for each, form into 20 crabcakes. Place the remaining ½ cup bread crumbs in a shallow bowl. Coat each crabcake with bread crumbs, pressing to adhere. Place on a wax paper–lined baking sheet. (The crab cakes can be prepared up to 4 hours ahead, covered tightly with plastic wrap, and refrigerated.)

3. In a very large skillet (or in two medium skillets, using a bit more oil), heat the oil over medium heat until very hot but not smoking. Add the crab cakes and cook, turning once, until golden brown, about 5 minutes. Transfer to paper towels to drain briefly.

4. Toss the greens with 1 cup of the dressing. Divide the salad between large dinner plates, placing the salad to one side of the plate. Place 2 crab cakes on each plate opposite the greens. Drizzle about 2 teaspoons of the remaining dressing around each crab cake. Sprinkle with the chives, if desired. Serve immediately.

Scalloped Oysters with Mushrooms and Leeks

Makes 8 servings

Make Ahead: The bread cubes can be prepared, then stored in an airtight container at room temperature for up to 1 day. The vegetable mixture can be prepared up to 4 hours ahead, stored at room temperature.

While neither soup nor salad, scalloped oysters are a first-course mainstay of the Yankee holiday table. Raw oysters and other shellfish on the half shell show up at many Christmas dinners, but most of my friends prefer their bivalves cooked. Scalloped oysters are usually a very simple dish: creamed oysters layered with crumbled cracker crumbs, and not much else. This version is enhanced with mushrooms and leeks and buttery bread cubes. The dish should be assembled just before serving, but the components can be prepared ahead of time.

- *Instead of shucking fresh oysters, I use containers of preshucked oysters. Buy large, plump "select"-sized oysters. Smaller oysters may be overcooked by the time the cream comes to a boil in the oven.*

- *If you wish, bake the scalloped oysters in individual servings. Butter eight 1-cup ramekins or 1¼-cup (300 ml) large glass custard cups. Place a layer of bread cubes in the ramekins. Divide the oysters and mushroom mixture evenly among the ramekins. Pour in the heavy cream–oyster juice mixture. Top with equal amounts of bread cubes. Bake until the cream bubbles, about 15 minutes. Top with chopped parsley.*

- *Leeks are very sandy and need to be well rinsed. Trim the leeks, and chop the white and pale green parts only, discarding the leafy dark green tops. Place the chopped leeks in a wire sieve and rinse well under cold running water, rubbing the leeks between your fingers to separate and expose the layers to the water. Drain well.*

6 tablespoons unsalted butter

10 slices firm white sandwich bread, cut into ¼-inch cubes

12 ounces white mushrooms, sliced

1 large leek, chopped, white and pale green parts only (1 cup)

¼ teaspoon salt

¼ teaspoon freshly milled white pepper

1½ pints shucked "select" oysters

¾ cup heavy cream

Chopped fresh parsley, for garnish

1. Position a rack in the center of the oven and preheat to 375°F. Lightly butter an 11½ × 8-inch (2-quart) baking dish.

2. In a small saucepan over low heat, melt 4 tablespoons of the butter. In a 15½ × 10½-inch jelly-roll pan, toss the butter with the bread cubes. Bake, stirring occasionally, until the bread cubes are very lightly toasted and crisp, about 15 minutes. Set aside. (The bread cubes can be prepared, stored in an airtight container at room temperature for up to 1 day.)

3. In a large skillet, melt the remaining 2 tablespoons butter over medium heat. Add the mushrooms and cook until they give off their liquid, about 4 minutes. Stir in the leek, salt, and pepper. Cook until the leek softens and the mushroom liquid evaporates, about 4 more minutes. Transfer to a bowl and set aside. (The vegetable mixture can be prepared up to 4 hours ahead, cooled, covered, and stored at room temperature.)

4. In a large sieve or colander set over a bowl, drain the oysters, reserving the oyster liquid. In the same skillet, boil the oyster liquid over high heat, about 3 minutes. Stir in the heavy cream and set aside.

5. Layer half of the bread cubes in the bottom of the prepared dish. Top with the oysters, then the mushroom mixture. Pour over the heavy-cream mixture. Top with the remaining bread cubes. Place the dish on a baking sheet.

6. Bake until the cream bubbles and the oysters turn opaque, about 25 minutes. If the cubes are browning too deeply, cover loosely with aluminum foil.

7. To serve, spoon the scalloped oysters onto salad plates and sprinkle with the parsley. Serve hot.

 **Beet and Apple Salad**

Makes 8 servings

Make Ahead: The beets can be prepared up to 1 day ahead. The salad can be prepared 1 day ahead, covered, and refrigerated. Garnish with the cheese and nuts just before serving.

This is one of my most popular dinner party salads. Even people who think they do not like beets love it, which is understandable because roasted beets have it all over the canned variety. This salad has many different textures and flavors that meld together into a beautiful, crimson mélange.

Dressing
2 tablespoons balsamic vinegar
2 tablespoons cider vinegar
$^1/_2$ teaspoon sugar
$^1/_2$ teaspoon salt
$^1/_4$ teaspoon freshly milled black pepper
$^2/_3$ cup vegetable oil

3 large beets (about 2 pounds)
3 Granny Smith apples, peeled, cored, and
   chopped into $^1/_2$-inch dice
8 large red lettuce leaves
5 ounces Roquefort or blue cheese, crumbled
$^1/_2$ cup toasted, peeled, and coarsely chopped
   hazelnuts

1. To make the dressing, in a medium bowl, whisk the balsamic and cider vinegars, sugar, salt, and pepper. Gradually whisk in the oil. Cover and set aside at room temperature.

2. Preheat the oven to 400°F. If the beets have their greens attached, trim the greens, leaving about 1 inch of the stems attached to the beets. Scrub the beets under cold running water. Wrap each beet in aluminum foil and place on a baking sheet. Bake until the beets are tender when pierced with the tip of a long, sharp knife, about $1^1/_2$ hours, depending on the size of the beets. Cool completely, without unwrapping the beets.

3. Unwrap the beets and peel them. Cut into $^3/_4$-inch cubes. Place in a self-sealing plastic bag and refrigerate until chilled, at least 2 hours. (The beets can be prepared up to 1 day ahead.)

4. In a large bowl, toss the beets and apples with the dressing. (The salad can be prepared up to 1 day ahead, stored in self-sealing plastic bags, and refrigerated.) Place a lettuce leaf on each plate, and spoon the salad onto the lettuce. Top each salad with the cheese and walnuts. Serve chilled.

Salmon and Spinach Terrine with Cucumber-Dill Sauce

Makes 12 servings

Make Ahead: The terrine must be chilled at least 4 hours or overnight. It can be prepared up to 2 days ahead of serving, tightly covered, and refrigerated. The sauce can be prepared up to 1 day ahead, tightly covered, and refrigerated.

This is a gorgeous and elegant first course to serve at your finest dinner party. For a fancy appetizer, it comes together very quickly, and has the added attraction of being totally make-ahead. You can also serve it as a spread at a cocktail party.

1 tablespoon unsalted butter

3 tablespoons finely chopped shallots

$^1/_2$ cup dry vermouth

20 ounces skinless salmon fillets

4 ounces sea scallops

$^1/_2$ cup fresh bread crumbs (make in a food
   processor or blender)

1 large egg

$1^1/_4$ teaspoons salt

$^1/_4$ teaspoon freshly milled white pepper

$^1/_8$ teaspoon hot red pepper sauce

$1^1/_2$ cups heavy cream

One 10-ounce package frozen chopped spinach,
   thawed, squeezed well to remove liquid

Fresh watercress or dill sprigs, for garnish

Cucumber-Dill Sauce

1 medium cucumber, peeled, seeded, and
   cut into $^1/_4$-inch dice

Salt

$^3/_4$ cup sour cream

2 tablespoons milk

2 tablespoons chopped fresh dill

$^1/_8$ teaspoon freshly milled white pepper

1. Preheat the oven to 325°F. Lightly oil an $8^1/_2 \times 4^1/_2 \times 2^1/_2$-inch loaf pan. Line the bottom of the pan with wax paper. In a small saucepan, melt the butter over medium-low heat. Add the shallots and cook until softened, about 2 minutes. Add the vermouth and cook until reduced to 1 tablespoon; cool.

2. In a food processor, pulse the salmon and scallops until finely chopped. Add the shallot mixture, bread crumbs, egg, salt, white pepper, and red pepper sauce. With the machine running, gradually add the heavy cream. Transfer 1 cup puree to a medium bowl. Stir in the spinach.

3. Spread half of the salmon puree in the loaf pan, then spread with the spinach puree. Top with the remaining salmon puree. Cover with buttered wax paper, buttered side down.

4. Place the loaf pan in a larger roasting pan and place in the oven. Add enough hot water to the roasting pan to come $^1/_2$ inch up the sides of the loaf pan. Bake until an instant-read thermometer inserted in the center of the terrine registers 140°F, about 1 hour. Cool completely in the pan on a wire rack. Invert and remove the wax paper. Tightly wrap the terrine in plastic wrap. Refrigerate at least 4 hours or overnight.

5. Meanwhile, make the sauce. In a small bowl, toss the cucumber with $^1/_2$ teaspoon salt. Let stand for 30 minutes. Rinse well. Pat dry with paper towels. Squeeze the cucumber to remove excess moisture.

6. In a medium bowl, mix the cucumber, sour cream, milk, dill, and pepper. Season with salt to taste. Cover with plastic wrap and refrigerate until chilled, at least 1 hour.

7. Cut the terrine into 12 slices. Divide the slices between 12 dinner plates. Spoon equal amounts of the sauce next to each slice. Garnish with the watercress. Serve immediately.

Cauliflower Salad with Red Pesto Dressing

Makes 8 to 12 servings

Make Ahead: The salad can be prepared up to 1 day ahead, covered, and refrigerated.

Cauliflower is a useful winter vegetable that is very often (and unfairly) demoted to the side-dish category, where it can be treated with apathy. It makes a terrific salad that lives up to my strict standards for a buffet dish: It looks great, tastes great, and holds up well at room temperature.

Red Pesto Dressing

1 cup (6 ounces) oil-packed sun-dried tomatoes, drained
¼ cup balsamic vinegar
1 garlic clove, crushed through a press
¼ teaspoon salt
¼ teaspoon crushed hot red pepper
1 cup extra virgin olive oil

2 medium heads cauliflower (3 pounds total)
Chopped fresh parsley, for garnish

1. To make the dressing, place the sun-dried tomatoes, vinegar, garlic, salt, and crushed red pepper in a food processor fitted with the metal blade. With the machine running, gradually add oil in a thin stream, and process until the dressing is thick. Set aside.

2. Trim the cauliflower and cut into bite-sized florets. Bring a large pot of salted water to a boil over high heat. Add the cauliflower and cook until barely tender, 4 to 6 minutes. Rinse under cold water and drain well.

3. Transfer the cauliflower to a large bowl and toss with the dressing. Cover and refrigerate until chilled, at least 2 hours. Sprinkle with the parsley before serving.

Mushroom and Parmesan Salad

Makes 8 servings

Make Ahead: The dressing can be prepared up to 1 day ahead. Toss the salad just before serving.

Topped with curls of Parmesan cheese, this salad has a festive look especially suited for the holidays. For the best flavor, use only real Parmigiano-Reggiano cheese— look for the identifying stamp on the rind.

Dressing

⅓ cup fresh lemon juice
½ teaspoon salt
¼ teaspoon freshly milled black pepper
1¼ cups olive oil

2½ pounds fresh white mushrooms, thinly sliced
⅓ cup finely chopped shallots
2 tablespoons chopped fresh parsley
8 cups (about 7 ounces) mixed baby greens (mesclun)
One 4-ounce chunk Parmigiano-Reggiano cheese

1. To make the dressing, in a medium bowl, whisk the lemon juice, salt, and pepper. Gradually whisk in the oil. (The dressing can be prepared up to 1 day ahead, covered, and refrigerated. Whisk well before using.)

2. Just before serving, in a medium bowl, toss ¾ cup of the dressing with the mushrooms, shallots, and parsley. In a large bowl, toss the greens with the remaining ½ cup dressing. On each of 8 large plates, place portions of the mushroom salad and greens next to each other. Using a vegetable peeler, shave curls of Parmesan cheese over each salad. (You won't use all of the cheese, but you need a good-sized piece to make the curls.) Serve immediately.

It Wouldn't Be the Holidays Without . . . Caviar

Rare, costly, sublime—caviar is all of these. There are few foods that state elegance more implicitly.

True caviar from the Caspian Sea has become a holiday luxury because of its processing cycle. One catch takes place in October (the other in March), and it takes about a month to process and ship the caviar. Stored at perfect conditions (in a very narrow range of 28° to 32°F), it will remain fresh for about six months, or just in time for the next batch to arrive.

Caspian caviar is processed from sturgeon eggs; the variety of sturgeon designates the size, color, and flavor of the eggs. The most common varieties are *beluga* (the most expensive, with large grains, firm texture, and a light gray color), *osetra* (smaller berries than beluga, with a more intense flavor; the color ranges from golden yellow to brown), and *sevruga* (a good bargain; fine flavor, small berries, dark gray to black color).

There are very good American sturgeon caviars from California and Oregon that are worth experimenting with, but Caspian caviar remains the king. Salmon roe, or red caviar, has a very strong flavor, and is best served as an ingredient in an appetizer, rather than on its own. Lumpfish caviar is the dyed black stuff sold at supermarkets—it's not very good, and the dye can stain your lips. Don't use it for a special holiday dish.

When serving caviar, simplicity is the key. If you want to serve it as an hors d'oeuvre, the best way is to spoon it onto toast (cut rounds of firm, white sandwich bread and toast them lightly). Or serve the caviar in a traditional caviar *servior,* which will keep the eggs ice-cold. You can simulate the servior by nestling a glass bowl in a larger bowl of ice. Caviar aficionados insist that metal spoons should never touch caviar, for fear that the metal will transfer its flavor to the delicate morsels. They recommend bone, wood, or ivory spoons, but I use a Bakelite espresso spoon. No matter how you serve caviar, don't overwhelm its saline flavor and pleasantly crunchy texture with lots of competing ingredients. If you want to extend it, offer small bowls of minced onion, crème fraîche or sour cream, separately chopped hard-boiled egg yolks and whites and, of course, thin wedges of lemon. But do not encourage your guests to look at the caviar as an upscale salad bar.

Unfortunately, the high cost of caviar is not always an indication of quality, which can change with each catch. Also, caviar is very delicate and requires very careful handling and constant refrigeration, or the flavor and texture will suffer. Find a trustworthy local purveyor, preferably one with a large turnover of product. Excellent caviar can also be mail-ordered from Caviarteria (1-800-422-8427) and Caviar Russe (1-800-692-2842).

Yukon Gold Potatoes with Caviar and Crème Fraîche

Makes 4 servings

When you bring out the caviar, your guests will know that you hold them in high regard. Since good caviar is never inexpensive, I reserve it for my best friends and very special occasions. The humble potato is the perfect match for the elegant caviar. Here is one of the easiest, yet most satisfying, first courses around.

- *Yukon Gold potatoes are my first choice for this dish. They have a yellow-gold, buttery flesh that bakes beautifully. These potatoes sometimes have other generic names, so ask the produce manager if you aren't sure you have the right thing. Small russet, Idaho, or Maine potatoes are an alternative. Choose small-to-medium potatoes—this is an appetizer, not a side dish to a steak.*

- *Baking the potatoes on a bed of kosher salt helps draw out the moisture from the potatoes, giving them an especially fluffy texture. If you can't find kosher salt, use large-crystal sea salt, available at natural food stores and many supermarkets. Table salt will work, but not as well.*

- *The amount of caviar you use is up to you. Caviar is rich. While you will need at least 1 ounce per person, more than 2 ounces will be excessive. Check your bank account, and then take it from there.*

- *Crème fraîche can be described as French sour cream, but it is more buttery and less tangy, and it won't overpower the caviar as American sour cream might. It can be found in many supermarkets or specialty food stores with refrigerated food departments. However, it is easy to make your own, and I've included the recipe here.*

- *Serve the crème fraîche or sour cream next to the potato, not dolloped on top. Also, sprinkle the chives lightly around the potato and crème fraîche. That way,*

each guest can decide how much to use—some people prefer to savor the clean, saline flavor of caviar with as few accoutrements as possible, while others like to gild the lily.

2 cups kosher or coarse sea salt, for baking (approximately)
4 small Yukon Gold potatoes (4 ounces each), scrubbed but not peeled, pierced a few times with a fork
4 to 8 ounces caviar
½ cup crème fraîche (see Note) or sour cream, at room temperature
Chopped fresh chives, for garnish

1. Position a rack in the center of the oven and preheat to 400°F. Spread enough salt in an 8-inch square baking dish to make a thick layer. Nestle the potatoes in the salt. Bake until the potatoes are tender, about 45 minutes.

2. Brush the salt from the potatoes. Place each potato on a salad plate. Cut the potatoes lengthwise, then squeeze to open them up. Spoon equal amounts of caviar on each potato. Place a dollop of crème fraîche next to each potato. Sprinkle the chives on each plate around the potatoes and crème fraîche. Serve immediately.

Note: To make your own crème fraîche: In a small bowl (fill the bowl with boiling water and let stand for 5 minutes, drain, and dry), mix 1 cup heavy cream (not ultrapasteurized) and 2 tablespoons buttermilk. Cover loosely with plastic wrap. Let stand in a warm place until thickened, at least 12 hours and up to 24 hours, depending on the temperature. Do not let the crème fraîche get too thick, as it will thicken further when refrigerated. Transfer to a jar or airtight container and refrigerate until ready to use, up to 2 weeks.

Orange and Red Onion Salad with Cranberry-Orange Vinaigrette

Makes 8 servings

Make Ahead. The cranberry balsamic vinegar must be made 1 week ahead. The oranges and dressing can be prepared up to 1 day ahead.

Cranberry balsamic vinegar is one of my favorite gifts from my kitchen. It takes no time to make, and can be multiplied as many times as you have room in your pot. And it's a great way to perk up a so-so bottle of inexpensive supermarket balsamic. (It is not intended to be made with a fine artisanal balsamico.) This salad makes a light, refreshing opener to a holiday meal that more likely than not will be on the rich and heavy side. A short marinating period helps mellow the pungent red onion.

Dressing

1/4 cup Cranberry Balsamic Vinegar (recipe
   follows) or regular balsamic vinegar
Grated zest of 1 orange
1 tablespoon light brown sugar (optional,
   if using regular balsamic vinegar)
1/2 teaspoon salt
1/4 teaspoon freshly milled black pepper
3/4 cup olive oil

4 large oranges
1 small red onion, thinly sliced
2 heads Belgian endive, wiped with a moist
   paper towel (do not rinse)
1 large head red leaf lettuce, torn into
   bite-sized pieces
1 medium head radicchio, torn into
   bite-sized pieces
1/2 cup dried cranberries

1. To make the dressing, in a medium bowl, whisk the vinegar, orange zest, brown sugar, if using, salt, and pepper. Gradually whisk in the oil. (The dressing can be prepared up to 1 day ahead, covered, and refrigerated. Whisk well before serving.)

2. Using a serrated knife, cut off the skin, including the thick white pith, from the oranges. Cut between the membranes to remove the segments, and let the segments drop into a bowl. Cover tightly and refrigerate. (The oranges can be prepared up to 1 day ahead.)

3. About 30 minutes before serving, in a small bowl, toss the red onion with 2 tablespoons of the dressing. Cover and set aside.

4. Using a sharp knife, cut the endive crosswise into 1/2-inch wide pieces. Separate the endive pieces into strips, discarding any tough, solid center pieces.

5. When ready to serve, in a large bowl, toss the lettuce, radicchio, and endive with the remaining dressing. Spoon an equal amount of salad onto each plate. Top with the orange segments and red onions, and sprinkle with the cranberries. Serve immediately.

Cranberry Balsamic Vinegar: In a medium, nonreactive saucepan, combine 2 cups balsamic vinegar (supermarket quality), one 12-ounce bag cranberries, rinsed and sorted, and 1/3 cup packed light brown sugar. Cook, stirring occasionally, over medium-low heat until the vinegar begins to simmer and the cranberries have collapsed, about 20 minutes. Strain in a wire sieve over a medium bowl, pressing gently on the cranberries to extract all of the juice and vinegar, but do not press any pulp through the sieve. Let drain for a few minutes. Cool and transfer to a glass bottle for gift giving.

The Original Ambrosia

Makes 12 servings

Make Ahead: The salad can be prepared up to 1 day ahead, covered tightly with plastic wrap, and refrigerated.

What my grandma called ambrosia was concocted entirely of canned fruits and mortared with sour cream and marshmallows. This recipe takes ambrosia back to its roots, using only fresh fruit to make a superior dish that works as a first course, buffet salad, or dessert. The liquor is totally optional, but a nice touch.

- *Preparing fresh coconut is a labor of love, but like so many other kitchen chores, it's easy to master once you get the hang of it. The coconut meat should be finely shredded—if it is too thick, it is unpleasant to eat. Unless you have a food processor with a fine shredding blade (which sometimes has to be special-ordered separately from the large shredding blade that comes with most machines), shred the coconut by hand on the medium-sized holes of a box grater. Or shred chunks of the coconut in a hand-held rotary grater.*

- *If desired, substitute ⅔ cup unsweetened flaked coconut found in the frozen food section of some supermarkets (not desiccated coconut) for the fresh coconut. Or place regular sweetened flaked coconut in a wire sieve and rinse under hot water to remove the sugar coating. Drain and pat dry with paper towels.*

1 medium coconut

6 medium seedless oranges

1 ripe pineapple

**¼ cup Grand Marnier, dark rum, or
  fresh orange juice**

1. Position a rack in the center of the oven and preheat to 350°F. Pierce the eyes (the soft indentations on one end of the coconut) with a clean screwdriver and a hammer. Drain out the liquid. Place the coconut on a baking sheet. Bake for 30 minutes.

2. Using the hammer, rap the coconut around its circumference to crack it in half. Using a sturdy paring knife, pry the coconut in pieces from the shell. Using a vegetable peeler, remove the dark brown skin from the coconut. Shred the coconut.

3. Cut thin slices from the tops and bottoms of the oranges so they will stand. Using a serrated knife, cut off the thick rind from the oranges where it meets the flesh. Cut the oranges into ½-inch thick rounds.

4. Cut off the top of the pineapple, including the leafy crown. Cut the thick rind from the pineapple where it meets the flesh. Remove the dark eyes in the flesh. Cut the pineapple lengthwise into quarters, and cut the hard core from each quarter. Cut each quarter lengthwise again, then into bite-sized pieces.

5. In a large glass bowl, toss the pineapple, orange rounds, coconut, and Grand Marnier. Cover tightly with plastic wrap and refrigerate until well chilled, about 2 hours. Serve chilled. (The salad can be prepared up to 1 day ahead, covered tightly with plastic wrap, and refrigerated.)

Tortellini Antipasto Salad

Makes 8 to 12 servings

Make Ahead: This salad is best served the day it is made.

Of all the dishes on the buffet table, it is safe to say that pasta salad will be one of the first you'll have to replenish. This salad is loaded with the goodies you might find on an antipasti platter: Italian-style pickled vegetables (giardiniera), salami, roasted red pepper, and olives. Pasta salads have a tendency to soak up their dressings, and their flavor will change on standing. So it's a good idea to reserve some of the dressing to perk up the salad just before serving.

Dressing

¼ cup red wine vinegar

1 garlic clove, crushed through a press

½ teaspoon salt

¼ teaspoon freshly milled black pepper

1 cup extra virgin olive oil

2 pounds frozen cheese tortellini

One 24-ounce jar giardiniera, drained and
   coarsely chopped

6 ounces sliced (¼-inch thick) Genoa-style
   salami, cut into ½-inch square pieces

1 cup pimiento-stuffed green olives, coarsely
   chopped

1 large red bell pepper, roasted, cored, seeded,
   and cut into ½-inch square pieces (see Note)

3 scallions, white and green parts, chopped

3 tablespoons chopped fresh basil, oregano, or
   parsley

1. To make the dressing, place the vinegar, garlic, salt, and pepper in a blender. With the machine running, gradually add the oil and process until thick and smooth. Set aside.

2. Cook the tortellini in boiling salted water according to the package instructions. Drain, rinse under cold running water, and drain well.

3. Transfer the pasta to a large bowl. Add the giardiniera, salami, olives, red bell pepper, scallions, and basil. Toss with three-fourths of the dressing, covering and reserving the remaining dressing. Cover the pasta salad and refrigerate until chilled, at least 2 hours and up to 6 hours.

4. Just before serving, toss with the reserved dressing. Taste for seasoning, and add more salt and pepper, if needed. Serve chilled.

Note: There's more than one way to roast a pepper. Most methods ask the cook to turn the pepper over an open flame, but the technique here takes much less attention. To roast a red bell pepper, position the broiler rack about 6 inches from the source of heat and preheat the broiler. Cut off the top of the pepper, just below and including the stem, then cut off ½ inch from the bottom. Slit the pepper down the side, open it up, and cut out the ribs and seeds. Spread out the pepper, skin side up, and press on it to flatten. Broil, skin side up, until the skin is blackened and blistered, 5 to 10 minutes. Be careful not to burn a hole through the pepper—only the skin should blacken. (The flattened pepper can also be grilled over a hot charcoal fire or in a gas grill heated to the High setting.) Using kitchen tongs, transfer to a plate and cover with aluminum foil. Let stand until cool enough to handle. Using a small knife, peel and scrape off the skin. Try not to rinse the pepper under cold running water unless absolutely necessary.

Shrimp, Zucchini, and Red Pepper Bisque

Makes 8 servings

Make Ahead: The bisque can be prepared, up to the point of adding the half-and-half, up to 1 day ahead, covered, and refrigerated. Reheat gently before proceeding.

This creamy bisque makes an outstanding first course. The chunky, colorful sautéed shrimp-and-vegetable mixture not only provides the bulk of the flavor, it acts as a garnish, too. To avoid last-minute work, have all the sauté ingredients ready, then quickly cook them just before serving. For the easiest serving procedure, you could stir the cooked shrimp and vegetables into the bisque. I much prefer to bring a tureen of the soup to the table along with a bowl of the shrimp and vegetables, and I spoon the sautéed mixture into each bowl—the splash of green, red, and pink in the creamy soup looks terrific.

1 pound medium shrimp

7 tablespoons unsalted butter

1 small onion, chopped

1 small celery rib with leaves, chopped

2 cups bottled clam juice

1 cup dry white wine

2 sprigs fresh parsley

$\frac{1}{8}$ teaspoon dried thyme

$\frac{1}{8}$ teaspoon peppercorns

$\frac{1}{4}$ cup all-purpose flour

2 tablespoons Madeira or dry sherry

1 tablespoon tomato paste

2 cups half-and-half

$\frac{1}{4}$ teaspoon salt

$\frac{1}{4}$ teaspoon freshly milled black pepper

1 medium zucchini, cut into $\frac{1}{4}$-inch dice

1 medium red bell pepper, cored, seeded, and cut into $\frac{1}{4}$-inch dice

1. Peel and devein the shrimp, reserving the shells. Coarsely chop the shrimp; cover, and refrigerate.

2. In a medium saucepan, heat 1 tablespoon of the butter over medium heat. Add the onion and celery. Cover and cook until softened, about 5 minutes. Add the shrimp shells, 3 cups cold water, clam juice, wine, parsley, thyme, and peppercorns. Bring to a boil over high heat. Reduce the heat to low and simmer for 30 minutes. Strain and reserve the stock (you should have 5 cups; add water as needed.)

3. In a large, heavy pot, melt 4 tablespoons butter over low heat. Whisk in the flour and let bubble without browning for 1 minute. Whisk in the Madeira and tomato paste, then the reserved shrimp stock. Bring to a simmer over medium heat and cook until lightly thickened, about 3 minutes. (The bisque can be prepared to this point up to 1 day ahead, cooled, covered, and refrigerated. Reheat gently before proceeding.) Add the half-and-half and cook until very hot but not simmering. Season with $\frac{1}{8}$ teaspoon salt and $\frac{1}{8}$ teaspoon pepper.

4. In a large skillet, melt the remaining 2 tablespoons butter over medium-high heat. Add the zucchini and red bell pepper and sauté until just tender, about 7 minutes. Add the shrimp and cook until pink and firm, about 3 minutes. Season with the remaining salt and pepper. Transfer to a warmed bowl.

5. Pour the bisque into a warmed soup tureen. To serve, ladle the bisque into soup bowls, topping each serving with a spoonful of the shrimp and vegetable mixture.

Sangria Jell-O Mold

Makes 8 to 12 servings

Make Ahead: The mold can be prepared up to 2 days ahead.

To many Americans, a holiday dinner means a molded Jell-O salad. Beth Hensperger, author of many baking books, told me that she always puts wine in her Jell-O mold to give it a little sophistication. While the salad can be presented as a first course, I prefer to serve it as a side dish or on a buffet table with many other offerings. With this inspiration, here is a recipe that brings this old favorite into the new millennium.

- *You will need a 6-cup mold for this salad. A metal ring mold will do, but the Jell-O company makes a beautifully designed plastic one that I am very partial to. The Holiday Ring Mold is available in some supermarkets during the holidays, or you can order it through the Jell-O web site, www.jell-o.com (go to the "Corner Store," and look for the "Jell-O Molds" section).*

- *This recipe is easily halved again to fill a 9-cup mold (use three 3-ounce packages of Jell-O) or doubled to fit a large mold. Just be sure that the Jell-O mixture reaches the top of the mold, or it will be difficult to unmold.*

- *There are some tips for making a good Jell-O mold. First, be sure the gelatin is completely dissolved, which takes 2 minutes of constant stirring. Don't cheat, or the mold won't set properly. Second, the Jell-O must be partially set in order to support the weight of the added fruit, or the chunks will sink to the bottom of the mold. You can chill it in the refrigerator for about 1 1/2 hours, but chilling it in an ice-water bath cuts the time, and allows you to keep an eye on the progress.*

- *You should have 3 cups of combined orange segments, grape halves, and sliced strawberries for this salad. The*

exact proportion of each fruit doesn't matter, and you can add raspberries, peeled, cored and diced apple or pear, or cubed bananas, if you wish.

1 1/2 cups fruity red wine, such as Merlot
One 6-ounce package raspberry-flavored gelatin
1 tablespoon fresh lemon or lime juice
3 large seedless oranges
1 cup red or green (or a combination)
  seedless grapes, cut into halves lengthwise
1 cup sliced strawberries or raspberries
Nonstick vegetable spray, for the mold

1. In a small saucepan, bring the wine to a boil over high heat. In a stainless steel or glass (not plastic) bowl, using a rubber spatula, stir the Jell-O with the hot wine until the gelatin is completely dissolved, occasionally scraping down the sides of the bowl, about 2 minutes. Stir in 1 1/2 cups cold water and the lemon juice. Place the bowl in a larger bowl of ice water. Let stand, stirring occasionally, until the Jell-O is partially set and the spoon briefly cuts a swath that allows you to see the bottom of the bowl, about 20 minutes.

2. Meanwhile, grate the zest from one orange and set aside. To cut the oranges into segments, use a serrated knife to cut off the tops and bottoms from each orange. Following the curve of each orange, cut off the thick white pith where it meets the orange flesh. Working over a bowl, cut between the thin membranes to release the orange segments, letting them drop into the bowl. Drain the oranges before using.

3. Fold the orange segments, orange zest, grapes, and strawberries into the partially set Jell-O. Lightly spray a 6-cup decorative mold with nonstick vegetable spray. Pour the Jell-O into the mold and cover with plastic wrap. Refrigerate until set, at least 4 hours or overnight.

4. To unmold, run a knife around the inside edge of the mold to break the "seal." Lightly moisten a serving platter (this will allow you to move the unmolded salad on the platter, if you need to). Place the platter upside down over the top of the mold. Holding the mold and platter together, invert and shake firmly to unmold the salad. If the salad doesn't unmold, dip the outside of the mold briefly (less that 5 seconds) in a bowl of warm tap water. Dry the outside of the mold and try again. Serve chilled.

Parsnip and Leek Soup with Bacon

Makes 8 servings

Make Ahead: The soup can be prepared up to 1 day ahead, cooled, covered, and refrigerated. Reheat over very low heat, stirring often.

The sweet, earthy flavors of parsnips and leeks create a smooth and elegant soup that will have your guests trying to guess the ingredients. A crisp topping of crumbled bacon is the perfect garnish.

2 tablespoons unsalted butter
3 large leeks, chopped, white and pale green parts only (1½ cups)
1 pound parsnips, peeled and cut into 1-inch pieces
2 pounds baking potatoes, such as russet or Idaho, peeled and cut into 1-inch pieces
5 cups Homemade White Chicken Stock (page 41) or canned low-sodium chicken broth
¾ teaspoon salt
¼ teaspoon freshly milled white or black pepper
4 slices bacon

1. In a large pot, heat the butter over medium heat. Add the leeks and cook until softened, about 5 minutes. Add the parsnips and potatoes. Stir in the stock. Bring to a simmer. Reduce the heat to low and cover. Cook until the vegetables are tender, about 25 minutes.

2. In batches, puree the soup in a blender or food processor. Return to the pot and season with the salt and pepper. (The soup can be prepared up to 1 day ahead, cooled, covered, and refrigerated. Reheat over very low heat, stirring often.)

3. Meanwhile, in a medium skillet, cook the bacon, turning once, until crisp and browned, about 5 minutes. Transfer to paper towels to drain and cool. Crumble the bacon and set aside.

4. Ladle the soup into soup bowls and top with the crumbled bacon. Serve hot.

Homemade Brown Stock 101

Makes about 2 ½ quarts

Make Ahead: The stock can be prepared and refrigerated up to 3 days ahead or frozen up to 3 months.

Nothing beats homemade stock. Just like most home cooks, I use canned broth (a good low-sodium brand, but never bouillon cubes, which are too salty and artificial-tasting) for the majority of my cooking, but for a special holiday meal, I bring out the stockpot. Stock takes very little actual work, and it can be made well ahead of time and frozen. The only problem is, no matter how much you make and store, it always seems to disappear too quickly. This basic recipe can be altered by using different meaty bones to make different stocks. Following are a few pointers about stock.

- *This rich brown stock is made from roasted bones—preferred for meat sauces and gravies. For soups and white sauces, you can make White Chicken Stock (recipe follows), as its color is more neutral and the finished dish will look and taste lighter.*

- *What's the difference between a stock and a broth? A stock is generally made from bones, but a broth is the cooking liquid of braised meat or poultry. The biggest distinction, however, comes from the use of salt. Stock is unsalted, used in a recipe as an ingredient, and then the final dish is seasoned. Broth is usually seasoned and can be enjoyed on its own, like a soup.*

- *Never let stock come to a rolling boil, or it will become cloudy and have a less refined flavor. Cook the stock uncovered.*

- *Add the herbs to the stock after you've skimmed it. If you add them at the beginning, they will rise to the surface and be skimmed off with the foam. By the way, the foam isn't unwholesome—it's just the coagulating proteins in the bones. The foam is removed to make the stock clearer.*

- *The longer a stock simmers, the better, up to 12 hours. Replace the water as needed as it evaporates. While I trust my stove to simmer the stock overnight, some of my students have been shocked at the idea of leaving a pot unattended. A great alternative is to make the stock in a 5½-quart slow cooker. Transfer the browned bones and cooked vegetable mixture to the cooker, add the herbs, and pour in enough cold water to cover well. Cook on Low, covered, for 12 hours. This makes a clear, delicious stock. As a slow cooker holds less liquid than a stockpot, the stock will be very full-flavored. You may choose to use fewer bones and vegetables (especially if you make the stock in a 3½-quart pot), or dilute the finished stock with water, if you wish.*

- *If time is a factor, just simmer the stock for an hour or two—it will still be better than using water or canned broth to make your gravy. You may want to add a can of broth to boost the flavor, though. (It's cheating, but I won't tell.) Or, make some well ahead of Thanksgiving and freeze it.*

- *Be sure the stock is cooled before refrigerating or freezing. To speed the cooling, place the stockpot in a sink filled with cold water, changing the water as necessary to keep it as cold as possible. Stir occasionally until the stock is cool.*

- *Don't add salt to your stock. The stock is often used in recipes where it will be reduced, and the final dish could end up too salty.*

3 pounds chicken wings, chopped into 2- to 3-inch pieces

2 tablespoons vegetable oil

1 medium onion, chopped

1 medium carrot, chopped

1 medium celery rib with leaves, chopped

6 fresh parsley sprigs

½ teaspoon dried thyme

¼ teaspoon whole black peppercorns

1 bay leaf

1. Position a rack in the upper third of the oven and preheat to 450°F. Place the chicken wings in a large roasting pan. Roast, turning occasionally, until golden brown, about 45 minutes.

2. Meanwhile, in a large pot, heat the oil over medium-high heat. Add the onion, carrot, and celery to the pot and cook, stirring often, until softened, about 6 minutes.

3. Transfer the wings to the pot. Pour off all the fat in the roasting pan. Place the pan over two burners on high heat. Add 1 cup water, scraping up the browned bits in the pan with a wooden spoon. Pour into the pot. Add enough cold water to cover the wings by 2 inches. Bring to a boil, skimming off the foam that rises to the surface. Add the parsley, thyme, peppercorns, and bay leaf. Reduce the heat to low. Cook at a bare simmer for at least 2 hours and up to 12 hours. Add more water to the pot as needed, to keep the bones covered.

4. Strain the stock through a colander into a large bowl. Let stand for 5 minutes and skim off the clear yellow fat that rises to the surface. Cool the stock completely before refrigerating or freezing. (Chicken stock can be prepared up to 3 days ahead, cooled completely, covered, and refrigerated. It can also be frozen in airtight containers for up to 3 months.)

Homemade Turkey Stock: Substitute 3 pounds turkey wings for the chicken wings. Using a heavy cleaver, chop the wings into 2- to 3-inch pieces (you may want to ask the butcher to do this, as turkey bones are often too heavy to chop at home). Add the turkey neck (chopped into 2- to 3-inch pieces), heart, and gizzard to the pot, but don't use the liver, which will give the stock a bitter flavor.

Homemade Duck Stock: Substitute the carcasses, giblets (no liver), wing tips, and necks (chopped into 2- to 3-inch pieces) of two ducks for the chicken wings.

Homemade Goose Stock: You won't have enough bones from one goose to make a full-flavored stock, so use canned chicken broth to boost the flavor. Substitute the goose wing tips, neck (chopped into 1- to 3-inch pieces), and giblets (no liver) for the chicken wings. Substitute two 13¾-ounce cans of low-sodium chicken broth for 3½ cups of the water.

Homemade Beef Stock: Substitute 3 pounds beef bones (preferably 2 pounds beef bones and 1 pound beef shin, as the bit of meat on the shin will give the stock a richer flavor) for the chicken wings.

Homemade White Chicken Stock: Make the stock as directed, but do not roast the wings. Add the raw wings to the pot after the vegetables have softened.

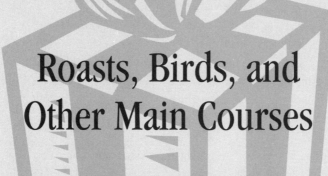

Roasts, Birds, and Other Main Courses

The Groaning Board

he Christmas tradition of serving an extravagant array of victuals goes way back to Old England. The feudal lords were expected (nay, obligated) to feed their serfs throughout the holiday season. They literally opened their houses to the underlings—the beginning of today's "open house." The serfs didn't want a few canapés and a glass of wine, either. They expected, and got, a groaning board of food. If they didn't, they could find ways to make life pretty miserable for the lord.

Today's holiday dinners are centered around at least one roast or bird. I know many cooks who bake a ham, a turkey, and a few dishes of lasagna, just for starters. This can pose more than a few problems for the cook. But the good news is that roasts are really easy to prepare. A lot of the guesswork is sidestepped simply by choosing a good cut of meat (see Beefing Up on page 45).

For my own Christmas dinner, I usually choose prime rib or crown roast of pork. Since each of these is delicious, the final decision really comes down to the size of the guest list. If the meal is for eight people, prime rib is just the thing. For groups of eight to twelve, I often prepare a crown roast. Roasts always need to stand for at least 20 minutes before carving, which gives me plenty of time to finish up the side dishes.

Not all holiday meals are sit-down affairs, of course, and buffets need main courses, too. You'll find many dihes here that will be perfect for an open house or cocktail party buffet.

Rib Roast "Au Jus" 101

Makes 8 to 10 servings

The verdict is in. My Christmas entrée of choice is a gorgeous standing beef rib roast. It is a surefire way to hear sighs of appreciation from guests. (At my house, we have to raffle off the roasted rib bones for post-supper gnawing.) With a rib roast, let the meat speak for itself. Keep the seasonings very simple and serve with a beef stock–based "au jus" sauce. I often offer horse-radish sauce for those who must have it.

- Buy a prime-grade rib roast. While we use "prime rib" as a generic term to describe any rib roast, that is incorrect unless the meat is officially graded USDA prime. This is the highest grade available, which virtually guarantees tender, well-aged, flavorful meat. It is expensive and only found at the finest butchers, but for Christmas dinner, get the best. Most supermarket beef is graded choice, which can be excellent, but it is aged differently than prime and has less fat (and in beef, fat equals flavor). Choice beef will benefit from a 5-day aging period in your refrigerator. For details, see Beefing Up on page 45.

- The rib section of a steer has 12 ribs, but home cooks rarely serve a whole 12-rib roast. Try to buy a roast from the "small end" of the rib section, as it will have less fat and more meat to the pound. To serve eight to ten people, buy a 4-rib roast. For smaller or larger roasts, just use the roasting-time estimates that follow. If you are having a small crowd, it's advisable to buy a 3-rib roast, as 2-rib roasts are hard to roast evenly.

- Some rib roasts are sold with the thick fat cap on top of the meat intact, and some are trimmed. I prefer to keep most of the fat cap intact, and I trim it myself to a ⅛- to ¼-inch thickness, if necessary. In any case, some meat will be exposed. If you trim away a good amount of fat, the purchased weight of the roast will be reduced, so adjust your cooking time as needed. While a kitchen scale is the best way to weigh the meat, of course, you can simply estimate the difference.

- After the grade of the meat, timing is the next most important thing to keep in mind. Check the internal temperature with a good instant-read or digital thermometer. Be sure to remove the roast from the oven 10° to 15°F before it reaches the desired internal temperature! The residual heat in the roast will continue to cook the meat, even outside of the oven. So, if you want medium-rare meat at 130°F, remove the roast when the thermometer reaches 120°F (or even a few degrees lower if you are a rare-meat fan). If you and your guests prefer medium meat at 140°F, remove the roast when it reaches an internal temperature of 130°F. It is a waste of money to cook a rib roast beyond 140°F, because the rich, beefy flavor is lost. If you have guests who prefer well-done meat, serve them the end cuts, or place their sliced meat back in the oven for a few minutes (or microwave it until it looks the way they want it).

- My perfect roast beef has a tasty, crisply browned crust and a juicy interior. For a rib roast of any size, follow this roasting-time estimate. Place the roast in a pre-heated 450°F oven and roast for 15 minutes. Reduce the heat to 350°F and continue roasting until done. Allow about 15 minutes per pound for medium-rare meat, and 17 minutes per pound for medium (calculate the time from when the roast goes in the oven, not from when the temperature is reduced). During the last 30 minutes of roasting time, be sure to check the roast's internal temperature occasionally to avoid overdone meat.

- Let the roast stand for at least 20 minutes before serving. If you are making Herbed Yorkshire Puddings (page 75) in the same oven, it will take about 35 minutes to heat the oven to 400°F and bake the puddings. As long as the roast is served within an hour, do not worry about the roast cooling off.

- "Au jus" sauce is nothing more than beef stock stirred into the degreased roasting pan and brought to a boil.

It is not thick like a typical sauce or gravy. The "au jus" will only be as good as your stock, so I strongly recommend that you use Homemade Beef Stock (page 41). If you must use canned stock, buy the best you can find, but forget about using salty, artificially flavored bouillon cubes.

One 4-rib standing beef rib roast, preferably prime grade (about 8 pounds)

2 large garlic cloves, peeled

1½ teaspoons salt

1 teaspoon dried thyme

1 teaspoon dried rosemary, crumbled

½ teaspoon freshly milled black pepper

3 cups Homemade Beef Stock (page 41) or canned low-sodium beef broth

Sour Cream Horseradish Sauce (recipe follows), optional

1. Position a rack in the lower third of the oven and preheat *thoroughly* to 450°F.

2. Using a sharp, thin knife, trim any fat on the top of the roast to ¼-inch thickness. With a large knife, finely chop the garlic on a work surface. Sprinkle with ½ teaspoon of the salt, and mash and smear the garlic on the work surface to make a paste. Scrape into a small bowl. Add the remaining 1 teaspoon salt, and the thyme, rosemary, and pepper. Rub the seasoning mixture all over the roast, including the underside.

3. Place the rib roast, rib side down, in a large roasting pan. (No need to use a roasting rack, as the bones create a natural one.) Roast for 15 minutes. Reduce the oven temperature to 350°F. (Do not open the oven door.) Continue roasting until an instant-read thermometer inserted in the center of the roast reads 115° to 120°F, about 2 hours total roasting time for medium-rare meat. For an accurate reading, be sure the tip of the thermometer is positioned in the center of the meat. Transfer the roast to a carving board. Let stand for 20 minutes.

4. While the meat is standing, make the "au jus" sauce: Pour out all of the fat from the roasting pan and discard (or reserve if making Herbed Yorkshire Puddings on page 75). Place the roasting pan over two burners on medium heat. Add the beef stock and stir to release any browned bits in the pan. Bring to a boil and cook until the stock is slightly reduced, about 2 minutes. Transfer to a gravy boat.

5. To carve the roast, using a meat fork and a long, thin carving knife, stand the roast on its end. Carve off the rib section in one piece, and set aside. Slice the meat, cut the ribs into individual pieces, and serve immediately, with a spoonful of the "au jus" sauce poured over each serving. Pass the horseradish sauce on the side, if desired.

Sour Cream Horseradish Sauce: In a medium bowl, mix 1 pint sour cream, ½ cup prepared horseradish, well drained, ¼ cup chopped chives (optional), ½ teaspoon salt, and ¼ teaspoon freshly milled black pepper. If desired, add more drained horseradish to taste. Let stand at room temperature for 1 hour before serving.

Beefing Up

The perfect roast beef is tender, juicy, and full of meaty flavor. The USDA grades meat according to tenderness. Two main factors are the age of the steer (the older the beef, the tougher the meat), and the amount of fat marbled through its flesh (this inner marbling moistens the meat as it cooks). The most common grades are prime, choice, and standard. Beef has the most grades. Lamb and veal have fewer grades, and only the highest grades make it to market. Pork is so consistent, only one grade is sold directly to consumers.

Only about 2 percent of all beef is graded prime. This is the very best meat you can buy and accordingly expensive. One of the reasons why it's so pricey is that it has gone through a special dry-aging process. All beef is aged after slaughter so the enzymes can break down and tenderize the flesh. Most beef is wet-aged in its juices in sealed plastic bags (like the ones for sale at wholesale clubs). But dry-aged beef is allowed to stand uncovered in special refrigerators for about 3 weeks or more. This special aging process evaporates excess moisture from the meat. As the exposed surface must be trimmed away, dry-aged meat makes for a good amount of waste, so the price of the meat goes up.

Most of the meat sold in supermarkets is wet-aged and graded choice. It's very good, but it lacks the depth of flavor of prime meat. If you roasted a choice rib roast without any special treatment, it would taste just fine but not really great. However, there is a way to simulate dry-aging for choice cuts of meat at home, if you are willing to make space in your refrigerator for 5 days.

I have been doing this "quick" dry-aging method ever since I saw it outlined in Jane Frieman's *Dinner Parties,* but it has recently been popularized by Pam Anderson in her book *The Perfect Recipe.* Before you start, be sure your refrigerator is 40°F or below (use a refrigerator thermometer and don't just guess). And be aware that between the moisture evaporation and post-aging trimming, you will lose about 20 percent of the roast's purchase weight. The last time I aged a rib roast like this, I began with a 10-pound roast that cost $50. After aging and trimming, the roast weighed 8 pounds, so I "lost" $10 worth of meat. For my money, the improved flavor was worth every penny. At the premium butcher in my neighborhood, an 8-pound prime rib roast would have cost about $100. (You do the math.)

Purchase the roast 5 days before you plan to serve it. Unwrap the roast and place on a wire rack on a jelly-roll pan. Refrigerate it for 5 days. The outside surface of the meat will dry out, but don't worry about it. When you are ready to roast the meat, use a sharp, thin-bladed knife to trim away all of the dried surface. The meat is now ready to roast.

This method only works with very large untrimmed pieces of meat, like a rib roast or leg of lamb. Don't try it with steaks or chops.

Marinated Beef Tenderloin

Makes 8 to 12 main-course servings, and 16 to 20 buffet servings

Make Ahead: The beef should be marinated for 2 to 4 hours before roasting.

Marinated, roasted beef tenderloin is one of the most versatile dishes in a cook's repertoire. Served hot, it can be the main course of a holiday sit-down dinner. Cooled and thinly sliced, it is often the centerpiece of an open-house buffet. The citrus–red wine–balsamic vinegar marinade is tasty but very strong—don't marinate the beef for too long or the acids in the marinade could give the meat a mushy texture.

- *This recipe assumes that you will be buying a whole, untrimmed beef tenderloin, available in Cryovac packages at large supermarkets and wholesale clubs. Even though you will trim the beef yourself, there will still be a fair amount of waste: A whole tenderloin weighing 6 pounds trims down to about 3½ pounds, plus about ¾ pound of meat culled from the trimmings to put to another use. I prefer to trim off the disproportionately large clod of meat that is attached to the thinner main muscle and cut it into strips for a stir-fry). Or, you can buy a 3½- to 4-pound trimmed tenderloin.*

One 6-pound beef tenderloin, untrimmed

Marinade

1 cup hearty red wine, such as Zinfandel

Grated zest and juice of 1 large orange

⅓ cup soy sauce

⅓ cup extra virgin olive oil

¼ cup balsamic vinegar

2 garlic cloves, crushed under a knife

1½ teaspoons dried rosemary

1½ teaspoons dried thymne

½ teaspoon whole black peppercorns

1 tablespoon extra virgin olive oil

½ teaspoon salt

½ teaspoon freshly milled black pepper

1. Drain the beef, rinse under cold running water, and pat dry with paper towels. (Do not be concerned about any odor—it will dissipate in a minute or so.) Using a sharp, thin-bladed knife, trim away any fat, including the large lump at the wide end, and discard. Pull and cut away the long, thin "chain" muscle that runs the length of the tenderloin. (If you wish, trim away the fat from the chain and reserve the meat for an-other use.) Following the natural muscle separation, cut away the large clod of meat at the wide end and reserve for another use. At one end of the meat, make an incision under the silver sinew covering the meat. Slip the knife under the sinew, and pull and trim it away. Work lengthwise down the tenderloin until it is completely free of sinew and fat.

2. Fold the thin ends of the meat underneath so the tenderloin is the same thickness throughout its length, and tie with kitchen string. Tie the roast crosswise at 2- to 3-inch intervals.

3. To make the marinade, whisk all of the ingredients in a large bowl to combine. Immerse the tenderloin in the marinade. Cover and refrigerate, turning occasionally, for at least 2 hours and up to 4 hours. Drain the tenderloin and let stand at room temperature for 1 hour before roasting.

4. Position a rack in the center of the oven and preheat to 425°F. Rub the tenderloin with the oil, and season with the salt and pepper. Place in a large roasting pan (no need to use a roasting rack). Roast until an instant-read thermometer inserted in the center of the roast reads 120° to 125°F for medium-rare meat (the internal temperature of the meat will continue to rise about 10°F outside of the oven), about 35 minutes.

5. If serving hot, let stand for 10 to 15 minutes before carving. For a buffet, cool for at least 30 minutes, then carve and serve within 2 hours. Or cool completely, wrap tightly in foil, and refrigerate for up to 2 days before carving and serving at room temperature.

It Wouldn't Be the Holidays Without . . . Roasts

There are many reasons why you'll usually find a big roast on a Christmas dinner table. First of all, roast meat is delicious, and it is a pretty easy way to feed a crowd. However, the tradition of serving a large cut of meat during the biggest winter holiday goes way back to Roman times.

Today, we take refrigeration for granted. If we want fresh meat, no problem. But until about a hundred years ago, most meat was preserved by salting, corning, or smoking. The main butchering took place in the winter, when it was cold and the meat could be naturally refrigerated. Winter was about the only time that the average peasant could enjoy fresh meat.

In Roman times the main winter holiday occurred on December 25, the "Birthday of the Invincible Sun God," Mithras. Mithraism was the main religion of the Roman empire, and the sun god's birthday was a big feast day.

Of course, it made sense to use up as much of the fresh meat possible before it spoiled, and when better than during one of those big Roman feasts that you see in the movies?

The early Christians did not want to celebrate Christ's birthday, as they thought that kind of natal day was the province of Pharaohs and other false gods.

When Christianity established itself, the Church Fathers usurped Mithras, and declared December 25 as Christ's birthday. In order to persuade former pagans to commemorate Christ's birth, the Church had to change its former position on celebrating the day. Mithraists were allowed to keep the winter festival, as long as Mithras had nothing to do with it. Many of the old pagan traditions took centuries to die, and some of them, like serving big roasts on the most important winter holiday, never went away.

Baked Ham with Pineapple and Seeded Mustard Glaze

Makes 16 to 24 servings

Make Ahead: The ham should be served within 2 hours of baking.

A sweet and tangy glazed smoked ham is another versatile holiday entrée, equally at home on the dinner or buffet table. (Not to mention the bonus of leftover ham for postparty sandwiches and casseroles.) This recipe features the familiar flavors of glazed ham without resorting to the usual brown sugar, pineapple slices, and maraschino cherries. If you can't find pineapple preserves, substitute apricot preserves.

- *In my opinion, a bone-in smoked ham gives the most flavor for the money. Other hams, such as canned hams, country ham (Smithfield or Virginia types), or partially cooked hams have different flavors, textures, and cooking techniques. I prefer a shank-end ham because it looks more dramatic than the butt portion. My second choice is an unglazed, boneless spiral-sliced ham because it is easy to serve. If you purchase a glazed spiral-sliced ham, cook it according to the accompanying instructions and omit the pineapple glaze.*

- *This recipe uses an average 8-pound ham, but larger or smaller hams can be used to accommodate the number of people you want to serve (and the leftovers you want to have!). Allow 15 minutes per pound at 325°F, glazing the ham during the last hour of baking, and make more or less glaze as needed.*

- *Sure, baked ham is delicious, but it also looks terrific on a buffet because it stands tall on the platter, and height adds visual interest to the display. I found a ham holder at a garage sale. It is a metal ring with prongs attached to a wooden board that lifts the whole ham up and holds it securely for slicing. If you find one at a kitchenware or restaurant supply store (or at a garage sale or secondhand shop), grab it. A conical ham holder, which holds a shank-end ham straight up, is available by mail order from Kitchen Glamor (1-800-641-1252). Don't confuse it with an Italian prosciutto holder, which is too narrow to hold an American ham.*

- *Common food-safety precautions require that meat stand no longer than 2 hours at room temperature before serving. This isn't always easy to do. If necessary, serve chilled sliced ham and replenish the platter as needed.*

**One 8-pound bone-in smoked ham,
  preferably the shank end**
1 cup pineapple preserves
2 tablespoons Dijon mustard
1½ teaspoons yellow mustard seeds

1. Position a rack in the center of the oven and preheat to 350°F. Line a roasting pan with aluminum foil.

2. Using a sharp knife, trim off all of the skin, except for a 1- to 2-inch band around the shank. Trim off all of the fat, leaving a less than ¼-inch thick layer.

3. In a small bowl, whisk the preserves, Dijon mustard, and mustard seeds, and set aside.

4. Place the ham on a roasting rack in the pan and bake until a meat thermometer inserted in the thickest part of the ham (without touching a bone) registers 140°F, about 2 hours (allow 15 minutes per pound). After 1 hour, baste with half of the glaze. After 30 minutes, baste with the remaining glaze.

5. Transfer the ham to a carving board or platter. Let stand for 15 to 30 minutes before carving.

Crown Roast of Pork with Apple Stuffing and Hard Cider Sauce

Makes 10 generous servings

Make Ahead: The seasoned pork roast must be refrigerated overnight.

Truly one of the most magnificent of all holiday entrees, a crown roast of pork is surprisingly simple to prepare.

- *Order your roast well ahead of time from the butcher. Be flexible about the actual size of the roast—the weight can vary quite a bit from roast to roast, even with the same number of ribs. Allow about 20 minutes per pound, roasting until the meat is cooked to 155°F, and you'll be fine.*

- *The butcher usually grinds the trimmings from the crown roast to supply the ground pork for the stuffing. If necessary, ask for additional ground pork to make up the 2 pounds total.*

- *Make the stuffing just before roasting so it is warmed slightly by the sautéed vegetables. A slightly warm stuffing will cook more quickly and evenly than a chilled one.*

- *The crown roast will usually come from the butcher on some kind of support to help transfer the roast to the serving platter. If not, you can use the flat bottom of a springform or tart pan.*

One 8½-pound (12-rib) crown roast of pork
2 tablespoons vegetable oil
1 teaspoon salt
1 teaspoon sugar
½ teaspoon crumbled dried sage
½ teaspoon dried rosemary
½ teaspoon dried thyme
½ teaspoon freshly milled black pepper

Stuffing

2 tablespoons vegetable oil
2 medium celery ribs with leaves, chopped
⅓ cup chopped shallots
2 garlic cloves, minced
2 pounds ground pork
1 cup unflavored dried bread crumbs
3 large eggs, beaten
⅓ cup chopped fresh parsley
2 teaspoons dried sage
1 teaspoon dried rosemary
¼ teaspoon ground allspice
2 teaspoons salt
¾ teaspoon freshly milled black pepper
1 cup (4 ounces) packed coarsely chopped
    dried apples

Sauce

1½ cups Homemade Beef Stock (page 41)
    or canned low-sodium beef broth
1 cup hard apple cider
2 teaspoons cornstarch
2 tablespoons applejack or Calvados

1. The night before, brush the crown roast inside and out (including the underside) with the oil. Combine the salt, sugar, sage, rosemary, thyme, and pepper, and rub all over the roast. Place the roast in a roasting pan, cover loosely with plastic wrap, and refrigerate overnight. Remove the meat from the refrigerator 1 hour before roasting.

2. To make the stuffing, in a large skillet, heat the oil over medium heat. Add the celery and cook, stirring often, until softened, about 3 minutes. Add the shallots and garlic and cook, stirring often, until shallots soften, about 2 minutes. Transfer to a large bowl. Add the ground pork, bread crumbs, eggs, parsley, sage, rosemary, allspice, salt, and pepper, and mix well. Mix in the dried apples.

3. Position a rack in the bottom third of the oven and preheat to 450°F. Fill the center of the roast with stuffing. Cover the stuffing with aluminum foil. Cover each bone tip with a small piece of foil.

4. Roast for 10 minutes. Reduce the oven temperature to 325°F. Cook until a thermometer inserted in the thickest part of the roast, without touching a bone, reads 155°F, about 2 hours, 30 minutes. During the last 15 minutes of cooking time, remove the foil from the stuffing and bone tips to allow them to brown. Using a large spatula to help support the roast, transfer the roast to a serving platter. Let stand for 15 minutes before carving.

5. Meanwhile, pour off any drippings from the pan into a glass measuring cup. Skim off and discard any clear fat that rises to the surface. Reserve the dark juices in the cup. Place the roasting pan over two burners on high heat. Add the beef stock, cider, and reserved juices, and bring to a boil, scraping up any browned bits on the bottom of the pan. In a small bowl, dissolve the cornstarch in the applejack. Whisk into the pan and cook until the sauce is lightly thickened. Season with salt and pepper to taste. Strain through a wire sieve into a small bowl. Pour the sauce into a warmed sauceboat.

6. Using a long, sharp knife, cut the roast into 1-rib servings. Serve with a spoonful of the stuffing, and pass the sauce on the side.

Chicken Cassoulet

Makes 12 to 16 servings

Make Ahead: The cassoulet can be prepared up to 1 day ahead (without the bread crumbs and parsley topping), cooled, covered, and refrigerated. Stir 2 cups chicken broth or water into the cassoulet and add the topping just before reheating.

Cassoulet, the extravagant French version of pork and beans, is probably one of the most filling dishes on the planet, which makes it a good choice for an open-house entrée. The classic recipe can take days to create. It usually includes confit (duck or goose cooked and aged in fat), an essential ingredient if you live in the southwest of France . . . and I don't! Even my most discriminating foodie friends agree that this easy recipe is just as good as the time-consuming original. If you have guests who don't eat red meat, make the cassoulet with turkey sausage, then they can dig in.

- *The cassoulet looks especially good when baked and served from a large 7- to 8-quart Dutch oven, preferably made of enameled cast iron. I have one left over from my catering days, and it is one of my most used cooking utensils. The bean mixture can also be prepared in a standard 6-quart Dutch oven, then divided between two standard 3½-quart casseroles. When ready to bake, stir 1 cup chicken broth or water into each casserole, and add the bread-crumb topping.*

1 teaspoon dried thyme

1 teaspoon dried rosemary

1 teaspoon dried sage

1 teaspoon dried oregano

¾ teaspoon salt

½ teaspoon freshly milled black pepper

3 tablespoons vegetable oil

3 pounds boneless, skinless chicken thighs,
  cut into 1-inch cubes (see Note)

1 cup dry vermouth or white wine

One 28-ounce can tomatoes in juice, chopped,
  juices reserved

2 cups Homemade White Chicken Stock
  (page 41) or canned reduced-sodium
  chicken broth

1 bay leaf

1½ pounds sweet Italian pork or turkey sausage,
  casings removed

2 medium onions, chopped

1 large red bell pepper, cored, seeded, and
  chopped

2 garlic cloves, chopped

Six 15- to 19-ounce cans cannellini (white kidney)
  beans, rinsed and drained

½ cup dried bread crumbs

¼ cup chopped fresh parsley

1. Position a rack in the center of the oven and preheat to 350°F.

2. In a small bowl, mix the thyme, rosemary, sage, oregano, salt, and pepper. Set the seasoning mixture aside.

3. In a very large (7- to 8-quart) Dutch oven, preferably enameled cast-iron, heat 1 tablespoon of the oil over medium-high heat. In batches without crowding, cook the chicken thighs, turning occasionally, until browned lightly on all sides, about 10 minutes. Using a slotted spoon, transfer the browned chicken to a platter. Return the browned chicken to the Dutch oven. Sprinkle the seasoning mixture over the chicken, mixing well. Add the vermouth and bring to a boil, scraping up any browned bits on the bottom of the pan with a wooden spoon. Add the tomatoes with their juices, the chicken stock, and the bay leaf. Bring to a simmer.

4. Meanwhile, in a large skillet, heat the remaining 1 tablespoon oil over medium heat. Add the sausage and cook, breaking up with the side of a large spoon into bite-sized pieces, until it loses its pink look, about 8 minutes. Add the onions, red bell pepper, and garlic. Cook, stirring occasionally, until the onions are softened, about 6 minutes. Stir into the chicken mixture. Stir in the beans. (The cassoulet can be prepared up to this point up to 1 day ahead, cooled, covered, and refrigerated. Stir 2 additional cups chicken stock or water into the cassoulet before proceeding.)

5. In a small bowl, mix the bread crumbs and parsley. Sprinkle over the top of the cassoulet. Bake for 30 minutes. Using a large spoon, gently press the thin crust that has formed on the cassoulet just under the surface. Continue baking until the cassoulet is simmering and a second thin crust has formed, about 30 minutes. Let stand for 10 minutes. Serve hot.

Note: Instead of paying a premium price for boneless and skinless chicken thighs, purchase 5 pounds chicken thighs with the skin and bones, and remove the skin and bones yourself. It's a quick and easy procedure.

Two-Way Duck with Pecan-Orange Wild Rice

Makes 4 servings

Make Ahead: Cut up the ducks, make the stock, and render the fat the day before serving. The sauce can be prepared up to 1 day ahead, cooled, covered, and refrigerated. The duck quarters can be steamed up to 1½ hours before roasting, and set aside at room temperature.

Roast duck is a popular dish at my house, but frankly, a single duck is really just enough for two people. When I want to serve duck to friends, fitting two birds into my oven just doesn't work. So I devised this solution, based on the way that many restaurants serve duck: Cut the ducks into parts, then cook each one so they are at their best: Roast the leg quarters until crisp, cook the boneless duck breast in a skillet until medium-rare, turn the bony carcass and giblets into a luscious classic demi-glace sauce, and render the excess skin and fat. Each one of these steps is very easy, so please do not be intimidated by the long recipe. I've also included suggested side dishes here because they serve only four people, and the other recipes in the book are for larger groups.

- *Like goose, duck gives off a lot of fat. In France, where the word "cholesterol" is rarely uttered, rendered duck and goose fat are prized cooking ingredients. To accommodate the American phobia about animal fats, you could certainly substitute butter or vegetable oil for the rendered fat in these recipes, but try the rendered fat as a special treat.*

- *Pecan-Orange Wild Rice is the perfect side dish for duck. Wild rice varies greatly from brand to brand and it is hard to gauge its cooking time and rate of liquid absorption. Hand-harvested wild rice is expensive, but it has an excellent, robust flavor and firm texture. It takes somewhat longer to cook than the less expen-*

sive, machine-harvested variety. If you have excess liquid in the pot when the rice is tender, simply drain it off. On the other hand, if the rice absorbs the liquid before it is done, add more stock (or water) as needed. Because of these variables, it may be best to make the rice ahead of serving, and reheat it in a skillet or the microwave oven.

Two 5½- to 6-pound Long Island (Peking) ducks
2 quarts Homemade Duck Stock (page 41),
  made with reserved wings, giblets, necks, and
  carcass bones
½ teaspoon salt
¼ teaspoon freshly milled black pepper
½ teaspoon dried thyme

Pecan-Orange Wild Rice (recipe follows)
Sautéed Spinach (recipe follows)

1. Prepare the ducks and stock the day before serving. Using a large, heavy knife, cut off the wings and reserve. Reserve the giblets (not the livers; save them for another use or discard). Chop the necks into 2- to 3-inch pieces. Set the wings, giblets, and necks aside for the stock.

2. Using a sharp, thin knife, cut off the leg quarters (thigh and drumstick together) at the thigh joints. Make an incision down each side of the breastbone. With the knife tip pointing toward the rib bones, cut away the breast meat (with the skin still attached), pulling the meat away from the ribs as you cut. Cut off the breast section when you reach the wing joint and the bottom of the rib cage. Trim away excess skin from the perimeters of the duck quarters and reserve the skin pieces. Pull the skin off the duck breasts and reserve. You will have four duck leg quarters and four boneless and skinless breasts. Season the duck with salt, pepper, and thyme. Cover with plastic wrap and refrigerate.

3. To make the stock, using a heavy cleaver chop the

duck carcasses into manageable pieces to fit your stockpot, and use to make the duck stock according to the directions on page 41.

4. To make the salsa verde, pull out the clumps of fat inside the duck body cavity on either side of the tail, coarsely chop, and set aside. Cut off any remaining skin from the carcass and cut into thin strips. Render according to the instructions in Roast Goose with Port Gravy.

5. To make the sauce, place the duck stock in a large pot. Bring to a boil over high heat. Boil until the stock is reduced to about 1 quart, 1 to 1½ hours. Transfer to a medium saucepan and boil until reduced to about 1½ cups, about 30 minutes. (The sauce can be prepared up to 1 day ahead, cooled, covered, and refrigerated. Reheat before serving.)

6. Fit a large pot with a collapsible aluminum steamer rack and fill the pot with enough water to almost reach the rack. Add the duck leg quarters and bring to a boil over high heat. Cover tightly and reduce the heat to medium-low. Steam the duck leg quarters for 45 minutes. Remove from the pot and transfer to a roasting pan. (The duck quarters can be prepared up to this point 1½ hours before roasting, covered, and set aside at room temperature.)

7. Position a rack in the top third of the oven and preheat to 450°F. Roast the steamed duck leg quarters, turning occasionally, until crisp and golden brown, 30 to 40 minutes. Remove the duck breasts from the refrigerator and let stand at room temperature while the duck legs are roasting.

8. About 15 minutes before serving, heat 2 tablespoons of the rendered duck fat in a very large skillet over medium-high heat. Add the duck breasts and cook, turning once, until lightly browned and medium-rare, 6 to 8 minutes. (You can use a small, sharp knife to make an incision in the thickest part of the breast to check for doneness. Or press the duck with your finger—it should feel somewhat soft in the center. The firmer the meat, the more well done it is.) Transfer the

duck to a carving board and cover loosely with aluminum foil. Let stand for about 3 minutes for the juices to settle.

9. To serve, using a sharp carving knife, slice each breast into thin diagonal slices. Slip the knife under each breast and transfer to a dinner plate, fanning out the slices slightly. (If you wish, serve a whole breast, unsliced, on each plate.) Place a duck leg quarter on each plate. Divide the wild rice and the spinach among the plates. Spoon some of the duck sauce around the duck, and serve immediately.

Pecan-Orange Wild Rice: In a medium saucepan, heat 2 tablespoons rendered duck fat over medium heat. Add 2 tablespoons finely chopped shallots and cook until softened, about 1 minute. Stir in 1 cup (6 ounces) wild rice, rinsed and drained. Add 2⅔ cups Homemade Duck Stock (page 41) or canned low-sodium chicken broth, ⅓ cup fresh orange juice, the grated zest of ½ large orange, ¾ teaspoon salt, and ¼ teaspoon freshly milled black pepper. Bring to a boil over high heat. Reduce the heat to medium-low and cover tightly. Cook until the rice is tender and puffed, about 1 hour. Be flexible with the cooking time, as it will vary with different brands of rice. Stir in ½ cup finely chopped pecans. Cover and let stand for 10 minutes. If necessary, drain any excess liquid from the wild rice before serving hot. (The rice can be prepared up to 2 hours ahead. If necessary, reheat, covered, over low heat, stirring often. Or place in a covered, microwave-safe bowl, and microwave on Medium-High, or 70% power, stirring occasionally, until heated through, about 5 minutes.)

Sautéed Spinach: Fill a sink or very large bowl with cold water. Wash 2 pounds fresh spinach, tough stems removed. Shake the spinach to remove excess water, but do not dry completely. (The spinach can be cleaned up to 2 hours before cooking, stored at room temperature.) In a large saucepan, heat 2 tablespoons unsalted butter over medium-high heat. Add 1 small garlic clove, finely chopped, and cook until fragrant, about 1 minute. In batches, stir in the spinach, waiting for the first batch to wilt before adding another. Cook until the spinach is tender, about 5 minutes. Season with ½ teaspoon salt and ¼ teaspoon pepper. (The spinach can be prepared up to 1 hour ahead. Reheat over low heat, stirring often.) Serve hot, using a slotted spoon to leave excess liquid in the pot.

Roast Goose with Port Wine Gravy

Makes 6 to 8 servings

Make Ahead: The goose must be refrigerated uncovered 2 days before serving. The rendered goose fat and stock can be prepared up to 2 days ahead, cooled, covered, and refrigerated.

There is a lot of romance about roast goose for Christmas, probably stemming from the Yuletide dinner scenes in British tales or from the German culinary tradition. Goose is a big bird, but first-time cooks should know that its size is deceiving—it doesn't yield a lot of meat. That said, the meat is dark, rich, and flavorful, reminiscent of both roast duck and well-done roast beef. In order to stretch the servings, offer lots of side dishes, like braised Red Cabbage with Apples and Bacon (page 66), Chestnut and Prune Stuffing (page 76), and Giant Potato and Leek Rösti (page 69).

- *If possible, order a fresh goose from a specialty butcher. Frozen geese are also available, and are quite good. For best results, thaw thoroughly in the refrigerator, allowing 2 to 3 days.*
- *Goose gives off a great amount of fat during cooking (around 3 cups!), which is a blessing in disguise. Goose fat is an excellent medium for frying and sautéing, especially for potato dishes like Giant Potato*

and Leek Rösti (page 69). There is plenty of visible fat that can be removed from around the tail area, chopped, and melted in a saucepan. However, most of it is hidden in the skin, and it needs to be cooked out, or the skin will be unappetizingly rubbery and greasy. My method uses two tricks to get the fat out (culled from recipes for crisp-skinned Peking duck): First, leave the goose uncovered in the refrigerator for a day or two to dry and stretch the skin, which opens the pores and helps the fat run out of the skin during roasting. Second, steam the goose on a rack in a covered oval roasting pan (such as an old-fashioned turkey roaster) on top of the stove, a procedure that draws out the initial amount of fat better than roasting.

- *Unlike turkey, the entire batch of stuffing should fit in the goose body cavity. Also, unlike turkey, the large opening to a stuffed goose needs to be sewn shut. Trussing needles are hard to find, even at professional restaurant supply stores. Mattress or canvas needles are easily available at sewing or hobby shops. These needles are long and sturdy, with large eyes that can thread cotton butcher's twine. I store my "goose needle" in my kitchen gadget drawer, taped to the inside of the drawer with a large piece of masking tape so it can't get lost.*
- *Make Homemade Goose Stock to flavor the stuffing and make the gravy. The bony wing tips are always removed from the goose before roasting because they have a tendency to burn. Along with the goose neck and heart (the liver would make the stock bitter and is used in the stuffing), the wing tips are the beginning of a great stock, but a bit of chicken stock boosts the poultry flavor. If you don't own a heavy cleaver that will cut through the strong bones, have the butcher remove the wing tips and chop them along with the goose neck before you bring the bird home.*
- *Goose should be cooked to 180°F, like a turkey, but don't expect it to be tender like turkey. The joints of a goose, especially at the hip, are very tight, and it always takes some work to pry them from the body. The*

skin is one of the best parts of the goose, and should be served in generous portions.

One 10- to 12-pound goose, neck chopped into 2- to 3-inch pieces, and giblets reserved to make Homemade Goose Stock (page 41)

Chestnut and Prune Stuffing (page 76)
Salt
Freshly milled black pepper
4 tablespoons rendered goose fat or butter
¼ cup all-purpose flour
2⅔ cups Homemade Goose Stock (page 41)
⅓ cup tawny or ruby port

1. One to two days before roasting, rinse the goose and pat dry with paper towels. Pull out the clumps of pale yellow fat from around the tail cavity and reserve. Cut off any excess neck skin and reserve. Cut off the wings at the second joints, leaving only the last wing segment attached to the goose. Use the neck, giblets (no liver), and wing tips to make the stock. Wrap the liver tightly in plastic wrap, and refrigerate until ready to make the stuffing.

2. Place the goose on a rack in a roasting pan. Refrigerate uncovered at least overnight and up to 48 hours. The skin will dry out, but that's what you want.

3. Meanwhile, render the goose fat: Coarsely chop the goose fat and cut the skin into thin strips. Place in a medium saucepan and add ¼ cup warm water. Cook over medium-low heat until the fat has rendered into a golden liquid and the skin strips are lightly browned, about 2 hours. Strain into a bowl and let cool to room temperature. Store the fat in small containers (1-cup deli containers work well), as you will use only small amounts of it at a time. Makes about 2 cups. (The rendered fat can be stored, covered and refrigerated, for up to 3 weeks or frozen for up to 3 months.)

4. Fill the body cavity with the stuffing. Using a trussing needle and kitchen twine, sew up the opening.

With the tip of the needle, prick the goose skin all over (without piercing the meat), especially in the thigh area.

5. Place the goose on a rack in a covered oval roasting pan. Add 2 cups water to the pan and bring to a boil on top of the stove over high heat. Cover tightly and reduce the heat to low. Steam the goose for 1 hour. Remove the goose and the rack from the pan, and pour out the liquid in the pan. Return the goose and the rack to the pan, and season the goose with 1 teaspoon salt and ¼ teaspoon pepper.

6. Preheat the oven to 350°F. Roast the goose, uncovered, until an instant-read thermometer inserted in the thickest part of the thigh (without touching a bone) reads 170°F, about 1½ hours. During the last 15 minutes of roasting, increase the oven temperature to 400°F to crisp the skin. As the goose roasts and rendered fat accumulates in the pan, use a bulb baster to remove the fat and add it to the rendered fat from Step 2, if desired, or discard. Transfer the goose to a serving platter and let stand for 20 to 30 minutes before carving.

7. To make the gravy, pour all of the rendered fat out of the pan into the reserved fat. Set the roasting pan on two burners over medium-low heat. Add 4 tablespoons of the rendered goose fat to the pan. Sprinkle the flour into the pan, whisking constantly. Let the mixture bubble until it turns beige, 1 to 2 minutes. Whisk in the stock and port, scraping up the browned bits on the bottom of the pan. (Save the remaining stock for another use. It is an excellent substitute for chicken stock.) Simmer for about 5 minutes, whisking occasionally. Season the gravy with salt and pepper. If desired, strain the gravy. Transfer to a warmed sauceboat.

8. Carve the goose (see Carving Up, page 58), and serve with a spoonful of the stuffing and a portion of the crisp skin. Pass the gravy on the side.

Roast Turkey with Bourbon Gravy

Makes about 12 servings, plus leftovers

Some families think of turkey as strictly for Thanksgiving, but others wouldn't dream of having a Christmas meal without the bird making a return appearance. Turkey is a big bird, and a big subject. I have roasted hundreds of turkeys in just about every way possible. But this is the tried-and-true method that has given me my reputation as Mr. Turkey (for an in-depth discussion, see Thanksgiving 101. In the meantime, here are the most important things to remember:

- There is no flavor difference between a tom and a hen turkey, only size. Toms weigh about 15 pounds and above, and hens average between 8 and 15 pounds. Choose your turkey size by how many people you want to serve, allowing about 1 pound per person, which allows for seconds and leftovers. Toms are bred to have large breasts, so you will get more white meat for your money with a big bird. Use the chart below to calculate the roasting times.

- I prefer the flavor and moistness of a fresh turkey. If you must use a frozen turkey, defrost it properly in the refrigerator, never at room temperature. Allow a full 24 hours in the refrigerator to defrost each 5 pounds of turkey. A 25-pound bird will take a full 5 days to defrost. If you are a novice cook, buy a self-basting bird; these are injected with broth and fats to help keep the bird moist. Self-basting birds don't have a true turkey flavor, but they are practically fail-proof. But, I guarantee, once you learn how to roast a beautiful, fresh, all-natural turkey, there is no turning back. Organic and free-range birds are excellent, but the added cost depends on your guests (will they really appreciate the difference?).

- Invest in few essential tools that you will use time and again to roast your holiday birds (and roasts). A high-quality roasting pan *will make the best, beautifully browned gravy drippings, and, unlike those cheap disposable aluminum foil pans, you won't have to worry about the pan buckling under the weight of a heavy bird. My favorite pan is heavy-duty aluminum with an anodized aluminum exterior and a nonstick interior and measures 16 × 13 × 3 inches. Buy a* roasting rack

 Estimated Turkey Roasting Times

(Oven Temperature 325°F)

*A*dd an extra 30 minutes to the roasting time to allow for variations in roasting conditions. It's better to have a bird done ahead of time than to keep hungry people waiting for it to finish roasting.

Unstuffed Turkey		Stuffed Turkey	
8 to 12 pounds	2³/₄ to 3 hours	8 to 12 pounds	3 to 3¹/₂ hours
12 to 14 pounds	3 to 3³/₄ hours	12 to 14 pounds	3¹/₂ to 4 hours
14 to 18 pounds	3³/₄ to 4¹/₄ hours	14 to 18 pounds	4 to 4¹/₄ hours
18 to 20 pounds	4¹/₄ to 4¹/₂ hours	18 to 20 pounds	4¹/₄ to 4³/₄ hours
20 to 24 pounds	4¹/₂ to 5 hours	20 to 24 pounds	4³/₄ to 5¹/₄ hours

to fit the pan so the turkey doesn't stew in its own juices. A meat thermometer, *preferably instant-read, is the best way to tell when the bird is cooked. Don't trust pop-up thermometers as they often get glued shut by the turkey juices. A* bulb baster *helps distribute the cooking juices over the bird. And don't forget an* oven thermometer— *many oven thermostats are inaccurate. A* flat whisk *(buy a hard plastic one for a nonstick pan) helps you get into the corners of the pan to whisk the flour and butter into the drippings for the gravy.*

- *You will never be able to fit all of the stuffing into the bird, so plan on baking leftover stuffing on the side. Fill the bird loosely with the stuffing, as it will expand during cooking.*

- *The trick with roast turkey is have the white meat remain moist and succulent while the dark meat is thoroughly cooked and at its peak of flavor. White meat is cooked at 170°F, and after that point, it begins to dry out. Unfortunately, dark meat needs to be cooked to 180°F in order for it to be tasty. Many cookbooks and cooking magazines instruct the cook to roast the bird to 170°F, which does give moist white meat, but undercooked, pinkish dark meat. It's not unhealthy to eat the dark meat—I just don't like the soft texture and underroasted flavor. I correct the problem by wrapping—not tenting—the breast area with aluminum foil. Steam collects under the foil and helps keep the breast tender and juicy. Baste under the foil (basting promotes a crisp, brown skin) every 20 to 30 minutes. During the last hour of roasting, remove the foil and allow the skin to brown.*

- *Use Homemade Turkey Stock (page 41) for the best gravy and stuffing. If you wish, make Quick Turkey Stock (page 58) from the neck and giblets. To make any amount of gravy, follow the recipe below, allowing 1 1/2 tablespoons each of turkey fat and flour for every cup of combined stock and degreased turkey drippings.*

One 18-pound fresh turkey

Corn Bread–Succotash Stuffing (page 74) or your favorite recipe

6 tablespoons (3/4 stick) unsalted butter, softened

Salt and freshly milled black pepper

8 1/2 cups Homemade Turkey Stock (page 41) or Quick Turkey Stock (recipe follows), approximately

1/2 cup plus 1 tablespoon all-purpose flour

3 tablespoons bourbon (optional)

1. Preheat the oven to 325°F. Remove the neck and giblets. Reserve or use to make stock. Rinse the turkey well with cold water and pat dry with paper towels. Remove the fat from the tail area; reserve. (If there isn't any fat, don't worry.) Turn the turkey on its breast. Loosely fill the neck cavity with stuffing. Pin the neck skin to the back skin with a thin wooden or metal skewer. Fold the wings akimbo behind the back or tie them to the body with kitchen string. Loosely fill the body cavity with stuffing. Place any remaining stuffing in a lightly buttered casserole, cover, and refrigerate to bake as a side dish. Secure the drumsticks at the tail with a clip or tie them with kitchen string. Place the turkey, breast side up, on a rack in a large roasting pan. Rub the turkey with the softened butter. Season with salt and pepper. Place the reserved turkey fat in the pan. Tightly cover the breast area with aluminum foil. Pour 2 cups of the stock in the bottom of the pan.

2. Roast, basting every 30 minutes with the drippings in the pan (lift up the foil to reach the breast area), until an instant-read thermometer inserted into the thickest part of the thigh (not touching a bone) reads 180° to 185°F and the stuffing at least 165°F, about 4 1/2 hours. As the drippings in the pan evaporate, add 2 cups water. During the last hour, remove the foil to allow the skin to brown.

3. Transfer the turkey to a large serving platter. Let stand for 20 to 30 minutes before carving. Increase the

Carving Up

Here are step-by-step instructions on carving a roast turkey.

1. First, allow the bird to stand at room temperature for at least 20 minutes and up to 40 minutes before carving. This allows the juices to settle into the meat. If you carve it too soon, the juices will run out of the flesh, and you'll have dry turkey.

2. Remove the drumsticks to make the breast easier to reach and carve. Cut off each drumstick at the knee joint. If the turkey is properly cooked (that is, to at least 180°F), they will pull away without any trouble, making the joints easy to sever. Do not remove the thighs at this point, or the bird will roll around on the platter while you try to carve it. Transfer the drumsticks to a platter. To allow more people to enjoy the dark meat, tilt each drumstick, holding it from the foot end, and cut downward along the bone to slice the meat.

3. Hold the breast firmly with the meat fork. One side at a time, make a deep incision, cutting parallel to the table, down near the wing. Cut down along the side of the breast to carve it into thin slices. Every slice will stop at the parallel cut. Transfer the sliced breast to the platter. Turn the turkey around to carve the other side.

4. Pry the thighs away from the hips to reveal the ball joints, and sever at the joints. Transfer the thighs to the platter. To carve each thigh, hold the thigh with a meat fork, and carve the meat parallel to the bone.

5. Pry the wings away from the shoulder joints and sever at the joints. Transfer to the platter.

If you still feel nervous about carving in front of your guests, present the whole roast bird at the table in all its glory. Then, run back into the kitchen and carve the meat where no one is looking. Serve it carved on a platter, or use two platters, separating the dark and white meat. This actually works better, because the guests can serve themselves more easily.

Carving a goose follows the same general idea, but with some important distinctions. The goose joints are very tight, and they will not sever as easily as the turkey. Also, a goose is all dark meat.

---

oven temperature to 375°F. Drizzle the stuffing in the casserole with ½ cup turkey broth, cover, and bake until heated through, about 30 minutes.

4. Meanwhile, pour the drippings from the pan into a large glass bowl or measuring cup. Let stand for 5 minutes; skim off and reserve the clear yellow fat on the surface. Add enough turkey stock to the skimmed drippings to make 6 cups total.

5. Place the roasting pan over two stove burners on medium heat. Add ½ cup plus 1 tablespoon of the reserved turkey fat (if necessary, add melted butter to make up any shortage). Whisk in the flour, scraping up the browned bits on the bottom of the pan, and cook for 2 minutes. Whisk in the turkey stock and optional bourbon. Reduce the heat to low and simmer for 5 minutes. (If the gravy seems too thick, add more stock or water.) Season with salt and pepper. Strain the gravy, if desired. Transfer to a warmed gravy boat. Carve the turkey (see Carving Up, above), and serve the gravy and stuffing alongside.

Quick Turkey Stock: In a large saucepan, heat 1 tablespoon oil over medium-high heat. Add the turkey neck, chopped into 2- to 3-inch pieces, and the giblets (no liver). Cook, turning occasionally, until browned, about 8 minutes. Add 1 small onion, 1 small carrot, 1 small celery rib with leaves, all chopped, and cook until softened, about 6 minutes. Add three 13¾-ounce cans low-sodium chicken broth and 1 quart water. Bring to a simmer, skimming off any foam that rises to the surface. Add 3 fresh parsley sprigs, ¼ teaspoon dried thyme, 8 peppercorns, and 1 bay leaf. Simmer for 1½ hours, the longer the better. Strain. Cool and skim any clear yellow fat that rises to the surface. Makes about 8½ cups.

Baked Salmon Fillets with Salsa Verde

Makes 16 to 20 buffet servings

Make Ahead: The salmon can be prepared up to 1 day ahead, cooled, covered, and refrigerated.

A chilled, whole poached salmon with herb mayonnaise has been the centerpiece of many a buffet. But, honestly, how many cooks have a salmon poacher? In this up-dated version boneless salmon fillets are slathered with an herbed sauce, then baked to make a no-fuss, lovely main course for a serve-yourself feast. If you want to serve a hot fish main course at a large dinner party, bake the salmon fillets, but do not cool them.

Salsa Verde

½ cup coarsely chopped fresh parsley
½ cup packed fresh basil leaves
¼ cup sliced blanched almonds
2 tablespoons fresh lemon juice
1 tablespoon Dijon mustard
1 garlic clove, crushed through a press
½ teaspoon salt

¼ **teaspoon freshly milled black pepper**
½ **cup extra virgin olive oil**

Vegetable oil, for brushing
Two 3-pound salmon fillets, skin on
Lemon wedges, for serving

1. To make the salsa verde: In a food processor fitted with the metal blade, process all of the ingredients except the oil. With the machine running, gradually add the oil. Process, occasionally stopping the machine to scrape down the sides of the bowl, until the salsa is smooth, about 45 seconds. Set aside.

2. Position the racks in the center and top third of the oven and preheat to 350°F. Brush a 2-foot long sheet of extrawide aluminum foil well with oil. Rub your fingers over the surface of a fillet and use tweezers to remove any stray bones. (Sterilize the tweezers first over an open flame.) Place the fillet, skin side down, on the foil and spread with half of the salsa. Bring the long sides of the foil up to meet over the fillet, and fold tightly to seal. Fold the short sides closed. Place on a large baking sheet. Repeat with the other fillet and the remaining salsa.

3. Bake for 20 minutes. Switch the position of the fillets from top to bottom. Continue baking until the fish is done, about 20 more minutes. To check for doneness, open the foil and insert a knife between the flakes of flesh in the center of the fillets—it will be evenly opaque or have just a blush of pink in the center.

4. Open the foil and let the fillets stand until cooled to room temperature. Rewrap and refrigerate until well chilled, at least 4 hours or overnight. To serve, slide the fillets onto a platter. Cut the salmon on the platter into individual portions. Serve with the lemon wedges on the side.

Red and Green Lasagna

Makes 12 servings

Make Ahead: The lasagna can be prepared 6 hours before baking, covered, and refrigerated.

With a more delicate flavor than the typical beefy lasagna, this delicious chicken-and-spinach–filled version is especially welcome at holiday time, where its green and red ingredients tie into the season's colors. In addition to tomato sauce, it has a creamy white sauce that gives the dish a northern Italian flair. Yes, it is a bit more complicated than other lasagnas, but the results are hard to beat.

- *Some cooks like to make and freeze lasagna 2 to 3 weeks before baking. The last time I cooked a frozen batch of this dense lasagna, it took 2½ hours to cook through! In my opinion, the convenience of freezing isn't worth the lengthy baking time. (Of course, you could defrost the lasagna first.) I prefer to make and freeze the tomato sauce, chicken, and stock for up to 1 month. When I'm ready to make the lasagna, I defrost them, make the filling and white sauce, and assemble.*

Chicken and Broth
One 3½-pound chicken, cut into 8 pieces
1 medium onion, chopped
1 medium celery rib with leaves, chopped
1 medium carrot, chopped (optional)
2 sprigs fresh parsley
¼ teaspoon dried thyme
¼ teaspoon whole black peppercorns

Tomato Sauce
2 tablespoons olive oil
1 large onion, chopped
2 garlic cloves, minced
One 28-ounce can tomatoes in juice, chopped, juices reserved
One 6-ounce can tomato paste
1½ cups Homemade White Chicken Stock (page 41) or canned low-sodium chicken broth
1½ teaspoons dried basil
1½ teaspoons dried oregano
¼ teaspoon crushed hot red pepper

White Sauce
8 tablespoons (1 stick) unsalted butter
½ cup all-purpose flour
3½ cups Homemade White Chicken Stock (page 41) or canned low-sodium chicken broth, heated until hot
¼ cup heavy cream
¼ teaspoon salt
¼ teaspoon freshly milled white or black pepper

Filling
Two 10-ounce packages frozen chopped spinach
1½ cups dried bread crumbs
½ cup heavy cream
1½ cups ricotta
½ cup freshly grated Parmesan
2 large eggs, beaten
⅓ cup chopped fresh parsley
¼ teaspoon freshly grated nutmeg
¼ teaspoon salt
¼ teaspoon freshly ground black pepper
1 pound dried lasagna noodles
3 cups (12 ounces) shredded mozzarella

1. To prepare the chicken and broth, place the chicken, onion, celery, and carrot, if using, in a large pot and add enough cold water to cover. Bring to a boil over high heat, skimming off the foam that rises to the surface. Add the parsley, thyme, and peppercorns. Reduce the heat to medium-low. Cook, uncovered, for 30 minutes. Remove from the heat and cover tightly. Let stand for 30 minutes to allow the chicken to cook through.

2. Strain over a large bowl, reserving the chicken broth. Cool the chicken until easy to handle. Discard the skin and bones, and coarsely chop the chicken meat. Set the meat aside. (The chicken and broth can be prepared 1 day ahead, separately cooled, covered, and refrigerated, or frozen for up to 1 month.)

3. To make the tomato sauce, heat the oil in a large saucepan over medium heat. Add the onion and cook until softened, about 5 minutes. Add the garlic and cook for 1 minute. Stir in the tomatoes with their juices, tomato paste, chicken stock, basil, oregano, and crushed red pepper, and mix to dissolve the tomato paste. Bring to a boil. Reduce the heat to low. Simmer, uncovered, until thickened and reduced to about 6 cups, about 40 minutes. (The tomato sauce can be prepared 1 day ahead, cooled, covered, and refrigerated, or frozen for up to 1 month.)

4. To make the white sauce, in a medium, heavy-bottomed saucepan, melt the butter over medium-low heat. Whisk in the flour and let bubble, without browning, for 2 minutes. Whisk in the hot stock and bring to a simmer. Cook, stirring often, until thick, about 3 minutes. Stir in the heavy cream. Season with the salt and pepper. Transfer to a medium bowl. Cover with plastic wrap, pressing the wrap directly on the surface of the sauce, and pierce a few holes in the wrap to allow the steam to escape (this prevents a skin from forming on the surface of the sauce). Set aside.

5. To make the filling, put the spinach in a wire sieve and rinse under warm water until thawed. A handful at a time, squeeze the moisture out of the spinach, and transfer the spinach to a large bowl.

6. In a small bowl, mix the bread crumbs and heavy cream, and let stand until softened, about 5 minutes. Scrape into the bowl with the spinach. Add the chopped chicken, ricotta and Parmesan, eggs, parsley, nutmeg, salt and pepper. Set aside.

7. Bring a large pot of lightly salted water to a boil over high heat. One a time, stir the lasagna noodles into the water. Cover and bring the water back to a boil. Immediately uncover the pot, and cook the pasta until barely tender, about 7 minutes. (The pasta will cook further in the oven, so it should still have some "bite" to its texture.) Drain into a colander and rinse under cold running water. (If not using immediately, toss the pasta with 1 tablespoon olive oil and set aside in the colander for up to 1 hour.)

8. Position a rack in the center of the oven and preheat to 350°F. Lightly oil a 15 × 10-inch baking dish.

9. Spread about $1/2$ cup of the tomato sauce on the bottom of the dish. Arrange 5 lasagna noodles (4 horizontally and 1 vertically), slightly overlapping and cut to fit, in the dish. Spoon one-third of the tomato sauce over the noodles. Scatter half of the chicken-spinach filling over the noodles, then spoon half of the white sauce on top. Arrange another 5 noodles in the dish. Top with half of the remaining tomato sauce, then the remaining filling, remaining white sauce, and 1 cup of the mozzarella. Arrange a final layer of noodles, spread with the remaining tomato sauce, and sprinkle with the remaining mozzarella. Cover the lasagna tightly with aluminum foil. (The lasagna can be prepared up to 6 hours ahead, cooled, covered tightly, and refrigerated.)

10. Bake for 30 minutes. Remove the foil and continue baking until the sauce is bubbling throughout, or until a meat thermometer inserted in the center of the lasagna registers 165°F, about 30 more minutes. Let the lasagna stand for 10 minutes before serving.

Savory Sausage and Cheese Bread Pudding

Makes 6 to 8 servings

Make Ahead: The pudding can be prepared the night before, covered tightly with plastic wrap, and refrigerated.

Here's a carefree, delicious way to serve Christmas brunch. Layers of bread with sausage and vegetables, held together with a cheesy custard, this dish is sometimes called strata ("layers" in Italian). The pudding can be made the night before, so when you are up to your neck in Christmas-morning wrapping paper, all the pudding needs is a trip to the oven. Serve it with a winter fruit salad of sliced apples and pears, orange sections, and pomegranate seeds, tossed with a bit of Grand Marnier.

- *Before assembling the pudding, remember to let the bread stand out at room temperature for at least 8 hours so it dries out a bit. If necessary, bake in a preheated 300°F oven until it is dried out but not toasted or crisp, 20 to 30 minutes—the bread will firm up more out of the oven.*

- *If you wish, the pudding can also be prepared right before it goes into the oven. To reduce the baking time, heat the milk in a medium saucepan until bubbles appear around the edges. Slowly whisk the hot milk into the eggs. Bake the pudding until a knife inserted in the center comes out clean, about 1 hour.*

2 tablespoons extra virgin olive oil
1 large onion, chopped
1 medium red bell pepper, cored, seeded, and chopped
1 pound sweet Italian pork or turkey sausage, casings removed
6 large eggs
2 tablespoons Dijon mustard
1½ teaspoons Italian herb seasoning
½ teaspoon salt
¼ teaspoon freshly milled black pepper
1 quart milk
12 slices day-old, firm white sandwich bread, crusts trimmed
2 cups (8 ounces) shredded sharp Cheddar

1. In a large skillet, heat the oil over medium heat. Add the onion and red bell pepper. Cook, stirring occasionally, until softened, 5 to 7 minutes. Add the sausage and cook, breaking up the sausage with the side of a spoon until it loses its pink color, about 10 minutes. Drain off any liquid in the skillet and set the sausage mixture aside.

2. In a large bowl, whisk the eggs, mustard, Italian seasoning, salt, and pepper. Gradually whisk in the milk. Set aside.

3. Lightly butter a 13 × 9-inch glass baking dish. Line the bottom of the prepared dish with the bread slices, trimming to fit, if needed. Sprinkle the bread with half of the cheese, then spread with all of the sausage mixture. Top with the remaining bread slices. Slowly pour the egg mixture over the bread, allowing it to soak in. Sprinkle the top with the remaining cheese. (The pudding can be prepared the night before, covered tightly with plastic wrap, and refrigerated.)

4. Position a rack in the center of the oven and preheat to 325°F. Uncover the pudding and bake until a knife inserted in the center comes out clean, about 1½ hours. Let stand for 10 minutes before serving.

Side Dishes and Stuffings

From Cranberries to Black-Eyed Peas

What would roast beef be without potatoes or Yorkshire pudding serve alongside? Roast goose without red cabbage and potato pancakes? Or, the ultimate in holiday unthinkables, turkey without cranberry sauce? Never underestimate the importance of side dishes. In my family we look forward to Mom's cheesy scalloped potatoes just as much as we do her delicious ham.

To serve your side dishes at their best, follow these tips:

- Unless you plan accordingly, you could easily have a traffic jam in the oven trying to reheat all those sides. Be sure that at least one dish is prepared on top of the stove to lessen the load.

- Many side dishes can be prepared ahead and stored in the refrigerator until ready to serve. Increase the baking times by 10 to 15 minutes if the dishes have been chilled.

- Allow at least 20 minutes for the food to heat through in the oven. Cover dishes with their lids or aluminum foil.

- Warm the serving dishes (in a preheated 200°F oven for a few minutes or by filling with hot water) before adding the food.

- If a hot dish is going to be served in the casserole or baked dish it was cooked in, have pot holders and trivets at the table to make the serving easier.

Black-Eyed Pea Stew (Hoppin' John)

Makes 12 to 16 side-dish servings; 8 to 12 main-course servings

Make Ahead: The black-eyed peas can be prepared up to 1 day ahead and reheated. Add the cooked rice just before serving.

Another Southern holiday tradition, black-eyed peas are always served at New Year's celebrations because they represent the countless coins that we hope to accumulate during the upcoming prosperous year. Hoppin' John is a black-eyed pea and rice stew that is hearty enough to serve as a main course, but I serve it as a side dish for baked ham. There are many ideas on how it got its unusual name, but one seems to make the most sense. The dish arrived in our country via the African slaves from French Caribbean islands, where a rice and pigeon pea stew was cooked. "Hoppin' John" is an Americanization of pois à pigeon, French for pigeon peas, which are related to black-eyed peas.

- *Black-eyed peas have a distinctively earthy flavor. Because they have thin skins, they don't have to be soaked like many other dried legumes. However, it is difficult to gauge their cooking time (some beans are just drier than others). So, keep an eye on the pot, and check often for tenderness.*

- *While there are many, many ways to make Hoppin' John, this version uses a ham hock stock. This step takes little effort, just a bit of patience. If you are serving Hoppin' John as a main course, cut the meat from the cooked hocks, reserve, and stir it into the finished peas. To serve it as a side dish, reserve the ham for another use, and do not add it to the peas (unless you want a filling side dish).*

- *For a buffet, serve Hoppin' John from the Dutch oven,*

placed on a warming plate, or transfer it to a chafing dish or slow cooker.

2 ham hocks, about 1¼ pounds total (see Note)
2 medium onions, chopped
3 medium celery ribs, chopped
2 tablespoons vegetable oil
1 medium red bell pepper, cored, seeded, and chopped
2 garlic cloves, minced
1½ tablespoons Cajun Seasoning (recipe follows) or a salt-free, store-bought blend
1 pound black-eyed peas, picked over to remove stones, rinsed, and drained
Salt
1 cup long-grain rice
Hot red pepper sauce

1. Place the ham hocks, 1 onion, and 1 celery rib in a large pot, and add 3 quarts cold water. Bring to a boil over high heat. Reduce the heat to medium-low and partially cover. Simmer until the ham hocks are tender, about 1½ hours. Strain over a large bowl, reserving the liquid. You should have about 2½ quarts stock; add water, if necessary. Remove the meat from the hocks, discarding the skin and bones. Coarsely chop the meat and set aside (or reserve for another use).

2. In a Dutch oven, heat the oil over medium heat. Add the remaining onion and celery ribs, and the red bell pepper. Cook, stirring often, until softened, about 5 minutes. Add the garlic and Cajun seasoning, and stir until fragrant, about 30 seconds. Add the black-eyed peas and enough of the ham stock to cover the peas by 1 inch, about 2 quarts. Bring to a boil over high heat.

3. Reduce the heat to medium-low and partially cover. Cook, stirring occasionally, until the peas are tender, about 40 to 60 minutes. Add water, if needed, to keep the beans barely covered with liquid. If desired, stir in the ham meat during the last 5 minutes. The mixture will be somewhat soupy. (The black-eyed peas can be prepared up to this point up to 1 day ahead, cooled, covered, and refrigerated. Reheat gently over medium-low heat, adding about 1 cup water to return it to its former soupy consistency.)

4. Meanwhile, in a medium saucepan, bring the rice, 2 cups of the remaining ham stock, and ½ teaspoon salt to a boil over medium heat. Reduce the heat to low and cover tightly. Cook until the rice is tender and has absorbed the liquid, 15 to 17 minutes. Remove the pan from the heat and let stand, covered, for at least 5 minutes. (The rice will stay hot for at least 30 minutes.)

5. To serve, fluff the rice with a fork and stir into the black-eyed peas. Season with salt and hot pepper sauce. Serve immediately.

Cajun Seasoning: In a small bowl, combine 2 tablespoons sweet paprika (preferably Hungarian), 1 tablespoon each dried thyme and dried basil, 1 teaspoon each garlic powder and onion powder, ½ teaspoon freshly milled black pepper, and ⅛ teaspoon cayenne pepper. Store leftover seasoning tightly covered in a cool, dark place. Use to season grilled poultry, fish, or pork, or to sprinkle on popcorn.

Note: Ham hocks are the traditional seasoning meat in Southern cooking. With an eye to reduced-fat cooking, most of my Southern and African-American friends substitute smoked turkey wings for ham hocks—an excellent alternative. Substitute two 1-pound smoked turkey wings, cut into 2-inch pieces, for the ham hocks. Simmer for 1 hour. Remove the skin and bones from the wings and chop the meat.

Brussels Sprouts with Pancetta

Makes 8 to 10 servings

While Brussels sprouts are popular on winter menus, they often need a bit of gussying up for a holiday meal. Pancetta, a peppered, unsmoked, and rolled bacon available at Italian delicatessens and many supermarkets, gives a boost to the humble sprouts. If you want to substitute regular bacon, blanch it first to remove the smoky taste: Place the bacon strips in a skillet, add cold water to cover, and bring to a simmer over low heat. Drain, rinse, pat dry with paper towels, and chop coarsely.

4 ounces sliced (¼-inch thick) pancetta, coarsely chopped
1 tablespoon olive oil
⅓ cup chopped shallots
Three 10-ounce containers Brussels sprouts, trimmed and cut lengthwise into ½-inch thick slices
1 cup Homemade Brown Stock (page 40), Homemade Turkey Stock (page 41), or canned low-sodium chicken broth
½ teaspoon salt
¼ teaspoon freshly milled black pepper

1. In a large skillet, cook the pancetta in the oil over medium heat, turning occasionally, until crisp and brown, about 5 minutes. Add the shallots and stir until softened, about 1 minute. Stir in the Brussels sprouts. Add the stock and season with the salt and pepper.

2. Cover and reduce the heat to medium-low. Simmer until the Brussels sprouts are tender when pierced with the tip of a small, sharp knife, about 20 minutes. If any broth remains in the skillet, increase the heat to medium-high and cook until it evaporates. Serve hot.

Maple-Glazed Butternut Squash

Makes 8 servings

Make Ahead: The squash can be peeled and cubed up to 8 hours before cooking, covered, and refrigerated.

Sautéed cubes of butternut squash with a simple maple syrup glaze are an excellent side dish, and are much easier to prepare than many winter squash recipes that require long baking. Unlike other hard squash, butternut squash has a thin skin that is easy to remove with a vegetable peeler (some of the other varieties need a machete to peel and chop). Real maple syrup gives the squash a subtly sweet flavor; if you want a more maply taste, use pancake syrup, which gets its punch from artificial flavorings. Instead of finely ground black pepper, use a coarse grind—it works well to accent the sweet glaze.

4 pounds butternut squash
3 tablespoons unsalted butter
6 tablespoons maple syrup
1 teaspoon salt
$^1/_2$ teaspoon coarsely cracked black pepper
   (crush in a mortar or under a heavy saucepan)

1. Peel the squash and discard the seeds. Using a large knife, cut into 1-inch pieces. (The squash can be prepared, covered, and refrigerated for up to 8 hours.)
2. In a very large skillet, heat the butter over medium-high heat. Add the squash and cover. Cook, stirring occasionally, until the squash is lightly browned and almost tender, about 12 minutes.
3. Stir in the maple syrup and season with the salt and pepper. Cook, uncovered, stirring occasionally, until the cooking liquid has reduced to a glaze and the squash is tender, about 5 minutes. Serve immediately.

Red Cabbage with Apples and Bacon

Makes 8 to 12 servings

Make Ahead: The cabbage can be prepared up to 1 day ahead, cooled, covered, and refrigerated. Reheat over medium-low heat.

This sweet-and-sour dish only gets better if made a day ahead. It's equally at home with roast goose or pork. When not gracing the holiday table, this dish is excellent served alongside grilled pork chops.

6 slices bacon
1 tablespoon vegetable oil
1 medium onion, thinly sliced
2 Granny Smith apples, peeled, cored, and
   thinly sliced
6 tablespoons cider vinegar
$^1/_3$ cup packed light brown sugar
1 medium red cabbage ($2^1/_2$ pounds), quartered,
   cored, and thinly cut crosswise
1 cup Homemade Beef Stock (page 41) or
   canned low-sodium beef broth
1 teaspoon dried thyme
1 bay leaf
$^1/_2$ teaspoon salt
$^1/_4$ teaspoon freshly milled black pepper

1. Place the bacon in a cold Dutch oven. Cook over medium heat, turning the bacon once, until crisp and brown, about 6 minutes. Using a slotted spatula, transfer the bacon to paper towels to drain, leaving the bacon fat in the pot.
2. Add the onion to the pot and cook, stirring often, until golden brown, about 8 minutes. Add the apples and stir for 1 minute. Stir in the vinegar and brown sugar. Gradually stir in the red cabbage, then the beef broth,

thyme, bay leaf, salt, and pepper. Cover and reduce the heat to medium-low. Simmer until the cabbage is very tender, about 45 minutes. (The cabbage can be prepared up to 1 day ahead, cooled, covered, and refrigerated. Reheat gently over medium-low heat.) Chop the bacon and stir into the cabbage. Serve hot.

Baby Carrots and Green Beans in Tarragon Butter

Makes 8 servings

Make Ahead: The carrots and green beans can be prepared up to 1 day ahead, cooled, wrapped in paper towels in self-sealing bags, and refrigerated.

When the main course calls for a brightly colored, crisp-tender side dish, this is the one you want. Here's the technique to use: The night before, blanch the baby carrots and beans, rinse them under cold running water, and pat dry. They can now be refrigerated overnight. When it's time for dinner, just give them a quick sauté in butter together with some shallots to heat them up. Voilá! Other vegetables and herbs work well in this dish. Broccoli and cauliflower florets are a nice winter combination, sprinkled with fresh thyme.

12 ounces trimmed baby carrots, peeled

12 ounces trimmed green beans, preferably haricots verts

2 tablespoons unsalted butter

2 tablespoons finely chopped shallots

1 tablespoon chopped fresh tarragon or 1 teaspoon dried tarragon

$\frac{1}{4}$ teaspoon salt

$\frac{1}{4}$ teaspoon freshly milled black pepper

1. Bring a large pot of lightly salted water to boil over high heat. Add the carrots and cook until barely tender, about 5 minutes. Remove from the water with a skimmer and place in a colander. Rinse under cold water. Pat dry with paper towels.

2. In the same pot of boiling water, cook the green beans until barely tender, about 3 minutes. Drain and rinse under cold water. Pat dry. (The vegetables can be prepared 1 day ahead, wrapped in paper towels, stored in self-sealing plastic bags, and refrigerated.)

3. In a very large skillet, melt the butter over medium heat. Add the shallots and cook for 1 minutes. Add the carrots and green beans, and cook, stirring occasionally, until heated through, about 6 minutes. Stir in the tarragon. Season with the salt and pepper. Transfer to a warmed serving dish and serve hot.

Long-Simmered Greens

Makes 8 to 12 servings

Make Ahead: The greens can be prepared up to 1 day ahead, cooled, covered, and refrigerated. Reheat before serving.

Just as Southern cooks make Hoppin' John on New Year's because the black-eyed peas represent coins, simmered greens are another must-have, since they resemble the loads of greenback bills we hope to gather in the coming year. Long-cooked greens are a perfect accompaniment to baked ham, too, which graces many a holiday buffet or dinner. There is a trend to quickly sauté greens, but in my opinion, those cooks are very misguided—the assertive flavor of greens needs plenty of cooking time to mellow.

- *There are many varieties of greens that are appropriate for long simmering: Kale, curly kale, collards, mustard greens, turnip greens, and dandelions are the most popular. They all have distinctive tastes, from the relatively mild collards to the peppery mustard greens. If you don't have a preference, I suggest collards. You can also mix different greens to come up with a personal blend.*

- *Many African-American cooks use turkey wings instead of ham hocks in traditional soul-food fare. The belief is that turkey wings are less fatty than ham hocks; however, there is still plenty of fat in turkey skin. At any rate, the wings are reasonably priced and have a good smoky flavor all their own.*

- *Savvy cooks sip the greens' cooking liquor, known colloquially as "pot likker"—it's especially good as a dunk for corn bread. To be sure that the pot likker is as full-flavored and delicious as it can be, use chicken broth as part of the cooking liquid. Southern restaurants often serve greens and the likker in individual serving dishes so you have plenty of likker for dunking (and the juices won't run all over the plate).*

5 pounds dark, strong-flavored greens
   (kale, curly kale, collards, or mustard,
   turnip or dandelion greens)
2 tablespoons vegetable oil
1 large onion, chopped
2 garlic cloves, finely chopped
1 cup Homemade White Chicken Stock
   (page 41) or canned low-sodium
   chicken broth, optional
1 teaspoon salt
¼ teaspoon crushed hot red pepper
One 1-pound smoked turkey wing, chopped into
   2-inch pieces
1 tablespoon cider vinegar

1. Remove the thick stalks from the greens and discard. Stack the leaves and cut crosswise into 1-inch wide strips. Fill a sink with tepid water (lukewarm water helps loosen any grit better than ice-cold water). Swish the greens in the water and let stand for 1 minute. Lift the greens from the water, trying not to disturb the grit on the bottom of the sink, and place the greens in a large bowl. Do not drain the greens.

2. In a large pot, heat the oil over medium heat. Add the onion and cook until softened, about 4 minutes. Stir in the garlic and cook for 1 minute. Add 2 cups water (or, if desired, 1 cup water and the chicken stock). In batches, stir in the greens with any water clinging to them, covering the pot and letting the first batch wilt before adding the next batch. Stir in the salt and crushed red pepper. Bury the turkey wing in the greens.

3. Cover and reduce the heat to low. Simmer, stirring occasionally, until the greens are very tender, about 45 minutes. Remove the turkey wings, discard the skin and bones, and chop the meat. Stir the turkey meat back into the greens, then stir in the vinegar. (The greens can be prepared up to 1 day ahead, cooled, covered, and refrigerated. Reheat before serving.) Transfer the greens and cooking liquid to a warmed serving dish. Serve hot, using a slotted spoon.

Giant Potato and Leek Rösti

Makes 6 to 8 servings

Make Ahead: The potatoes must be chilled, so prepare them the day before serving. The leeks can be prepared up to 1 day ahead, cooled, covered, and refrigerated.

Rösti, a big potato pancake, is a specialty of Switzerland. This is a great side dish for roast goose, as it uses some of the copious amounts of tasty goose fat that the bird gives off. The pancake turns out crispy and golden brown with a surprise filling of tender leeks. It can bake in the oven while the goose rests before carving. Try it for brunch with a dollop of sour cream, poached eggs, and slices of bacon or ham.

6 large baking potatoes, such as russet or Idaho, scrubbed but unpeeled (3 pounds)
2 tablespoons butter
3 medium leeks, chopped, white and pale green parts only
1 teaspoon salt
½ teaspoon freshly milled black pepper
4 tablespoons rendered goose fat or vegetable oil
Chopped fresh chives, for garnish (optional)

1. Place the potatoes in a large pot of lightly salted water and bring to a boil over high heat. Reduce the heat to medium. Cook, uncovered, until the potatoes are tender when pierced with a knife, 25 to 35 minutes. Drain and rinse under cold water. Cool completely. Cover and refrigerate until chilled, at least 4 hours and preferably overnight.

2. Position a rack in the center of the oven and preheat to 400°F. In a very large (12-inch) nonstick skillet (if the skillet handle isn't heatproof, wrap it in a double thickness of aluminum foil), heat the butter over medium heat. Add the leeks and cook until tender, stirring often, about 4 minutes. In a small bowl, mix the salt and pepper. Season the leeks with ¼ teaspoon of the salt-and-pepper mixture. Transfer to a small bowl and set aside. (The leeks can be prepared up to 1 day ahead, cooled, covered, and refrigerated.)

3. Peel the potatoes and shred on the large holes of a box grater. In the skillet, heat 2 tablespoons of the goose fat over medium-high heat until very hot but not smoking. Spread half of the potatoes in the skillet in a layer. Season with ½ teaspoon of the salt-and-pepper mixture. Spread with the leeks, leaving a 1-inch border around the edges. Top with the remaining potatoes, and season with the remaining ½ teaspoon salt and pepper.

4. Cook until the edges of the pancake are golden brown, about 5 minutes. Hold a flat round skillet top, plate, or pizza pan on top of the skillet. Invert the skillet and the skillet top together so the pancake falls, upside down, onto the skillet top. (If this seems too heavy to handle, slide the pancake carefully out of the skillet onto a plate. Place a second plate on top, and invert.) Return the skillet to the stove and heat the remaining tablespoons goose fat until very hot. Slide the pancake back into the skillet, browned side up. Cook until the underside is browned, 5 to 7 minutes.

5. Bake for 10 minutes. Turn the pancake as before, and bake it until crisp, about 10 more minutes.

6. Transfer to a warm round platter and sprinkle with the chives, if desired. Serve hot, cut into wedgers.

Scalloped Potatoes 101

Makes 12 servings

Make Ahead: The potatoes are best served immediately after baking. They can be prepared up to 1 day ahead. Reheat, covered, in a preheated 350°F oven for 30 minutes.

Good, old-fashioned scalloped potatoes, layered with milk and sharp Cheddar cheese, have a special place in the hearts of American cooks. French-style gratins, made with heavy cream and sometimes no cheese at all, have sneaked onto some dinner menus, and they have their own admirable qualities. But when you want a piece of hot, cheesy, down-home goodness to go alongside your glazed ham, it's got to be scalloped potatoes, not something French! Here's a classic derived from my own mom's recipe.

- *Many a holiday dinner has been delayed because the scalloped potatoes weren't ready yet. To speed things along, cut the potatoes evenly and on the thin side (a mandoline or plastic V-slicer helps), and heat the milk. Scalloped potatoes made with cold milk take forever to bake through.*

- *Use starchy baking potatoes, such as russet or Idaho. They will give off their starch and help thicken the milk, along with the butter and flour. You may store peeled, unsliced potatoes in cold water to cover for a few hours before slicing. But do not store sliced potatoes in water, or you will wash off the valuable starch.*

- *Scalloped potatoes are best served immediately after baking. If you must reheat them, bake 2 to 3 hours ahead of serving, and let stand at room temperature. Cover with aluminum foil and place in a preheated 350°F oven until heated through, about 30 minutes. Or cover with plastic wrap and reheat in a microwave oven on Medium for about 10 minutes.*

3 cups milk (not reduced-fat)

1¼ teaspoons salt

½ teaspoon freshly milled black pepper

8 medium baking potatoes, such as russet or Idaho, peeled and sliced into ³⁄₁₆-inch thick rounds (4 pounds)

4 tablespoons unsalted butter, cut into small pieces

1½ cups shredded extra-sharp Cheddar

3 tablespoons minced onion

3 tablespoons all-purpose flour

1. Position a rack in the center of the oven and preheat to 400°F. Lightly butter a 13 × 9-inch glass baking dish.

2. In a medium saucepan over medium-high heat, heat the milk until small bubbles appear around the edges. Mix the salt and pepper together.

3. Layer half of the potatoes in the prepared dish. Season with half of the salt and pepper, and dot with half of the butter. Sprinkle with 1 cup of the cheese, the onion, and the flour. Spread the remaining potatoes on top. Season with the remaining salt-and-pepper mixture, and dot with the remaining 2 tablespoons butter. Pour the hot milk over all. Cover tightly with aluminum foil. Place the dish on a baking sheet.

4. Bake for 45 minutes. Uncover and sprinkle with the remaining ½ cup cheese. Continue baking, uncovered, until the potatoes are tender, about 45 minutes. Let stand for 10 minutes before serving. Serve hot.

Potato, Mushroom, and Roquefort Gratin

Makes 8 to 12 servings

Make Ahead: The gratin can be prepared 6 hours ahead, cooled, covered with aluminum foil, and refrigerated. Reheat in a 350°F oven until heated through, about 30 minutes. Or, cover with plastic wrap and reheat in a microwave oven on Medium for about 10 minutes.

A gratin is the French way to make scalloped potatoes. The main difference between the two is that a gratin uses heavy cream. The high butterfat content in cream allows it to cook for a long time without curdling, so a gratin can be prepared without the butter and flour that are needed to thicken the milk in scalloped potatoes. The result is rich and luxurious. Try this gratin with roast beef or tenderloin.

2 tablespoons unsalted butter

1 pound shiitake mushrooms, stemmed and
   cut into $1/2$-inch slices

$1/3$ cup chopped shallots

2 cups heavy cream

1 cup chicken stock, preferably Homemade
   White Chicken Stock (page 41) or canned
   low-sodium chicken broth

5 large Idaho, russet, or Eastern potatoes,
   peeled and thinly sliced (about $3^1/4$ pounds)

6 ounces Roquefort or blue cheese, crumbled

$1/2$ teaspoon salt

$1/4$ teaspoon freshly milled black pepper

1. Position a rack in the top third of the oven and preheat to 350°F. Lightly butter a 9 × 13-inch baking dish.

2. In a large skillet, heat the butter over medium heat. Add the mushrooms and cook, stirring often, until tender, about 10 minutes. Stir in the shallots and cook until softened, about 1 minute. Set aside.

3. In a medium saucepan, bring the cream and stock just to a simmer over medium heat. Remove from the heat and stir in the cheese until melted.

4. Spread half of the potatoes in the prepared dish and sprinkle with half of the salt and pepper. Top with the mushrooms, then the remaining potatoes. Season with the remaining salt and pepper. Pour the hot cream mixture over all. Cover tightly with aluminum foil.

5. Bake for 40 minutes. Remove the foil and continue baking until the potatoes are tender and the top is golden, about 40 more minutes. Let stand for 10 minutes before serving.

Sour Cream and Chive Mashed Potatoes

 ## Cranberry-Kumquat Chutney

Makes 8 to 12 servings

Makes about 3 cups

Make Ahead: The potatoes can be peeled and cut in advance, placed in the cooking pot and covered with cold water, and stored in a cool place for up to 4 hours.

These incredible mashed potatoes are based on the ones I learned to make when working with chef Alfred Portale on his book, The Gotham Bar and Grill Cookbook.

5 pounds baking potatoes (such as russet, Idaho, Burbank, or Eastern)
Salt
1 cup (2 sticks) unsalted butter, at room temperature
1 cup sour cream
¼ cup chopped fresh chives
½ teaspoon freshly milled white pepper

1. Fill a large pot (5 quarts or larger) halfway with cold water. Peel the potatoes, cut into chunks about 1½ inch square, and drop them into the pot. Add more cold water to cover the potatoes by 1 to 2 inches. (The potatoes can be prepared up to this point up to 4 hours ahead and stored at cool room temperature.)
2. Stir in enough salt until the water tastes mildly salted. Cover tightly and bring to a boil over high heat.
3. Reduce the heat to medium-low and set the lid askew. Cook at a moderate boil until the potatoes are tender when pierced with the tip of a small, sharp knife, 15 to 20 minutes; add more boiling water, if needed, to keep the potatoes covered. Do not overcook.
4. Drain the potatoes well and return to the warm cooking pot. Add the butter. Using a hand-held electric mixer at medium speed, add the butter and mash the potatoes. Mix in the sour cream and chives. Season with 1 teaspoon salt and the pepper. Transfer to a warmed serving dish and serve immediately.

Make Ahead: The chutney can be prepared up to 2 weeks ahead, cooled, covered tightly, and refrigerated.

Winter is the time for kumquats. They look like tiny, elongated oranges, with a pungent citrusy flavor. Kumquats can be eaten uncooked, but they really shine when simmered into a jam or chutney like this one. Buy extra kumquats to use as a garnish—they are gorgeous and usually come attached to a spray of shiny, dark green leaves.

12 ounces fresh cranberries
8 ounces kumquats, cut into ¼-inch thick rounds
1½ cups packed brown sugar
⅓ cup finely chopped onion
2 tablespoons shredded fresh ginger
1 teaspoon minced garlic
1 teaspoon yellow mustard seeds
1 cinnamon stick
¼ teaspoon salt
¼ teaspoon crushed hot red pepper

Combine all the ingredients in a heavy-bottomed, nonreactive medium saucepan. Bring to a boil over medium heat, stirring often. Reduce the heat to medium-low. Simmer, uncovered, stirring often, until the chutney is thick and kumquats are translucent, about 20 minutes. Cool completely. Remove the cinnamon stick. (The chutney can be prepared up to 2 weeks ahead, cooled, covered, and refrigerated.)

Yam and Pineapple Pudding

Makes 8 servings

Make Ahead: The pudding, without the egg whites, can be prepared up to 2 hours ahead, loosely covered with plastic wrap and stored at room temperature. Beat the whites and fold in just before baking. Or, the pudding can be baked up to 1 day ahead, cooled, covered with aluminum foil, and refrigerated. Reheat in a 350°F oven until heated through, about 30 minutes. Or, cover with plastic wrap and reheat in a microwave oven on Medium for about 10 minutes.

I used to say that I didn't like yams. (Yams are the orange-fleshed tubers that many people call sweet potatoes but, in fact, sweet potatoes are yellow-fleshed and not very sweet at all.) I found out what I didn't like was ooey-gooey, sweet-enough-to-set-your-teeth-on-edge recipes. This one is just sweet enough. If you insist on marshmallows, delete the pecan topping and sprinkle 2 cups of tiny marshmallows on top of the pudding during the last 5 minutes of baking.

Pudding

4 pounds orange-fleshed (Louisiana or jewel) yams, scrubbed (5 large yams)

4 tablespoons unsalted butter

½ cup heavy cream

½ cup packed light brown sugar

One 20-ounce can crushed pineapple, drained well

4 large eggs, at room temperature, separated

½ teaspoon ground cinnamon

½ teaspoon ground cloves

Zest of 1 lemon

Topping

¼ cup packed light brown sugar

2 tablespoons unsalted butter, at room temperature

2 tablespoons all-purpose flour

½ cup coarsely chopped pecans

1. To make the pudding: Place the yams in a large pot and add enough lightly salted water to cover. Bring to a boil over high heat. Reduce the heat to medium and partially cover. Cook until the yams are tender when pierced with a knife, about 30 minutes. Drain and rinse under cold water until cool enough to handle. Peel and place in a large bowl.

2. Position a rack in the center of the oven and preheat to 350°F. Lightly butter a deep 2½-quart casserole.

3. Using a hand-held electric mixer at low speed, mash the yams with the butter. Beat in the cream and brown sugar, beating to dissolve the sugar. Add the crushed pineapple. One at a time, beat in the yolks, mixing well after each addition, then the cinnamon, cloves, and lemon zest. (The pudding can be prepared ahead up to this point 2 hours ahead, loosely covered with plastic wrap, and stored at room temperature.)

4. In a medium bowl, using clean beaters, beat the egg whites at high speed until soft peaks form. Stir about one-fourth of the whites into the pudding, then fold in the rest. Transfer to the prepared dish and spread evenly.

5. To make the topping: In a small bowl, using your fingers, work the brown sugar, butter, and flour until combined. Work in the pecans. Sprinkle over the pudding.

6. Bake until the pudding is slightly puffed and lightly browned, about 1 hour. Serve immediately. The pudding can be baked up to 1 day ahead, cooled, covered with aluminum foil, and refrigerated. Reheat in a 350°F oven until heated through, about 30 minutes. Or, cover with plastic wrap and reheat in a microwave oven on Medium for about 10 minutes.

⚇ Corn Bread–Succotash Stuffing

Makes 12 generous servings

Make Ahead: The corn bread should be prepared 1 day ahead, crumbled, and stored at room temperature to dry out. The stuffing should be assembled just before using.

I can never decide what kind of stuffing to make for turkey, but corn bread stuffing continues to be a strong annual contender. (Truth be known, I usually break down and make two stuffings, including an old-fashioned bread-and-herb kind to keep traditionalists happy.) This one is filled with colorful vegetables and is flavor-packed.

- *If you need more inspiration, let me guide you toward either* Thanksgiving 101 *or* 50 Best Stuffings and Dressings *(Broadway Books). If the recipe you want to make isn't in either of those books, then, well, you just don't like stuffing.*
- *For the best stuffing, you must make your own corn bread. Corn bread mixes are usually oversweetened. This recipe makes a firm, unsweetened corn bread that can be turned into a very fine stuffing. (Call it dressing, if you prefer—it still tastes the same.)*
- *It is safe to stuff a turkey, if you take some simple precautions. Stuff the bird with warm, freshly prepared stuffing, never with ice-cold stuffing. And absolutely never stuff the turkey the night before, even if you plan to refrigerate it.*
- *Use an instant-read thermometer, inserted deep into the stuffing, to be sure it has cooked to 165°F. If the turkey is done but the stuffing isn't hot enough, remove the stuffing, transfer it to a casserole, and bake until heated through.*

Corn Bread

1¼ cups yellow cornmeal, preferably stone ground

¾ cup all-purpose flour

2 teaspoons baking soda

½ teaspoon salt

1 cup milk

3 tablespoons unsalted butter, melted

1 large egg, beaten

Stuffing

½ cup (1 stick) unsalted butter

2 medium onions, chopped

2 medium red bell peppers, cored, seeded, and chopped

2 medium celery ribs with leaves, chopped

One 10-ounce package frozen lima beans, thawed

2 cups frozen corn kernels, thawed

⅓ cup chopped fresh parsley

1 tablespoon dried sage

1 tablespoon dried thyme

2 teaspoons crumbled dried rosemary

1 large egg, beaten

½ cup Homemade Turkey Stock (page 41) or canned low-sodium chicken broth, as needed

1 teaspoon salt

½ teaspoon freshly milled black pepper.

1. The day before preparing the stuffing, bake the corn bread: Position a rack in the center of the oven and preheat to 375°F. Lightly butter an 8-inch square baking pan.

2. In a medium bowl, whisk the cornmeal, flour, baking soda, and salt. Make a well in the center and pour in the milk, butter, and egg. Using a wooden spoon, stir just until smooth. Spread the batter in the prepared pan.

3. Bake until the top springs back when gently pressed in the center, about 20 minutes. Cool in the pan on a wire cake rack. Coarsely crumble and spread onto a jelly-roll pan. Let stand overnight, uncovered, at room temperature.

4. To make the stuffing: In a large skillet, melt the butter over medium heat. Add the onions, red bell peppers, and celery. Cook, stirring occasionally, until softened, about 10 minutes. Transfer to a large bowl.

5. Add the corn bread, lima beans, corn kernels, parsley, sage, thyme, and rosemary. Stir in the egg and enough stock to thoroughly moisten the stuffing without making it soggy. Season with the salt and pepper. Use immediately to stuff the turkey. Place any remaining stuffing in a buttered baking dish, cool, cover, and refrigerate. To reheat, drizzle with about 1/4 cup additional stock and bake, covered, in a preheated 350°F oven until heated through, 20 to 30 minutes.

☓ Herbed Yorkshire Puddings

Makes 12 puddings

These light, puffy popovers are irresistibly crisp on the outside and tender within. They are a classic accompaniment to roast beef, as they use the rendered beef fat in the roasting pan. Some cooks make a big rectangular pudding, but I like to make individual puddings in a muffin pan. Vary the herbs to go with your menu or leave the herbs out entirely.

- *Don't trim the fat cap on the rib roast too closely before roasting, or you may not have enough fat in the pan to make the puddings. Some butchers trim the fat cap to a faretheewell, so you may not have a choice. To gather the rendered beef fat from a beef rib roast, pour the clear light brown drippings out of the roasting pan, leaving the brown bits in the pan. Add melted butter to make up for any shortage of beef drippings.*

- *The puddings are baked in a hot oven while the roast is standing during its precarving wait. Heat the oven thoroughly to 400°F before baking the puddings—most ovens take 10 minutes to climb up from 325°F. Do not be concerned that the roast might cool down while the puddings bake. Just store the roast, loosely tented with aluminum foil, in a warm place near the stove. The internal temperature of the roast will actually rise 10° to 15°F before it starts to cool.*

9 tablespoons rendered beef fat from roasting pan (see instructions above)

1 1/2 cups all-purpose flour
1/2 teaspoon dried thyme
1/2 teaspoon dried rosemary
3/4 teaspoon salt
Generous 1/4 teaspoon freshly milled black pepper
1 1/2 cups milk
3 large eggs, beaten

1. Position a rack in the top third of the oven and preheat to 400°F. Measure 3 tablespoons of the beef fat and set aside. Spoon about 1/2 tablespoon of the remaining fat into each of 12 nonstick muffin tins.

2. In a medium bowl, whisk the flour, thyme, rosemary, salt, and pepper to combine. Make a well in the center of the flour mixture and pour in the milk, eggs, and reserved beef fat. Using a whisk, mix the liquid ingredients a bit to combine, then whisk them into the flour mixture, just until smooth. Do not overbeat.

3. Pour or ladle equal amounts of the batter into the prepared muffin tins, filling them about three-fourths full. Bake until the puddings are puffed, golden brown, and crisp, about 30 minutes. Serve immediately.

Chestnut and Prune Stuffing

Makes 8 to 12 servings

Make Ahead: Make the stuffing just before using.

This is a very rich stuffing that was created to accompany roast goose; it is also delicious with roast turkey. In either case, reserve the goose or turkey liver to use in the stuffing. The stuffing is also excellent baked in a shallow casserole as a side dish to roast pork (just leave out the liver).

- *Chestnuts are a popular winter food, but preparing them can be trying—you almost always discover a few inedible ones during peeling. It's hard to judge the freshness of chestnuts because they are imported, usually from Italy. Buy a few more chestnuts than you need, just to be sure.*

¾ cup (½-inch dice) pitted prunes

½ cup tawny port

5 tablespoons rendered goose fat (see page 55) or unsalted butter

1 goose or turkey liver, trimmed of membranes

1 large onion, chopped

2 medium celery ribs with leaves, chopped

1 pound chestnuts, roasted, peeled, and coarsely chopped (see below)

⅓ cup chopped fresh parsley

2 tablespoons chopped fresh sage or 1 tablespoon dried sage

½ teaspoon salt

¼ teaspoon freshly milled black pepper

12 ounces day-old, firm white sandwich bread, cut into ½-inch cubes (6 cups)

3 tablespoons unsalted butter, melted

¾ cup Homemade Goose Stock (see page 41) or canned low-sodium chicken broth, as needed

1. In a small bowl, combine the prunes with the port and let stand at room temperature for 1 hour. Drain the prunes, reserving the port, and set both aside.

2. In a small skillet, heat 1 tablespoon of the goose fat over medium heat. Add the liver and cook, turning occasionally, just until the liver is cooked through, 8 to 10 minutes. Cool, then cut the liver into ½-inch cubes. Set aside.

3. In a large skillet, heat the remaining 4 tablespoons goose fat over medium heat. Add the onion and celery. Cook, stirring occasionally, until the onion is golden, about 10 minutes. Add the port and cook until evaporated to a glaze, about 1 minute. Stir in the reserved liver and prunes, and the chestnuts, parsley, and sage. Season with the salt and pepper. Transfer to a large bowl. Add the bread cubes and stir in the butter. Stir in enough of the stock to moisten the stuffing. Use immediately to stuff the bird. (To bake the stuffing separately, transfer it to a lightly buttered 10 × 15-inch baking dish. Drizzle the stuffing with an additional ¼ cup stock or broth. Cover with aluminum foil. Bake in a preheated 350°F oven until heated through, about 30 minutes.)

Roasted Chestnuts: Preheat the oven to 400°F. Using a small, sharp knife, cut a deep X in the flatter side of each chestnut. Place in a single layer on a baking sheet and bake until the outer skin is split and crisp, about 30 minutes. They never seem to be done at the same time, so work with the ones that are ready and continue roasting the others. Place the roasted chestnuts in a kitchen towel to keep them warm. Using a small, sharp knife, peel off both the tough outer and thin inner skins. To loosen the peels on stubborn, hard-to-peel chestnuts, return to the oven for an additional 5 to 10 minutes or microwave on High for 1 minute. You can also use one 15-ounce jar vacuum-packed chestnuts, available at specialty food stores. (Avoid canned chestnuts, which don't have much flavor.)

Festive Breads

Comfort and Joy

While the enticing aroma of baking bread is not restricted to the holidays, this is the time for extra-special breads, many of which have been handed down from generation to generation. No matter how good it was, Christmas was the only time of year my great-aunt would bake her gügelhopf. My friends say it is the same with their families' breads. Some of them are sweet, like stollen and panettone, and others are savory and stuffed with salami or prosciutto.

Bread baking is one of the most satisfying of all kitchen techniques. It connects the baker to the food in so many ways. If you like to roll up your sleeves and knead the bread by hand, great. But if you feel more confident with a machine to help you do the work, that's fine too.

Here are some basics that will help you create Christmas breads for carrying on the traditions.

Equipment: For mixing most doughs, all you need is a big bowl and a sturdy wooden spoon. Choose a thick pottery, glass, or ceramic bowl rather than a metal bowl—the former retains warmth better. If you plan to knead by hand, have a large work surface cleared and ready.

Heavy-duty electric mixers with large mixing bowls, such as KitchenAid, make short work of the dough-making process. Most hand-held electric mixers aren't strong enough to mix yeast doughs. Mix the ingredients with the paddle blade until the dough comes together and clears the bowl, then switch to the dough hook.

I don't recommend using food processors for these recipes, because most of them can only handle doughs containing about 3 cups of flour, and many of these recipes call for higher amounts.

Check your oven temperature with an oven thermometer. Some bakers use baking stones to give their breads a flat, even baking surface. The stones are nice for hard, crusty breads, but not that necessary for sweet, thin-crusted loaves. If you have a baking stone, place it on the oven rack, positioned as recommended in the recipe, and preheat the oven. Place the baking sheet with the bread directly on the stone.

Ingredients: The three most important ingredients in bread making are flour, yeast, and salt. Use *unbleached* or *bread flour.* Its high gluten content gives a well-risen, firm-crumbed loaf. Organic unbleached flour makes incredible bread, and is worth an extra trip to a natural food store and any extra cost.

Yeast, of course, causes the bread to rise. The live yeast grows in the dough, feeding on the sugars in the dough, and as it multiplies, it gives off carbon dioxide. The gas is trapped in the dough, making it rise. (If the yeast is too old or killed by hot water, the dough won't rise.) *Active dry yeast* in $1/4$-ounce packets (about 2 teaspoons per envelope) is the most convenient form available. Be sure to note the expiration date, as the yeast quickly loses potency after that. Store yeast in the refrigerator to keep it fresh. Other yeasts (cake, fast-rising, instant) can be used, but follow the directions on each package to make the substitutions.

The yeast must be dissolved in warm water, about 105° to 110°F. If the water is too hot, the yeast will be killed. If the water is too cold, the yeast won't dissolve properly. (If you have to err, err on the cold side.) You can check the temperature with an instant-read thermometer. After a few times, you will be able to test the water with your fingers—it will be just warmer than body temperature. If another liquid, such as milk, is added to the dough, it should be warm, too.

Salt adds flavor to the bread and helps retard the rising action of the yeast. (Without a little salt, the yeast could grow too rapidly.) I prefer iodized salt because it dissolves easily with liquids. If you substitute fine sea salt or kosher salt, remember that these salts are about half as salty as iodized, so use about twice as much.

Mixing the Dough: As with any recipe, it helps to have all the ingredients measured out before proceeding. But with bread making, keep one important thing in mind. The exact amount of flour needed to make the dough will vary, due to the amount of humidity stored in the flour and in the air. Be flexible, and try not to add too much flour. Take special care with sweet breads containing butter, eggs, and sugar that make the dough feel sticky.

Sprinkle the yeast over the warm water and let it stand for 5 to 10 minutes to soften. It will usually look creamy—not all yeasts get foamy when moistened. Stir well to dissolve the yeast. (In some cases, the yeast and water are mixed with some of the flour to make a thick batter called a "sponge," which is allowed to rise before proceeding. This lengthens the rising period by an hour or so, and adds extra flavor to the bread.)

In a large bowl or the bowl of a heavy-duty mixer fitted with the paddle blade at low speed, mix the dissolved yeast with the remaining liquid ingredients (and butter, if using). Gradually mix in enough of the flour to get a stiff dough that clears the sides of the bowl. The dough is now ready for kneading.

Kneading: Manipulating the dough by hand or by machine actives the gluten in the flour, strengthening the dough so it won't collapse when the yeast multiplies and gives off its carbon dioxide.

To knead by hand, first, lightly flour the work surface. Turn the dough onto the work surface. Fold about one-fourth of the dough over onto the top of the remaining dough and press it down. Give the dough a quarter-turn, and repeat. Keep repeating the folding and turning, adding more flour as needed to keep the dough from sticking to the work surface (but not so much that the dough becomes dry). Do this rhythmically and enjoy the sensual pleasure of handling the dough. After 8 to 10 min-

utes, the dough will be smooth, somewhat firm, and elastic (if you pull the opposite ends of the dough apart slightly, the dough will snap back into shape).

To knead in a heavy-duty mixer, change to the dough hook. Knead the dough, adding more flour as needed, until smooth and elastic. Sweet, soft doughs have a tendency to climb up on the hook— just stop the machine, form the dough into a rough ball, and resume kneading. Knead for the minimum amount of time, as the motor is strong and it is easy to overknead. To check the consistency, transfer the dough to an unfloured work surface and knead by hand. If the dough doesn't stick to the surface, it has enough flour.

To add fruit or nuts to the dough, press the dough into a thick disk. Sprinkle with some of the fruit, roll up, and knead a couple of times. Continue the procedure until all of the fruit is incorporated. With a mixer, gradually mix in the fruit—don't add it all at once.

Rising: Lightly oil or butter a clean, large bowl. Form the dough into a ball. (Place your hands on the opposite sides of the dough, and tuck them under the dough to stretch the top surface of the dough. Rotate the dough and repeat the tucking movement. After a few tucks, the dough will shape itself into a ball.) Place the ball, smooth side down, in the bowl and coat the underside with oil. Turn the dough oiled side up and cover tightly with plastic wrap. Let the dough stand in a warm place (near a turned-on stove or water heater is ideal, as is the top of a running clothes dryer) until it doubles in volume. To check the volume, push your finger ½ inch into the dough. If the indentation remains, the dough has risen enough.

Shaping: Follow the individual instructions for shaping the loaves. If any seams are formed, pinch them shut. Place the loaves on nonstick baking sheets (or in their molds or pans), cover loosely with plastic wrap, and let rise until they look doubled in volume (use the finger test again, if you wish).

Baking: Preheat the oven thoroughly before baking the bread. Sweet breads with sugar and butter have a tendency to brown quickly, and should be baked at moderate temperatures around 375°F. If the bread browns too fast, tent it with aluminum foil. The bread is done when it is golden brown and sounds hollow when tapped on the bottom with your knuckles. An absolutely fail-proof method of checking doneness is to insert an instant-read thermometer in the center of the loaf—it will read 195°F or above.

Cooling: Bread baked in a pan or mold should be cooled in the pan for a few minutes, then removed from the pan, or trapped steam will make the bread soggy. Cool the bread on a wire cake rack for at least 30 minutes before slicing. If sliced too soon, steam will escape, and you'll have bread that dries out before its time.

Moravian Sugar Cake

Makes 4 cakes

Make Ahead: The cakes can be prepared up to 2 days ahead, stored in a self-sealing plastic bag at room temperature. To refresh, wrap in aluminum foil and bake in a preheated 350°F oven for 15 to 20 minutes until heated through.

The culinary traditions of the Moravian sect run strong near Winston-Salem, North Carolina, where every Christmas bakeries struggle to keep up with the demand for these flat coffee cakes with a sugary topping. This home-baked recipe was supplied by Cary Kirk's sister, Grigg K. Murdoch (although she leaves out the cinnamon). The cakes can be baked in four 9-inch round cake pans (aluminum foil pans are fine) or in two jellyroll pans, then cut in halves vertically to make 4 cakes.

**2 medium baking potatoes, peeled and cut
    into 1-inch chunks**
Two ¼-ounce packages active dry yeast
**12 tablespoons (1½ sticks) unsalted butter,
    at room temperature**
½ cup granulated sugar
1 teaspoon salt
2 large eggs, at room temperature
**6½ cups unbleached all-purpose flour,
    approximately**

Topping
**¾ cup plus 2 tablespoons packed light brown
    sugar**
6 tablespoons (¾ stick) unsalted butter
½ teaspoon ground cinnamon

1. Place the potatoes in a medium saucepan and add enough cold water to cover by 2 inches. Do not add salt.

Bring to a boil over high heat. Reduce the heat to medium-low and cook until the potatoes are very tender, about 20 minutes. Drain the potatoes, reserving the potato cooking liquid. Rub the potatoes through a wire sieve. Measure 1 packed cup of the potatoes, and set aside at room temperature; discard any remaining potatoes. Cool the potato cooking water to 105° to 110°F.

2. In a small bowl, combine the warm potato water with the yeast and let stand until the yeast is creamy, about 5 minutes. Stir to dissolve the yeast.

3. In a large mixing bowl, using a hand-held electric mixer, or the large bowl of a heavy-duty mixer fitted with the paddle blade, beat the butter and sugar until light in texture, about 2 minutes. Beat in the cooled potatoes and salt, then the eggs. Beat in the yeast mixture (the mixture may look curdled, but don't worry). Gradually beat in enough of the flour to form a soft, shaggy dough that just clears the sides of the bowl.

4. Turn out the dough onto a lightly floured work surface and knead, adding more flour as needed, until the dough is smooth and elastic but still somewhat soft and slightly sticky, about 10 minutes.

If kneading by machine, switch from the paddle to the dough hook and knead on medium-low speed, adding more flour as needed, about 8 minutes. If desired, transfer the dough to a floured surface and knead briefly by hand to check the consistency; it should be slightly sticky but smooth.

5. Shape the dough into a ball. Place into a buttered large bowl and turn to lightly coat the underside with butter. Cover tightly with plastic wrap and let stand in a warm place until doubled in volume, about 1 hour.

6. Lightly butter four 9-inch round cake pans or two 15½ × 10½ × 1-inch jelly-roll pans. Stretch and pat the dough into the prepared pans. Cover with plastic wrap and let stand in a warm place until puffy, about 30 minutes.

7. To make the topping, bring ¾ cup brown sugar, 4 tablespoons of the butter, and 2 tablespoons water to a boil over medium heat, stirring often. Pour into a glass measuring cup and let stand until cooled but pourable, about 30 minutes.

8. Melt the remaining 2 tablespoons butter. Brush the tops of the cakes lightly with the melted butter. Using your finger, punch 12 evenly spaced indentations into each round pan of dough (if the dough is in jelly-roll pans, punch 24 indentations into each). Pour the syrup into the indentations. In a small bowl, combine the remaining 2 tablespoons brown sugar and cinnamon with your fingers, and sprinkle over the cakes.

9. Position racks in the top third and center of the oven and preheat to 375°F. Bake, switching the position of the pans from top to bottom and front to back halfway through baking, until the cakes are golden brown, about 35 minutes. Cool in the pans for 10 minutes. Slide the cakes out of the pans onto racks and cool right sides up. If baking in jelly-roll pans, cut each cake in half vertically to make 4 cakes. (The cakes can be prepared up to 2 days ahead, stored in a self-sealing plastic bag at room temperature. To refresh, wrap in aluminum foil and bake in a preheated 350°F oven for 15 to 20 minutes until heated through.)

Prosciutto, Rosemary, and Pepper Bread

Makes one large loaf, about 12 servings

Make Ahead: The bread is best served the day baked.

With the additions of prosciutto, fresh rosemary, and cracked pepper, a basic bread becomes a festive loaf. The extra rising period gives the bread a more compact crumb and deeper flavor. If your main course is a simple roast, this bread goes well with dinner, or you can slice and serve it as an appetizer with a glass of wine.

1 package (2¹⁄₂ teaspoons) active dry yeast

¹⁄₄ cup warm (105° to 110°F) water

2 tablespoons extra virgin olive oil

1¹⁄₂ teaspoons salt

³⁄₄ teaspoon coarsely cracked black pepper

3¹⁄₂ cups bread or unbleached all-purpose flour, approximately

4 ounces (¹⁄₄-inch thick) sliced prosciutto, chopped into ¹⁄₄-inch dice

1¹⁄₂ tablespoons chopped fresh rosemary or 2 teaspoons dried rosemary

1. In a large bowl or in the bowl of a heavy-duty electric mixer, sprinkle the yeast over the water and stir. Let stand until the yeast softens, about 10 minutes. Stir to dissolve the yeast.

2. Using a wooden spoon or the paddle blade of the mixer, stir in the oil, salt, and pepper. Gradually beat in enough of the flour to make a shaggy dough that clears the sides of the bowl.

3. If kneading by hand, turn out the dough onto a lightly floured work surface. Knead the dough, adding more flour as needed, until the dough is smooth and elastic, about 10 minutes.

If kneading by machine, change to the dough hook and knead on medium-low speed until the dough is smooth and elastic, about 8 minutes. If desired, knead on the work surface to check the consistency.

4. Shape the dough into a ball. Transfer the dough to a lightly oiled large bowl. Turn to coat the dough with oil. Cover tightly with plastic wrap. Let stand in a warm place until doubled in volume, about 1 hour.

5. Punch down the dough and shape into a ball. Return the dough to the bowl, turn to coat with oil, cover, and let rise until doubled again, about 45 minutes.

6. Position a rack in the center of the oven and preheat to 400°F. Lightly oil a large baking sheet.

7. Turn out the dough onto the work surface. Knead, gradually working in the prosciutto and rosemary. Flatten the dough into a 12-inch disk. Starting at a long end, roll up jelly-roll style. Pinch the seams shut. Place on the baking sheet, seam side down. Cover loosely with plastic wrap. Let rise until doubled in volume, about 30 minutes.

8. Using a very sharp knife, cut 3 shallow diagonal slashes in the top of the bread. Bake until the bread is golden brown and sounds hollow when tapped on the bottom, 35 to 40 minutes. Cool completely on a wire rack. If desired, wrap in aluminum foil and store at room temperature up to 8 hours before serving.

Salami and Cheese-Stuffed Bread

Makes one long loaf, about 16 servings

Make Ahead: The bread is best served the day baked.

Put slices of this bread out on a buffet and watch it disappear. It looks great, and tastes even better. Shirley Corriher, author of the indispensable Cookwise, *taught me to bake this immediately after stuffing (without a second proofing) so that the bread rises in a thinner layer that will help the filling adhere to the bread without any gaps.*

1 package (2½ teaspoons) active dry yeast
¼ cup warm (105° to 110°F) water
2 tablespoons extra virgin olive oil
1½ teaspoons salt
3½ cups unbleached all-purpose flour,
   approximately

1 cup (4 ounces) shredded mozzarella
4 ounces thinly sliced Genoa salami
1 cup (4 ounces) shredded provolone
2 tablespoons finely chopped fresh basil
   or 1½ teaspoons dried basil
1 teaspoon dried oregano
¼ teaspoon crushed hot red pepper
2 tablespoons milk
1 large egg yolk
2 teaspoons sesame seeds

1. In a large bowl or in the bowl of a heavy-duty electric mixer, sprinkle the yeast over the water. Let stand until the yeast softens, about 10 minutes. Stir until the yeast dissolves.

2. Using a wooden spoon or the paddle blade, stir in the oil and salt. Gradually beat in enough of the flour to make a shaggy dough that clears the sides of the bowl.

3. Turn out the dough and knead, adding more flour as necessary, until smooth and elastic, about 10 minutes.

If kneading by machine, switch to the dough hook and knead on medium-low speed until the dough is smooth and elastic, about 8 minutes. If desired, transfer the dough to a work surface and knead briefly by hand to check the consistency.

4. Shape the dough into a ball. Transfer the dough to a lightly oiled large bowl. Turn to coat the ball with oil. Cover tightly with plastic wrap. Let stand in a warm place until doubled in volume, about 1 hour.

5. Position a rack in the center of the oven and preheat to 375°F. Lightly oil a 17½ × 11½ × 1-inch jelly-roll pan (preferably nonstick).

6. Punch down the dough to deflate, and knead briefly on the work surface. Place the dough in the pan and pat it out to fit the pan. (If the dough seems too elastic, and snaps back instead of staying in place, cover the dough in the jelly-roll pan with plastic wrap and let stand for 5 to 10 minutes to relax, and try stretching again.) Sprinkle the dough with the mozzarella, leaving a ½-inch border. Layer the salami over the mozzarella, then sprinkle with the provolone. Sprinkle with the basil, oregano, and hot red pepper. Starting at a long end, roll up the dough as tightly as possible and pinch the seams shut. Arrange the dough so the long seam is down.

7. In a small bowl, mix the milk and yolk well. Lightly brush the top of the roll with some of the mixture, then sprinkle the dough with the sesame seeds. Using a very sharp knife, cut 3 shallow diagonal slashes in the top of the bread. Bake until the bread is golden brown, about 35 minutes. Cool completely on a wire rack. If desired, wrap in aluminum foil and store at room temperature up to 8 hours before serving.

 # Gügelhopf

Makes one large loaf, 12 to 16 servings

Make Ahead: The cake can be baked up to 2 days ahead, cooled, wrapped in plastic wrap, and stored at room temperature.

Another one of my Aunt Gisela's specialties, this beautiful sweet bread (sometimes called kügelhopf) can be found year-round at bakeries in northern Europe, but Gisela made her homemade version as a holiday treat. It has a light, dry texture that's perfect for dipping into hot tea or coffee. The sticky batterlike dough requires a heavy-duty standing mixer or a hand-held mixer with a strong motor and kneading beaters. It is usually made in the traditional turban-shaped gügelhopf pan (see page 163 for mail-order sources), but any 10- to 12-cup tube cake pan will do.

1 cup raisins
3 tablespoons dark rum

Sponge
One ¼-ounce package active dry yeast
¼ cup warm (105° to 110°F) water
¾ cup milk
1 cup all-purpose flour

Gügelhopf
1 cup (2 sticks) unsalted butter, at room
   temperature
¾ cup granulated sugar
5 large eggs, at room temperature
½ teaspoon salt
½ teaspoon pure lemon oil or 1 teaspoon
   lemon extract
Grated zest of 1 lemon
3 cups all-purpose flour

Glaze
1 cup confectioners' sugar
3 tablespoons dark rum
2 tablespoons sliced almonds

1. Place the raisins in a small bowl and sprinkle with the rum. Let stand for 1 hour or up to overnight.

2. To make the sponge: In a medium bowl, sprinkle the yeast over the water. Let stand 5 minutes and stir to dissolve the yeast.

3. In a small saucepan or a microwave oven, heat the milk to 105° to 110°F. Stir the warmed milk into the yeast mixture. Add the flour and stir with a wooden spoon for 100 strokes. (This helps develop gluten and improves the cake's texture.) Scrape down the bowl and cover tightly with plastic wrap. Let stand in a warm place until the sponge doubles in volume, about 1½ hours.

4. Butter well a 10-inch gügelhopf mold (or use a plain or fluted tube pan). Drain the raisins well (if desired, save any drained rum to use in the glaze) and set aside.

5. To make the gügelhopf: Using a heavy-duty standing mixer fitted with the paddle blade, on medium speed, beat the butter and granulated sugar until light in color and texture, about 3 minutes. One at a time, beat in the eggs, then the salt, lemon oil, and lemon zest. The mixture will be soupy. Reduce the speed to low. Scrape the sponge into the butter mixture. Gradually beat in the flour, ½ cup at a time, to make a thick batter. Beat for about 10 minutes. The batter will feel sticky, look elastic, and cling to the sides of the bowl. Beat in the raisins, just until incorporated.

6. Spread the batter evenly into the prepared pan. Cover tightly with plastic wrap and let stand in a warm place until the batter rises to the top of the pan, about 1¼ hours.

7. Position a rack in the center of the oven and preheat to 350°F. Bake until the top is golden brown and a long wooden skewer inserted in the center of the bread comes out clean, about 1 hour. Cool on a wire cake rack for 10 minutes. Run a sharp knife around the inside of the mold and the tube to release the bread. Unmold onto the rack and cool completely.

8. To make the glaze: In a small bowl, using a rubber spatula, mix the confectioners' sugar with the rum until very smooth. Place the cooled bread on the wire rack over a piece of wax paper. Pour the glaze over the top and around the sides of the bread, then thinly spread the glaze all over the bread with a pastry brush. Immediately sprinkle the almonds over the wet glaze, patting them, if necessary, to adhere. Allow the glaze to set, about 30 minutes. Serve immediately or wrap tightly in plastic wrap and store at room temperature.

Panettone

Makes 1 large loaf

Make Ahead: The panettone can be prepared up to 5 days ahead, cooled, wrapped in plastic wrap, and stored at room temperature.

In Italian-American neighborhoods, the holiday season is announced by the arrival of panettone, the dome-shaped Christmas bread of Italy. The factory-baked varieties are good (and seem to stay fresh forever thanks to a special commercial yeast), but like so many other things, homemade is better. Panettone is great to serve to friends with a cup of dark roast coffee. Slightly stale slices are revived by a light toasting or they can be turned into excellent French toast. There is a fairy tale–like story on how panettone got its name. A poor baker named Antonio (nicknamed Tone) created a special bread to convince the stubborn king that he should be allowed to marry his beautiful daughter. Tone's bread (or pane di Tone) did the trick, and the couple lived happily ever after.

½ cup dark raisins
½ cup golden raisins
½ cup chopped Candied Orange Peel (page 93), store-bought candied peel, or glacéed orange slices
3 tablespoons grappa, brandy, or dark rum

Sponge
1 cup warm (105° to 110°F) milk
One ¼-ounce package active dry yeast
1 cup unbleached all-purpose flour

Dough
8 tablespoons (1 stick) unsalted butter, at room temperature
½ cup sugar
3 large eggs plus 1 large egg yolk
1 teaspoon vanilla extract
Grated zest of 1 orange
½ teaspoon salt
3 cups unbleached all-purpose flour, approximately

1 large egg white, beaten, for glaze
2 tablespoons sliced almonds, for garnish

1. In a medium bowl, mix the raisins, golden raisins, and candied orange peel with the brandy. Cover and let stand for 1 hour.

2. To make the sponge, in another medium bowl, mix the milk and yeast (no need to dissolve the yeast). Add the flour and stir for 100 strokes to make a thick batter. Cover tightly with plastic wrap and let stand in a warm place until the sponge is bubbly, about 1 hour.

3. To make the dough, drain the fruit, reserving the grappa. Pat the fruit dry with paper towels and set aside. In a large bowl, using a hand-held electric mixer, or in the work bowl of a heavy-duty electric mixer fitted with the paddle blade, beat the butter until creamy, about 1 minute. Add the sugar and beat until light in color and texture, about 2 minutes. Beat in the eggs, one at a time. Beat in the reserved grappa, vanilla, orange zest, and salt. Beat in the sponge. Gradually beat in enough of the flour to form a soft, shaggy dough that just clears the sides of the bowl. When using a hand-held mixer, switch to a wooden spoon when necessary.

4. Turn out the dough onto a lightly floured work surface and knead until supple but still slightly sticky, about 5 minutes. If the dough holds its shape when formed into a ball, it has been kneaded enough. Do not add too much flour. Gradually knead in the fruit.

If kneading by machine, switch from the paddle to the dough hook and knead on medium-low speed until the dough is supple but still slightly sticky, about 5 minutes. Gradually add the fruit and knead until incorporated. If desired, transfer the dough to a floured surface and knead briefly by hand to check the consistency.

5. Shape the dough into a ball. Place in a buttered large bowl and turn to lightly coat the underside with butter. Cover tightly with plastic wrap and let stand in a warm place until doubled in volume, about 2 hours.

6. Position a rack in the center of the oven and preheat to 350°F. Lightly butter an 8½-inch springform pan with 3-inch sides.

7. Turn out the dough onto the work surface and knead briefly. Shape into a flat disk and transfer to the prepared pan, stretching the dough to fill the pan. Cover with plastic wrap and let stand in a warm place until the dough barely reaches the top of the pan, about 45 minutes.

8. Brush the top of the bread lightly with egg white and sprinkle with the almonds. Bake for 40 minutes. Loosely cover the top of the bread with aluminum foil, and continue baking until the top is golden brown and a thin knife inserted in the center comes out clean, about 35 minutes. Do not overbake. Cool on a wire rack for 15 minutes. Remove the sides and bottom of the pan, and cool completely on the rack. (The panettone can be stored at room temperature, wrapped well in plastic wrap, for up to 3 days. Stale panettone is excellent toasted.)

Overnight Maple-Pecan Sticky Buns

Makes 16 buns

Make Ahead: The sticky buns can be prepared the night before serving, covered tightly with plastic wrap, and refrigerated. The buns are best served the day baked.

What's better than waking up to freshly baked sweet rolls? With this recipe, you don't have to get up at the crack of dawn to enjoy the aroma of sugar and spice wafting through the kitchen. Make a pan of sticky buns the night before and refrigerate them until ready to bake the next morning—the dough will slowly rise and develop flavor.

- *The buttermilk gives the dough a light flakiness. Although dried buttermilk powder is available, I always use liquid dairy buttermilk because it is thicker and has more flavor. Reconstituted buttermilk powder is too thin, and the dough may require too much flour. Heat the dairy buttermilk in a small saucepan over low heat or in the microwave. It should be just above body temperature.*

- *Maple syrup is one of Mother Nature's great culinary gifts, but it has a mild flavor that is best savored over pancakes or waffles. Maple-flavored pancake syrup works best here. Not only does it give the buns more maple flavor, it remains gooey when the buns cool, while the true maple syrup hardens.*

One ¼-ounce package active dry yeast

¼ cup warm (105° to 110°F) water

¾ cup warm (105° to 110°F) buttermilk

¼ cup granulated sugar

4 tablespoons (½ stick) unsalted butter, melted

1 large egg plus 1 large egg yolk

½ teaspoon salt

¼ teaspoon baking soda

2¾ cups unbleached flour, approximately

5 tablespoons unsalted butter, melted

⅓ cup packed light brown sugar

½ cup chopped pecans

¾ cup maple-flavored pancake syrup

1. In a small bowl, sprinkle the yeast over the warm water. Let stand until the yeast is creamy, about 10 minutes. Stir to dissolve the yeast.

2. In a large bowl or the bowl of a heavy-duty electric mixer, mix the yeast mixture with the warm buttermilk, granulated sugar, melted butter, egg, egg yolk, salt, and baking soda. Using a wooden spoon or the paddle blade on low speed, add enough of the flour to make a soft dough.

3. If kneading by hand, turn out the dough onto a lightly floured work surface. Knead the dough, adding more flour as necessary, until the dough is smooth and elastic, about 10 minutes.

If kneading by machine, change to the dough hook and knead on medium-low speed until the dough is smooth and elastic, about 8 minutes. If desired, knead on the work surface to check the consistency.

4. Shape the dough into a ball. Place in a lightly buttered bowl and turn to coat the dough with butter. Cover tightly with plastic wrap and let stand in a warm place until the dough doubles in volume, about 1¼ hours.

5. Turn out the dough onto a lightly floured work surface. Roll, pat, and stretch the dough into a 14 × 10-inch rectangle. Brush the dough with 1 tablespoon of the melted butter. Leaving a 1-inch border at the long ends, sprinkle with the brown sugar, then the pecans. Starting at a long end, roll up the dough into a long cylinder. Pinch the long seam shut.

6. Using a sharp knife, cut the dough into 16 slices. Pour the remaining 4 tablespoons melted butter into a 13 × 9-inch metal baking dish. Brush the butter evenly onto the bottom and sides of the pan. Pour the maple syrup into the pan, tilting to coat the bottom of the pan. Place the dough slices, flat sides down, side by side in the pan. Cover tightly with plastic wrap and refrigerate for at least 8 and up to 12 hours.

7. Position a rack in the center of the oven and preheat to 375°F. Remove the pan of prepared buns from the refrigerator and let stand in a warm spot near the stove while the oven preheats.

8. Uncover the pan. Bake until the rolls are golden brown, about 30 minutes. Immediately invert the rolls onto a large platter. Let cool for 5 minutes, then cut or break apart into individual rolls. Serve warm or cooled to room temperature.

 # Stollen

Makes 2 large stollen, about 10 servings each

Make Ahead: The stollen can be prepared 1 day ahead, cooled, wrapped in plastic wrap, and stored at room temperature.

Stollen are the festive Christmas breads of Germany. Their unusual folded shape is said to represent the baby Jesus in swaddling clothes. They are an authentic dessert for a German-style dinner of roast goose.

¹/₂ cup dried cranberries or chopped candied
  red cherries
¹/₂ cup chopped Candied Orange Peel (page 93),
  store-bought candied peel, or glacéed
  orange slices
¹/₂ cup dark raisins
¹/₂ cup golden raisins
¹/₂ cup dark rum

Sponge
1 cup warm (105° to 110°F) milk
Two ¹/₄-ounce packages active dry yeast
1 cup unbleached all-purpose flour

Dough
12 tablespoons (1¹/₂ sticks) unsalted butter,
  at room temperature
¹/₂ cup granulated sugar
2 large eggs
Grated zest of 1 lemon
¹/₂ teaspoon salt
3¹/₂ to 4 cups unbleached all-purpose flour,
  approximately
1 cup slivered almonds

4 tablespoons unsalted butter, melted,
  for assembly
4 tablespoons sugar, for assembly
Confectioners' sugar, for serving

1. In a medium bowl, mix the cranberries, orange peel, dark raisins, and golden raisins with the rum. Cover and let stand for 1 hour.

2. To make the sponge, in another medium bowl, mix the milk and yeast to combine (no need to dissolve the yeast). Add the flour and stir for 100 strokes to make a thick batter. Cover tightly with plastic wrap and let stand in a warm place until the sponge is bubbly, about 1 hour.

3. To make the dough, drain the fruit, reserving the rum. Pat the fruit dry with paper towels and set aside. In a large bowl, using a hand-held electric mixer, or in the work bowl of a heavy-duty electric mixer fitted with the paddle blade, beat the butter until creamy, about 1 minute. Add the sugar and beat until light in color and texture, about 2 minutes. Beat in the eggs, one at a time. (The mixture may curdle, but don't worry.) Beat in the reserved rum, the lemon zest, and salt. Beat in the sponge. Gradually beat in enough of the flour to form a soft, shaggy dough that just clears the sides of the bowl. Switch to a wooden spoon when necessary when using a hand-held mixer.

4. Turn out the dough onto a lightly floured work surface and knead until supple but still slightly sticky, about 5 minutes. If the dough holds its shape when formed into a ball, it has been kneaded enough. Do not add too much flour. Gradually knead in the fruit and almonds.

If kneading by machine, switch from the paddle to the dough hook and knead on medium-low speed until the dough is supple but still slightly sticky, about 5 minutes. Gradually add the fruit and almonds and knead until incorporated. If desired, transfer the dough to a floured surface and knead briefly by hand to check the consistency.

5. Shape the dough into a ball. Place in a buttered large bowl and turn to coat the dough with butter. Cover tightly with plastic wrap and let stand in a warm place until doubled in volume, about 1 hour.

6. Position the racks in the center and top third of the oven (see Note) and preheat to 350°F. Lightly butter two large baking sheets.

7. Turn out the dough onto the work surface and knead briefly. Cut the dough in half. On a prepared baking sheet, stretch and pat out the dough to form a 12 × 8-inch oval. (If the dough resists shaping, cover with plastic wrap and let rest for 5 minutes, then try again.) Brush the dough with 1 tablespoon melted butter, and sprinkle with 1 tablespoon sugar. Fold one long side of the dough over, about 1 inch past the cen-

ter. Fold the other side of the dough over, about 1 inch past the center. Pinch the seams closed. Brush with 1 tablespoon melted butter and sprinkle with 1 tablespoon sugar. Cover with plastic wrap and let stand in a warm place until almost doubled in volume, about 30 minutes. Repeat with the remaining dough.

8. Bake until the tops are golden brown and a thin knife inserted in the thickest part of the dough comes out clean, about 45 minutes. Cool completely on a wire rack. Dust with confectioners' sugar just before serving.

Note:

If your oven isn't big enough to accommodate both stollen at the same time, position the rack in the center of the oven. Bake the first stollen, refrigerating the second one while the first bakes.

Candies

Visions of Sugarplums

For most of the year, making candy at home isn't a top priority. Then, at Christmas, cooks bring out their favorite recipes for gift giving and filling up the holiday candy dish, and rediscover how much fun candy making can be. My dad always makes a few pounds of rocky road to hand out, a tradition he carries on from Grandma Rodgers.

Candies don't have to be complicated or difficult to make. The recipes offered in this chapter are among the easiest around, and you will get lots of sweets for your efforts. Only a few of them even call for using a candy thermometer. But it helps to have an understanding of the basic techniques. You could just leave all the responsibility to a candy thermometer, but take a minute to read these tips, and the mysteries of candy making won't seem daunting at all.

Cooked Syrup Temperatures: Many candies are based on a cooked sugar syrup. As the sugar boils, the water evaporates and the syrup becomes denser. The higher the temperature, the denser the syrup. The different syrup stages are identified by how the syrup behaves when a spoonful is dropped into a glass of cold water, which imitates how the candy will set when cooled. For example, when cooked to 300° to 310°F, the syrup is at the hard-crack stage, and the cooled candy will be brittle. On the other hand, if the syrup if cooked to only 270°F, the soft-crack stage, the candy will harden but have a softer texture. Because I do not use the entire range of cooked syrup temperatures in this book, I will not go into more detail, but that's the general idea.

Usually, syrups are cooked without stirring. If a foreign object like a spoon is introduced into the syrup, the sugar crystals attach themselves to the intruder, and the syrup could crystallize, resulting in grainy candy—if you get it to turn into candy at all. Butter—and some other foods, like corn syrup—will hinder the crystallization process, so candies with a high proportion of these ingredients can be stirred while cooking to ensure that the mixture doesn't scorch.

A good candy thermometer is an important tool. Plaque-attached, mercury candy thermometers are best because the tip of the thermometer is raised off the bottom of the pot (if it touches the bottom, it will give an inaccurate reading). If you have a dial, clip-type thermometer, adjust it so it doesn't touch the bottom of the pot.

One very important piece of advice. *Do not make sugar-syrup based candy in humid or rainy weather.* The moisture in the air wreaks havoc with the syrup. The only two recipes in this book that have this caveat are Macadamia Milk Chocolate Toffee (page 98) and Homemade Peppermint Taffy (page 95).

Types of Chocolate: Buy the best chocolate you can afford. For most of my chocolate making, I prefer a high-quality European bittersweet chocolate, such as Lindt. These chocolates have a high cocoa-butter content, which gives them a high gloss and that unmistakable, melt-in-your-mouth quality.

Unsweetened chocolate is pure chocolate liquor, the dark brown mass obtained from grinding cacao beans. It is most often used in baking, like in The Best Chocolate-Pecan Brownies (page 126).

Bittersweet chocolate is unsweetened chocolate that has been mildly sweetened and flavored. Many manufacturers are now selling chocolates with varying amounts of chocolate liquor in them. The amount is usually stated in a percentage on the label. A "70% cocoa" so-called bittersweet chocolate will be quite a bit more bitter than one with a "64% cocoa" content. Most European chocolates are bittersweet. I use Lindt Excellence. *Semisweet* chocolate is slightly sweeter, and in most cases, interchangeable with bittersweet. Baker's is a reliable brand. *Milk chocolate* is flavored not only with sugar, but with milk. It scorches easily, so watch out when melting it. I prefer Hershey's milk chocolate. *White chocolate* (not used in this book) is not chocolate at all, but sweetened cocoa butter. *Chocolate chips* include lecithin, which acts as an emulsifier.

Chocolate is delicious but temperamental. Take care when melting chocolate, as it hates water and high heat. A single drop of water in melted chocolate will make it clump up and "seize" into a thick mass. When chocolate is overheated, it gets grainy.

The best way to melt chocolate is in a double

boiler. Chop the chocolate finely with a large knife, as it will melt more evenly and quickly. Don't try to save time by chopping it in a food processor—the friction in the bowl will heat up the chocolate and melt it. Place the chopped chocolate in the double-boiler insert or a heatproof bowl. Bring the water to the boil, then turn it off. If the water isn't simmering, it won't build up steam that could collect and drip into the bowl of chocolate. Set the insert over the hot water (it should not touch the water) and let stand, stirring occasionally, until the chocolate is smoothly melted.

Chocolate can also be melted in a microwave oven at Medium (50%) power. Microwave the chocolate in 1-minute intervals, stirring after each interval (the chocolate may look shiny and unmelted, but will smooth out when stirred), until melted. I prefer the double-boiler method because it is easy to scorch chocolate in a microwave unless you are very attentive.

Finishing Touches: It used to be that you didn't have much choice when it came to giving your homemade candies to friends. You just put them in a jar or a box of some kind, and added a ribbon. Now, kitchenware catalogues abound with candy boxes, cellophane bags, and candy papers to present your handiwork. Williams-Sonoma (1-800-541-2233) is a good source. For an especially nice gift, put the candies in a candy dish and wrap in colored plastic wrap.

S'Mores Rocky Road

Makes about 2¼ pounds

Make Ahead: The candy can be prepared up to 2 weeks ahead, stored in an airtight container at room temperature.

My dad is the family candy maker, and his holiday specialty is rocky road. I stir graham crackers into my version for a delicious variation on the S'Mores theme.

1½ **pounds milk chocolate, finely chopped**
6 **ounces marshmallows, snipped into**
    quarters with lightly oiled scissors
1 **cup coarsely chopped walnuts**
1 **cup mini-graham crackers (or break**
    large crackers into bite-sized pieces)

1. Line a baking sheet with aluminum foil and lightly butter the foil. In a large stainless steel bowl set over a large saucepan of *barely* simmering water, melt the chocolate, stirring occasionally, until almost but not completely melted. (The water must be at the barest simmer to melt this amount of chocolate efficiently.) Remove from the water and let stand, stirring occasionally, until the chocolate is completely melted and slightly thickened.

2. Stir in the marshmallows, nuts, and graham crackers. Scrape the mixture out onto the prepared baking sheet and spread into a 1-inch thick layer. Refrigerate until the chocolate is firm. Using a sharp knife, cut into 1- to 2-inch pieces. (The rocky road can be prepared up to 2 weeks ahead, stored in an airtight container at room temperature.)

Candied Citrus Peels

Makes about ³/₄ pound

Make Ahead: The candied peels must stand overnight before rolling in sugar. They can then be stored, in an airtight container at room temperature, for up to 1 month.

In my Christmastime kitchen, candied citrus peels serve a double purpose. Candied grapefruit peels are easy-to-make treats that make great gifts. I also use the same technique to prepare my own candied orange and lemon peels for chopping and baking into desserts. Really good candied fruit peels aren't that easy to find, yet many Yuletide baked goods call for them. I would much rather use delicious homemade fruit peels in my fruit-cake, mincemeat, and sweet breads than the tasteless supermarket stuff. This recipe makes enough syrup to candy 2 grapefruits, or 3 oranges, or 4 lemons.

2 medium grapefruits
1¹/₂ cups granulated sugar plus additional
   for coating
¹/₃ cup light corn syrup

1. Using a sharp knife, cut off the tops and bottoms of the grapefruits so they can stand. Cut off the rinds in thick, wide strips where the rind meets the fruit. Cut the rind into long strips about ¹/₂ inch wide. Place in a medium saucepan and cover with cold water. Bring to a boil over high heat, then reduce the heat to medium and cook at a gentle boil for 5 minutes. Drain and rinse under cold running water. Return to the pan, cover with water, and repeat the procedure.
2. In a medium saucepan, bring the sugar, corn syrup, and 1¹/₄ cups water to a boil, stirring to dissolve the sugar. Add the peels and reduce the heat to medium-low. Simmer until the peels are translucent and tender, 20 to 30 minutes. Drain the peels. Arrange the peels, not touching each other, on a wire cake rack set over a baking sheet. Let stand at room temperature overnight. Roll the peels in additional sugar to coat. (The candied grapefruit peel can be prepared up to 1 month ahead, stored in an airtight container at room temperature.)

Candied Orange Peel: Substitute 3 large seedless oranges for the grapefruit. Simmer the peel strips in the syrup until tender and translucent, 30 to 40 minutes. Chop the peels just before using. Makes about ³/₄ pound or 1 cup chopped peels.

Candied Lemon Peel: Substitute 4 lemons for the grapefruit. Simmer the peel strips in the syrup until tender and translucent, 30 to 40 minutes. Chop the peels just before using. Makes about ³/₄ pound or 1 cup chopped peels.

Chocolate, Cranberry, and Walnut Fudge

Makes about 2¼ pounds

Make Ahead: The fudge must stand overnight before serving. It can be prepared up to 1 week ahead, stored in an airtight container at room temperature.

There are a lot of fudge recipes out there, but most of them are for experienced candy makers. This one is carefree, as it "fudges" with the help of marshmallows.

8 tablespoons (1 stick) unsalted butter,
   cut into pieces
6 ounces semisweet chocolate, coarsely chopped
1¾ cups miniature marshmallows (3 ounces)
¾ cup (3 ounces) coarsely chopped walnuts
½ cup (2 ounces) dried cranberries
1 ounce unsweetened chocolate, finely chopped
1 teaspoon vanilla extract
2¼ cups sugar
⅔ cup evaporated milk

1. Line an 8- or 9-inch baking pan with a double thickness of aluminum foil so that the foil extends 2 inches over the opposite ends of the pan. Fold the overhang to form handles. Butter the inside of the foil-lined pan.

2. In a large bowl, combine the butter, semisweet chocolate, marshmallows, walnuts, cranberries, unsweetened chocolate, and vanilla.

3. In a large, heavy-bottomed saucepan, combine the sugar and evaporated milk. Lightly butter the exposed sides of the saucepan above the surface of the sugar mixture. Bring to a boil over medium heat, stirring constantly with a flat wooden spatula to prevent scorching. Attach a candy thermometer to the pan.

Boil, stirring constantly, until the mixture reaches 238°F (soft-ball stage).

4. Pour the hot mixture over the ingredients in the bowl. Let stand for 30 seconds. Stir with a wooden spoon until the mixture thickens and begins to develop its sheen, about 1 minute. Spread evenly in the prepared pan. Let stand at room temperature to cool and mellow the flavors, at least 8 hours or overnight.

5. Lift up on the foil handles to remove the fudge from the pan. Using a sharp knife, cut the fudge into squares and lift it up from the foil. (It can be prepared up to 1 week ahead, stored in an airtight container at room temperature.)

 Homemade Peppermint Taffy

Makes about 14 ounces

Make Ahead: The candy can be prepared up to 1 month ahead, stored in an airtight container at room temperature.

If you hanker to make homemade candy canes, they are very difficult (if not impossible) to master at home. Make these good, old-fashioned pulled-taffy hard candies instead—they're not difficult to make at all. Supply yourself with a pair of rubber gloves to protect your hands from the heat of the candy during the pulling process, and you can have a batch ready in no time. Do not make taffy in humid or rainy weather. Peppermint candies make a wonderful gift, packaged in a beribboned glass jar.

- *This basic recipe can be flavored with any kind of good-quality oil or extract and tinted with food coloring to identify the flavor. Oil-based flavorings are preferred, because the flavor won't evaporate when it hits the hot syrup. Alcohol-based extracts will evaporate a bit, so the amount should be increased slightly. A large variety of flavoring oils and extracts are available from Kitchen Glamor (1-800-641-1252). High-quality citrus oils and mint, fruit, and spice flavorings (which aren't oils but are very strong and good for candy making) can be mail-ordered from Williams-Sonoma (1-800-541-2233).*

Nonstick vegetable oil spray
1½ cups granulated sugar
½ cup corn syrup
¼ cup water
2 tablespoons unsalted butter
⅛ teaspoon salt

½ teaspoon peppermint oil or ¾ teaspoon clear peppermint extract
Red liquid food coloring

1. Lightly butter a nonstick baking sheet. Spray a pair of kitchen scissors with the nonstick spray.

2. In a medium saucepan, fitted with a candy thermometer, bring the sugar, corn syrup, water, butter, and salt to a boil over high heat, stirring constantly to help dissolve the sugar. Reduce the heat to medium. Cook, occasionally swirling the saucepan by the handle, until the syrup reaches 270°F.

3. Remove the saucepan from the heat. Add the peppermint oil to the syrup. Color the syrup with 2 or 3 drops of red food coloring. Holding the handle of the saucepan, swirl the syrup to incorporate the oil and coloring and tint the syrup pink. Pour onto the prepared baking sheet.

4. Let the syrup cool until a skin begins to form on top, about 3 minutes. Put on rubber gloves (to protect your hands from the heat while pulling the candy) and lightly oil the gloves (to keep the candy from sticking to them). Using a lightly oiled metal spatula, continuously fold the syrup back on itself until it is cool enough to handle. Pick up the mass of syrup and pull the candy, stretching it between your hands and folding it back on itself until it is white and opaque, but still warm, about 3 minutes, depending on the heat of the kitchen.

5. Twist and pull the candy into a long rope about ¾ inch thick, letting the rope fall onto the baking sheet as it is pulled. Work quickly, as the candy hardens as it cools. Using the oiled scissors, snip the candy rope into ¾-inch long pieces. (If the candy cools until hard, crack it into pieces.) Cool completely. (The candy can be prepared up to 1 month ahead, stored in an airtight container at room temperature.)

It Wouldn't Be the Holidays Without . . . Candy Canes

The hooked shape of the candy cane represents the crook of the shepherds who were present at the Nativity. Surprisingly, cellophane-wrapped red-and-white–striped candy canes are a fairly recent addition to the list of edible Christmas traditions.

The first candy canes were created in 1670, when the choirmaster at the Cologne Cathedral handed out candy sticks to the children in his choir to keep them quiet during the long Living Nativity ceremony. To keep the children in a religious state of mind, he bent the sticks into shepherds' crooks to remind them that they were no longer just eating candy but commemorating the Nativity itself. Eventually, hooked candy canes became a German holiday tradition.

Like many other Yuletide traditions (notably the Christmas tree), the candy cane came to America with the first wave of German immigrants in the early 1800s. Its first documented stateside appearance was in 1847, on the Christmas tree of Wooster, Ohio citizen August Imgard, a German-Swedish immigrant.

But how did the American candy cane become the red-and-white–striped, peppermint-flavored Christmas icon we know today? The technical advances of the Industrial Revolution made sugar inexpensive and mechanized candy making. One of the most popular sweets of the nineteenth century was the peppermint stick. Its shape was perfect for bending into a crooked candy cane, but this still had to be done by hand, one cane at a time. The cooling menthol flavor of peppermint was distinctly wintry, and to some, the red-and-white coloring was a metaphor for Christ's blood and the purity of the Christ child.

In the 1920s, a candy manufacturer in Albany, Georgia, Bob McCormack of Bobs Candies, began making handmade candy canes. Because they were so difficult to make and too fragile to transport, they were reserved for his family and local customers. And so they remained until the 1950s, when Bob's brother-in-law, Gregory Keller, a Catholic priest, invented a machine to automate candy cane production. Packaging innovations such as the individual cellophane wrap (pioneered by Bobs Candies in the 1920s when they became the first candy manufacturer to use the transparent paper) and special boxes to nestle the canes soon made Bobs the largest producer of candy canes in the world.

If you want to mail-order the granddaddy of all contemporary candy canes (which now come in such flavors as piña colada and bubble gum), call Bobs Candies at 1-800-569-4033, or visit their web site at www.bobscandies.com.

 ## Sweet and Spicy Candied Walnuts

Makes ³/₄ pound

Make Ahead: The walnuts can be prepared up to 1 week ahead, stored in an airtight container at room temperature.

It's a toss-up. Should I make candied walnuts with the familiar cinnamon-and-spice flavors? Or do I give them a savory twist with orange zest, rosemary, and cracked pepper? They're so easy, why not make them both?

1 large egg white
¹/₄ cup sugar
¹/₂ teaspoon salt
¹/₂ teaspoon ground cinnamon
¹/₄ teaspoon ground ginger
¹/₄ teaspoon ground nutmeg
¹/₄ teaspoon ground cloves
12 ounces walnuts, preferably walnut halves

1. Position a rack in the center of the oven and preheat to 300°F.
2. In a medium bowl, whisk the egg white, sugar, and salt until very foamy. Whisk in the cinnamon, ginger, nutmeg, and cloves. Add the walnuts and stir to coat.
3. Spread the nuts on an ungreased baking sheet. Bake for 10 minutes. Stir and separate any walnuts that are sticking together. Bake for another 10 minutes. Stir and continue baking until the coating is dry and walnuts are crisp, 5 to 10 minutes. Cool completely.

Savory Orange-Rosemary Walnuts: Substitute the grated zest of 1 orange, 1 teaspoon crumbled dried rosemary, and 1 teaspoon coarsely cracked black pepper for the cinnamon, ginger, nutmeg, and cloves. If desired, substitute pecans for the walnuts.

 ## Chocolate Peanut-Butter Meltaways

Makes about 4 dozen candies

Make Ahead: The candies can be prepared up to 2 weeks ahead, stored in an airtight container, and refrigerated.

A few Christmases ago, Marion Hampton was our houseguest. A holiday "CARE" package arrived from her mother, Caroline Cox, and it included a box of these chocolate morsels. It wasn't long before I was on the phone getting the recipe.

One 12-ounce jar peanut butter, preferably chunky
5 tablespoons (¹/₂ stick plus 1 tablespoon)
   unsalted butter, at room temperature (see Note)
2 cups confectioners' sugar, sifted
1¹/₂ cups crispy rice cereal
11 ounces bittersweet or semisweet chocolate,
   finely chopped
1 tablespoon vegetable shortening

1. Line a baking sheet with aluminum foil. In a medium bowl, using a wooden spoon, cream the peanut butter and butter until combined. Gradually stir in the confectioners' sugar. Stir in the cereal, which will crumble (see Note). Using about 1 tablespoon for each, roll the mixture into balls, placing them on the prepared baking sheet. Refrigerate the balls while melting the chocolate.
2. In the top part of a double boiler over hot, not simmering, water, melt the chocolate and shortening, stirring occasionally until smooth and an instant-read thermometer inserted in the chocolate reads 115° to 120°F. Remove from the heat. Transfer the chocolate mixture to a small bowl and let cool slightly.
3. Place a dab of the chocolate in the palm of one

hand. Pick up a ball and roll it between your palms to coat lightly with the chocolate. Return the chocolate-coated ball to the foil-lined baking sheet. Repeat with the remaining balls. Refrigerate until the chocolate is set and the balls release easily from the foil, about 30 minutes. (The candies can be prepared up to 2 weeks ahead, stored in airtight containers, and refrigerated.)

Note: The moisture in peanut butter varies from brand to brand. If the mixture seems too crumbly, mix in additional softened butter.

Macadamia Milk Chocolate Toffee

Makes about 35 pieces

Make Ahead: The toffee can be prepared up to 2 weeks ahead, stored in an airtight container at room temperature.

Make a batch of this buttery, crunchy toffee for gift giving, and you may end up keeping a good bit of it for yourself. Use other nuts if you like—cashews, almonds, or even peanuts. Do not make toffee in humid or rainy weather.

2 cups sugar

1½ cups (3 sticks) unsalted butter, cut up

1 cup (4 ounces) macadamia nuts, rinsed of salt, patted dry, and coarsely chopped

6 ounces milk chocolate, finely chopped

1. Lightly butter a 15½ × 10½ × 1-inch jelly-roll pan. In a large, heavy-bottomed saucepan, stirring constantly, cook the sugar and butter over medium-high heat until the mixture comes to a boil.

2. Attach a candy thermometer to the pan and continue to cook and stir until the thermometer reads 310°F, 5 to 10 minutes. Remove the pan from the heat and stir in ½ cup of the nuts. Pour the mixture into the prepared pan, letting it spread naturally. Let stand for 10 minutes to cool slightly.

3. Sprinkle the chocolate in a single layer over the surface of the hot toffee. Let stand until the chocolate softens, about 5 minutes. Using a metal spatula, spread the chocolate evenly over the surface of the toffee. Sprinkle with the remaining ½ cup nuts. Using a large, sharp knife, score the toffee into 2-inch pieces. As the toffee cools, retrace the score lines occasionally with the knife to reach the bottom of the pan so the toffee will break apart easily.

4. When the toffee has cooled and the chocolate is firm, use a metal spatula to remove the toffee from the pan. Following the score lines, break into pieces and serve. (The toffee can be made up to 2 weeks ahead, stored in a airtight container at room temperature.)

Chocolate-Orange Truffles

Makes about 4 dozen truffles

Make Ahead: The truffles can be prepared up to 1 week ahead, stored in an airtight container, and refrigerated, or frozen for up to 2 months.

There's a very nice story connected with these truffles. When I was working as a Manhattan restaurant manager, I became friendly with many customers, but Susan Ginsburg was a favorite. She always gave me a bottle of Grand Marnier for Christmas, and I used it to make these truffles to give to her. Years went by, and we lost track of each other until we accidentally crossed paths again. She is now my literary agent. When I became a caterer, I took out the recipe again and turned these out by the thousands. Now I make them in more modest batches, but I always try to have some tucked away in the freezer to finish holiday meals with a flourish.

- To serve these at home, roll the truffles in cocoa powder and refrigerate them. But if you plan to give them as a gift, consider coating the truffles in melted, quick-tempered chocolate to help them stay firm out of refrigeration.

- Dutch-processed cocoa has been treated with alkali. Because it has a milder flavor than natural, nonalkalized cocoa, it is preferred for rolling the truffles, but regular cocoa will do. If you want to cut the bitterness of either cocoa, sift ¼ cup cocoa with ¼ cup confectioners' sugar, and use the mixture for rolling the truffles.

- It's simple to vary the flavors with different preserves and liqueurs. Instead of orange marmalade and Grand Marnier, substitute strawberry preserves and brandy, strained raspberry preserves (not seedless preserves, which are too thin) and Chambord or framboise, apricot preserves and dark rum, or cherry preserves and kirschwasser.

12 tablespoons (1½ sticks) unsalted butter, cut into pieces

1 pound bittersweet chocolate, finely chopped

½ cup orange marmalade, preferably bitter orange

¼ cup Grand Marnier or other orange-flavored liqueur

½ cup Dutch-process cocoa powder, such as Droste, for rolling

1. In a medium heatproof bowl set over a large saucepan of hot, not simmering, water, melt the butter. Add the chocolate and melt, stirring often, until smooth. Remove from the heat. Whisk in the marmalade and the liqueur. Cover loosely with plastic wrap and refrigerate until firm and chilled, at least 4 hours or overnight.

2. Place the cocoa in a shallow medium bowl. Line a baking sheet with aluminum foil. Using a melon baller, scoop the chilled chocolate mixture and roll between your palms to form a round truffle. (If the chocolate is too firm, let stand at room temperature to soften slightly.) Roll the truffle in the cocoa and place on the prepared baking sheet. Repeat with the remaining chocolate. (The truffles can be prepared up to 1 week ahead, stored in airtight containers, and refrigerated, or frozen for up to 2 months.) Remove the truffles from the refrigerator 10 minutes before serving.

Amaretto and Apricot Truffles: This is an especially delicious combination. Substitute ½ cup apricot preserves for the marmalade, and Amaretto for the Grand Marnier. Instead of rolling the truffles in cocoa powder, use 1½ cups (6 ounces) finely chopped sliced almonds.

Chocolate-Dipped Truffles: Do not roll the truffles in cocoa powder. Refrigerate the truffles on the foil-lined baking sheet for 10 minutes. In the top part of a double boiler over hot, not simmering, water, melt 12 ounces finely chopped bittersweet chocolate, stirring often, until smooth and an instant-read thermometer inserted in the chocolate reads 115° to 120°F. Remove from the heat and cool, stirring occasionally, until the chocolate is about 90°F. Place a dab of chocolate in the center of your palm. Pick up a truffle and roll it between your palms to coat with the chocolate. Place the truffle on the foil-lined baking sheet. Repeat with the remaining truffles and chocolate. Refrigerate until the chocolate is set and the truffles release easily from the foil, about 30 minutes. If desired, roll the coated truffles in cocoa to give them their traditional look (which is supposed to resemble a fresh truffle coated with earth, with the cocoa representing the dirt). Transfer the truffles to airtight containers to store.

Cookies

The Christmas Cookie Jar

O f all the Christmas edibles, cookies are most beloved. Every year, I bake sheet after sheet of my favorites, then pack them up for delivery to my friends (keeping plenty for myself). I love everything about the process: poring over cookbooks to decide which new recipes to try, mixing the dough, the rhythm of rolling the dough, searching kitchenware stores and catalogues for new cookie cutters, inhaling the aromas of sugar and spice from the oven as they fill the kitchen, packing up the trays and boxes of cookies, and most of all, the look and sounds of pleasure as my friends bite into their cookies. However, none of this happens without advance planning. Here are a few tips.

Balance your cookie menu just like you balance a dinner menu. Choose cookies to give a variety of visual looks and flavors. You don't want them all to be homey (but delicious) drop cookies, nor do you want them all to be heavily spiced with ginger and cinnamon. Also, try to bake cookies that are specific to Christmas. But if you are pressed for time and you want a familiar recipe to "flesh out" a cookie platter, then bake the chocolate chip cookie you make the rest of the year.

By nature, many traditional Christmas cookies are a bit time-consuming. I am a very experienced baker, and I can tell you that there are aren't too many shortcuts to baking and decorating gorgeous cut-out cookies. But you can balance the more time-intensive, hands-on cookies with some that are quickly made. In this chapter, I share plenty of easy recipes that my friends, many of whom are food professionals, and I have baked for years. We all agree that our favorites are often the ones that give the cook the most cookies with least effort.

In the spirit of a basic cookie cooking class (this is *Christmas 101,* not *202),* I stayed away from recipes that required special equipment (including German *springerle* and Dutch *spekulatias,* which call for special molds to stamp them with intricate designs). I do include a recipe for Spritz Butter Cookies (page 126), requiring a cookie press, because even though the press isn't an absolutely necessary kitchen utensil, it can be used throughout the year. But don't look for a gingerbread house. It takes too much time. And as no one has the nerve to bite into such an ornate creation, I think it's a waste of time and ingredients.

Set up your cookie-baking kitchen like an assembly line. In other words, get organized, and finish one job before you move on to the next. With cookie baking, having an assembly-line frame of mind really helps. Don't let those bowls and spoons pile up in the sink. Owning more than one or two cookie sheets will definitely move things along. Have the entire batch of cookies baked and cooled before you begin any icing or decorating. Keep plenty of small custard cups or paper cups with separate spoons ready to hold different colored icings.

Whenever possible, enlist another pair of hands. Cookie making is so much easier, quicker, and more

fun when you are sharing the work with a friend. Every year, Diane Kniss and I get together to bake her Ultimate Thumbprints cookies (page 124). In a couple of hours, we have made literally hundreds of them.

Types of Cookies

The most basic cookie categories are rolled cookies, formed cookies, drop cookies, and bar cookies.

Rolled cookies are created from chilled, rolled-out dough, and are usually cut into shapes and decorated with icing. Sugar cookies and gingerbread cookies, two Christmas traditions, are examples of rolled cookies. The dough must be chilled to give it a firm texture that can be rolled out. Let the chilled dough stand at room temperature for a few minutes to warm and soften slightly, or it may crack during rolling. The work surface should be floured somewhat generously to cut down on sticking. Don't forget to dust the top of the dough with flour, too, so the rolling pin doesn't stick to it. During rolling, occasionally run a long, thin knife or metal spatula under the dough to be sure it isn't sticking. If you wish, roll out the dough between lightly floured, large pieces of wax paper or parchment paper, but check often to be sure that the dough and paper aren't buckling.

Formed cookies are made into shapes without the help of cookie cutters, although other utensils or your hands may be used. The dough can be chilled or at room temperature. When forming balls of dough, use measured amounts (I generally use 1 level tablespoon) so the cookies are uniform. Measure out all of the dough balls at once, placing them on an extra cookie sheet or jelly-roll pan (or even in a shallow baking dish). When cutting out squares or strips, use a ruler as a guide. Thin doughs are best cut with a pizza wheel. To give the cookies attractive wavy edges, use a fluted ravioli wheel.

Drop cookies are made from dough dropped in measured amounts onto baking sheets. They spread quite a bit, so always allow 2 inches between the cookies so they don't run into each other when baked. They aren't the prettiest cookies, but they are among the most popular.

Bar cookies are baked in a baking pan, cooled, and cut into bars. They are very sturdy, and great cookies for mailing. I used to be frustrated digging the first bar out of the pan, ruining it in the process (well, I did get to eat it . . .), so I developed a method to solve the problem. To remove bar cookies easily from the baking pan, line the bottom and short sides of the pan with a long piece of aluminum foil, folding the excess foil to form handles. When the cookies are baked and cooled, lift up on the handles to remove the cookies from the pan in one piece. They can now be cut into uniform bars without any waste.

Ingredients

As I always say in my cooking classes, baking is nothing but chemistry that tastes good. It is impor-tant to understand the ingredients that go into the recipes. Too often cooks are tempted to substitute in-gredients, then have problems. During the holiday season, when I know I will be doing a lot of baking, I buy many of my staple ingredients in quantity at a wholesale club to get the best prices.

Butter and Other Fats: Fats add tenderness and moisture to baked goods. There are many cook-ing fats available, and they all have unique quali-ties that make them behave differently in recipes.

Butter is the fat backbone for most cookies. Butter gives cookies a crisp texture and an irreplaceable flavor. Buy a high-quality butter for the best results. Some inexpensive brands have off flavors or a high water content that will affect the taste and texture of the dough. Most bakers prefer *unsalted butter* for many reasons. First, unsalted butter allows the baker to be in control of how much salt is needed to bring out the flavors in the dough. Also, because the addition of salt to butter hides off flavors and ran-cidity, unsalted butter will always be fresher than salted. If you must use salted butter, omit the salt in the recipe. There are reduced-fat butters on the market, but I have not tested these recipes with them, and do not guarantee the results.

In most recipes, to start the dough, butter is creamed with sugar. Properly softened butter is the key, because you want to use the electric mixer to beat in little bubbles of air that will expand in the oven (thanks to the chemical reaction of the baking soda or baking powder). If the butter is too warm or too cold, the bubbles won't form properly, and you'll have hard, flat cookies.

To soften butter, cut the chilled butter into 1-inch pieces and place in the mixing bowl. Let stand until soft but pliable, about 30 minutes in an average-temperature kitchen. The butter shouldn't look shiny or oily. To save time, using the large holes on a box grater, grate the cold butter into the bowl. It will be softened by the time you gather the rest of the ingredients. Butter can also be softened in a microwave oven, if you keep an eye on it. The exact length of time depends on the wattage power of the oven. Use Low (20%) power, as higher settings tend to melt the butter before it is completely softened.

Margarine is softer and more oily than butter. Some bakers indiscriminately substitute it for butter, but the cookies will have a softer texture. I rarely bake with margarine because I like the flavor and texture of butter-baked cookies, but some recipes (there are none in this book) require it to give the cookies a tender crumb. If you use margarine, select a reliable stick brand. Never use tub or whipped margarine (or butter, for that matter), as its added water makes it unreliable for cooking.

Vegetable shortening is used in some recipes to lend extra tenderness to the cookie. Measure shortening in level amounts in a metal measuring cup. Shortening now comes in easy-to-measure sticks, which are especially convenient to use during the busy holiday baking season.

Eggs: Use large, Grade A eggs. If you substitute another egg size, you could throw off the liquid content of the recipe. Store eggs in their carton in the refrigerator, not in the egg holders in the refrigerator door (it really isn't cold enough in the door, which reduces the time the eggs stay fresh). When a recipe calls for room-temperature eggs, remove them from the refrigerator about 1 hour before using. Never let eggs stand at room temperature for longer than 2 hours. To speed the warming-up process, place the whole, uncracked eggs in a bowl and cover with hot tap water. Let the eggs stand for 3 to 5 minutes, and the hot water will remove their chill. Drain and use the eggs.

Royal icing, a common decorating icing, is usually made with raw egg whites. Knowing that some cooks prefer to avoid uncooked eggs, I specify dehydrated egg-white powder (which is salmonella-safe) in my royal icing. It is available in most supermarkets or by mail order from The Baker's Catalogue (1-800-827-6836).

Flour: *Bleached, all-purpose flour* is preferred for cookie baking. It has a moderate amount of gluten, the protein combination that gives strength to dough. *Unbleached flour* (even if it is called "all-purpose") has a high gluten content, and is really best for yeast dough. *Cake flour* has a very low gluten content, and should only be used in recipes that call for it. *Use the flour indicated in the recipe.*

White rice flour, available in natural food stores, or *cornstarch* (both gluten-free ingredients) is sometimes added to cookie dough to further reduce the gluten content and give the cookies a meltingly tender crumb.

These recipes were tested by using the dip-and-sweep method of measuring. Dip the metal measuring cup or measuring spoon into the bag of flour (or any dry ingredient) and fill the cup without packing the ingredient. Using the flat side of a knife, sweep the excess from the top of the cup to get a level measurement. (When following a recipe in other cookbooks, read the introductory remarks to see what dry measuring method the cook prefers. Some bakers insist that you spoon the flour into a cup and level it off, but that makes a mess. Others insist that you weigh the flour on a scale.)

Sugar Products: Most cookie doughs use *granulated sugar.* I have come to experience that there is a difference in quality among sugars (some are coarser than others), so buy a well-known brand.

Confectioners' sugar, sometimes called powdered sugar, is used primarily for icings and decorating. Confectioners' sugar is usually sifted over baked cookies as a garnish. If you plan to garnish a lot of cookies, purchase a confectioners' sugar shaker with a mesh wire top (available at kitchenware stores and from catalogues) so you don't have wash a sieve every time you need a little sprinkle of sugar.

Light brown sugar is granulated sugar with mo-

lasses added. *Dark brown sugar* simply has more molasses. They are interchangeable, but I find light brown sugar milder and more versatile. Always store brown sugar at room temperature in an airtight container or tightly closed in its plastic bag (I secure mine with a sturdy rubber band), or it will dry out and harden. There are a number of methods of softening hard brown sugar (place a wedge of apple in the bag for a couple of days, for example), but none is faster or easier than buying a new, inexpensive box of fresh brown sugar. I do not use "granulated" brown sugar or liquid brown sugar. Brown sugar should be measured in packed, level amounts.

Molasses is a by-product of the sugar refining process. *Unsulfured molasses* (often called light molasses) is extracted from the sugar cane without sulfur dioxide. *Sulfured molasses* (sometimes labeled "robust") is strong-flavored. *Blackstrap molasses* is very bitter. I only use unsulfured molasses. When measuring molasses, lightly spray the inside of the liquid measuring cup with nonstick vegetable oil spray, and it won't stick as much.

Honey is often categorized by the type of flower nectar that the bees collect in the vicinity of their hive—thyme, lavender, and so on. I prefer a full-flavored, high-quality, blended supermarket honey like Golden Blossom because I can be sure of the flavor from jar to jar.

Nuts: Many holiday cookies are loaded with nuts. For the best price (and usually the best, freshest flavor because of fast turnover), buy nuts in bulk at natural food stores. The high oil content of nuts encourages rancidity, so store them, tightly wrapped, in the refrigerator or freezer, not at room temperature.

Baking Perfect Cookies

Get Organized: Before you start baking, read the entire recipe to be sure you have all the ingredients and utensils. Measure all of the ingredients accurately, and have them ready in the order used. Prepare all of the baking sheets according to the recipe (although most of the recipes here use non-stick baking sheets). Adjust the oven racks in the recommended positions before preheating the oven.

Baking Basics: Do you want great cookies? Then get good cookie sheets. After fussing with many different baking sheets over the years, hassling with greasing and flouring them, cursing the flimsy thin ones that made the edges of the cookies burn, I finally went out and bought high-quality, nonstick insulated cookie sheets. What a difference! The double-thick insulation helps reduce burning, and the nonstick surface speaks for itself.

During the holidays, you will appreciate having more than one baking sheet. Three or four sheets are ideal. If you don't want to buy nonstick insulated sheets (they are relatively expensive), purchase the heaviest you can afford. Ideally, cookie sheets have no sides at all or just a handle at one end. This allows the heat to circulate around the cookies and promotes even browning. If possible, do not bake cookies on baking sheets with sides higher than $1/2$ inch, or turn them upside down and bake the cookies on the flat, rimless bottom. Dark, old, stained cookie sheets should be lined with aluminum foil, shiny side up, before using—dark cookie sheets promote burned cookies. It's best to simply throw away the old cookie sheets.

For uniform baking, the cookies should all be the same size. Measure out the cookie dough with a measuring spoon to get exact portions every time. I have given very precise measurements (by measuring spoon and size) because if your cookies are much bigger or smaller than mine, the baking time won't be the same.

In a gas oven, the heat rises from the bottom, so the cookies in the top third of the oven will bake more quickly than those in the center. Therefore, the positions of the baking sheets should be switched from top to bottom and from front to back to ensure even baking. For the best results, *bake the cookies one sheet at a time on the center rack.* This may be absolutely necessary in electric ovens with top-heating elements. If you have a convection oven, you can bake on two or even three racks, but lower the oven temperature by 25°F, and reduce the estimated baking time by about one-third.

Check the cookies for doneness at the beginning of the recommended baking time. Not all cookies turn golden brown when done—I have given specific visual tests as well as timings. It is a good idea to make a test run of the first tray so you can judge if you like the cookies more or less baked according to your taste. I prefer soft, just-baked cookies myself, but you may like them well done and crisp.

Remove the cookies from the sheets immediately after baking, unless indicated otherwise. Cool them on wire cake racks. I love my stackable cake racks, which are especially helpful in a cramped kitchen. Cool cookies completely before decorating, stacking, or storing.

Allow the cookie sheets to cool completely before baking another batch. If you put the dough on warm cookie sheets, the cookies will melt and spread before they have a chance to bake. There is a trick to save the cooling time. Arrange the cookies on aluminum foil (or parchment paper) cut to fit the cookie sheet, and slide the cookie-covered foil onto the warm cookie sheets. The foil will protect the dough from the hot sheets. However, it is still better just to have plenty of cookie sheets.

Making Masterpieces: Some cookies come out of the oven looking beautiful. Others want to be decorated. Those blond-gold sugar cookies aren't really Christmas cookies until they are embellished with icing and dusted with colored sugar or sprinkles.

With little more than some good food coloring to create nicely tinted icing, and a selection of attractive sugars, jimmies, and sprinkles, I can accomplish a lot. And a collection of well-shaped cookie cutters also helps. Some people are driven to create

cookies that are so intricately painted that I don't see how anyone can bear to bite into them! Just use your imagination, and your color sense, and you'll do fine.

If you don't consider yourself an artist and are afraid of garnishing your cookies with mismatched colors, just go to an art supply store and purchase an inexpensive color wheel. This is a tool that artists use to match up colors. The colors opposite each other on the wheel are considered compatible. Purple and yellow, for example, are opposites but compatible. Now you don't have to let your own (possibly misguided) sense of color lead you astray.

Most cookies can be decorated with only two icings. For a shiny icing to spread over cookies use the Decorating Icing on page 129. To pipe line decorations from a pastry bag, use the Royal Icing on page 130. If you wish, frost the cookie with an undercoat of decorating icing, and let dry, then add detail with the royal icing. (Usually, that is as complicated as I get.) When not using the icings, cover them with plastic wrap or moist paper towels pressed onto the surface so they don't crust over. A metal icing spatula, preferably offset, makes icing the cookies a breeze. I have two sizes, one large and one small, to use on different sizes of cookies.

Both these icings can be colored. For the truest, brightest tones, use high-quality food colorings, available at kitchenware stores. Spectrum and Chefmaster are two excellent brands. (Supermarket-quality food colorings are only okay. Their colors aren't very exciting, and the icing often ends up pastel no matter how much coloring is added.) Use these colorings in very judicious amounts, stirring the icing well before you judge the color—it is easy to go overboard. Food-coloring drops or gels are the easiest to use because they mix well with the icing. Pastes give very intensely colored results, but need to be scooped out of the jar with the tip of a toothpick or wooden skewer and require a good amount of stirring to dissolve.

When mixing different colors of icing, use disposable cups and spoons because they can be thrown away. When washing the bowls and utensils later, be careful not to splash colored water all over the sink and kitchen.

Cookies can also be painted *before baking* with an egg yolk–based glaze. For each color, stir 1 large egg yolk with $1/4$ teaspoon water in a small bowl, custard cup, or disposable cup. With a small whisk or spoon (a whisk works best), whisk in the desired amount of high-quality food-coloring drops. You must use good food coloring to override the bright yellow of the yolk. Small paint brushes are useful to paint unbaked cookies. It's up to you how intricate you want to get.

Storing Cookies: Store cookies in airtight containers. Throughout the year, I look for covered metal boxes or containers (such as those that hold gift bottles of liquor and coffee cans with snap-shut plastic lids) that I can press into service. During the holidays, decorated boxes show up in party stores and the seasonal section of chain variety stores, but these can be expensive. I also like plastic food containers with snap-shut lids. When layering cookies, separate the layers with double sheets of wax paper. Some sturdy cookies can be stored in self-sealing plastic bags. Wrap bar cookies individually in plastic wrap. Especially during the holidays, supermarkets carry colored plastic wrap which will give the cookies a holiday look.

For long-term storage, do not store different cookies in the same container, as they may pick up flavors from each other. Also, when combined, moist cookies will soften the crisp ones. Of course, you can't help mixing cookies if you are giving someone a selection, but in general, with cookies, it's never mix, never worry.

Mailing Cookies: Use a gift box just large enough to hold the amount of cookies you want to send. Choose sturdy cookies—bar and drop cookies, for example—and wrap them individually with plastic wrap. If baking and sending rolled cookies, roll them on the thick side so they hold up better during shipping. Place double layers of wax paper between the layers. Crumple wax paper to fill any spaces in the gift box. Place the gift box in a larger mailing box, surround the gift box with plastic pellets, and seal.

🎄 Sugar Cookies 101

Makes about 3½ dozen cookies, depending on size

Make Ahead: The dough must chill for at least 1½ hours. The cookies can be prepared 1 week ahead, stored in an airtight container at room temperature.

A perfect sugar cookie must have buttery flavor, melt-in-your-mouth texture, yet be firm enough to stand up to decorating. In typical sugar cookie recipes, the butter and sugar are creamed together, but I cut the butter into the dry ingredients like a pie dough to increase the cookies' flakiness. For added tenderness, I also combine shortening with the butter and cornstarch with the flour.

• *If you want to freeze these, I recommend freezing them undecorated, as the icing won't hold up well. They can be kept frozen for up to 1 month. About a week before serving, defrost the cookies, decorate, and store in airtight containers at room temperature.*

2¾ cups all-purpose flour

¼ cup cornstarch

1 cup sugar

1½ teaspoons baking powder

½ teaspoon salt

8 tablespoons (1 stick) unsalted butter,
   at room temperature

½ cup vegetable shortening, at room temperature

⅓ cup heavy cream

1 large egg plus 1 large yolk

1½ teaspoons vanilla extract

Decorating Icing (page 129)

1. Position the racks in the top and bottom thirds of the oven and preheat to 350°F.

2. In a large bowl, whisk the flour, cornstarch, sugar, baking powder, and salt to combine. Add the butter and shortening. Using a hand-held electric mixer at low speed, move the beaters through the mixture until the butter and shortening are uniformly cut into tiny crumbs and the mixture resembles coarse cornmeal, 2 to 3 minutes. In a small bowl, mix the cream, egg, egg yolk, and vanilla well. Using a wooden spoon, stir the cream mixture into the dry ingredients, and mix well to form a soft dough. Gather the dough together and divide into two thick disks. Wrap each disk in plastic wrap. Refrigerate until chilled, about 1½ hours. (The dough can be prepared up to 1 day ahead.)

3. Remove one disk of dough from the refrigerator and let stand at room temperature, 5 to 10 minutes. (If the dough has been chilled for longer than 1½ hours, it may take a few more minutes.) Unwrap the dough and place on a floured work surface. Lightly sprinkle the top of the dough with flour. Roll out the dough ⅛ inch thick, or slightly thicker for softer cookies. As you roll out the dough, it will become easier to work with, and tiny cracks on the surface will smooth out and disappear. Occasionally run a long knife under the dough so it doesn't stick to the work surface, and dust more flour under the dough, if needed. If the kitchen is warm, roll out the dough on a large piece of lightly floured wax paper, checking to be sure that the dough doesn't buckle. Slip the paper onto a large baking sheet and refrigerate for about 10 minutes before cutting out cookies.

4. Using cookie cutters, cut out the cookies and transfer to nonstick cookie sheets, placing the cookies 1 inch apart. Gently knead the scraps together and form into another disk. Wrap and chill for 5 minutes before rolling out again to cut out more cookies.

5. Bake, switching the positions of the cookie sheets from top to bottom and front to back halfway through baking, just until the edges of the cookies are barely beginning to turn golden, about 10 minutes. Do not overbake. Let stand on the cookie sheets for 2 minutes, then transfer to wire cooling racks to cool completely. Decorate as desired with Decorating Icing.

Gingerbread Cookies 101

Makes about 3 dozen (3-inch) cookies, depending on size

Make Ahead: The dough must be chilled for at least 3 hours and up to 2 days. The cookies can be prepared up to 1 week ahead, stored in an airtight container at room temperature.

I had to bake many batches to finally accomplish the perfect gingerbread cookie. When the dough is rolled thin, it will bake crisp and almost crackerlike. Yet, when rolled thick (my preference), the cookies turn out plump and moist. In either case, the flavor will be complex and almost hot-spicy. I use large gingerbread cookies as placecards for my holiday dinner table, with the guest's name written onto each, and everyone gets to take theirs home (if they don't nibble it with their coffee after dinner).

3 cups all-purpose flour

1 teaspoon baking soda

¾ teaspoon ground cinnamon

¾ teaspoon ground ginger

½ teaspoon ground allspice

½ teaspoon ground cloves

½ teaspoon salt

¼ teaspoon freshly milled black pepper

8 tablespoons (1 stick) unsalted butter, at room temperature

¼ cup vegetable shortening, at room temperature

½ cup packed light brown sugar

⅔ cup unsulfured molasses

1 large egg

Royal Icing (page 130)

1. Position the racks in the top and bottom thirds of the oven and preheat to 350°F.

2. Sift the flour, baking soda, cinnamon, ginger, allspice, cloves, salt, and pepper through a wire sieve into a medium bowl. Set aside.

3. In a large bowl, using a hand-held electric mixer at high speed, beat the butter and vegetable shortening until well combined, about 1 minute. Add the brown sugar and beat until the mixture is light in texture and color, about 2 minutes. Beat in the molasses and egg. Using a wooden spoon, gradually mix in the flour mixture to make a stiff dough. Divide the dough into two thick disks and wrap each disk in plastic wrap. Refrigerate until chilled, about 3 hours. (The dough can be prepared up to 2 days ahead.)

4. To roll out the cookies, work with one disk at a time, keeping the other disk refrigerated. Remove the dough from the refrigerator and let stand at room temperature until just warm enough to roll out without cracking, about 10 minutes. (If the dough has been chilled for longer than 3 hours, it may need a few more minutes.) Place the dough on a lightly floured work surface and sprinkle the top of the dough with flour. Roll out the dough ⅛ inch thick, being sure that the dough isn't sticking to the work surface (run a long metal spatula or knife under the dough occasionally just to be sure, and dust the surface with more flour, if needed). For softer cookies, roll out slightly thicker. Using cookie cutters, cut out the cookies and transfer to nonstick cookie sheets, placing the cookies 1 inch apart. Gently knead the scraps together and form into another disk. Wrap and chill for 5 minutes before rolling out again to cut out more cookies.

5. Bake, switching the positions of the cookies from top to bottom and back to front halfway through baking, until the edges of the cookies are set and crisp, 10 to 12 minutes. Cool on the sheets for 2 minutes, then transfer to wire cake racks to cool completely. Decorate with Royal Icing. (The cookies can be prepared up to 1 week ahead, stored in airtight containers at room temperature.)

Chocolate-Hazelnut Biscotti

Makes about 28 biscotti

Make Ahead: The biscotti can be prepared up to 2 weeks ahead, stored in an airtight container at room temperature.

Biscotti are great for gift giving because they get better as they age a bit. Dip these into hot coffee or tea, or even a sweet wine. (Since biscotti are especially nice dipped into wine, a bottle of port makes a nice auxiliary gift.)

½ cup (2 ounces) hazelnuts

2 cups plus 2 tablespoons all-purpose flour

1 teaspoon baking powder

¼ teaspoon salt

8 tablespoons (1 stick) unsalted butter,
  at room temperature

1 cup sugar

Grated zest of 1 large orange

2 large eggs

1 teaspoon vanilla extract

½ cup (3 ounces) mini-chocolate chips

1. Position the racks in the top third and center of the oven and preheat to 350°F. Spread the hazelnuts on a baking sheet. Bake until the skins are cracked, about 10 minutes. Place the hazelnuts in a clean kitchen towel and rub together to remove as much skin as possible. (Some skin will remain on the nuts, but that's fine.) Cool completely, then chop coarsely.

2. In a medium bowl, whisk the flour, baking powder, and salt together to combine; set aside. In a large bowl, using a hand-held electric mixer at high speed, beat the butter, sugar, and orange zest until very light in color and texture, about 2 minutes. One at a time, beat in the eggs, then the vanilla.

3. Using a wooden spoon, gradually beat in the flour mixture, just until a smooth dough forms. Using a wooden spoon, stir in the chocolate chips and chopped hazelnuts.

4. Divide the dough in half. Using lightly floured hands, on a floured work surface, form the dough into two 10 × 2-inch rectangular logs. Place the logs on an ungreased large baking sheet, at least 2 inches apart. Bake on the center rack until the logs are set and golden brown, about 30 minutes. Remove from the oven and let cool on the baking sheet for 20 minutes.

5. Transfer the logs to a work surface. Using a serrated knife and a sawing motion, carefully cut the logs into diagonal slices about ½ inch wide. Place the slices on ungreased baking sheets. Bake until the undersides of the biscotti are lightly browned, about 8 minutes. Turn the biscotti over. Switch the position of the baking sheets from top to bottom and front to back. Continue baking until lightly browned on the other side, about 8 minutes longer. Cool completely on wire cake racks. (The biscotti can be prepared up to 2 weeks ahead, stored in an airtight container at room temperature.)

Cinnamon Stars

Makes about 3 dozen cookies

Make Ahead: The dough must stand at room temperature for 1 hour before rolling out. The cookies can be baked up to 2 weeks ahead, stored in airtight containers at room temperature.

The recipe for these cookies was brought by my great-grandmother Kindle from the old country, where they are called Zimt Sternen, literally "cinnamon stars." Using ground almonds instead of flour gives the cookies an intense flavor and crisp texture. It may seem like an advanced recipe because of the nut grinding, but it is really an easy chore and the results are wonderful. Do allow about an hour for the ground almonds in the dough to soak up the moisture from the egg whites before rolling out. These are good cookies for making well ahead of time.

- *There are many ways to grind the nuts. I use a tabletop Zylis-brand rotary grinder that is good not only for nuts, but hard cheese. Use the attachment with the finest holes. The almonds can also be ground in a hand-held rotary grater. With a hand grater, use whole blanched almonds.*

- *To grind the nuts in a food processor, combine blanched sliced almonds with 2 tablespoons of the confectioners' sugar from the recipe. (The confectioners' sugar acts as a buffer to keep the almonds from turning into almond butter. In Step 2, beat the egg whites, lemon zest, and cinnamon with the remaining confectioners' sugar.) Pulse until the almonds are very finely ground but not oily, about 25 pulses. Use as directed.*

- *It is best to bake these cookies one sheet at a time in the center of the oven. If you only have one cookie sheet, be sure to let it cool completely before placing the next batch of dough onto the sheet. To roll out all of the cookies at once, place them on a sheet of parchment paper trimmed to fit your cookie sheet. When ready to bake, slip the parchment paper onto the cooled baking sheet.*

2 cups confectioners' sugar
3 large egg whites
Grated zest of 1 lemon
½ teaspoon ground cinnamon
2 cups (8 ounces) blanched sliced almonds, ground

1. Sift the confectioners' sugar into a medium bowl. Add the egg whites, lemon zest, and cinnamon. Using a hand-held electric mixer at high speed, beat until the mixture is thick and shiny, about 5 minutes. Transfer ¾ cup of the meringue mixture to a small bowl, cover tightly with plastic wrap, and set aside. Add the ground almonds to the remaining meringue and stir to make a soft dough. Cover with plastic wrap and set aside until the mixture is stiff enough to roll out, about 1 hour. (The exact length of time depends on the humidity when the dough is made.)

2. Position a rack in the center of the oven and preheat to 350°F.

3. On a lightly floured work surface, roll out the dough to ⅛-inch thickness. Using a 2½-inch star-shaped cookie cutter, cut out the cookies and place about 1 inch apart on a nonstick baking sheet. Spoon about ½ teaspoon of the meringue onto the center of each cookie, and use the back of the spoon to spread to the edges of the cookie.

4. Bake one sheet at a time until the glaze is set and the tips of the cookies are barely beginning to brown, about 12 minutes. Cool on the sheets for 1 minute, then transfer to a wire cake rack to cool completely. Knead the dough scraps and repeat the procedure to bake more cookies. You will have leftover meringue. (The cookies can be baked up to 2 weeks ahead, stored in airtight containers at room temperature.)

 Lebkuchen

Makes about 40 cookies

Make Ahead: The dough must be chilled for at least 4 hours or overnight. The cookies can be baked up to 2 months ahead, stored in airtight containers at room temperature. If possible, store the cookies for at least 3 days before serving.

In my family, these cookies epitomized Christmas baking. Great-Auntie Gisela would bake her lebkuchen into large oblong cookies, and decorate them with paper stamps of Saint Nicholas, using the glaze as glue. The stamps were imported and beautifully designed in an Old World attention to detail. Nonetheless, my cousin Lisa and I would complain that our friends didn't have to scrape paper off their cookies. Now, as adults, we have great nostalgia for Gisela's famous lebkuchen, and got all choked up when we found the same paper stamps during an antique shopping trip.

Full of honey and spices, these aromatic, hard bars keep forever. Cousin Suzie still has some of Gisela's old Saint Nick lebkuchen stashed away with her ornaments and brings them out every year to admire—if not eat. (There are tales of lebkuchen getting better with years of aging.) If you prefer softer cookies, place a sliced apple on wax paper in the closed cookie container for a day or two.

3 cups all-purpose flour
1 teaspoon baking soda
1 teaspoon ground cinnamon
1/2 teaspoon freshly grated nutmeg
1/2 teaspoon ground cloves
1/2 teaspoon salt
1 cup honey
3/4 cup packed light brown sugar
1 large egg

Zest of 1 lemon
1 tablespoon fresh lemon juice
1 cup (4 ounces) very finely chopped walnuts
1/2 cup very finely chopped Candied Orange Peel (page 93) or store-bought candied orange peel

Icing
1 cup confectioners' sugar
1 teaspoon fresh lemon juice
1/2 teaspoon almond extract

1. Sift the flour, baking soda, cinnamon, nutmeg, cloves, and salt into a medium bowl, and set aside. In a large bowl, whisk the honey, brown sugar, egg, lemon zest and juice, and 2 tablespoons water. Gradually stir in the flour mixture, then the walnuts and candied orange peel. If the dough seems too dry, sprinkle with water, 1 tablespoon at a time, and mix with your hands until moistened. Gather up the dough. Divide the dough into two flat disks and wrap in plastic wrap. Refrigerate until firm and chilled, at least 4 hours or overnight. (If chilled overnight, allow the dough to stand at room temperature for 30 minutes before rolling out. The dough will crack if it is too cold.)

2. Position the racks in the center and top third of the oven and preheat to 375°F.

3. On a lightly floured work surface, roll out one disk of dough into a 1/2-inch rectangle, about 12 × 8 inches. Using a sharp knife, trim the dough to a 7 1/2 × 10-inch rectangle, discarding the trimmings. Cut the dough into 20 bars. Place the bars on nonstick cookie sheets, about 1 inch apart. Repeat the procedure with the remaining dough.

4. Bake, switching the positions of the cookies from top to bottom and back to front halfway through baking, until the edges of the cookies are beginning to brown, about 15 minutes. Transfer to wire cake racks and cool completely.

5. To make the icing, sift the confectioners' sugar into a small bowl. Add the lemon juice and almond extract. Stir in 2 tablespoons water to make a thin, spreadable icing. Using a small metal spatula, spread the icing over the tops of the cookies, and let stand until the icing is dry. (The cookies can be baked up to 2 months ahead, stored in airtight containers at room temperature. If possible, store the cookies for at least 3 days before serving.)

Tannenbaum Cookies

Makes about 4 dozen cookies

Make Ahead: The dough must chill for 3 hours. The cookies can be prepared up to 1 week ahead, stored in an airtight container at room temperature.

Christmas cookies don't come much prettier than this. With the help of a pastry tube, round holes are cut out from Christmas tree–shaped butter cookies. The holes are filled with crushed sour-ball candies that melt during baking and resemble glass ornaments. They are a little fussy to make, but worth the effort.

- *Don't crush an entire 10-ounce bag of sour balls, crush only the colors you prefer (the white ones don't look like much when melted). You'll need about ¹/₂ cup crushed candies for the total batch, so 2 tablespoons each of 4 colors will be plenty.*

2¹/₂ cups all-purpose flour

1 teaspoon baking powder

¹/₂ teaspoon salt

8 tablespoons (1 stick) unsalted butter, at room temperature

2 large eggs, at room temperature

1 teaspoon vanilla extract

About 5 ounces (half a 10-ounce bag) sour-ball candies

Nonstick cooking oil spray

1. In a medium bowl, whisk the flour, baking powder, and salt. In another medium bowl, using a hand-held electric mixer on high speed, beat the butter until creamy, about 1 minute. Add the sugar and beat until light in color and texture, about 2 minutes. Beat in the eggs, one at a time, then the vanilla. Using a wooden spoon, gradually stir in the flour mixture. Gather up the dough and divide into two flat disks. Wrap in wax paper and refrigerate until chilled, about 3 hours.

2. Unwrap the candies and separate them by color. Place each color in a small plastic bag and crush with a rolling pin or flat meat pounder. Set aside.

3. Position the racks in the center and top third of the oven and preheat to 350°F. Line cookie sheets with aluminum foil and spray with nonstick cooking spray.

4. Working with one disk at a time, on a lightly floured work surface, dust the top of the dough with flour and roll out to ¹/₈-inch thickness. Using a 3-inch tree-shaped cookie cutter, cut out the cookies. Place the cookies 1 inch apart on the foil. Using a plain pastry tip with a ¹/₂-inch opening (such as Ateco No. 5), cut out 3 or 4 holes from each cookie. Using a small spoon (an espresso spoon works well), fill the holes with the crushed candies. (You will have leftover candies.)

5. Bake, switching the positions of the cookies from top to bottom and back to front halfway through baking, until the cookies are lightly browned and the candies have melted, 10 to 12 minutes. Cool completely on the baking sheets. If you wish, let stand 5 minutes, then slide foil with the cookies off the sheets to cool. (The cookies can be prepared 1 week ahead, stored in an airtight container at room temperature.)

Moravian Spice Wafers

Makes about 10 dozen

Make Ahead: The dough must be chilled for at least 4 hours or overnight. The cookies can be baked up to 2 months ahead, stored in airtight containers at room temperature.

The Moravians were a Protestant sect that settled in Pennsylvania and North Carolina. They were well known for their belief in the spiritual rejuvenation that comes from breaking bread with loved ones. (Their religious services were called "love feasts," and lasted so long that refreshments of coffee and buns had to be served.) These plain-looking but delicately crisp wafers have been baked for generations by families around Winston-Salem, and they are one of my absolute favorites, especially for gift giving.

- *Bakers who enjoy the "zen" of rolling dough should try making these cookies, because the dough is rolled quite thin. Even if you don't consider yourself a master "roller-outer," the dough is very easy to work with. And don't let the large yield scare you off. When you get into a rhythm, you'll knock out the entire batch in no time, and you'll have a mountain of cookies that store very well.*

2³/₄ cups all-purpose flour
1 teaspoon baking soda
1 teaspoon ground cinnamon
¹/₂ teaspoon ground ginger
¹/₂ teaspoon ground cloves
¹/₂ teaspoon ground allspice
¹/₂ teaspoon freshly grated nutmeg
¹/₂ teaspoon salt
¹/₂ cup vegetable shortening
¹/₂ cup packed light brown sugar

1 cup unsulfured molasses
1 tablespoon brandy

1. Sift the flour, baking soda, cinnamon, ginger, cloves, allspice, nutmeg, and salt into a medium bowl. In a large bowl, using a hand-held electric mixer at high speed, beat the shortening and brown sugar until light in color and texture, about 2 minutes. Beat in molasses and brandy. Using a wooden spoon, gradually stir in the flour to make a stiff dough. (If the dough seems too dry, sprinkle with additional brandy and mix with your hands until moistened.) Gather up the dough and divide into four thick disks. Wrap each disk in plastic wrap. Refrigerate until well chilled, at least 4 hours or overnight.

2. Position a rack in the center of the oven and preheat to 350°F. (These cookies are best when baked one sheet at a time in the center of the oven.)

3. Work with one disk of chilled dough at a time. (Unlike many other refrigerated doughs, this dough is easy to roll, even when chilled.) Unwrap the dough, place on a lightly floured work surface, and sprinkle the top of the dough with flour. Roll out the dough ¹/₁₆ inch thick, being sure that the dough isn't sticking to the work surface (run a long metal spatula or knife under the dough occasionally and dust the surface with more flour, if needed). Using a 2-inch round cookie cutter (preferably with a fluted edge), cut out the cookies. Place the cookies ¹/₂ inch apart on nonstick cookie sheets. Place the scraps in a plastic bag.

4. Bake the cookies, one sheet at a time, turning the sheet from front to back halfway during cooking, until the edges are very lightly browned, about 8 minutes. Do not overbake the cookies or they will taste bitter. Transfer to wire cake racks to cool completely. Repeat the procedure with the remaining dough, placing any scraps in the plastic bag.

5. To bake more cookies, knead all of the scraps from the four disks together. (If the dough seems dry, sprinkle with 2 teaspoons brandy and knead until moistened.) Working with half of the dough at a time, roll out more cookies and bake. Do not roll out the scraps a third time, as they will have picked up too much flour and be tough. (The cookies can be baked 2 months ahead, stored in airtight containers at room temperature.)

Linzer Cookies

Makes about 3¹/₂ dozen cookies

Make Ahead: The cookies can be baked up to 5 days ahead, stored in an airtight container at room temperature.

The Austrian city of Linz is famous for its special, lattice-topped tart created from a cinnamon-scented nut dough filled with raspberry jam. This recipe makes beautiful sandwich cookies from the same formula. You will need two fluted round cookie or biscuit cutters, one 2 inches in diameter, and other ³/₄ inch in diameter.

1¹/₂ cups (6 ounces) walnuts
³/₄ cup sugar
2 cups all-purpose flour
¹/₂ teaspoon baking powder
¹/₂ teaspoon ground cinnamon
¹/₄ teaspoon ground cloves
1 cup (2 sticks) unsalted butter, chilled,
  cut into small cubes
2 large eggs
¹/₂ cup raspberry preserves (not jelly or jam)
Confectioners' sugar, for serving (optional)

1. Position the racks in the center and top third of the oven and preheat to 350°F.

2. In a food processor fitted with the metal blade, pulse the walnuts with ¹/₄ cup of the sugar until finely ground, about 20 pulses. Transfer to a large bowl. Add the flour, the remaining ¹/₂ cup sugar, baking powder, cinnamon, and cloves, and mix well. Add the butter. Using a pastry blender, cut the butter into the flour mixture until it looks like cornmeal. In a small bowl, beat 1 egg and stir into the flour mixture to make a dough. Gather up the dough into a ball.

3. Work with half of the dough at a time, keeping the remaining dough covered with plastic wrap. On a lightly floured work surface, roll out the dough ¹/₈ inch thick. Using a 2-inch round cookie cutter (preferably with a fluted edge), cut out the cookies. Transfer to nonstick baking sheets, placing the cookies about 1 inch apart. Gather up the scraps and knead together briefly. Roll and cut more cookies until the first half of the dough is depleted. Place about ¹/₂ teaspoon of the raspberry preserves in the center of each cookie round.

4. On a lightly floured work surface, roll out the reserved dough ¹/₈ inch thick and cut out 2-inch round cookies. Using a ³/₄-inch round cookie cutter, cut holes in the center of each round. Place over the preserve-topped cookies with the holes centered over the preserves to make sandwiches, lightly pressing the edges of the two layers together. In a small bowl, beat the remaining egg well. Using a pastry brush, lightly brush the dough tops of the cookies with the egg. Repeat with the remaining dough, preserves, and egg.

5. Bake, switching the positions of the cookies from top to bottom and back to front halfway through baking, until the cookies are golden and the preserves are bubbling in the centers, about 15 minutes. Transfer the cookies to wire cake racks to cool completely. (The cookies can be baked 5 days ahead, stored in an airtight container at room temperature.) Just before serving, sift confectioners' sugar over the cookies, if desired.

 Polish Bowknots

Makes about 7 dozen

Make Ahead: The cookies can be prepared up to 3 days ahead, stored in airtight containers at room temperature.

Every European culture has a fried Christmas cookie, but this recipe for Polish chrusciki has become my favorite. The smooth silky dough, rich with sour cream and fragrant with a bit of rum, is a pleasure to roll out, and fries into flaky, delicate bowknot cookies. To ensure safe, easy deep-frying and the best cookies, take a few minutes to set up the proper procedure with a deep pot and a deep-frying thermometer. And above all, use fresh vegetable oil.

- *Deep-frying is an easy cooking technique to master if you have the right tools. Use a large (5-quart) heavy pot that will hold at least 2 to 3 inches of oil. Deep-fried food should swim in the oil so it can cook properly. The cookies will be greasy and heavy if you skimp on the oil and use less than is required.*

- *The type of oil isn't especially important, as long as it is tasteless. I usually use generic vegetable oil or vegetable shortening. Canola oil often leaves a thick, sticky coating behind on utensils, so I don't recommend it for deep-frying.*

- *Even if you are frugal, do not save the deep-frying oil for another use. Reheated oil never tastes the same, and subsequent food fried in it won't be as tasty. Just factor the cost of the oil into the recipe and discard it after you have finished.*

- *Use a deep-frying thermometer to check the temperature of the oil. Let the oil return to 360°F between batches. Do not crowd the cookies in the pot, or they bring down the temperature of the oil too much.*

- *Use a very large mesh wire strainer, like the kind that come with wok sets, to remove the cookies from the hot oil. A slotted spoon collects too much oil.*

- *Drain the fried cookies on wire cake racks set over a jelly-roll pan. This is much more effective than draining them on paper towels. When fried food is placed on paper towels, steam is created and trapped where the food touches the paper. This steam makes the food soggy. The cooled cookies can be placed on crumpled paper towels to remove any excess oil. (Crumpled paper towels get into the cookies' nooks and crannies better than flat paper.)*

3 large egg yolks
3 tablespoons sugar
¼ teaspoon salt
1 tablespoon dark rum or brandy
1⅔ cups all-purpose flour
½ cup sour cream, at room temperature
Vegetable oil, for deep-frying
Confectioners' sugar, for serving

1. In a medium bowl, using a hand-held electric mixer at high speed, beat the yolks, sugar, and salt until the yolks are thick and pale yellow, about 2 minutes. Beat in the rum. Using a wooden spoon, one-third at a time, alternately beat in the flour and sour cream, stirring well after each addition.

2. Transfer the dough to a floured surface and knead until smooth, about 3 minutes. Wrap in plastic wrap and let stand at room temperature for 20 minutes.

3. Work with half of the dough at a time, leaving the other half covered. On a lightly floured work surface, dust the dough with flour, and roll out to ¹⁄₁₆-inch thickness. Using a fluted ravioli cutter or pizza wheel, cut 1-inch wide strips of dough. Cut the dough crosswise into 3-inch lengths, cutting the ends on a slight diagonal. In the center of each strip, cut a slit about

1½ inches long. Pull one end of the dough through the slit to make a bow-tie shape. Place the cookies on cookie sheets. Repeat with the remaining dough.

4. Pour enough vegetable oil into a 5-quart pot to come halfway up the sides. Heat over high heat to 360°F. In batches, without crowding, fry the cookies until golden brown, turning halfway through frying, about 3 minutes. Using a large wire-mesh skimmer, transfer the cookies to wire cake racks set over jelly-roll pans to drain and cool. Place the cooled cookies on crumpled paper towels to remove any excess oil. (The cookies can be prepared up to 3 days ahead, stored in airtight containers at room temperature.) To serve, sift confectioners' sugar over the cookies.

Greek Snowballs

Makes about 30 cookies

Make Ahead: The cookies can be prepared up to 1 week ahead, stored in an airtight container at room temperature. Roll again in confectioners' sugar before serving.

Every Greek family has a recipe for these melt-in-your-mouth cookies. Known in Greece as kourambiedes, they are closely related to Nutty Angel Fingers (page 124), but here the dough is rolled into balls, not logs, and scented with brandy. You can substitute anise-flavored ouzo or sambuca for the brandy. Many bakers stud each cookie with a whole clove, but I prefer them plain.

1 cup (2 sticks) unsalted butter, at room
  temperature
⅓ cup confectioners' sugar plus
  additional ½ cup for rolling cookies

1 large egg yolk
1 tablespoon brandy or anise liqueur
1½ cups all-purpose flour
1 teaspoon baking powder
⅛ teaspoon salt
1 cup (5 ounces) finely chopped walnuts
  or almonds
About 30 whole cloves (optional)

1. Position the racks in the center and top third of the oven and preheat to 350°F.

2. In a medium bowl, using a hand-held electric mixer at high speed, beat the butter until light in color and texture, about 1 minute. Beat in ⅓ cup confectioners' sugar, then the egg yolk and brandy, just until combined. Using a wooden spoon, stir in the flour, baking powder, and salt, and then the walnuts, mixing just until smooth.

3. Using a level tablespoon for each, roll the dough into 1-inch balls. Place the balls 1 inch apart on a nonstick cookie sheet. If desired, stud each cookie in the center with a whole clove.

4. Bake, switching the positions of the cookie sheets from top to bottom and front to back halfway through baking, until the cookies are firm to the touch and lightly browned around the edges, about 20 minutes. Let the cookies cool on the sheets for 5 minutes. Roll the cookies in the remaining ½ cup confectioners' sugar, then transfer to wire cooling racks to cool completely. Before serving, roll the cookies again in more confectioners' sugar to freshen their coating. (The cookies will keep, covered tightly in an airtight container, for up to 1 week.)

It Wouldn't Be the Holidays Without . . . Cookies

*T*he word "cookie" comes from the Dutch *koeptje,* which means "little cake." The Dutch brought their recipes to America when they settled today's New York City, but the tradition of serving sweet little cakes at Christmas was already centuries old.

The first cookies were probably savory crackers. (To this day, sweet cookies are called "biscuits" in Britain.) Crisp baked cakes kept for a long time and were easy to transport on journeys, so they had a practical function. The Muslim invasion of Spain in the 700s, and later the Crusades, exposed Europe to Arabic foods. The Arabs loved sugar and spices, and European cooks soon incorporated both ingredients into their crackers, along with butter and other ingredients that lightened and tenderized the mix. However, the Arabs had a corner on the sugar market (they kept the refining process a secret for many centuries), so most cookies were sweetened with honey or dried fruits.

But it was in northern Europe, and Germany in particular, that the cookie reached its apotheosis. Nuremberg, a shipping center for the important spice trade, and with access to unlimited amounts of honey from the beekeepers in the nearby forest, perfected gingerbread. Fairs were important social and economic events in medieval Nuremberg (a custom that lives on in Germany with the annual Oktoberfest and Christmas market festivals). Gingerbread cookies, cut into shapes of people, hearts, and other everyday images, and occasionally crafted into small houses, were a specialty of these fairs.

The practice of baking gingerbread into people-shaped cookies probably evolved from the pagan human-sacrifice ceremonies that occurred around the winter solstice. Of course, human sacrifice was discouraged by the Church Fathers, so cookie-shaped people that could be dispatched with a bite replaced the real thing. The German fairy tale "Hansel and Gretel," with its gingerbread house, a witch that turns children into cookies, and a oven that turns out to be her sacrificial pyre, is a gold mine for sociologists, historians, and armchair psychologists alike.

 **Florentines**

Makes about 7½ dozen cookies

Make Ahead: The cookies can be prepared up to 1 week ahead, stored in an airtight container at room temperature.

Cooking teacher Vicki Caparulo says that these are among her favorite Christmas cookies, and she often makes them for gifts because they look so great but don't take much effort. Crisp and crunchy with a luscious caramel flavor and drizzled with chocolate, they are sometimes called lace cookies because of the tiny holes that form in the cookies during baking.

- *Be sure to leave plenty of room between the balls of dough so they can spread out without running into each other.*
- *Remove the cookies from the baking sheet when they are set but still warm. If they cool and can't be removed easily from the baking sheet, return them to the oven for a minute or two to warm up.*

8 tablespoons (1 stick) unsalted butter, cut up
½ cup light corn syrup
½ cup packed light brown sugar
1 cup all-purpose flour
1 cup (5 ounces) finely chopped walnuts
1 teaspoon vanilla extract
3 ounces bittersweet chocolate, finely chopped

1. Position the racks in the center and top third of the oven and preheat to 350°F.

2. In a medium saucepan, bring the butter, corn syrup, and brown sugar to a full boil over medium heat, stirring constantly. Remove from the heat and wait until the mixture stops bubbling. Stir in the flour, walnuts, and vanilla, and mix well. Transfer the dough to a bowl and cool for 20 minutes.

3. Using ½ teaspoon for each, form the dough into 1¾-inch balls and place 2 inches apart on nonstick baking sheets (or line regular baking sheets with parchment paper). Bake, switching the positions of the cookie sheets from top to bottom and front to back halfway through baking time, until the cookies are golden brown, bubbling, and covered with tiny holes, 8 to 10 minutes.

4. Let the cookies cool on the sheets until firm enough to remove but still warm, 1 to 2 minutes. Using a spatula, transfer the cookies to wire cooling racks to cool completely. When cooled, arrange the cookies in a single layer on paper towels on a work surface. (The paper towels will absorb any excess butter from the cookies.)

5. In the top part of a double boiler over hot, not simmering, water, melt the chocolate, stirring occasionally. Cool until slightly thickened, about 10 minutes. Transfer to a small plastic bag. Force the chocolate into the corner of the bag. Using scissors, snip a tiny hole from the corner. Drizzle the melted chocolate over the tops of the cookies. Let stand until the chocolate is firm. If the kitchen is warm, transfer the cookies to baking sheets and chill in the refrigerator until the chocolate sets. (The cookies can be prepared up to 1 week ahead, stored in an airtight container at room temperature.)

Florentine Sandwich Cookies: These cookies are doubly rich, but very impressive. Increase the chocolate to 6 ounces. Using a small icing spatula or a dinner knife, spread the flat back of a cookie with a thin layer of melted chocolate, then with a second cookie make a sandwich. Makes about 4 dozen cookies.

Mocha Nut Crinkles

Makes 4 dozen cookies

Make Ahead: The dough must be chilled for at least 2 hours. The cookies can be prepared up to 1 week ahead, stored in an airtight container at room temperature.

Deeply flavored with chocolate and espresso, these drop cookies are a mocha lover's dream. Kids love to make them because even though they're easy, there's a lot of fun hands-on work involved. Instant espresso coffee powder gives the strongest coffee flavor. You'll find it at Italian delicatessens and some supermarkets. If necessary, substitute regular instant coffee, although the flavor won't be as strong.

2 ounces unsweetened chocolate,
   finely chopped
2 cups all-purpose flour
2 teaspoons baking powder
¹/₂ teaspoon salt
1¹/₄ teaspoons instant espresso powder
¹/₃ cup milk
1²/₃ cups granulated sugar
¹/₂ cup vegetable shortening
2 large eggs, at room temperature
2 teaspoons vanilla extract
¹/₂ cup coarsely chopped walnuts
³/₄ cup confectioners' sugar, for rolling

1. In the top part of a double boiler, over barely simmering water, melt the chocolate, stirring occasionally. Remove from the water and cool the chocolate until tepid.

2. In a small bowl, whisk the flour, baking powder, and salt together to combine; set aside.

3. In a glass measuring cup, stir the espresso into the milk until dissolved; set aside.

4. In a medium bowl, using a hand-held electric mixer at high speed, beat the sugar and shortening until well combined. Beat in the eggs, one at a time, and the vanilla. Reduce the mixer speed to low. One-third at a time, alternately beat in the flour and milk mixtures. Stir in the walnuts. Cover with plastic wrap and refrigerate until chilled and firm, about 2 hours.

5. Position the racks in the center and top third of the oven and preheat to 350°F. Place the confectioners' sugar in a small bowl. Using 1 tablespoon for each, roll the dough into 1-inch balls. Roll the balls in the confectioners' sugar to coat, then place 2 inches apart on nonstick baking sheets.

6. Bake, switching the positions of the baking sheets from top to bottom and back to front halfway through baking, until the cookies are set with crisp edges, about 15 minutes. Cool on the baking sheets for 5 minutes, then transfer to wire cake racks to cool completely. (The cookies can be prepared up to 1 week ahead, stored in an airtight container at room temperature.)

 **Peppernuts**

Makes about 4 dozen cookies

Make Ahead: The cookies can be prepared up to 2 weeks ahead, stored in airtight containers at room temperature. If possible, store the cookies for 2 days before serving.

Just about every country in northern Europe has some version of these spicy drops in its Christmas cookie culture. The cookies are often allowed to dry out until they are rock hard. In my recipe, they aren't exactly soft, but they aren't dangerous to your teeth either. They are properly spicy-hot, loaded with ginger, pepper, cinnamon, cloves, and anise.

³/₄ cup honey

8 tablespoons (1 stick) unsalted butter, cut up

2 large eggs

4 cups all-purpose flour

¹/₂ cup granulated sugar

1¹/₂ teaspoons ground cinnamon

1 teaspoon aniseed, crushed in a mortar or
   under a heavy pot

1 teaspoon freshly milled black pepper

1 teaspoon freshly grated nutmeg

1 teaspoon baking soda

¹/₂ teaspoon ground cloves

¹/₂ teaspoon salt

¹/₂ cup finely chopped candied citron or
   candied lemon or orange peel

¹/₄ cup dark rum

Glaze

1¹/₂ cups confectioners' sugar, sifted

3 tablespoons water

1¹/₂ teaspoons dark rum

1. Position the racks in the center and top third of the oven and preheat to 350°F.

2. In a medium saucepan, bring the honey and butter to a boil over medium heat, stirring to melt the butter. Transfer to a large bowl and cool to room temperature. (To speed cooling, place the bowl on a wire cake rack in front of an open window, and stir often.) Add the eggs and mix well.

3. In a large bowl, whisk the flour, sugar, cinnamon, aniseed, pepper, nutmeg, baking soda, cloves, and salt until combined. In three additions, stir into the honey mixture, adding the citron with the last addition of flour. Stir in the rum to make a stiff dough.

4. Using a level tablespoon for each, roll the dough into 1-inch balls. Place the balls about 1 inch apart on a nonstick cookie sheet.

5. Bake, switching the positions of the cookies from top to bottom and back to front halfway through baking, until the cookies are lightly browned and feel firm when pressed with a finger, about 20 minutes. Cool for 5 minutes on the cookie sheet.

6. To make the glaze, mix the confectioners' sugar, water, and rum in a small bowl until smooth. One at a time, holding the cookies upside down, dip the tops of the cookies into the glaze. Let the excess glaze drip off, then place the cookies right side up on a wire cake rack to cool completely. (The cookies can be stored for up to 2 weeks in airtight containers at room temperature.) If possible, store the cookies for 2 days before serving.

 Chewy Molasses Drops

Makes about 3 dozen

Make Ahead: The dough must be chilled for at least 1 hour. The cookies can be prepared up to 1 week ahead, stored in an airtight container at room temperature.

Mary-Lynn Mondich's exceptional skills as a cookie baker led her to establish American Vintage, a bakery that specializes in her family's secret-recipe wine biscotti. So when Mary-Lynn shared this recipe with me many Christmases ago, I paid attention. Now a holiday baking season doesn't pass that I don't make these chewy, moist, spicy, I-could-eat-the-whole-batch cookies.

2 cups all-purpose flour
2 teaspoons baking soda
1 teaspoon ground cinnamon
½ teaspoon ground ginger
½ teaspoon salt
¼ teaspoon ground cloves
6 tablespoons (¾ stick) unsalted butter
6 tablespoons vegetable shortening
1⅓ cups sugar
¼ cup unsulfured molasses
1 large egg, at room temperature

1. Sift the flour, baking soda, cinnamon, ginger, salt, and cloves through a wire sieve into a bowl, and set aside. In a medium saucepan, melt the butter and shortening together over medium heat. Transfer to a medium bowl and let cool until tepid.

2. Whisk in 1 cup of the sugar, molasses, and egg. Using a wooden spoon, gradually stir in the flour mixture. Cover tightly with plastic wrap and refrigerate until chilled, about 1 hour.

3. Position the racks in the center and top third of the oven and preheat to 350°F. Place the remaining ⅓ cup sugar in a small bowl. Using 1 tablespoon of dough for each, roll into 1-inch balls. Roll in the sugar to coat, then place 2 inches apart on nonstick baking sheets.

4. Bake, switching the positions of the cookies from top to bottom and back to front halfway through baking, until the cookies are evenly browned and the edges are set, about 10 minutes. Cool briefly on the sheets for 3 minutes, then transfer to wire cake racks to cool completely. (The cookies can be prepared up to 1 week ahead, stored in an airtight container at room temperature.)

 Pine Nut Amaretti

Makes about 2 dozen cookies

Make Ahead: The cookies must stand at room temperature for 4 hours before baking. The cookies can be prepared up to 3 weeks ahead, stored in an airtight container at room temperature.

Amaretti are crisp Italian almond macaroons that can be bought at many specialty food shops. In this home-made version from Vicki Caparulo, the lily has been gilded by pressing pine nuts into cookies before baking. These cookies are almost ridiculously easy to make, and they are different from the others in this chapter. First, they are slowly baked in a low oven to create their special texture. Also, note that the cookies must dry at room temperature on their baking sheet for at least 4 hours before baking. If you do not have an extra cookie sheet handy, let them stand on a sheet of aluminum foil and slip the foil onto the sheet when ready to bake.

One 7-ounce tube almond paste (see Note)

2 large egg whites

½ cup sugar

½ cup pine nuts (2 ounces)

1. Using your fingertips, crumble the almond paste into a medium bowl until it is as fine as you can get it (within reason). Add the egg whites. Using a hand-held electric mixer at low speed, beat until the mixture is well combined. Add the sugar, increase the speed to medium-high, and beat until smooth.

2. Using a rounded teaspoon for each, roll the dough into ¾-inch balls. Place the balls about 1 inch apart on a large nonstick cookie sheet (or line a regular cookie sheet with parchment paper). Press the pine nuts into each cookie to cover. Set aside, uncovered, at room temperature for 4 hours.

3. Position a rack in the center of the oven and preheat to 300°F. Bake until the cookies are deep golden brown and the pine nuts are lightly toasted, about 40 minutes. Cool on the cookie sheet for 2 minutes, then transfer to wire cooling racks to cool completely. (The cookies can be prepared up to 3 weeks ahead, stored in an airtight container at room temperature.)

Note: Almond paste, made from ground almonds and sugar, is available at specialty food shops and many supermarkets. Do not confuse it with marzipan, which is prepared with ground almonds and syrup, and has a softer consistency and sweeter flavor.

🎄 Auntie Gisela's Cookies 🎄

The culinary highlight of the Christmas season in my family was Auntie Gisela's enormous cookie platter, wrapped in colored cellophane and delivered to my grandmother's house. Auntie Gisela had brought many of the recipes over with her from Liechtenstein in the early 1920s. Some of the cookies were Old World favorites. Spicy lebkuchen were cut into shapes, then topped with icing and stuck with paper stamps of Saint Nicholas. Crisp cinnamon stars were shiny with meringue glaze. Linz sandwich cookies had glistening raspberry preserves peeking through a small hole in the center of the top cookie. As an added attraction, she tucked in slices of her deluxe fruitcake and yeasty gügelhopf coffee cake.

It was food like this that got me interested in becoming a food professional. When I asked Mom how Auntie Gisela made these wonderful desserts, she said, "Ask her. She'd love to show you." And she did. After I moved to New York, Auntie Gisela would occasionally send me a recipe or two in her Christmas card, hinting that one of these days I'd get the entire collection of her cookbooks and notebooks. And after she passed away a few years ago, my cousin Suzie presented me with this treasure.

One day I found an example of why Auntie Gisela was such a wonderful baker: She was always trying to improve her skills. On a page of her stationery with the heading "Christmas 1975," she meticulously listed the cookies she baked, the yield of the recipe, how to improve them the next time (use different cutters and frostings), and what cookies to bake *next* year so as not to serve too many of the same kinds two years in a row! And people ask me where I get my sense of organization . . .

 Nutty Angel Fingers

Makes about 3 dozen

Make Ahead: The cookies can be prepared up to 1 week ahead, stored in an airtight container at room temperature.

My family calls these "angel fingers," although I've seen similar recipes called "Mexican wedding cakes" and "Russian tea cakes." The latter calls for the dough to be rolled into balls, but the Rodgerses have always rolled it into finger-shaped logs. Kids love to make these—they couldn't be easier and everyone loves them. My brother Doug, who isn't much of a baker at other times of the year, bakes these by the bushel every Christmas, to an appreciative audience of co-workers and family members.

1 cup (2 sticks) unsalted butter, at room
    temperature
6 tablespoons (⅓ cup plus 1 tablespoon)
    confectioners' sugar plus about 1 cup for
    coating the cookies
2 teaspoons vanilla extract
2 cups all-purpose flour
2 cups (8 ounces) finely chopped pecans
    or walnuts

1. Position the racks in the top and bottom thirds of the oven and preheat to 350°F.

2. In a large bowl, using a hand-held electric mixer on medium-high speed, beat the butter and 6 tablespoons confectioners' sugar until light in texture and color, about 2 minutes. Mix in the vanilla. Using a wooden spoon, work in the flour, then the chopped nuts, to make a crumbly dough. Gather up the dough and press it together.

3. Using 1 tablespoon of dough for each cookie,

squeeze the dough in your fist to make a rough 2½-inch log. Roll the log between your palms to smooth it. Place the logs 1 inch apart on nonstick cookie sheets. (These cookies don't spread during baking, but don't put them too close together or they won't brown as nicely.)

4. Bake, switching the positions of the cookies from top to bottom and back to front halfway through baking, until lightly browned, about 20 minutes. Don't underbake the cookies, or they will crumble. Place ½ cup confectioners' sugar in a small bowl. Let the cookies stand on the baking sheet for 5 minutes. Roll the warm cookies in the sugar, then transfer to wire cake racks to cool completely. Before serving, roll the cookies again in more confectioners' sugar to freshen their coating. (The cookies will keep, stored in an airtight container, for up to 1 week.)

 Diane's Ultimate Thumbprints

Makes about 5 dozen cookies

Make Ahead: The cookies can be prepared up to 1 week ahead, stored in an airtight container at room temperature.

Every holiday season Diane Kniss and I make mountains of these delectable walnut-coated cookies filled with glistening preserves. They are related to thumbprint cookies, but they are smaller and more delicate. Diane's original recipe card calls them "Sonja Henies," after the famous and elegant ice-skating star of the thirties and forties. Alas, Sonja's name doesn't mean much today, so we tried calling these "Kristi Yamaguchis" for a while, but it didn't have the right ring. The first time you make them, you may think they are somewhat time-consuming, but I've included some tips to help you along. And when you taste them, you won't mind the extra effort.

1 cup (2 sticks) unsalted butter, at room temperature

$1/2$ cup packed light or dark brown sugar

2 large eggs, separated

$1/2$ teaspoon vanilla extract

2 cups all-purpose flour

$1^1/2$ cups (6 ounces) walnuts

$1/4$ cup granulated sugar

Pinch of salt

$2/3$ cup fruit preserves, such as raspberry or apricot (see Note)

1. Position the racks in the top and bottom thirds of the oven and preheat to 350°F.

2. In a large bowl, using a hand-held electric mixer on medium-high speed, beat the butter until creamy, about 1 minute. Add the brown sugar and beat until light in color and texture, about 2 minutes. Beat in the egg yolks, then the vanilla. Using a wooden spoon, gradually mix in the flour to make a soft dough. Using a scant tablespoon for each, roll the dough into 1-inch balls. Place the balls on a baking sheet and let stand in a cool place (near an open window in cold weather or in the refrigerator) until slightly chilled and firmed, about 10 minutes. (Don't skip this step—the dough must be slightly chilled to make the holes in the dough that hold the preserve filling.)

3. In a food processor, pulse the walnuts and the granulated sugar until the walnuts are finely chopped. Set aside.

4. In a small bowl, beat the egg whites with the pinch of salt until foamy. Pour about one-third of the chopped walnut mixture into a shallow bowl. Dip each ball of dough in the egg whites, roll in the walnut

mixture to coat, and place 1 inch apart on nonstick cookie sheets. Holding a ball of dough on the sheet with one hand, use the tip of your little finger of the other hand to press a $1/4$-inch wide hole into the center, about $1/4$ inch deep. (If you have long fingernails, use the inverted tip of a $1/4$-inch wide wooden spoon handle or a dowel.) If the ball cracks, just press the crack together to smooth. Repeat with the other balls of dough, gradually adding more of the walnut mixture to the shallow bowl as needed. (It is important to use the walnut mixture in batches, as it will collect moisture from the egg whites, and if used all at once, it will get so wet it won't adhere properly. You will probably have leftover chopped walnuts, but that's better than running out of them.)

5. Bake until the cookies feel set but not completely baked, about 10 minutes. Meanwhile, place the preserves in a small, self-sealing plastic bag and squeeze the preserves into one corner of the bag. Using scissors, snip off the corner of the bag to make an opening about $1/4$ inch wide. When the cookies are set, remove them from the oven. Use the bag to pipe the preserves into the hole in each cookie. Return the cookies to the oven, switching the positions of the cookies from top to bottom and from front to back. Bake until the cookies are lightly browned, 5 to 8 more minutes. Cool on the baking sheets for 2 minutes. Transfer to wire cooling racks to cool completely. (The cookies can be prepared up to 1 week ahead, stored in an airtight container at room temperature.)

Note: Be sure to use preserves for the filling; jellies and jams are too thin and will melt into the cookies. If your preserves are especially chunky, chop up the fruit pieces in a bowl with a knife before using to avoid clogging the hole in the bag as you fill the cookies.

Spritz Butter Cookies

Makes about 5 dozen cookies

Make Ahead: The cookies can be baked up to 1 week ahead, stored in an airtight container at room temperature.

In the introduction to this chapter, I said that I didn't want to do any cookies that called for special equipment. These beautiful and buttery shaped cookies are the exception. Because you get a variety of shapes for your money, and the press can be used throughout the year to decorate appetizers and make shapes out of softened butter, I consider a cookie press a good investment and not an esoteric piece of kitchen equipment. Cookie presses are available at kitchenware shops, or by mail order (see page 163 for mail-order sources). To decorate these cookies, use high-quality dried or candied fruit.

1 cup (2 sticks) unsalted butter, at room
   temperature
³⁄₄ cup sugar
1 large egg
1 teaspoon vanilla extract
¹⁄₂ teaspoon almond extract (optional)
2 cups all-purpose flour
¹⁄₂ teaspoon baking powder
¹⁄₄ teaspoon salt
About 60 pieces of candied cherry halves or
   glacéed apricots, cut into ¹⁄₂-inch cubes,
   for decoration

1. Position the racks in the center and top third of the oven and preheat to 400°F.
2. In a large bowl, using a hand-held electric mixer at high speed, beat the butter and sugar until light in color and texture, about 2 minutes. Beat in the egg and vanilla, and almond extract, if using. Using a wooden spoon, add the flour, baking powder, and salt and mix to make a soft dough.

3. In batches, transfer the dough to the cookie press and fit with the desired plate. Holding the press about ¹⁄₂ inch above a nonstick baking sheet, press out cookies, placing them about 1 inch apart. Place a cherry half in the center of each cookie.

4. Bake, switching the positions of the cookie sheets from top to bottom and front to back halfway through baking, until the edges of the cookies are lightly browned, 8 to 10 minutes. Transfer to wire cake racks to cool completely. (The cookies can be baked up to 1 week ahead, stored in an airtight container at room temperature.)

The Best Chocolate-Pecan Brownies

Makes 24 brownies

Make Ahead: The brownies can be prepared up to 5 days ahead, wrapped individually in plastic wrap and stored at room temperature.

Brownies are just as appropriate for a Fourth of July celebration as a Christmas cookie platter. Yet I always find reasons to include them in the annual holiday selection. Everyone loves them, they are a great "bang for your buck" cookie (you get a lot of them with little work), and they are easy to send as gifts. Most important, this recipe is absolutely the best. Two kinds of chocolate give it a complex flavor (but still one that kids won't turn their noses up at), and the light corn syrup ensures that they will come out moist and chewy. (Be sure not to overbake them.)

1 cup (2 sticks) unsalted butter, cut into pieces

6 ounces bittersweet chocolate, finely chopped

4 ounces unsweetened chocolate, finely chopped

4 large eggs, at room temperature

2 cups packed light brown sugar

¼ cup light corn syrup

2 teaspoons vanilla extract

2½ cups all-purpose flour

½ teaspoon baking soda

½ teaspoon salt

2 cups (8 ounces) coarsely chopped pecans

1. Position a rack in the center of the oven and preheat to 350°F. Fold a 20-inch long piece of aluminum foil lengthwise to fit the bottom of a 13 × 9-inch baking pan, letting the ends of the foil hang over the sides as handles. Lightly butter the foil and sides of the pan, dust with flour, and tap out the excess.

2. In a large saucepan, melt the butter over medium heat. Remove the pan from the heat and add the bittersweet and unsweetened chocolates. Let stand until the chocolates soften, about 3 minutes. Whisk until smooth. Whisk in the brown sugar. One at a time, whisk in the eggs, then the corn syrup and vanilla.

3. In a small bowl, combine the flour, baking soda and salt, and sift the dry ingredients over the chocolate mixture. Using a rubber spatula, fold together until combined. The batter will be thick. Stir in the pecans.

4. Spread evenly into the prepared baking pan. Bake until a toothpick inserted in the center comes out with a moist crumb, 35 to 40 minutes. Do not overbake. Cool completely in the pan on a wire cake rack.

5. Run a knife around the inside edges of the pan to release the brownies from the sides. Lift up on the handles to remove the brownies. Cut into bars. (The brownies can be prepared up to 5 days ahead, wrapped individually in plastic wrap, stored at room temperature.)

Gingered Shortbread

Makes 12 large cookies

Make Ahead: The cookies can be prepared up to 5 days ahead, stored in an airtight container at room temperature.

Shortbread is the ultimate sugar cookie, crisp yet tender, and bursting with buttery flavor. It's a good cookie to make when the cookie monster in you growls but you don't have any eggs in the house. Gluten-free rice flour (cornstarch can be substituted) is used with regular flour to give it a delicate crumb.

- *The shortbread's ancestor is the bannock, a round oatmeal cake that symbolized the sun and was a part of pagan Yule celebrations. While some bakers roll and cut out shortbread dough into shapes, I prefer to mark the round of dough into the traditional "petticoat tail" wedges with the tines of a fork. If you make these around New Year's, and you are superstitious, you should know that it is considered unlucky to cut shortbread with a knife—you just break it along the perforations.*

1 cup (2 sticks) unsalted butter, at room temperature

½ cup sugar

1⅔ cups all-purpose flour

⅓ cup white rice flour (available at natural food stores and many supermarkets) or cornstarch

1 teaspoon ground ginger

½ cup (about 2 ounces) finely chopped crystallized ginger

1. Position a rack in the center of the oven and preheat to 350°F. Lightly butter a 9½-inch springform pan.

2. In a medium bowl, using a hand-held electric mixer at high speed, beat the butter until creamy, about 1 minute. Add the sugar and beat until the mixture is light in color and texture, about 2 minutes. Using a wooden spoon, stir in the flour, rice flour, and ground ginger to make a soft dough. Stir in the crystallized ginger. Press the dough evenly into the prepared pan. Using the tines of a fork, press around the perimeter of the dough. Prick the dough, reaching down to the bottom of the pan, into 12 wedges.

3. Bake until lightly browned, about 30 minutes. Cool completely in the pan. Remove the sides of the pan. Cut or break the shortbread into wedges, following the perforations in the dough. (The shortbread can be prepared up to 5 days ahead, stored in an airtight container at room temperature.)

Cranberry Oat Bars

Makes 16 bars

Make Ahead: The bars will keep up to 5 days, individually wrapped in plastic wrap and stored at room temperature.

Sturdy, hearty, and fruit-filled, these bars are great for mailing. I cut them into fairly large bars that are good for a lunchbox or an afternoon pick-me-up, but they can be cut into daintier pieces for a Christmas cookie platter. The foil lining allows you to lift out the baked cookie in one big piece before cutting it into bars.

Cranberry Filling

2 cups fresh or frozen cranberries
³/₄ cup granulated sugar
Grated zest of 1 orange

1¹/₂ cups all-purpose flour
1¹/₂ cups old-fashioned oatmeal

1 cup packed light brown sugar
1 teaspoon baking powder
¹/₂ teaspoon salt
12 tablespoons (1¹/₂ sticks) unsalted butter, cut into small cubes

1. Position a rack in the center of the oven and preheat to 350°F. Lightly butter an 8-inch square baking pan. Line the pan with a double thickness of aluminum foil so that the foil extends beyond the two opposite ends of the pan. Fold the overhang down to form handles. Lightly butter the foil.

2. To make the filling, bring the cranberries, sugar, and orange zest to a boil in a medium saucepan, stirring to dissolve the sugar. Reduce the heat to medium and cook, stirring often, until thick and reduced to 1 cup, about 5 minutes. Transfer to a bowl and cool completely.

3. In a medium bowl, mix the flour, oatmeal, brown sugar, baking powder, and salt. Add the butter. Using your fingertips, work the butter into the flour mixture until well combined and crumbly. Press half of the mixture firmly and evenly into the bottom of the prepared pan, and spread with the cranberry filling. Sprinkle the remaining mixture over the filling, and gently press into an even layer.

4. Bake until the top is evenly browned, about 40 minutes. Cool completely on a wire cake rack.

5. Run a knife around the inside edges of the pan to release the bars from the sides. Lift up on the foil handles to remove the bars from the pan. Using a large, sharp knife, cut into 16 bars. (The bars will keep up to 5 days, individually wrapped in plastic wrap and stored at room temperature.)

Brandied Fruitcake Drops

Makes 3 dozen

Make Ahead: The cookies can be baked up to 1 week ahead, stored in an airtight container at room temperature.

These moist and chewy cookies have been gobbled by many an unsuspecting professed fruitcake hater.

**8 tablespoons (1 stick) unsalted butter,
  at room temperature**
1 cup packed light brown sugar
1 large egg
$\frac{1}{2}$ cup buttermilk
$\frac{1}{4}$ cup brandy or bourbon
1 teaspoon vanilla extract
2 cups all-purpose flour
$\frac{1}{2}$ teaspoon baking soda
$\frac{1}{4}$ teaspoon salt
**1 cup chopped candied fruit for fruitcakes
  (a combination of candied orange and lemon
  peels, candied cherries, pineapple, and citron)
  or any dried or candied fruit you prefer**
$\frac{3}{4}$ cup coarsely chopped walnuts

36 walnut halves, for decoration

1. Position the racks in the center and top third of the oven and preheat to 350°F.
2. In a medium bowl, using a hand-held electric mixer at high speed, beat the butter and brown sugar until light in color, about 2 minutes. Beat in the egg. Add the buttermilk, brandy, and vanilla, and beat until the mixture is fluffy, about 1 minute. Using a wooden spoon, add the flour, baking soda, and salt, and mix to make a soft dough. Stir in the chopped candied fruit and walnuts.

3. Using about 1 tablespoon for each cookie, drop the mixture about 1 inch apart onto nonstick baking sheets. Press a walnut half into the center of each cookie. Bake, switching the positions of the cookie sheets from top to bottom and front to back halfway through baking time, until the edges of the cookies are lightly browned, about 20 minutes. Transfer the cookies to a wire cake rack and cool completely. (The cookies can be baked up to 1 week ahead, stored in an airtight container at room temperature.)

Decorating Icing

Makes about $\frac{3}{4}$ cup, enough for about 3 dozen cookies

When you want a shiny, slick surface on your cookies that can be sprinkled with colored sugar or other goodies, make this easy icing. For a thicker, opaque surface, use the minimum amount of milk. For a thinner, translucent look, use a bit more milk to make a thinner icing. The amount of milk needed to reach your desired thickness will vary, depending on the humidity.

2 cups confectioners' sugar
3 to 4 tablespoons milk, as needed
Food coloring, as needed (optional)

Sift the confectioners' sugar through a wire sieve into a medium bowl. Using a rubber spatula, blend enough milk into the sugar to reach the desired consistency. If desired, divide the icing into individual bowls or paper cups and tint with food coloring. When not using, to prevent a crust from forming, cover each bowl tightly with plastic wrap or press a moist paper towel directly on the icing surface.

Royal Icing

Makes about 2 cups, enough for about 4 dozen cookies, depending on size

Make Ahead: The icing can be prepared up to 2 days ahead, stored in an airtight container with a moist paper towel pressed directly on the icing surface, and refrigerated.

This icing hardens into shiny white lines, and is used for piping decorations on gingerbread people or other cookies. Traditional royal icing uses raw egg whites, but I prefer dried egg-white powder, available at most supermarkets, to avoid any concern about uncooked egg whites.

- *When using a pastry bag, practice your decorating skills before you ice the cookies. Just do a few trial runs to get the feel of the icing and the bag, piping the icing onto aluminum foil or wax paper. If you work quickly, you can use a metal spatula to scrape the test icing back into the batch.*

- *Dried egg-white powder is also available by mail order from The Baker's Catalogue, 1-800-827-6836. Meringue powder, which is dehydrated egg whites with sugar already added, also makes excellent royal icing; just follow the directions on the package. However, the plain unsweetened dried egg whites are more versatile, as they can be used in savory dishes, too. Meringue powder is available from Adventures in Cooking (1-800-305-1114) and The Baker's Catalogue.*

1 pound (4½ cups) confectioners' sugar
2 tablespoons dried egg-white powder
6 tablespoons water

1. In a medium bowl, using a hand-held electric mixer at low speed, beat the confectioners' sugar, egg-white powder, and water until combined. Increase the speed to high and beat, scraping down the sides of the bowl often, until very stiff, shiny, and thick enough to pipe; 3 to 5 minutes. (The icing can be prepared up to 2 days ahead, stored in an airtight container with a moist paper towel pressed directly on the icing surface, and refrigerated.)

2. To pipe line decorations, use a pastry bag fitted with a tube with a small writing tip about ⅛ inch wide, such as Ateco No. 7; it may be too difficult to squeeze the icing out of smaller tips. If necessary, thin the icing with a little warm water. To fill the pastry bag, fit it with the tube. Fold the top of the bag back to form a cuff, and hold it in one hand. (Or, place the bag in a tall glass, and fold the top back to form a cuff.) Using a rubber spatula, scoop the icing into the bag. Unfold the cuff and twist the top of the bag closed. Squeeze the icing down to fill the tube. Always practice first on a sheet of wax paper or aluminum foil to check the flow and consistency of the icing.

Traditional Royal Icing: Substitute 3 large egg whites for the powder and water.

Desserts

Oh, Bring Me a Figgy Pudding . . .

So many Christmas desserts have entered the collective consciousness, it's not an easy task to choose which ones to make. Fruitcake, mincemeat pie, gingerbread, plum pudding . . . each has its place of honor in the holiday dessert hall of fame. Every country with a substantial Christian population has its own special sweets, so the list is almost endless.

Yet there are common themes that run from dessert to dessert, and country to country. Many desserts, like plum pudding and fruitcake, are doused with liquor and made well ahead of serving to age and mellow. Aromatic spices such as ginger, cinnamon, cloves, nutmeg, and allspice are used.

Many Christmas desserts feature *candied fruits.* Supermarket candied fruits are not very good, since most of their natural flavor and color has been removed and artificially replaced. Specialty food stores and some candy stores carry high-quality candied fruits (although I still haven't met a candied cherry that I like). Instead of using candied orange peels, I often chop up glacéed orange slices.

Dried fruits also play a big role in many of these desserts. Sulfur dioxide, an ingredient that some people choose to avoid, is often used to process the fruits. Sulfured dried fruits do have a brighter color, but that isn't always necessary. Unsulfured fruits can be found at natural food stores. I prefer large, plump *Thompson raisins* for holiday baking, but regular raisins will do. *Golden raisins* add color variety, but you can always use more dark raisins. *Currants* aren't the summer berry at all, but small raisins. *Dried apricots and pineapple* are common, but use apricots that aren't too sour and pineapple that isn't too sweet. (Glacéed apricots are a great alternative to dried apricots.) When I see a recipe with candied cherries, I substitute tasty *dried cherries*. And *dried cranberries* are a delicious addition to holiday baked goods.

Excellent candied citrus peels and fruits are available from Economy Candy (1-800-352-4544), Adventures in Cooking (1-973-305-1114), and The Baker's Catalogue (1-800-827-6836).

Chocolate Bûche de Noël

Makes 8 to 12 servings

Make Ahead: The bûche de Noël can be prepared up to 1 day ahead. The chocolate leaves can be prepared up to 3 days ahead.

A spectacular finale to a Christmas meal, the French bûche de Noël is a dessert replica of the Yule log. (The Yule log was originally a Viking tradition, burned to scare off Jack Frost.) The log should be decorated to evoke its woodland origins, nestled on evergreen sprigs (use only nontoxic varieties like pine and juniper, and avoid holly) and garnished with chocolate truffles and leaves. If you can find them at a candy shop or specialty food store, meringue mushrooms are a nice touch. A dusting of cocoa will give the log a rustic look.

Chocolate Roll

6 large eggs, separated, at room temperature
¼ teaspoon cream of tartar
¾ cup granulated sugar
⅓ cup Dutch-process cocoa powder, such as Droste, sifted
2 tablespoons Dutch-process cocoa powder, such as Droste, for finishing cake

Filling

1 teaspoon unflavored gelatin
2 tablespoons boiling water
1½ cups heavy cream
2 tablespoons confectioners' sugar
Grated zest of ½ orange
½ teaspoon vanilla extract

Ganache

½ cup heavy cream
6 ounces bittersweet chocolate, finely chopped
2 tablespoons light corn syrup
1 tablespoon Grand Marnier or other orange-flavored liqueur, or frozen orange juice concentrate, thawed
Sprigs of fresh juniper or pine, for garnish

Chocolate Leaves (recipe follows), optional
10 to 12 Chocolate-Orange Truffles (page 98) or store-bought truffles
2 tablespoons Dutch-process cocoa powder, such as Droste, for garnish

1. To make the chocolate roll, position a rack in the center of the oven and preheat to 350°F. Lightly butter a 15½ × 10½ × 1-inch jelly-roll pan and line with wax paper.

2. In a grease-free, large bowl, using a hand-held mixer at low speed, beat the egg whites until foamy. Add the cream of tartar and increase the speed to high. Beat until soft peaks form. Gradually beat in $1/4$ cup of the sugar and beat until stiff peaks form. Set aside.

3. In another large bowl, beat the egg yolks with $1/3$ cup cocoa and the remaining $1/2$ cup sugar on high speed until the mixture forms a thick ribbon, about 2 minutes. Stir about one-fourth of the whites into the yolk mixture, then fold in the remaining whites. Scrape into the prepared pan and spread evenly.

4. Bake until the cake springs back when pressed in the center, 12 to 15 minutes. Cool completely in the pan on a wire cake rack. Sift 2 tablespoons cocoa over the top of the roll. Place a large sheet of aluminum foil over the cake. Place a baking sheet over the pan. Invert the cake onto the foil. Carefully peel off the wax paper. Cool completely.

5. To make the filling, in a small bowl, sprinkle the gelatin over the boiling water. Let stand for 10 minutes to soften the gelatin. In a small saucepan over medium-low heat, heat $1/4$ cup of the cream just until warm. Add to the gelatin mixture, stir dissolve the gelatin, and cool 10 minutes. In a chilled medium bowl, beat the remaining $11/4$ cups cream, confect-ioners' sugar, zest, and vanilla just until stiff. Beat in the gelatin mixture.

6. Spread the cake with the filling, leaving a 1-inch border. Using the foil as an aide, roll up the cake from a long end into a tight cylinder. Transfer the roll to a long platter, seam side down. Cover tightly and refrigerate until filling sets, about 1 hour or overnight.

7. To make the ganache, in a medium saucepan, bring the heavy cream to a simmer over medium-high heat. Remove from the heat and add the chocolate, corn syrup, and Grand Marnier. Let stand until the chocolate melts, about 5 minutes. Whisk until smooth and transfer to a medium bowl placed in a larger bowl of iced water. Let stand, stirring often, until chilled and thickened, about 5 minutes. Whisk just until soft peaks form. Do not overwhisk, or it will be grainy. (If this happens, melt the ganache over simmering water,

cool, and whisk again.) Immediately spread the ganache over the roll. Using the tines of a fork, make wavy lines in the ganache to simulate bark. (The roll can be prepared up to 1 day ahead, tented with aluminum foil, and refrigerated.)

8. To serve, tuck the evergreens under the roll, decorate the cake with the chocolate leaves and truffles. Sift the cocoa over all. Serve chilled or at cool room temperature.

Chocolate Leaves: Line a baking sheet with wax paper. Place 4 ounces finely chopped bittersweet chocolate in the top part of a double boiler over hot, not simmering, water. Stirring occasionally, heat the chocolate until almost completely melted, but not quite. Remove from the heat and let stand, stirring occasionally, until completely melted and tepid, about 10 minutes. Holding a gaalax (a wide shiny leaf available at florist shops) or lemon leaf in the palm of your hand and, using the back of a teaspoon, coat the underside of the leaf evenly with the melted chocolate. Avoid getting the chocolate on the top of the leaf. Place the coated leaves on the prepared baking sheet. Refrigerate until the chocolate is firm, at least 30 minutes. (The chocolate leaves can be prepared up to 3 days ahead and refrigerated.) Carefully pull the leaves away from the chocolate. Store the chocolate leaves in the refrigerator until ready to serve. Makes about 12.

Gisela's Deluxe Fruitcake

Makes 5 fruitcakes

Make Ahead: The fruitcakes must be made at least 1 day before serving. They can be stored, well wrapped in plastic wrap and aluminum foil, and brushed occasionally with liquor, for up to 2 months.

Don't tell me that you don't like fruitcake until you've tried my Auntie Gisela's recipe. I never could understand all of the jokes about fruitcake, because when I was growing up, I only ate Gisela's deluxe version, which wasn't made with the weird colored cherries and artificial booze flavor of commercial brands. The dried cranberries are my addition—Gisela stopped baking before the advent of dried cherries and cranberries; she used extra raisins. But, knowing her, she would have used the new dried fruits.

- *The fruitcake must age at least 24 hours before slicing. This allows the flavors to mellow and the fruit and applesauce to give off some moisture into the cake.*
- *Some people like well-aged fruitcakes. I age mine for only a few days, in the refrigerator. If you like a cake with a spirited brandy-and-rum kick, unwrap the cakes about once a week and brush them with a combination of brandy and rum, allowing about 2 tablespoons per cake. Rewrap the cakes and continue aging for up to 2 months.*
- *This recipe makes 5 loaves. It's a waste of time, money, and effort to make fewer. Because these cakes are so delicious, you can gladly give them as gifts. I assume that most people don't have five heavyweight loaf pans, so I give baking instructions for the typical 8½ × 3¾ × 2½-inch disposable foil pans. Sur La Table (1-800-243-0852) carries heavyweight paper baking pans that are especially suitable for gift giving.*
- *You will need a very large bowl (8 to 10 quarts) to mix the batter. If you don't have one this size, make the cake batter in the largest bowl you have, up to the point where the fruits and nuts are added. Scrape the batter into the largest kettle you own, and then stir in the nuts and fruits.*
- *If you wish, substitute apple juice for the cognac and dark rum. You can add ½ teaspoon each brandy or rum extract, or leave them out.*
- *Fruitcake bakes at a low temperature so that the fruit on the outside of the cake doesn't scorch. Bake only until a wooden skewer inserted in the center comes out clean, about 1¼ hours, or the cake will be dry.*

6 cups all-purpose flour

1½ teaspoons ground cinnamon

1½ teaspoons baking soda

1½ teaspoons baking powder

1½ teaspoons salt

¾ teaspoon ground cloves

¾ teaspoon freshly grated nutmeg

1½ cups (3 sticks) unsalted butter, at room temperature

2 cups packed light brown sugar

3 large eggs, at room temperature

1 cup store-bought applesauce

¼ cup Cognac or brandy

¼ cup dark rum

3 cups coarsely chopped pecans or walnuts

1½ cups (12 ounces) coarsely chopped glacéed oranges

2 cups (10 ounces) dark raisins

2 cups (10 ounces) golden raisins

1 cup (8 ounces) coarsely chopped pitted prunes

1 cup (6 ounces) coarsely chopped candied pineapple

1 cup (14 ounces) dried cranberries

¼ cup Cognac or brandy, for brushing

¼ cup dark rum, for brushing

It Wouldn't Be the Holidays Without . . . Fruitcake

It's ba-a-a-a-ck! Revered and reviled, resurrected and rejected, fruitcake remains a holiday icon. Its detractors may throw brickbats, but they bounce off fruitcake as if it was made of Teflon. And don't say that the last one you had tasted like it was!

Every European country has a version of fruitcake, but British colonists brought theirs to America. In Britain, Christmas fruitcake resembles ours, although American cooks often use bourbon in addition to or instead of rum or brandy. However, the British fruitcake is usually decorated with a sheet of marzipan, then frosted with a hard white icing. Ours remains unadorned. Scottish cooks create an especially rich, pastry-wrapped fruitcake, so dark with fruit and treacle (a kind of molasses) that it is called "black bun." On the other hand, the Irish bake a delicate, alcohol-free "white" fruitcake that has a light-colored batter.

Most American fruitcakes are dark and call for aging the cakes after baking. The "make-ahead" aspect made fruitcake especially attractive to cooks wanting to get some holiday chores out of the way before the hustle and bustle of the season set in. Alcohol plays a big part in these recipes, as it helps preserve the cakes.

If you have any lingering doubts about fruitcake, read "A Christmas Memory" by Truman Capote, with a fruitcake-baking scene that will send you straight into the kitchen to whip up a batch.

1. Position the racks in the center and bottom third of the oven and preheat to 300°F. Lightly butter and flour five $8^{1}/_{2} \times 3^{3}/_{4} \times 2^{1}/_{2}$-inch disposable aluminum-foil loaf pans. Line the bottom of the pans with wax paper.

2. Sift the flour, cinnamon, baking soda, baking powder, salt, cloves, and nutmeg through a wire strainer into a medium bowl. Set aside.

3. In a very large bowl, using a hand-held electric mixer at high speed, beat the butter until creamy, about 1 minute. Add the brown sugar and beat until light in texture and color, about 2 minutes. One at a time, beat in the eggs. Beat in the applesauce, Cognac, and rum. Using a wooden spoon, gradually stir in the flour mixture to make a stiff batter.

4. In a medium bowl, mix the pecans, glacéed oranges, raisins, golden raisins, prunes, pineapple, and dried cranberries. (Mixing the fruits first distributes them more evenly throughout the batter.) Stir the fruits into the batter until well distributed. Spread the batter evenly into the prepared pans, smoothing the tops. Place the pans on baking sheets (this makes it easier to get them in and out of the oven).

5. Bake for 45 minutes. Switch the baking sheets from top to bottom and front to back. Bake just until a wooden skewer inserted in the center of the cakes comes out clean, 30 to 40 minutes. Let cool in the pans on wire racks for 10 minutes.

6. Invert the cakes onto the racks and peel off the wax paper. In a small bowl, combine $1/_4$ cup each brandy and rum. Brush the mixture all over the cakes. Set the cakes right side up and cool completely.

7. Wrap each cake in plastic wrap, and then aluminum foil. Let stand at room temperature for 24 hours before slicing.

Deep Dark Stout Gingerbread

Makes 12 servings

Make Ahead: The gingerbread can be prepared up to 2 days ahead, covered tightly with plastic wrap and stored at room temperature.

A holiday season never goes by that I don't make this gingerbread at least once. The deep caramel notes of the stout complement the spices beautifully. The gingerbread is a regular on my buffet tables, because its tight crumb makes it easy for guests to eat it out of hand. Also, because it is firm and easy to transport, it is great to give as a present. Serve it warm from the oven for a real treat.

- *Open the stout and pour into a measuring cup about 1 hour before making the cake so the stout can go flat. Stir it occasionally to help expel the carbonation. Stout often comes in large bottles. If you have any left over, cover the spout tightly with plastic wrap and refrigerate for up to 1 week. You can use the flat stout in beef stew and, of course, plum pudding (page 144).*

2½ cups all-purpose flour

2 teaspoons ground ginger

2 teaspoons ground cinnamon

1½ teaspoons baking powder

½ teaspoon baking soda

½ teaspoon salt

1 cup (2 sticks) unsalted butter, at
  room temperature

1¼ cups packed light brown sugar

2 large eggs plus 1 large egg yolk

1 cup unsulfured molasses

¾ cup flat stout, at room temperature

Confectioners' sugar, for garnish

1. Position a rack in the center of the oven and preheat to 350°F. Lightly butter and flour the inside of a 12-cup fluted tube pan, tapping out the excess flour.

2. Sift the flour, ginger, cinnamon, baking powder, baking soda, and salt onto a piece of wax paper. Set aside.

3. In a large bowl, using a hand-held electric mixer at high speed, beat the butter until creamy, about 1 minute. Add the brown sugar and beat until the mixture is light in texture and color, about 2 minutes. One at a time, beat in the eggs, then the yolk. Beat in the molasses.

4. Reduce the mixer speed to low. In three additions, beat in the flour mixture, alternating with the stout, scraping down the sides of the bowl as needed, until the batter is smooth. Scrape into the prepared pan and smooth the top.

5. Bake until a toothpick inserted in the center of the cake comes out clean, 50 to 60 minutes. Cool on a wire cake rack for 10 minutes. Invert the cake onto the cake rack. Transfer to a serving platter, sift confectioners' sugar over the top, and serve warm. Or cool completely and serve at room temperature. (The gingerbread can be prepared up to 2 days ahead, covered tightly with plastic wrap and stored at room temperature.)

 ## Marie's Orange-Walnut Cake

Makes 12 servings

Make Ahead: The cake can be prepared up to 1 week ahead, wrapped tightly in plastic wrap and stored at room temperature.

Marie Instaschi has been baking this cake as a Christmas gift for friends for years. At first, I was just a lucky recipient, but as soon as I got her recipe, it became one of my holiday baking regulars, too. (In fact, I am copying this recipe from a page in my recipe book that is splattered with almost two decades' worth of batter.) Like Deep Dark Stout Gingerbread (page 136), it transports well (Marie's crosses the country to get to me, and it arrives in perfect condition). It also ages well—Marie always ages her cakes for a few days before giving them out, but I can never wait that long. Use Grand Marnier to make the cake—in my opinion, no other orange liqueur has the same flavor.

2 cups all-purpose flour
1 teaspoon baking powder
1 teaspoon baking soda
$^1/_2$ teaspoon salt
1 cup (2 sticks) unsalted butter,
  at room temperature
1 cup granulated sugar
3 large eggs, separated, at room temperature
Grated zest of 1 large orange
1 cup sour cream, at room temperature
$^3/_4$ cup (3 ounces) chopped pecans or walnuts

Glaze
$^1/_2$ cup Grand Marnier
$^1/_2$ cup confectioners' sugar
Juice of 1 large orange (about $^1/_4$ cup)

1. Position a rack in the center of the oven and preheat to 350°F. Lightly butter and flour the inside of a 12-cup fluted tube pan, tapping out the excess flour.

2. Sift the flour, baking powder, baking soda, and salt onto a piece of wax paper. Set aside.

3. In a large bowl, using a hand-held electric mixer at high speed, beat the butter until creamy, about 1 minute. Add the sugar and beat until light in color and texture, about 2 minutes. One at a time, beat in the egg yolks, then the orange zest.

4. Reduce the mixer speed to low. In three additions, beat in the flour mixture, alternating with the sour cream, scraping down the sides of the bowl as needed, until the batter is smooth. Stir in the walnuts.

5. In a grease-free, medium bowl, using the electric mixer with clean beaters, beat the egg whites just until stiff peaks form. Do not overbeat the whites, or they will look lumpy and watery. Using a rubber spatula, stir about one-fourth of the whites into the batter to lighten it. Pour the remaining whites on top, and fold them in until they are incorporated. Scrape the batter into the prepared pan and smooth the top.

6. Bake until a toothpick inserted in the center of the cake comes out clean, 50 to 60 minutes. Cool on a wire cake rack for 10 minutes.

7. To make the glaze, whisk the Grand Marnier, confectioners' sugar, and orange juice to dissolve the sugar. Brush about half of the glaze over the cake, letting it soak in. Invert the cake onto the cake rack, and place the cake rack over a jelly-roll pan. Brush the remaining glaze over the cake. Cool completely. (The cake can be prepared up to 1 week ahead, wrapped tightly in plastic wrap, and stored at room temperature.)

Mincemeat Lattice Tart

Makes 8 servings

Make Ahead: The mincemeat can be prepared up to 1 month ahead, cooled, covered tightly, and refrigerated. Once a week, stir in about ¼ cup combined brandy and dark rum. The tart can be baked up to 1 day ahead, covered with plastic wrap, and refrigerated. Serve warm or at room temperature.

Here's an encore of my favorite mincemeat recipe, originally in Thanksgiving 101. *This time, instead of making a pie, I serve the mincemeat in a sweetened tart crust, covered with a lattice topping. You will have about 3 cups leftover mincemeat. For a quick dessert, warm it over low heat, adding about ⅓ cup apple or orange juice to moisten, and spoon over ice cream.*

New-Fashioned Mincemeat

2 Golden Delicious apples, peeled and grated (use the large holes on a box grater)

One 12-ounce can (1½ cups) frozen apple juice concentrate, thawed

3 ounces (1 packed cup) chopped dried apples

¾ cup (3 ounces) dark raisins

¾ cup (3 ounces) golden raisins

¾ cup (3 ounces) dried currants

¾ cup (3 ounces) dried cranberries

⅔ cup chopped Candied Orange Peel (page 93), or store-bought candied orange peel

½ cup packed dark brown sugar

½ cup dark rum

½ cup Cognac or brandy

⅓ cup chopped Candied Lemon Peel (page 93) or store-bought candied lemon peel

4 tablespoons unsalted butter

½ teaspoon ground cinnamon

½ teaspoon ground allspice

½ teaspoon freshly grated nutmeg

½ teaspoon ground cloves

Sweet Tart Dough

2 cups all-purpose flour

¼ cup granulated sugar

¼ teaspoon salt

9 tablespoons (1 stick plus 1 tablespoon) unsalted butter, chilled, cut into ½-inch pieces

2 large egg yolks

6 tablespoons ice water

3 cups mincemeat

2 tablespoons unsalted butter, cut into pieces

1. To make the mincemeat, in a large Dutch oven, bring the fresh apples, apple juice concentrate, dried apples, raisins, golden raisins, currants, dried cranberries, candied orange peel, brown sugar, dark rum, Cognac, candied lemon peel, butter, cinnamon, allspice, nutmeg, and cloves to a boil over medium heat, stirring often. Reduce the heat to medium-low and cook, stirring often, until the fruits are softened and the liquid almost completely evaporates, about 25 minutes. Transfer to a medium bowl and cool completely. Cover tightly with plastic wrap and refrigerate overnight or up to 1 week. (To store the mincemeat up to 1 month, stir in an additional ¼ cup each dark rum and brandy every week or so.)

2. To make the tart dough, in a medium bowl, mix the flour, sugar, and salt to combine. Using a pastry blender, cut in the butter until the mixture resembles coarse crumbs. In a small bowl, beat the egg yolks with the water. Stirring the dry ingredients with a fork, gradually mix into the flour mixture until completely moistened and clumping together. Gather the dough together. Divide the dough into two disks, one slightly

The mincemeat we serve today is a throwback to the days when meats were preserved for long periods without refrigeration. Tough pieces of meat, offal, and suet were finely minced, and then cooked with sugar and liquor (for preservation) and spices and candied fruits (for flavor). The resulting confection could be topped off with more liquor for longer storage. Butchering usually took place in the winter, so the minced meat would age until the next year.

It can be argued that without meat, you can't call it mincemeat, but modern tastes have lightened the original recipe. Even in England, where holiday mincemeat tarts are piled high in bakery windows throughout the season, you would be hard put to find any with real meat or suet.

---

bigger than the other. Wrap in wax paper and refrigerate until chilled, about 1 hour.

3. Position a rack in the center of the oven, place a baking sheet on the rack, and preheat to 375°F. Lightly butter a 9-inch round tart pan with a removable bottom.

4. On a lightly floured work surface, dust the larger disk of dough with flour, and roll into a ⅛-inch thick circle. Fit into the prepared pan, being sure that the crust fits snugly into the corners. Trim the dough overhang to ½ inch. Fill the tart shell with the mincemeat and dot with the butter.

5. On the floured work surface, dust the smaller disk of dough with flour and roll into a ⅛-inch thick circle. Using a ruler and a pizza wheel (or a sharp knife), cut the dough into ¾-inch strips. Arrange the dough strips on top of the filling in a lattice pattern, trimming the edges of the strips where they touch the bottom crust. Fold over the edges of the bottom crust, and press against the top edge of the pan.

6. Place the tart on the hot baking sheet. Bake until the crust is lightly browned, about 45 minutes. Cool on a wire cake rack for 30 minutes. Serve warm or at room temperature. (The tart can be made up to 1 day ahead, covered with plastic wrap, and refrigerated.)

✦ Peppermint Profiteroles with Chocolate Sauce

Makes 8 servings

Make Ahead: The profiteroles can be prepared up to 1 week ahead, stored in self-sealing plastic bags, and frozen. The ice cream should be prepared at least 4 hours and up to 3 days ahead. The chocolate sauce can be prepared up to 2 days ahead, cooled, covered, and refrigerated.

The cooling flavor of peppermint is so refreshing after a big meal. I am not saying that these ice cream–stuffed cream puffs with a warm chocolate sauce are light—just delicious. This is a restaurant-style dessert that really is easy to duplicate at home. The components can all be made well ahead of time, and put together just before serving. (It does help to have someone help to fill the profiteroles.)

• *The profiteroles are most easily shaped with a pastry bag fitted with a ½-inch wide plain tip. Or drop the dough by teaspoonfuls onto the baking sheet.*

Cream Puffs

³/₄ cup water

6 tablespoons unsalted butter, chilled, cut into
¹/₂-inch pieces

1¹/₂ teaspoons sugar

¹/₈ teaspoon salt

³/₄ cup unbleached flour

4 large eggs, at room temperature

Ice Cream

23 hard red-and-white–striped peppermint
candies, crushed (about ¹/₃ cup)

1¹/₂ pints high-quality vanilla ice cream, slightly
softened

1¹/₂ teaspoons clear peppermint extract

Chocolate Sauce

1 cup heavy cream

9 ounces bittersweet or semisweet chocolate,
finely chopped

Additional red-and-white–striped candies,
crushed, for garnish

Fresh mint sprigs, for garnish

1. To make the cream puffs, position a rack in the center of the oven and preheat to 400°F. In a heavy-bottomed, medium saucepan, bring the water, butter, sugar, and salt to a full boil over high heat, stirring occasionally to melt the butter. Reduce the heat to medium. Add the flour and stir until the dough forms a ball that clears the sides of the pan and lightly films the bottom of the pan, about 2 minutes. Remove from the heat and cool for 10 minutes.

2. Using a hand-held electric mixer at low speed, one at a time, beat in 3 eggs. Transfer to a pastry bag fitted with a plain ¹/₂-inch tube (such as Ateco No. 5). Pipe sixteen 1¹/₂-inch wide mounds of dough onto an ungreased baking sheet. In a small bowl, beat the remaining egg. Lightly brush the tops of the mounds

with beaten egg, smoothing the pointed tops with a pastry brush. Do not drip egg onto the baking sheet.

3. Bake the cream puffs until golden, about 20 minutes. Reduce the oven temperature to 350°F and continue baking until the puffs are golden brown and crisp, about 10 minutes. Remove from the oven and pierce the side of each puff with small, sharp knife tip. Return to the oven and bake for 5 more minutes. Transfer to wire cake racks and cool completely. (The profiteroles can be prepared up to 1 week ahead, stored in self-sealing plastic bags, and frozen.)

4. At least 4 hours before serving, make the peppermint ice cream. Mix the ice cream, crushed candy, and peppermint extract in a medium bowl. Transfer to an airtight container, cover, and freeze until solid, at least 4 hours or up to 3 days.

5. To make the sauce, heat the cream in a medium saucepan over medium heat until simmering. Remove from the heat and add the chocolate. Let stand until the chocolate softens, about 5 minutes. Whisk until smooth. (The sauce can be prepared up to 2 days ahead, cooled, covered, and refrigerated. Reheat in a double boiler.)

6. To serve, split the pastries in half crosswise. Place one scoop of ice cream in the bottom of each puff. Cover with the tops. Spoon equal amounts of sauce into 8 shallow bowls. Place 2 profiteroles in each bowl. Sprinkle with crushed candy and garnish with mint sprigs. Serve immediately.

 **Pear and Cranberry Crisp**

Makes 8 to 13 servings

Make Ahead: The crisp can be prepared up to 8 hours ahead, cooled, covered, and stored at room temperature.

Sometimes, instead of the typical ornate Christmas sweet, I need a crowd-pleasing dessert. That's when I bake this homey, satisfying, and delicious crisp. If you wish, serve it with vanilla ice cream or sweetened whipped cream.

• *For best results, think ahead and buy the pears three or four days before you want to bake the crisp. Markets rarely carry ripe pears because they must be picked and transported while hard. Ripen them in a closed brown paper bag at room temperature. Do not put them in the refrigerator to get ripe. Not only will they never ripen, but the cores will be brown and soft.*

Filling

8 ripe medium Anjou or Bartlett pears, peeled, cored, and cut into 1/2-inch wedges

One 12-ounce bag of cranberries, rinsed

1 cup granulated sugar

2 tablespoons all-purpose flour

2 tablespoons unsalted butter, cut into small pieces, chilled

Topping

1/2 cup all-purpose flour

1/2 cup packed light brown sugar

6 tablespoons unsalted butter, cut into small pieces, chilled

1 teaspoon ground cinnamon

1 cup chopped walnuts

1. Position a rack in the center of the oven and preheat to 350°F. Lightly butter a 13 × 9-inch glass baking dish.

2. To make the filling, place the pears, cranberries, sugar, flour, and butter in the prepared dish. Mix well.

3. To make the topping, in a medium bowl, using your fingertips, work the flour, brown sugar, butter, and cinnamon until combined and crumbly. Work in the walnuts. Sprinkle the topping evenly over the filling. Place the dish on a baking sheet.

4. Bake until the juices are bubbling and the pears are tender, about 45 minutes. Serve hot, warm, or at room temperature. (The crisp can be prepared up to 8 hours ahead, cooled, covered, and stored at room temperature.)

It Wouldn't Be the Holidays Without . . . Spirits

The spirited, alcohol-spiked holiday dessert is a tradition that goes way, way back. Wherever feasible, for people who prefer to cook without alcohol, I suggest nonalcoholic substitutes. However, if a recipe just won't be the same without some alcohol flavor, I don't recommend an alternative (to my taste, mincemeat or plum pudding without the taste of rum or brandy are quite anemic). Just like cooking with wine, the flavor of the liquor will affect the finished dish, so buy the best brand you can afford, and if you don't drink much, purchase smaller bottles. I almost always cook with bottled liquor, and don't use extracts except in some cookies. If absolutely necessary, even though I don't wholeheartedly recommend it, for each 1/2 cup of dark rum or brandy you can substitute 1/2 cup apple juice or water and 1/4 teaspoon extract.

Shortcakes with Pears in Brandied Cream Sauce

Makes 12 servings

Make Ahead: The shortcakes can be prepared up to 8 hours before serving, cooled completely, and wrapped in aluminum foil. Reheat the foil-wrapped biscuits in a preheated 350°F oven for 10 minutes before using. The pears can be peeled and prepared up to 2 hours before serving, covered, and refrigerated.

Strawberry shortcake has its place as a summertime masterpiece, but other seasonal fruits can be used throughout the year. This version features sautéed pears in a creamy, brandy-spiked sauce. If possible, use star-shaped cookie cutters for the biscuits, as they will give a festive look to the dessert.

Biscuits

1³⁄₄ cups all-purpose flour

1 cup cake flour (not self-rising)

¹⁄₄ cup plus 1 teaspoon granulated sugar

4 teaspoons baking powder

¹⁄₂ teaspoon baking soda

³⁄₄ teaspoon salt

10 tablespoons (1¹⁄₄ sticks) chilled unsalted
    butter, cut into ¹⁄₂-inch pieces

1 cup buttermilk, approximately

1 large egg, beaten

Pear Filling

8 firm-ripe Bosc pears, peeled, cored, and
    cut into ¹⁄₂-inch thick wedges

2 tablespoons fresh lemon juice

2 tablespoons unsalted butter

¹⁄₃ cup Poire William (clear pear-flavored brandy),
    brandy, or canned pear juice

¹⁄₂ cup packed light brown sugar

2 cups heavy cream

Fresh mint sprigs, for garnish
Fresh raspberries, for garnish

1. To make the biscuits, position the racks in the center and top third of the oven and preheat to 400°F. Sift the flour, cake flour, ¹⁄₄ cup sugar, baking powder, baking soda, and salt into large bowl. Add the butter and cut in with pastry blender until mixture resembles coarse crumbs with a few pea-sized pieces. Stir in the buttermilk, adding a little more, if needed, to make a soft dough. Knead a few times in the bowl until the dough comes together.

2. On a lightly floured work surface, roll the dough out to ¹⁄₂-inch thickness. Using a 3-inch-diameter star-shaped biscuit cutter, cut out biscuits. Gather up the scraps, knead lightly, reroll, and cut out additional biscuits to make a total of 24. Place on two ungreased baking sheets, spacing 2 inches apart. Brush the tops of the biscuits lightly with the egg, then sprinkle with the remaining 1 teaspoon sugar.

3. Bake until golden brown, switching the positions of the baking sheets from top to bottom and front to back halfway through baking, 18 to 20 minutes. (The biscuits can be prepared up to 8 hours before serving, cooled completely, and wrapped in aluminum foil. Reheat the foil-wrapped biscuits in a preheated 350°F oven for 10 minutes before using.)

4. To make the pear filling, in a medium bowl, toss the pears with the lemon juice. (The pears can be prepared up to 2 hours ahead, covered, and refrigerated.)

5. In a very large skillet, melt the butter over medium heat. Add the pears and cook, stirring occasionally, just until tender, about 6 minutes. Stir in the pear brandy, then the brown sugar. Add the heavy cream, increase the heat to high, and bring to a boil. Cook until the cream reduces by about one-third (it should coat a wooden spoon), about 5 minutes.

6. To serve, divide the hot pears into 12 shallow bowls. Top each serving with 2 biscuits, garnish with mint sprigs and raspberries, and serve warm.

 **Figgy Pudding Noel**

Makes 6 to 8 servings

"Oh, bring me a figgy pudding . . ." Made famous by the carol "We Wish You a Merry Christmas" this pudding is a delicious dessert that is much lighter than other steamed puddings from the British Christmas tradition. If you want to flambé the pudding with Cognac or brandy, use apple juice to soak the figs, or your pudding will be too spirited. Be sure to use a firm, high-quality sandwich bread to make the crumbs.

Butter and flour, for preparing the mold

2¹⁄₂ cups fine, dry, freshly ground bread crumbs (made from about 12 slices stale bread, crusts trimmed)

¹⁄₂ cup milk

1 cup (about 8 ounces) finely chopped dried figs, preferably Calimyrna

3 tablespoons Cognac, brandy, or apple juice

3 large eggs, at room temperature

1 cup granulated sugar

4 tablespoons unsalted butter, melted

1¹⁄₂ teaspoons baking powder

¹⁄₂ teaspoon salt

1 cup heavy cream

2 tablespoons confectioners' sugar

¹⁄₂ teaspoon vanilla extract

1. Generously butter the inside of a 1¹⁄₂- to 2-quart covered tubed steamed-pudding mold. Dust with flour and tap out the excess.

2. In a medium bowl, moisten the bread crumbs with the milk. In a small bowl, combine the figs and Cognac. Let both mixtures stand for 10 minutes.

3. In a large bowl, whisk the eggs, sugar, melted butter, baking powder, and salt until combined. Stir in the soaked crumbs and the figs with their Cognac. Pour the batter into the prepared mold and cover with the lid.

4. Place a collapsible metal steamer in a large kettle. Add enough water to come just beneath the steamer and bring to a full boil over high heat. Place the mold on the steamer and cover tightly. Reduce the heat to low. Simmer, adding more boiling water as needed to keep a good head of steam, until a toothpick inserted in the center of the pudding comes out clean, about 2 hours. Let the pudding stand for 5 minutes.

5. Meanwhile, in a chilled medium bowl, using a hand-held electric mixer at high speed, beat the cream, confectioners' sugar, and vanilla until stiff. Set aside.

6. Run a sharp knife around the inside of the mold to release the pudding. Unmold the pudding onto a platter. Slice and serve warm with a dollop of the whipped cream.

✲🌲 Yuletide Plum Pudding 101

Makes 8 to 10 servings

Make Ahead: Plum pudding should be made at least 1 and up to 3 days ahead. Allow 5 hours for the pudding to steam.

Plum pudding is a Christmas classic that just doesn't get served at any other time of year. It is absolutely beloved by the British, but hasn't established itself as one of America's favorite Yuletide sweets. Nonetheless, I include it because the words "plum pudding" sing with holiday good cheer, and there is plenty of romance attached to it via Charles Dickens's well-known Christmas stories. And the proliferation of steamed-pudding molds in kitchenware shops in December shows that I am not alone in loving this kind of dessert! Thanks to my British friends Howard Shepherdson and Rod Marten for invaluable research assistance. Not only did they both supply their mums' recipes, but we had a taste-test of packaged plum puddings in their London kitchen. What a feast for my fellow plum pudding lovers.

- *In Britain and Australia, a homemade plum pudding is usually enormous and steamed in a big heatproof bowl for 8 hours or more. I use a typical 6-cup tubed steamed-pudding mold to reduce the cooking time, even though it still takes 5 hours. Plum pudding can be aged for days, weeks, or even months, just like a fruitcake, doused every week with about ¼ cup brandy, dark rum, or both. I find that for American tastes, a couple of days is enough. Steamed-pudding molds are available by mail order (see page 163) and at kitchenware shops.*

- *Old recipes for plum pudding call for suet, the hard, crisp fat around beef kidneys. I prefer to use butter because it's easier to find, but you can substitute shredded beef suet, if you want a plum pudding that the Cratchits would admire.*

- *The old-fashioned way to reheat a plum pudding is to steam it again until piping hot, but my British friends always use their microwave oven. The pudding is heated through when an instant-read thermometer inserted in the center reads 165°F. Be careful of the steam when you uncover the pudding.*

- *For the traditional spectacular presentation, flambé the pudding with warm brandy and display it with pride in a darkened room. Just be careful.*

- *Some hard-line traditional cooks wouldn't dream of serving plum pudding without hard sauce (creamed butter and confectioners' sugar spiked with brandy). I prefer the coolness of vanilla ice cream or whipped cream with the warm pudding. The choice is up to you.*

Butter and flour for the pudding mold

1 large Granny Smith apple, peeled, cored, and diced

½ cup (3 ounces) chopped pitted prunes

½ cup (2 ounces) dark raisins

½ cup (2 ounces) golden raisins

½ cup (2 ounces) dried currants or additional raisins

½ cup chopped Candied Lemon Peel, Candied Orange Peel, or a combination (page 93) or use storebought candied peels

½ cup (2 ounces) finely chopped almonds

1½ cups fresh bread crumbs, prepared from firm white sandwich bread

¾ cup packed light brown sugar

⅔ cup all-purpose flour

½ cup stout

2 large eggs, beaten

4 tablespoons (½ stick) cold unsalted butter, shredded on the coarse holes of a box grater

2 tablespoons brandy or dark rum

1 teaspoon ground cinnamon

1 teaspoon ground ginger

¹/₂ teaspoon salt

¹/₂ teaspoon ground allspice

¹/₄ teaspoon freshly grated nutmeg

¹/₄ teaspoon ground cloves

Grated zest of 1 orange

¹/₄ cup brandy, for flambéing

Hard Sauce (recipe follows), vanilla ice cream,
  or sweetened whipped cream, for serving

1. Butter well and flour the inside of a 1¹/₂-quart covered tubed steamed-pudding mold.

2. In a large bowl, combine the apple, prunes, raisins,
golden raisins, currants, candied citrus peel, and almonds. Add the bread crumbs, brown sugar, flour,
stout, eggs, butter, 2 tablespoons brandy, cinnamon,
ginger, salt, allspice, nutmeg, cloves, and orange zest.
Mix very well. Spoon into the prepared pudding mold,
smooth the top, and cover.

3. Place the pudding on a trivet or a collapsible
steamer rack in a large kettle. Fill the pot with enough
hot water to reach the bottom of the steamer rack.
Cover the pot tightly and bring the water to a boil over
high heat.

4. Reduce the heat to medium-low. Cook at a steady
simmer, keeping a full head of steam going and adding
boiling water to the pot as needed, for 5 hours. The pudding is done when it has lost its raw look, has a rich dark
brown color, and is firm to the touch. Of course, you will
have to remove the mold and open it to check the pudding's progress. Be careful of the steam and hot water!

5. Transfer the pudding mold to a wire cake rack and
let cool for 10 minutes. Invert the pudding onto a
plate. Cool completely. Wrap the pudding in aluminum foil and refrigerate for at least overnight and
up to 2 days.

6. To reheat, butter the steamed-pudding mold well.
Unwrap the pudding. To heat by steam, slip it back
into the mold. Place the mold in the pot and steam

again in simmering water until heated through, about
1 hour. To reheat in a microwave oven, place the pudding, upside down, in a large microwave-safe bowl.
Cover the pudding with plastic wrap. Cook on
Medium-High (70% power) until heated through, 5 to
10 minutes, depending on the wattage of your oven
(the higher the wattage, the less time needed to reheat
the pudding). The pudding is heated through when an
instant-read thermometer inserted in the center reads
165°F. Be careful of the steam when you uncover the
pudding. Invert the pudding onto a rimmed, heatproof plate.

7. In a small saucepan, heat the brandy over low heat
just until warm. Do not allow the brandy to come to a
boil. (Brandy won't flame unless it is warm, but if
overheated, it could unexpectedly ignite.) Pour the
warm brandy over the pudding and light the brandy
with a match. Present the flaming pudding, spooning
the brandy over the top of the pudding until it extin-
guishes. Serve hot with hard sauce.

Hard Sauce: In a medium bowl, using a hand-held
electric mixer at high speed, beat 1 cup (2 sticks) unsalted butter, at room temperature, until creamy,
about 1 minute. On low speed, gradually beat in 1 cup
confectioners' sugar. Beat in 2 tablespoons each
brandy and dark rum and ¹/₄ teaspoon freshly grated
nutmeg. Serve at room temperature. (The hard sauce
can be prepared up to 1 day ahead, covered tightly, and
refrigerated. Return to room temperature.)

It Wouldn't Be the Holidays Without . . . Plum Pudding

The "plum" in plum pudding refers to dried prunes. Over the years, some recipes have deleted the prunes in favor of raisins. Today, plum pudding can be made with all manner of dried and candied fruits.

Plum pudding is another Christmas food with origins older than Christianity itself. Druids believed that Daga, the god of plenty, celebrated the winter solstice by mixing up a pudding of the earth's bounty, including meats, fruits, and spices. For centuries the pudding was somewhat unceremoniously boiled in a sack. The Victorians were the ones who finally cosseted the pudding, placing it in a mold or basin to give it the more uniform shape we know today.

In England the fruits and liquors for the pudding are traditionally prepared on the last Sunday before Advent, called "Stir-Up Day." One of the prayers for that day's service begins "Stir up . . . ," which acts as a wake-up call for the task that awaits the parishioners when they return home. The mixture is stirred once a week or so by each family member for good luck (recipes prepared in this fashion rarely include eggs, and make a very heavy, but authentic, pudding), then steamed on Christmas morning.

Classic Raspberry and Sherry Trifle

Makes 10 to 12 servings

Make Ahead: The trifle should be prepared at least 8 hours ahead, and can be refrigerated for up to 1 day.

Here, pound cake is spread with raspberry jam, drizzled with sherry or apple juice, and layered in a glass trifle bowl with raspberries and custard sauce. These disparate ingredients marry into an impressively rich concoction that is perfect for feeding a crowd. But one word of advice: Trifle is only as good as its components. Buy a good pound cake from your favorite bakery, imported preserves, and a nice bottle of sherry, and you'll have a masterpiece that will more than satisfy lovers of gooey desserts!

- *A smooth custard sauce is one of the hallmarks of a good cook. It must be stirred constantly so the eggs do not overcook and become scrambled. A wooden spatula works better than a wooden spoon because it scrapes the bottom of the pan more thoroughly and can get into the corners more efficiently.*

- *The custard should cook just to the point when it is thick enough to coat the wooden spatula nicely. Until you've done this often enough that you recognize the proper thickness by sight, use an instant-read thermometer to gauge when the custard is cooked to 185°F. If you cook the custard much beyond this point, or anywhere near the boiling temperature of 212°F, it will become grainy. Some cooks rescue scrambled custard by whirling it in a blender until smooth again, but I find the fixed sauce tastes "eggy." If you do botch a batch, it's best to toss it out and start over again.*

- *Custards are strained before serving to remove any pieces of cooked egg white and ensure a silky smooth texture. Egg whites set at a lower temperature than egg yolks, so there will always be a few strands of stray egg white, or chalaza (the thin white cord attached to the yolks), in the sauce that should be removed.*

- *You can make the trifle in any 3-quart glass bowl, but a footed glass trifle bowl looks especially festive. (After the holidays, use the bowl to serve fruit or vegetable salads or tiramisù.) Trifle bowls are available at houseware stores during the holiday season, or by mail order (see page 163 for mail-order sources).*

Custard Sauce

2¹⁄₂ cups milk

¹⁄₂ cup granulated sugar

7 large egg yolks, at room temperature

1 teaspoon vanilla extract

One 16-ounce store-bought pound cake, cut into ¹⁄₂-inch thick slices

¹⁄₂ cup sweet sherry, such as cream or oloroso, or apple juice

1 cup high-quality raspberry preserves

2 pints fresh or frozen raspberries (see Note)

2 cups heavy cream

3 tablespoons confectioners' sugar

1¹⁄₂ teaspoons vanilla extract

¹⁄₃ cup sliced almonds, toasted

1. Start the trifle at least 8 hours before serving. To make the custard sauce, in a heavy-bottomed medium saucepan, heat the milk and sugar over medium-low heat until very hot, stirring occasionally to dissolve the sugar.

2. In a medium bowl, whisk the yolks to combine. Gradually stir about 1 cup of the hot milk mixture into the yolks, then whisk them into the saucepan. Cook over medium-low heat, stirring constantly with a wooden spatula, until the custard is thick enough to coat the spoon, about 3 minutes. An instant-read ther-

mometer inserted into the custard will read 185°F. Do not let the custard come to a boil. Strain the custard through a wire sieve into a medium bowl. Press a piece of plastic wrap directly onto the surface of the custard and pierce a few holes into the wrap with the tip of a sharp knife. Let stand on a wire cake rack until cooled to room temperature.

3. Stand cake slices around the inside of the bowl, and more on the bottom, trimming the cake as needed. Drizzle about ¹⁄₄ cup of the sherry over the cake. Using a rubber spatula, spread preserves on the exposed sides of the cake slices (this doesn't have to look perfect.) Fill the bowl with half of the raspberries. Top with more cake slices, spread with preserves, and sprinkle with 2 tablespoons sherry. Repeat with the remaining raspberries, cake slices, preserves, and sherry. (Don't be concerned if you have leftover cake or not quite enough.) Slowly pour the custard sauce over all. Cover tightly with plastic wrap and refrigerate for at least 8 hours, preferably overnight. (The trifle can be prepared up to this point 1 day ahead.)

4. Just before serving, in a chilled large bowl, using a hand-held electric mixer at high speed, beat the cream, confectioners' sugar, and vanilla until stiff. Spread over the top of the trifle and sprinkle with the almonds. Serve chilled, and include some of the whipped cream topping and almonds with each portion.

Note: Use individually frozen raspberries, not block-frozen berries. Place the frozen raspberries in a wire sieve and rinse under cold running water to remove any ice crystals. Do not thaw the raspberries completely.

Poached Pears with Zinfandel and Five-Spice Syrup

Makes 8 servings

Make Ahead: The pears can be prepared up to 1 day ahead, cooled, covered, and refrigerated.

Poached pears are a favorite winter dessert because they aren't too filling after a rich meal. The combination of star anise, Szechuan peppercorns, cinnamon, cloves, and fennel is a delightful Asian-inspired addition to the typical wine-poaching mixture. You'll need whole spices, as five-spice powder will give the wine syrup a gritty, dusty texture. Bosc pears hold their shape best after poaching, and Zinfandel wine has a peppery edge that is complemented by the spices. Serve the pears with crisp cookies (the Moravian Spice Wafers on page 114 are my favorite, but buttery, plain cookies are fine, too, either homemade or high-quality store-bought cookies).

• You may have to go to an Asian market to find star anise and rust-colored Szechuan peppercorns, where they will be very reasonably priced. (You can also order them from Penzeys Spices (1-414-679-7207). Asian markets also have cinnamon sticks and fennel seeds at bargain prices. You will have plenty of spices left over. Here are some ways you can use them.

Star anise makes a fine addition to mulled wine, or it can be ground in a spice grinder and mixed with ground cinnamon in cookies and apple pies.

Szechuan peppercorns have an aromatic menthol scent; add a few of them to poultry or meat broths or crush and use to season roasts.

The cinnamon in Asian markets is often soft-bark cassia, which has more flavor than the typical hard cinnamon sticks, but it can be used in the same way.

Fennel seeds, which have a mild licorice flavor, are frequently required in Mediterranean recipes.

Store the spices in tightly sealed containers in a cool

dark place. If you don't use them up after a year, toss them out, as they will have lost much of their flavor.

Eight 8-ounce firm-ripe Bosc pears
1 lemon, cut in half
One 750-milliliter bottle Zinfandel
¾ cup packed light brown sugar
2 star anise
2 cinnamon or cassia sticks
½ teaspoon Szechuan peppercorns
6 whole cloves
¼ teaspoon fennel seeds

1. Working one at a time and using a vegetable peeler, peel the pears, leaving the stems intact. With a small, sharp knife or the tip of a swivel-type vegetable peeler, working from the bottom of each pear, remove the bottom third of each core. If necessary, trim the bottom so the pear will stand up. As each pear is peeled and cored, rub the surface with a lemon half and set aside.

2. In a large, nonreactive (nonaluminum) saucepan large enough to hold the pears in a single layer, bring the wine, brown sugar, star anise, cinnamon, Szechuan peppercorns, cloves, and fennel seeds to a simmer over high heat. Add the pears, on their sides, and reduce the heat to medium-low. Cover tightly and simmer, turning the pears after 20 minutes, until they are tender when pierced with the tip of a sharp knife, about 45 minutes. Using a slotted spoon, stand the pears upright in a shallow dish.

3. Strain the cooking syrup through a fine-meshed wire sieve into a medium bowl and return to the pot. Discard the spices. Boil over high heat until the cooking liquid is thickened and reduced to about 1½ cups, 10 to 15 minutes. Cool completely. Cover and refrigerate until well chilled, at least 2 hours and up to 1 day.

4. To serve, place a pear in a soup plate, and drizzle with the syrup.

Holiday
Menu Planner

*H*ere are complete menus and timetables for five different holiday parties. I've included an all-dessert party, an open house that would work as a tree trimming event or a New Year's celebration, three separate sit-down dinners for moderately large groups, and an intimate New Year's Eve supper for four.

Photocopy the timetable and tape it up in the kitchen so you can mark off the steps as you finish them. Tape up the menu, too.

Before making a recipe, read it thoroughly, checking to ensure that you have the right utensils and any special ingredients. If you don't have a cookbook holder, or you just don't have enough counter space, photocopy the recipe and tape it up at eye level on a kitchen cabinet. This is a real space saver.

Most of the dishes for the buffets are make-ahead. Be sure you have enough refrigerator space for storage. Remember that large roasts should sit for 20 minutes before carving (a large turkey can stand for up to 45 minutes). This gives the cook time to finish the side dishes. Take advantage of this window of opportunity!

🎄 *Nutcracker Sweets Party* 🎄

*T*he holidays are the time for indulging, and this menu is Indulgence with a capital I. An all-dessert menu can be served as a late-afternoon tea or as an after-dinner party. Be sure to state "A Dessert Party" on the invitation so no one comes expecting dinner. Bake two orange-walnut cakes and two crisps, and single batches of the other recipes.

You can bake any cookies you like, but the ones here have been chosen to give a variety of shapes and flavors. Choose either gingerbread or sugar-cookie dough, and cut out cookies for decorating as you prefer. When I make this menu, I bake large cookies and write the name of each guest on each one to have as a party favor. (When baking large cookies, you may want to make a double batch of dough.) Decorating cookies takes time, but the other three cookies I've suggested are very easy to make.

Instead of wine, I set out a coffee bar so guests can make their own specialty coffees, if they want. Offer bottles of Irish whiskey, Kahlúa, brandy, and dark rum with bowls of lightly sweetened whipped cream and sugar cubes, and let people make coffee drinks to their taste. You will need a large-capacity coffeemaker. This menu will serve up to 24 guests.

Marie's Orange-Walnut Cake *(page 137)*

Pear and Cranberry Crisp *(page 140)*

Classic Raspberry and Sherry Trifle *(page 146)*

Gingerbread Cookies 101 *(page 109)*

or Sugar Cookies 101 *(page 108)*

Greek Snowballs *(page 117)*

Chewy Molasses Drops *(page 122)*

Cranberry Oat Bars *(page 128)*

Chocolate, Cranberry, and Walnut Fudge *(page 94)*

Hot Coffee

Cold Apple Cider

Assorted Liqueurs and Brandies

Bowls of Sweetened Whipped Cream and Sugar Cubes

Timetable

Up to 5 days ahead: Make orange-walnut cake; wrap airtight
      and store at room temperature
      Make fudge; store airtight

4 days ahead: Bake molasses cookies; store airtight

3 days ahead: Make gingerbread or sugar cookies;
      decorate and store airtight
      Bake snowball cookies; store airtight
      Bake cranberry bars; store airtight

1 day ahead: Make trifle; cover and refrigerate

4 hours ahead: Make crisp; store at room temperature

1 hour before guests arrive: Make coffee
      Whip cream; refrigerate

🎄 *A Tree-Trimming Open House* 🎄

*T*his is my kind of holiday party menu. Every dish is cooked ahead of time, and requires just an occasional refilling of bowls and platters as the party progresses. The menu is designed for 24 guests, but you may multiply the yield of these dishes to as many servings as you need. However, mix and bake the cakes one at a time, as cake recipes don't always work well when extended. Make double batches of the cauliflower and tortellini salads and the bread. You could make a double batch of the chicken cassoulet, but it is rich and most guests won't take much, especially with ham and salads on the table.

If you wish, you can offer plain apple cider and red and white wines with the holiday beverages, but the seasonal drinks will be pretty popular.

Santa Fe Crunch *(page 14)*

Sicilian Caponata with Garlic Crostini *(page 12)*

Caesar Dip with Crudités *(page 12)*

Stilton and Walnut Ball *(page 14)*

Salami and Cheese-Stuffed Bread *(page 83)*

Baked Ham with Pineapple and Seeded Mustard Glaze *(page 48)*

Chicken Cassoulet *(page 50)*

Cauliflower Salad with Red Pesto Dressing *(page 31)*

Tortellini Antipasto Salad *(page 36)*

Assorted Rolls and Mustards for Ham

Deep Dark Stout Gingerbread *(page 136)*

S'Mores Rocky Road *(page 92)*

Spritz Butter Cookies *(page 126)*

Old-Fashioned Eggnog *(page 17)*

Mulled Wine with Honey and Orange *(page 22)*

Timetable

Up to 5 days ahead:

Make crunch; store airtight at room temperature
Make caponata; refrigerate
Make cheese ball; refrigerate
Make rocky road; store airtight

3 days ahead:

Make Caesar dip; refrigerate
Bake spritz cookies; store airtight
Bake gingerbread; cover tightly and store at room temperature

1 day ahead:

Prepare crudités for dip; refrigerate
Make chicken cassoulet; refrigerate
Make cauliflower salad; refrigerate
Make eggnog; refrigerate

8 hours ahead:

Make dough for bread; let rise
Make tortellini salad; refrigerate
Bake crostini; store in paper bags at room temperature
Bake stuffed bread; cool and store at room temperature

3 hours ahead:

Bake ham

Just before guests arrive:

Stir broth into cassoulet and add bread topping; reheat
Make mulled wine; keep warm
Transfer eggnog to punch bowl; add ice cream to keep chilled
Thinly slice bread and place on platter

🎄 *Roast Beef for Dinner* 🎄

This celebratory meal is extravagant but not hard to make. While the dinner starts out rich, then gets richer, it concludes with refreshing, light poached pears in a spicy syrup.

If you aren't buying prime meat, and you choose to refrigerate-age your beef (see page 45), allow 3 to 5 days for aging. Time the dinner service from when the roast beef comes out of the oven. Slip the gratin into the oven, increase the heat to 400°F, and serve the soup. By the time the soup is cleared, the "au jus" sauce prepared, and the vegetables heated, the gratin should be hot. If you choose to make the Yorkshire puddings, the batter is very easy to mix up, but you will need a second oven or plan to reheat the gratin in a microwave oven. Preheat the oven to 400°F before baking the puddings—they need high heat to rise properly. The roast beef will stay perfectly warm, tented loosely with aluminum foil.

This is a meal for very good wines. Serve a crisp Sauvignon Blanc with the soup, then move on to an excellent, aged Cabernet Sauvignon. If you wish, serve port with dessert.

Sweet and Spicy Candied Walnuts *(page 97)*

Parsnip and Leek Soup with Bacon *(page 39)*

Roast Beef "Au Jus" 101 *(page 43)*

Sour Cream Horseradish Sauce *(page 44)*

Potato, Mushroom, and Roquefort Gratin *(page 71)*

Baby Carrots and Green Beans in Tarragon Butter *(page 67)*

Herbed Yorkshire Puddings *(page 75)*

Poached Pears with Zinfandel and Five-Spice Syrup *(page 148)*

Hot Coffee and Tea

Timetable

Up to 3 days ahead: Make walnuts; store airtight at room temperature

Up to 2 days ahead: Make pears; refrigerate

Up to 1 day ahead: Prepare crudités; refrigerate
Make soup; refrigerate
Make horseradish sauce; refrigerate
Make gratin; refrigerate
Blanch baby carrots and green beans; refrigerate

About 2 hours before serving: Roast beef
Cook and crumble bacon for soup;
    store at room temperature

1 hour before serving: Transfer horseradish sauce to serving bowl;
    let stand at room temperature

15 minutes before roast is done: Reheat soup; keep warm

When roast is done: Transfer roast to serving platter
Reheat gratin
Bake puddings
Serve soup

Just before serving roast: Make "au jus"; transfer to gravy boat
Heat baby carrots and green beans

After serving roast: Make coffee and tea
Serve pears

🎄 *A Plantation Turkey Feast* 🎄

*H*ere's a turkey dinner that features down-home, Southern flavors. It will serve up to 12 people. Personally, I try to keep my turkey menus under control by not serving too many side dishes. If I am already serving stuffing and sweet potatoes, I see no need to add mashed potatoes, even though tradition may dictate it. However, you can if you wish.

The time of the dinner centers around when the turkey is done. Remove the turkey from the oven and serve the crab cakes and salad. The pudding can be reheated in the oven while the turkey stands. Remember that the turkey must rest for at least 20 minutes before carving. If you wish, reheat the sugar cake before serving. I like to serve hard apple cider with this meal, but a Chardonnay is a good choice, too.

Spicy Cheese Straws *(page 15)*

Crab Cakes on Baby Greens with Lemon Vinaigrette *(page 27)*

Roast Turkey with Bourbon Gravy *(page 56)*

Corn Bread–Succotash Stuffing *(page 74)*

Yam and Pineapple Pudding *(page 73)*

Long-Simmered Greens *(page 68)*

Cranberry-Kumquat Chutney *(page 72)*

Moravian Sugar Cake *(page 80)*

The Original Ambrosia *(page 35)*

Hot Coffee and Tea

Timetable

1 week before serving:	Make chutney; refrigerate
2 days before serving:	Make corn bread; let stand at room temperature, uncovered, to stale
1 day before serving:	Make long-simmered greens; refrigerate Make sugar cake; store in self-sealing plastic bags at room temperature Make ambrosia; refrigerate Make lemon vinaigrette; refrigerate Make yam pudding; refrigerate Bake cheese straws; store airtight at room temperature
About 6 hours before serving:	Make stuffing; stuff turkey Roast turkey Make crab cakes; refrigerate
15 minutes before turkey is done:	Cook crab cakes; keep warm Transfer chutney to serving dish
When turkey is done:	Transfer turkey to serving platter Reheat pudding Reheat leftover stuffing Toss baby greens with vinaigrette; serve with crab cakes
Just before serving turkey:	Make gravy; transfer to gravy boat
After serving turkey:	Reheat sugar cake; serve Serve ambrosia Make coffee and tea

🌲 An Intimate New Year's Eve 🌲

We enjoy spending New Year's Eve with very close friends and a very special menu. This is a time for treats that you don't have every day of the year, like Champagne and caviar.

There are no tricks to this menu except for timing the potatoes. A second oven comes in handy here, as the potatoes cook ideally at 400°F, and the duck cooks at 450°F. If you wish, cook the potatoes in the same oven with the duck, but reduce their roasting time to about 30 minutes. If the potato skins seem to be browning too much, tent the potatoes with aluminum foil.

Start with a simple selection of your favorite cheeses served with walnuts and ripe pears. (I like a blue cheese, such as gorgonzola, with this combination.) After serving the first course, it will take about 12 minutes to cook the duck breasts and spinach and reheat the wild rice, so bring your guests into the kitchen with you to chat while you cook, if you wish. Serve Champagne with the caviar, and a Pinot Noir or Burgundy with the duck.

For dessert make the entire recipe, even though you will only be using half for this meal. The remaining cream puffs can be frozen for up to 1 month, the ice cream for up to 2 days, and the chocolate sauce can be refrigerated for up to 1 week.

Assorted Cheeses, Pears, and Walnuts

Yukon Gold Potatoes with Caviar and Crème Fraîche *(page 33)*

Two-Way Duck with Pecan-Orange Wild Rice *(page 52)*

Sautéed Spinach *(page 53)*

Peppermint Profiteroles with Chocolate Sauce *(page 139)*

Hot Coffee and Tea

Timetable

Up to 1 week ahead:	Make crème fraîche (if not purchasing)
	Bake profiteroles; freeze
Up to 3 days ahead:	Prepare ice cream; freeze
Up to 1 day ahead:	Cut up ducks; refrigerate
	Render duck fat; refrigerate
	Make duck stock; refrigerate
	Prepare chocolate sauce; refrigerate
	Make duck sauce; refrigerate
2 hours ahead:	Make wild rice; store at room temperature
	Cook spinach
1½ hours ahead:	Steam duck; store at room temperature
About 45 minutes before serving:	Roast potatoes
About 30 minutes before serving:	Roast duck
After serving potatoes:	Cook duck breast
	Reheat spinach
	Reheat wild rice
	Reheat duck sauce
After serving duck:	Make coffee and tea
	Reheat chocolate sauce
	Fill profiteroles; serve

⛄ 🎄 Gifts from the Kitchen 🎄 ⛄

A number of recipes in this book are perfect for holiday gift giving. Kitchenware shops and mail-order catalogues carry empty bottles, cookie tins, and candy boxes to lend your gift a finished, professional look. With cookies or baked items that keep best stored airtight, I often purchase covered plastic containers, and give the container along with the gift. A cake or cooked plum pudding in a tube pan or steamed-pudding mold with the recipe attached makes a wonderful present for a fellow cook.

Santa Fe Crunch *(page 14)*

Spicy Cheese Straws *(page 15)*

Cranberry Balsamic Vinegar *(page 34)*

Gügelhopf *(page 84)*

Moravian Sugar Cake *(page 80)*

Panettone *(page 85)*

Stollen *(page 88)*

Chocolate, Cranberry, and Walnut Fudge *(page 94)*

Chocolate Peanut-Butter Meltaways *(page 97)*

Candied Citrus Peels *(page 93)*

S'Mores Rocky Road *(page 92)*

Homemade Peppermint Taffy *(page 95)*

Chocolate-Orange Truffles *(page 98)*

Sweet and Spicy Candied Walnuts *(page 97)*

Sugar Cookies 101 *(page 108)*

Gingerbread Cookies 101 *(page 109)*

Chocolate-Hazelnut Biscotti *(page 110)*

Cinnamon Stars *(page 111)*

Lebkuchen *(page 112)*

Moravian Spice Wafers *(page 114)*

Mail-Order Sources

Adventures in Cooking

12 Legion Place

Wayne, NJ 07407

(973) 305-1114

www.adventuresincooking.com

One-stop kitchenware shopping with a personal touch. They carry everything from steamed pudding molds and cookie cutters to high-quality candied fruits and flavoring oils and extracts.

Baker's Catalogue

P.O. Box 876

Norwich, VT 05055-0876

(800) 827-6836

Everything for the baker and cookie maker; gügelhopf molds, cookie sheets, an array of decorating sugars and food coloring pastes and gels, European candied fruits and peels, and crystallized ginger.

Caviar Russe

538 Madison Avenue

New York, NY 10022

(212) 980-5908

(800) 692-2842 (N-Y-C-A-V-I-A-R)

A reliable mail-order source for fine caviar.

Caviarteria

4242 11th Street

Long Island City, NY 11101

(718) 482-8480

(800) 422-8427

Another place to mail-order imported caviar.

Economy Candy

108 Rivington

New York, NY 10002

(212) 254-1531

(800) 352-4544

www.economycandy.com

One of New York City's great stores, this enormous old-fashioned candy shop is a sweet-tooth's dream. I come here every year to buy reasonably-priced hard candies for my candy dish and candied fruit peels for baking.

Kitchen Glamor

Corporate Office

39049 Webb Court

Westland, MI 48185-7606

(800) 641-1252

An excellent source for common kitchen utensils, as well as hard-to-find items like ham holders, and flavoring oils for candies. They also have four stores throughout the metropolitan Detroit area.

Penzeys Spices
P.O. Box 933
W19362 Apollo Drive
Muskego, WI 53150
(800) 741-7787
www.penzeys.com
Call Penzeys when you want the best herbs and spices for holiday baking. They also carry Asian spices, such as Szechuan peppercorns and star anise, and excellent vanilla and almond extracts.

Sur La Table
Catalog Division
1765 Sixth Avenue South
Seattle, WA 98134-1608
(800) 243-0852
Based in Seattle, with other locations in California and Texas, Sur La Table has not only well-stocked kitchenware stores, but also two fine catalogues, one for serious cooks and one with more houseware items.

Williams-Sonoma
Mail-Order Department
P.O. Box 7456
San Francisco, CA 94120-7456
(800) 541-2233
As far as kitchenware shops go, Williams-Sonoma is no longer the only game in town, but it's still fun to curl up with their catalogue and pick out the items I just can't live without this holiday season. A great place to find gift boxes, bags, and ribbons for your homemade cookies and candies.

Index

About the Author

*R*ick Rodgers is a well-known cookbook author, cooking teacher, and radio and television guest chef. He has written over nineteen cookbooks on diverse subjects including *Thanksgiving 101, The Slow Cooker Ready* and *Waiting Cookbook, On Rice, Simply Shrimp, Fried and True,* and *Fondue: Great Food to Dunk, Dip, Savor and Swirl.* Rick's work has appeared in *Food and Wine, Chocolatier, Restaurant Business,* and *Newsday,* and he is a frequent contributor to *Bon Appétit.* He travels all over America teaching cooking classes, specializing in holiday menus. His website is www.rickrodgers.com.

The main course for the ultimate Thanksgiving dinner

Rick Rodgers's Thanksgiving 101 classes have been a hit for years. Now he serves up all of his know-how, trade secrets, recipes, and menus in one handy rescue manual. From the shopping to the chopping, *Thanksgiving 101* covers every detail of traditional turkey with all the trimmings as well as new ideas and regional favorites. For novice and experienced cooks alike, this is a foolproof, delicious education.

 IN TRADE PAPERBACK FROM BROADWAY BOOKS